ST. DRAGON GIRL

VOLUME EIGHT

 Story & Art by **Natsumi Matsumoto**

ST. ♥ DRAGON GIRL CHARACTERS

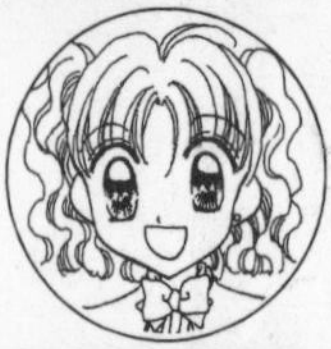

Shunran Kou

Ryuga's cousin and Momoka's best friend. Has psychic abilities.

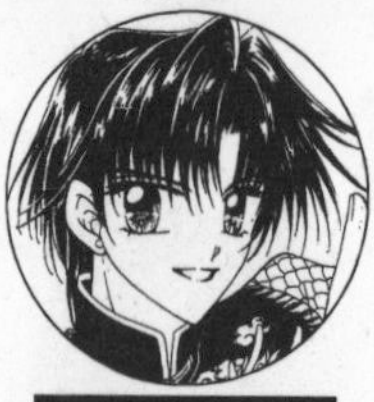

Ryuga Kou

Momoka's childhood friend and magic master.

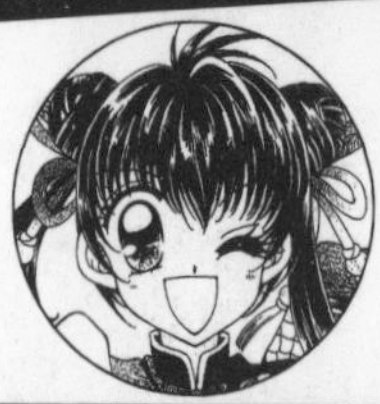

Momoka Sendou

She's possessed by a dragon spirit Ryuga summoned. She loves Ryuga. ♥

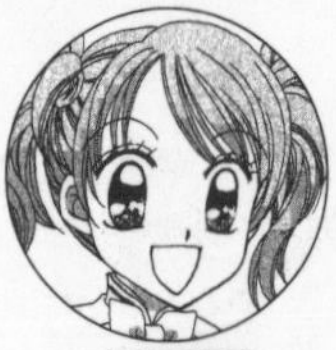

Mio

Mao's younger sister. Can use more powerful magic than Mao.

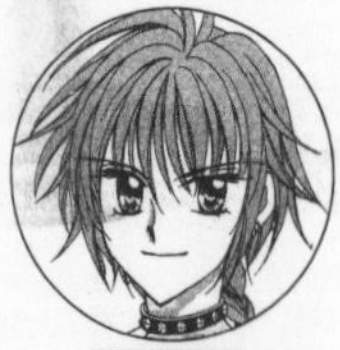

Mao

A magic master who is half demon. Has the appearance of a child by day.

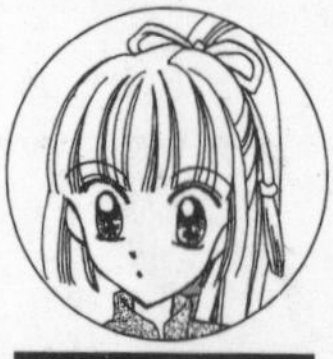

Ageha Inui

Momoka's friend. Member of the kenpo club.

STORY THUS FAR

Momoka is a member of the kenpo club at Yokohama's Tourin Academy. Her friends Ryuga and Shunran belong to a family of magic masters who can control dragons. Ever since the dragon Ryuga summoned possessed Momoka, she's been in danger many times. But every time, they manage to control the dragon and fight together.

A half-demon magic master called Mao tries to win over Momoka by dueling Ryuga, but Ryuga defeats him much to Momoka's relief.

After seeing Ryuga fight for her, Momoka makes up her mind to tell him her feelings, but Mao's younger sister Mio suddenly shows up. She uses her strong magic to tie her red string of fate to Ryuga's, severing Momoka and Ryuga's connection. Momoka and Ryuga were supposed to celebrate New Year's at an amusement park, but now Ryuga is lovey-dovey with Mio. What will Momoka's destiny be...?

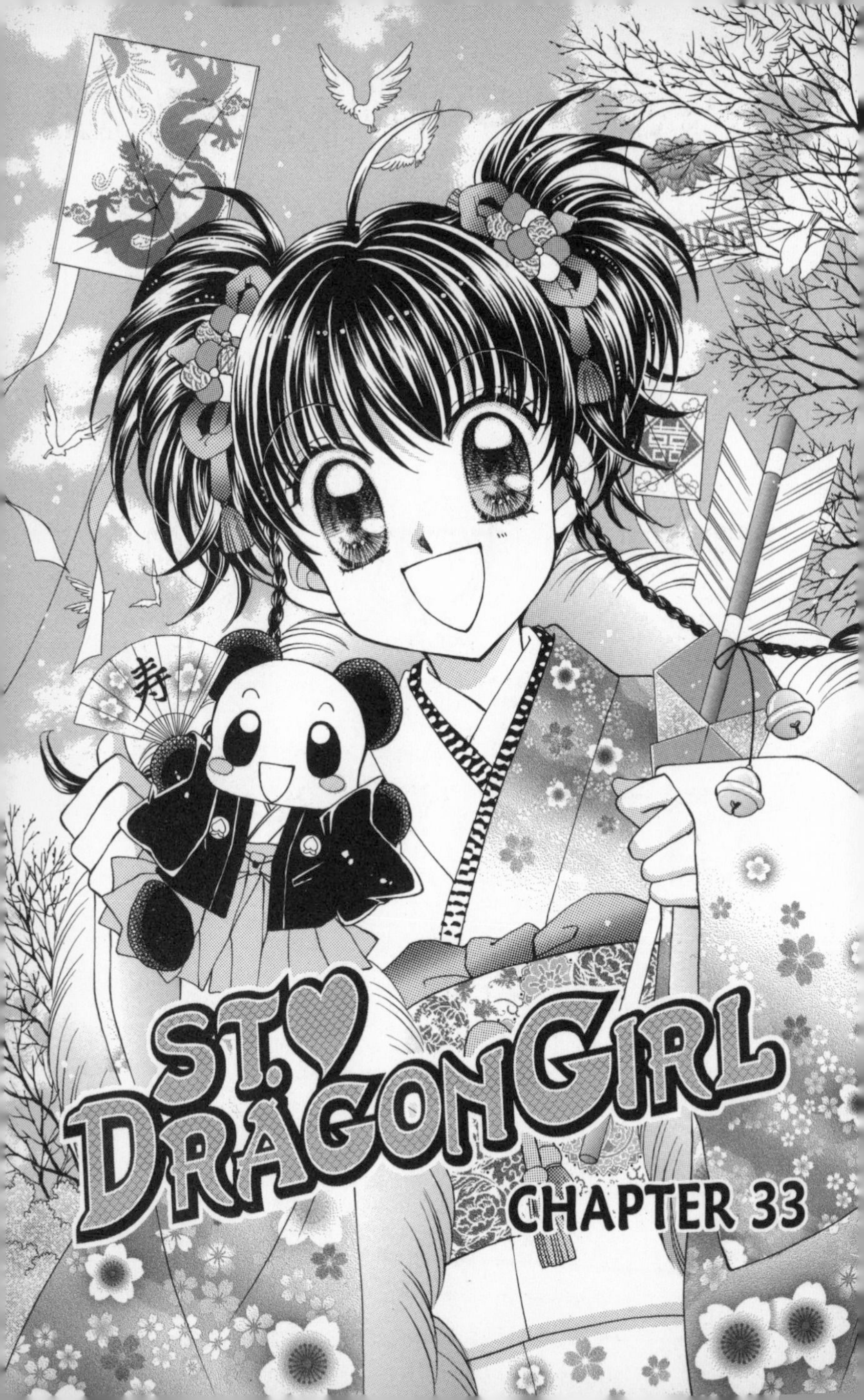
ST.♥DRAGON GIRL
CHAPTER 33
寿

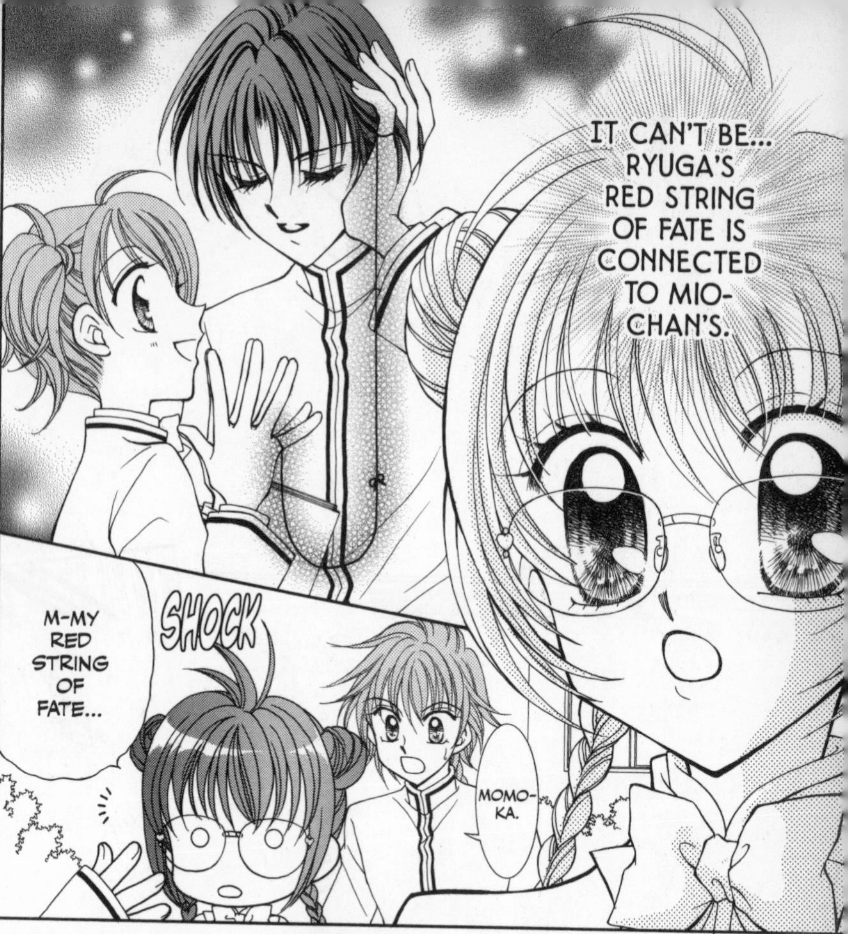
IT CAN'T BE... RYUGA'S RED STRING OF FATE IS CONNECTED TO MIO-CHAN'S.
M-MY RED STRING OF FATE...
SHOCK
MOMO-KA.

Reiji

Birthday: July 23. 17 years old.
Leo. Blood Type: A.

He's from a family of magic masters, and he is Mio's childhood friend. His specialty is ice magic. He's in love with Mio. He tends to be rather narcissistic but he loves wholeheartedly.

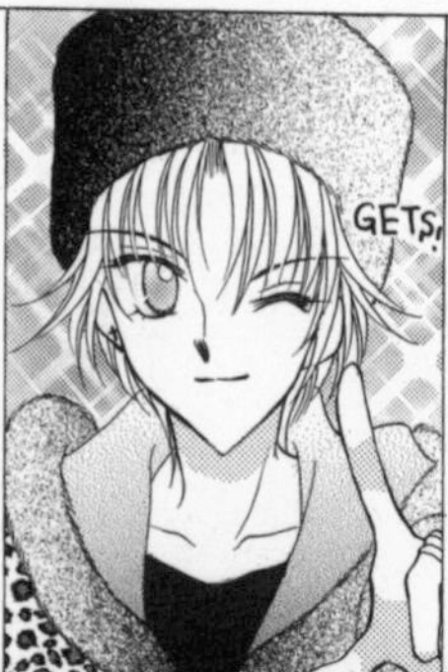
GETS!

Sorry for introducing such a hotheaded character in the middle of summer! Sometimes he says such stuck-up things you want to punch him, and he always wears over-the-top clothes. But don't you think it'll make him a good magic master someday?

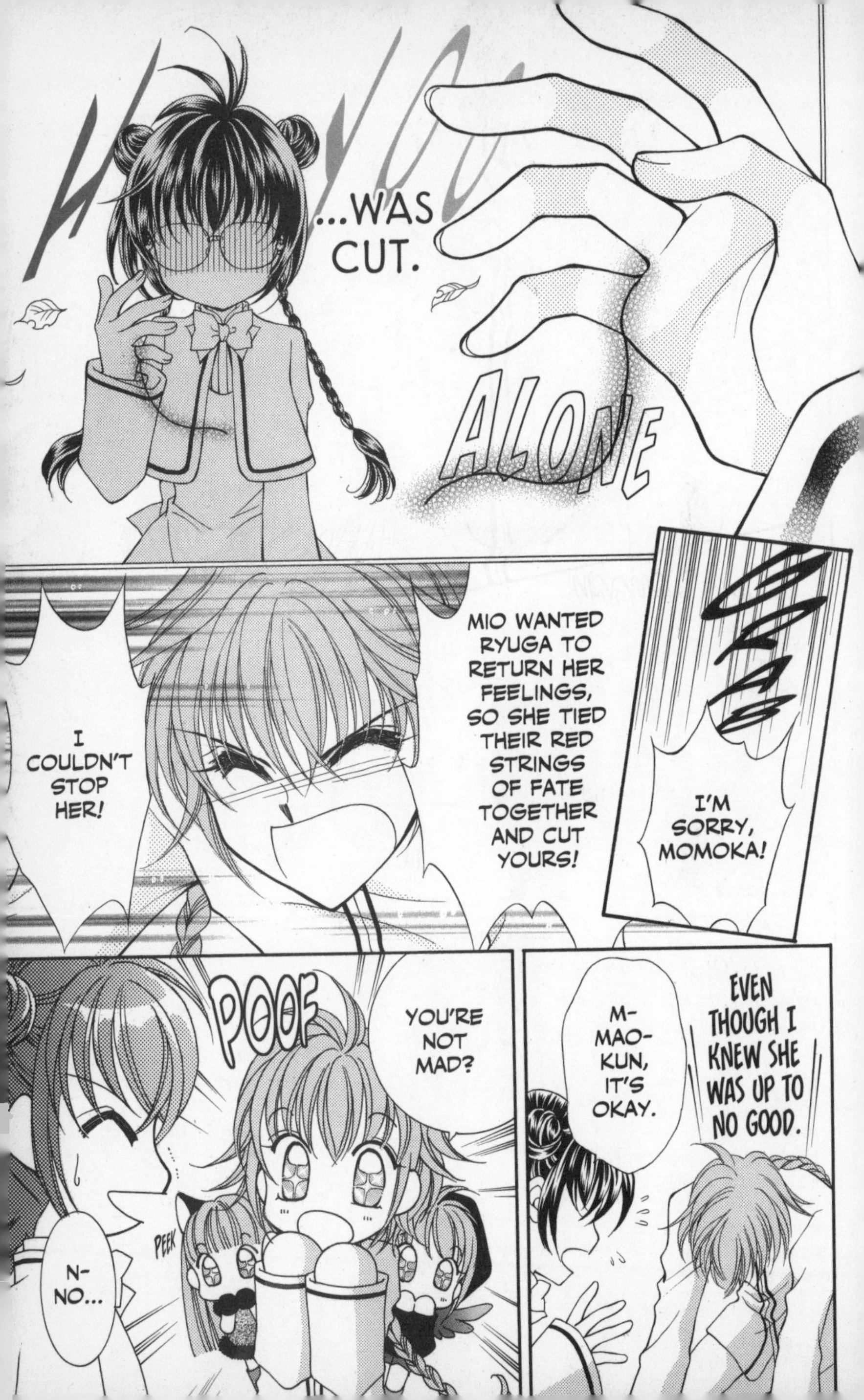
...WAS CUT.
ALONE
I'M SORRY, MOMOKA!
MIO WANTED RYUGA TO RETURN HER FEELINGS, SO SHE TIED THEIR RED STRINGS OF FATE TOGETHER AND CUT YOURS!
I COULDN'T STOP HER!
EVEN THOUGH I KNEW SHE WAS UP TO NO GOOD.
M-MAO-KUN, IT'S OKAY.
YOU'RE NOT MAD?
POOF
PEEK
N-NO...

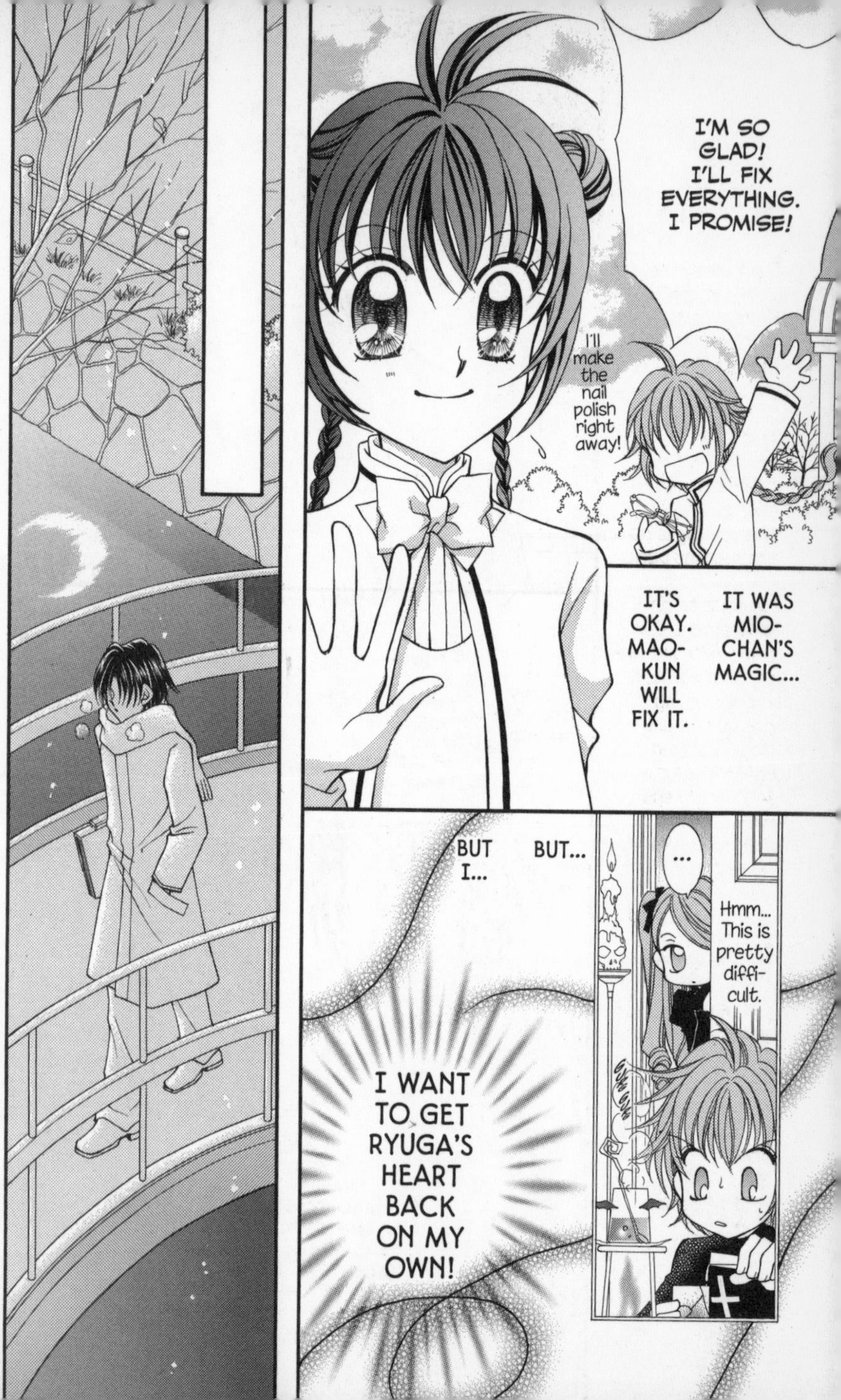
I'M SO GLAD! I'LL FIX EVERYTHING. I PROMISE!
I'll make the nail polish right away!
IT WAS MIO-CHAN'S MAGIC...
IT'S OKAY. MAO-KUN WILL FIX IT.
...
Hmm... This is pretty diffi-cult.
BUT...
BUT I...
I WANT TO GET RYUGA'S HEART BACK ON MY OWN!

1

Hello, everyone. How are you? Here's volume 8 of *St.♥Dragon Girl*! Sorry to keep you waiting.

This story is pretty lively—there are lots of characters, and the setting is at an amusement park.

I've gone to an amusement park on New Year's Eve too. I went there in the evening, ate dinner, and played around until midnight. An amusement park at night is romantic somehow. I had a lot of fun.

But it was so cold there that I caught the flu...💧

I ended up in bed all New Year's Day, and I swore from then on to stay home under the kotatsu and watch the Red and White Song Contest on TV for New Year's!

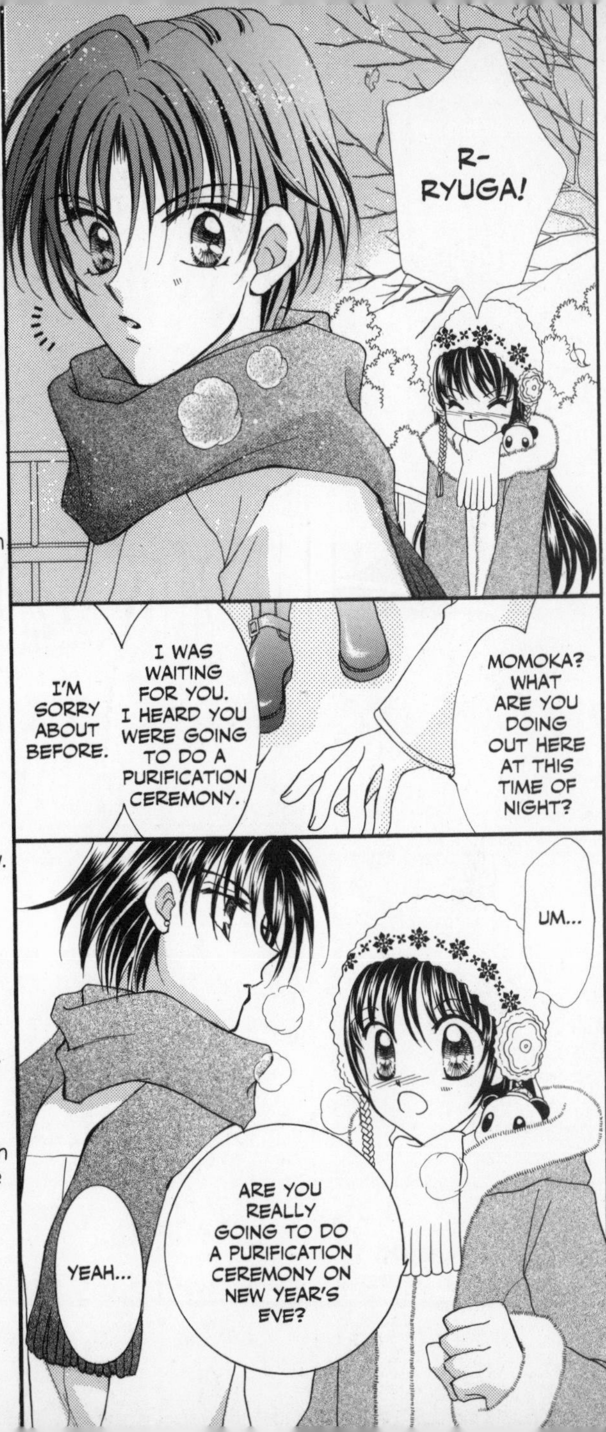
R-RYUGA!
MOMOKA? WHAT ARE YOU DOING OUT HERE AT THIS TIME OF NIGHT?
I WAS WAITING FOR YOU. I HEARD YOU WERE GOING TO DO A PURIFICATION CEREMONY.
I'M SORRY ABOUT BEFORE.
UM...
ARE YOU REALLY GOING TO DO A PURIFICATION CEREMONY ON NEW YEAR'S EVE?
YEAH...

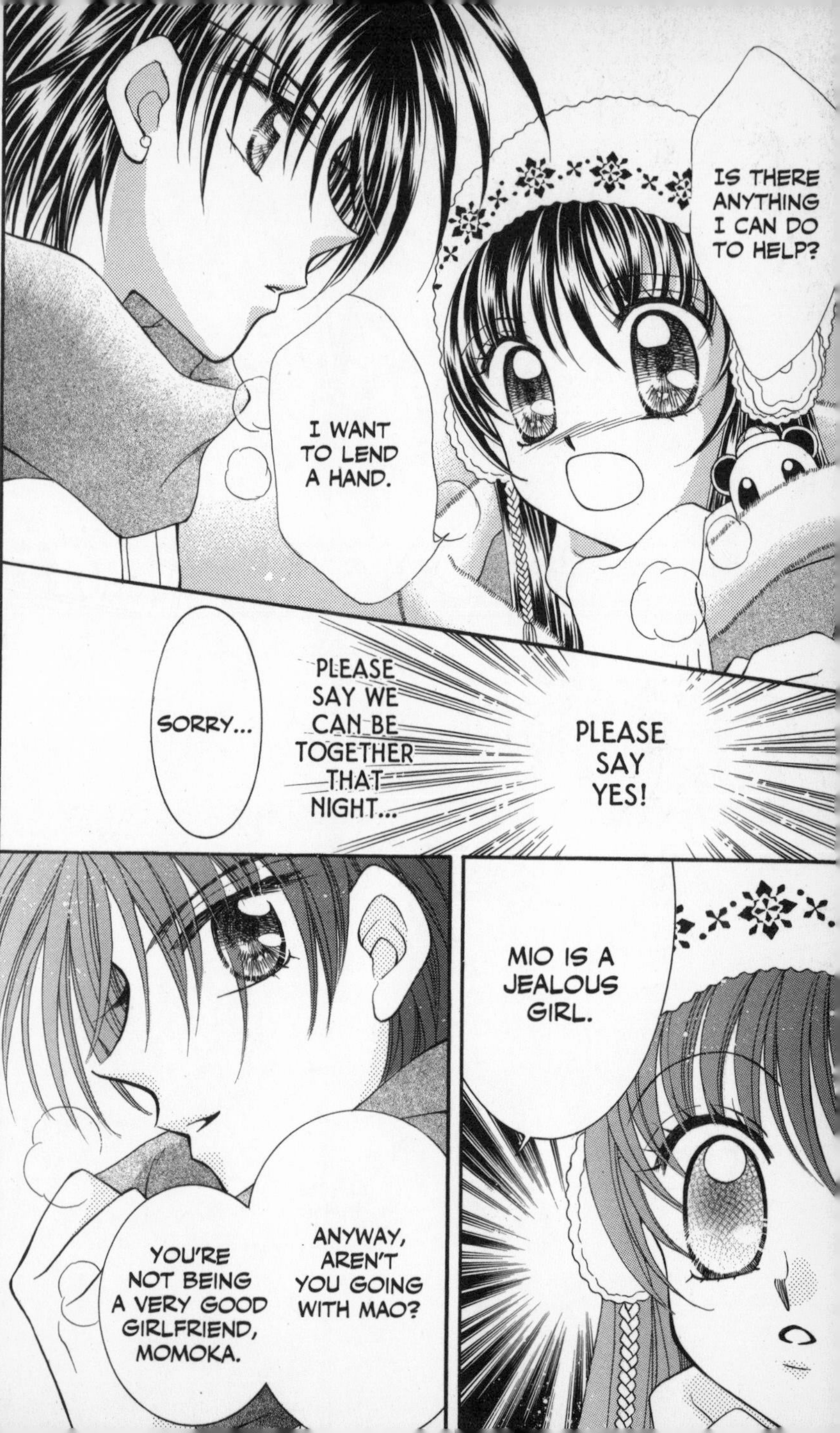
IS THERE ANYTHING I CAN DO TO HELP?
I WANT TO LEND A HAND.
PLEASE SAY YES!
PLEASE SAY WE CAN BE TOGETHER THAT NIGHT...
SORRY...
MIO IS A JEALOUS GIRL.
ANYWAY, AREN'T YOU GOING WITH MAO?
YOU'RE NOT BEING A VERY GOOD GIRLFRIEND, MOMOKA.

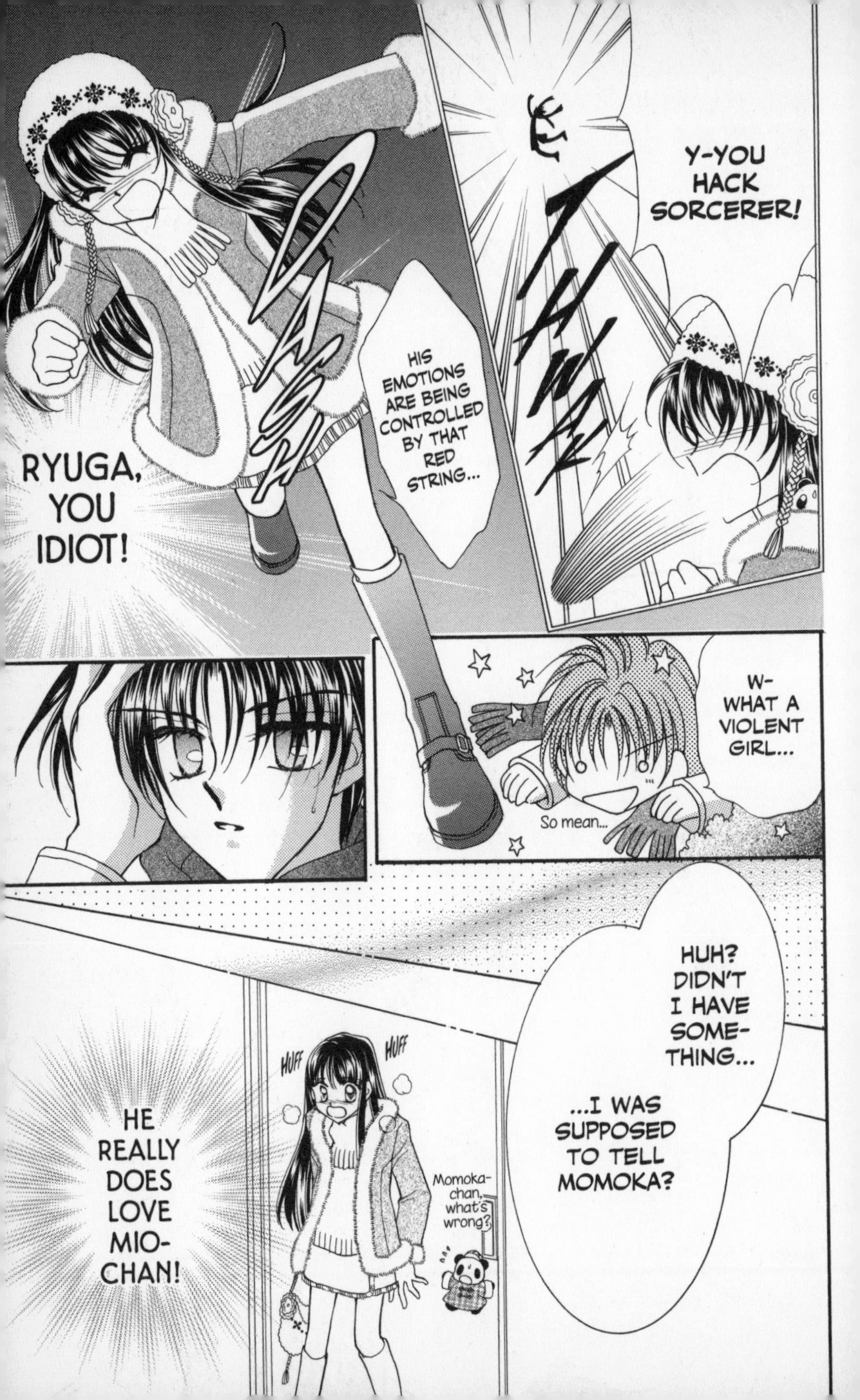
Y-YOU HACK SORCERER!
HIS EMOTIONS ARE BEING CONTROLLED BY THAT RED STRING...
RYUGA, YOU IDIOT!
W-WHAT A VIOLENT GIRL...
So mean...
HUH? DIDN'T I HAVE SOME-THING...
...I WAS SUPPOSED TO TELL MOMOKA?
Momoka-chan, what's wrong?
HUFF
HUFF
HE REALLY DOES LOVE MIO-CHAN!

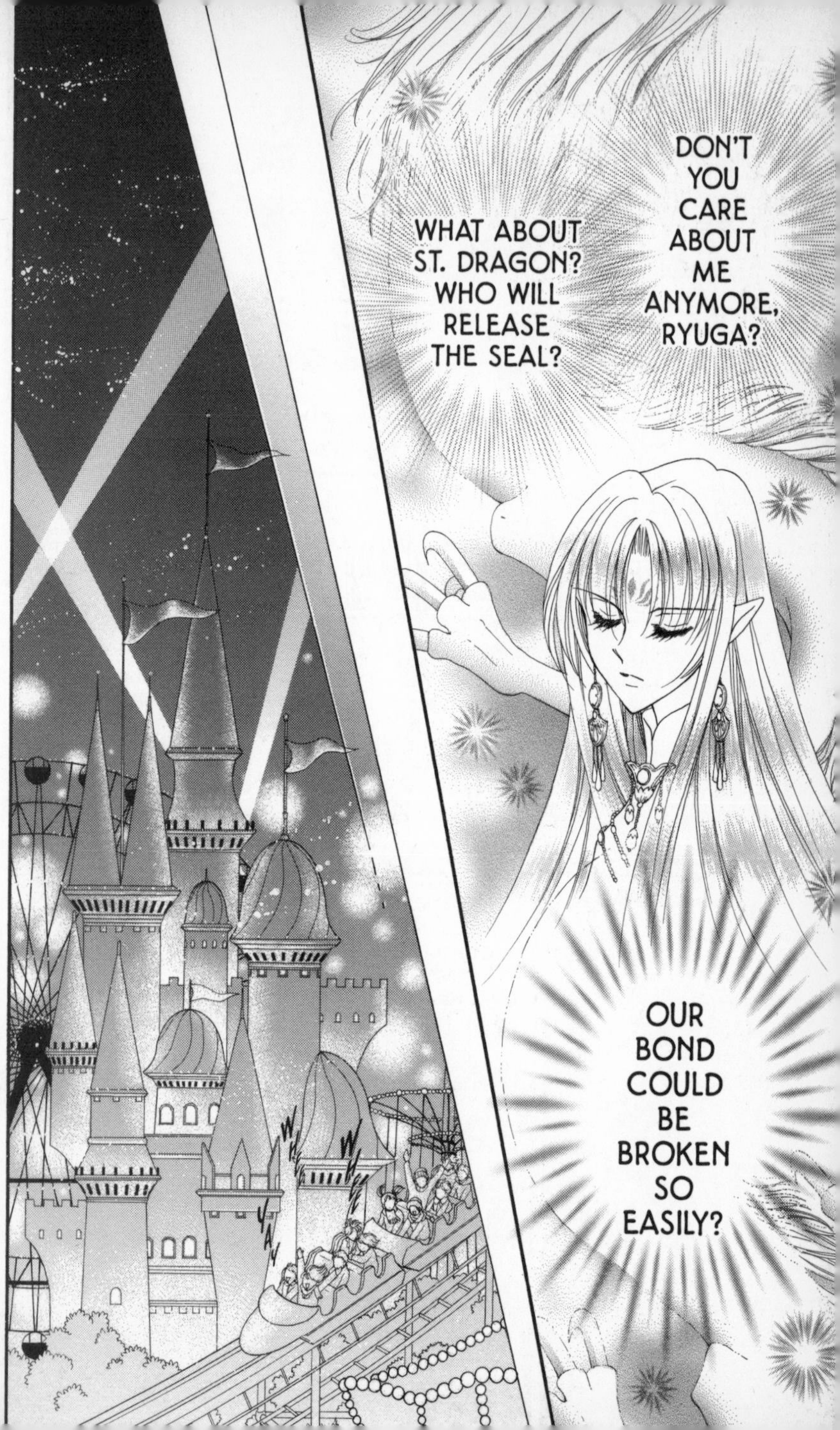
DON'T YOU CARE ABOUT ME ANYMORE, RYUGA?
WHAT ABOUT ST. DRAGON? WHO WILL RELEASE THE SEAL?
OUR BOND COULD BE BROKEN SO EASILY?

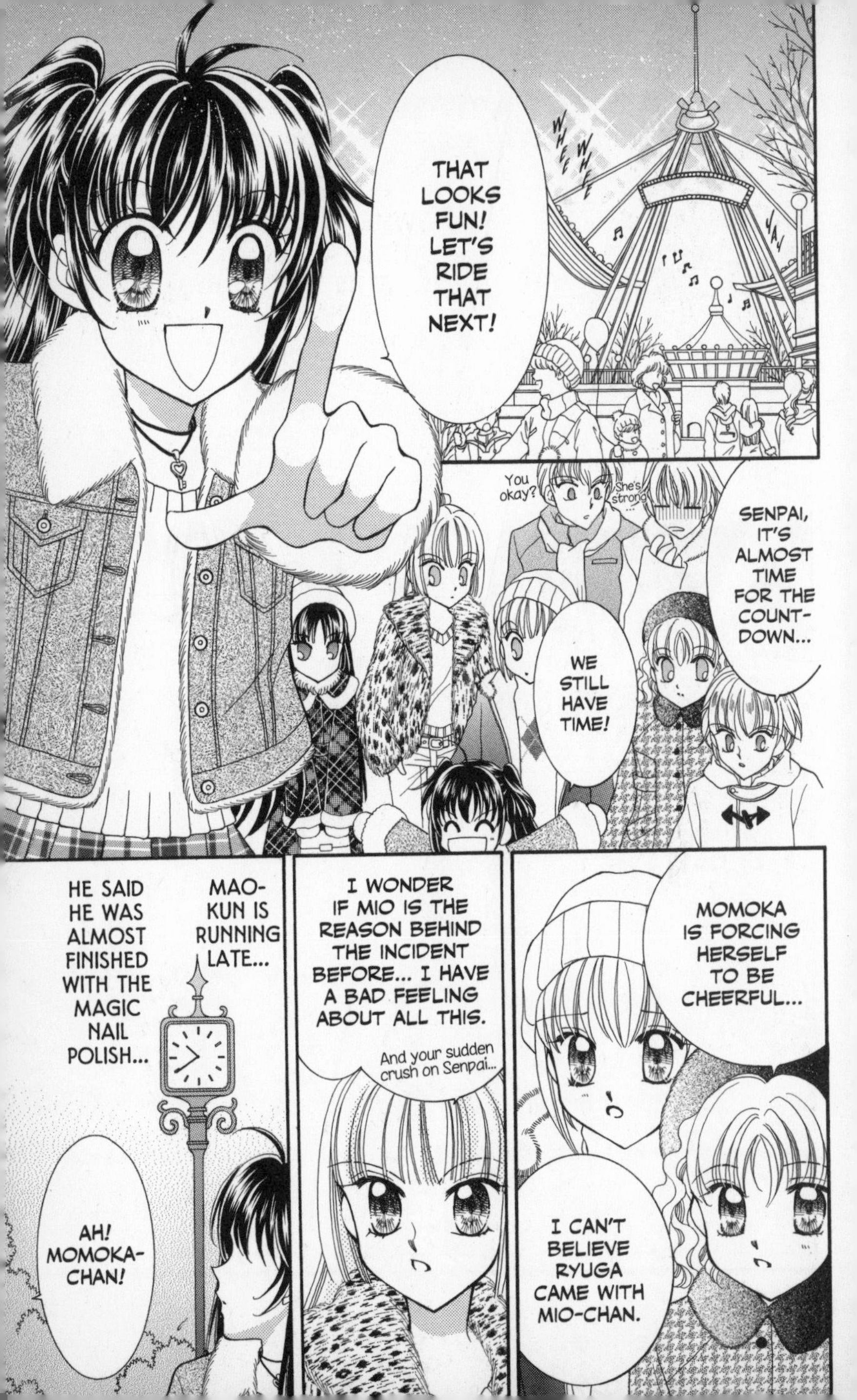
WHEE WHEE
YAY
THAT LOOKS FUN! LET'S RIDE THAT NEXT!
SENPAI, IT'S ALMOST TIME FOR THE COUNT-DOWN...
She's strong...
You okay?
WE STILL HAVE TIME!
MOMOKA IS FORCING HERSELF TO BE CHEERFUL...
I CAN'T BELIEVE RYUGA CAME WITH MIO-CHAN.
I WONDER IF MIO IS THE REASON BEHIND THE INCIDENT BEFORE... I HAVE A BAD FEELING ABOUT ALL THIS.
And your sudden crush on Senpai...
MAO-KUN IS RUNNING LATE...
HE SAID HE WAS ALMOST FINISHED WITH THE MAGIC NAIL POLISH...
AH! MOMOKA-CHAN!

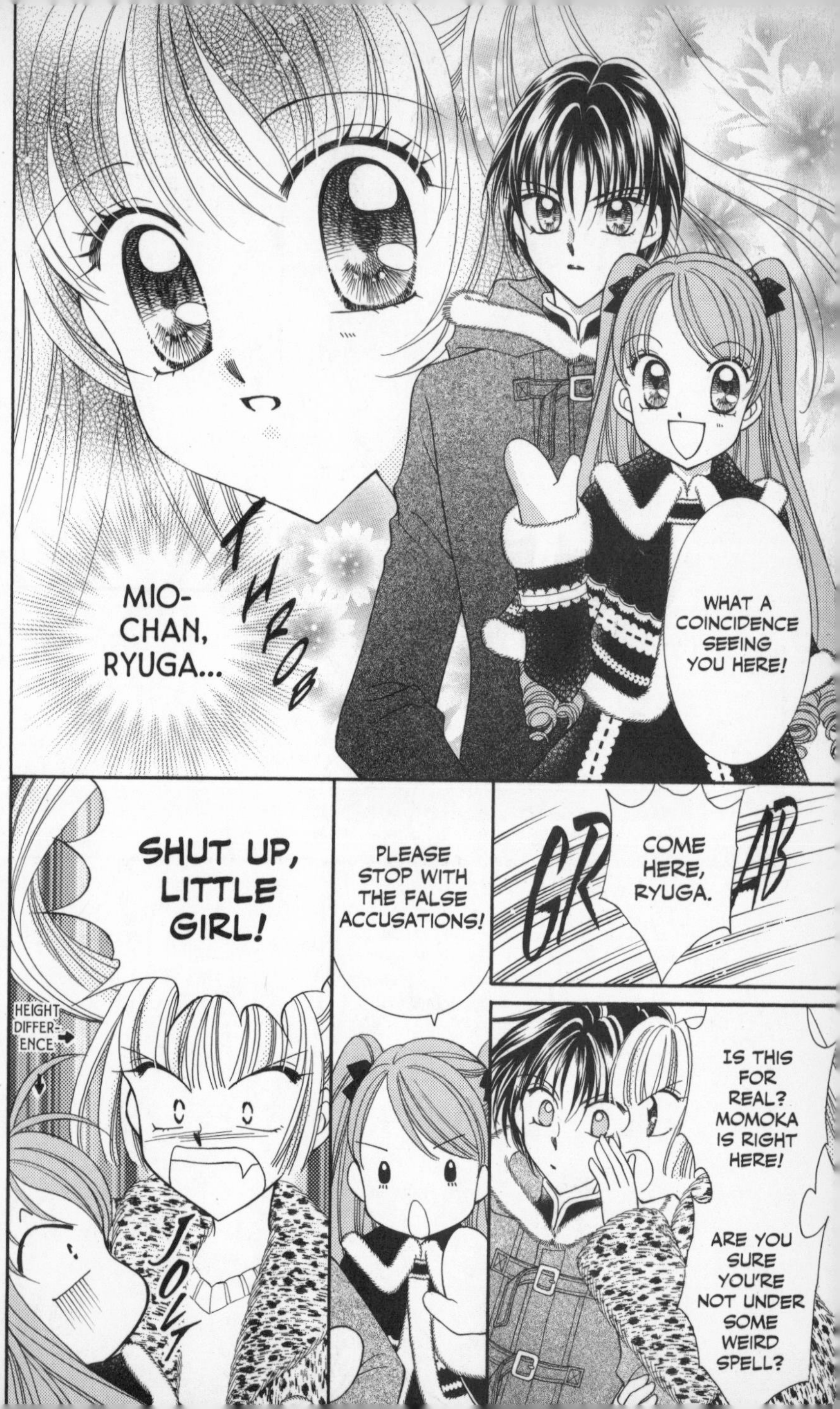
WHAT A COINCIDENCE SEEING YOU HERE!
THROB
MIO-CHAN, RYUGA...
GRAB
COME HERE, RYUGA.
IS THIS FOR REAL? MOMOKA IS RIGHT HERE!
ARE YOU SURE YOU'RE NOT UNDER SOME WEIRD SPELL?
PLEASE STOP WITH THE FALSE ACCUSATIONS!
SHUT UP, LITTLE GIRL!
HEIGHT DIFFERENCE
JOLT

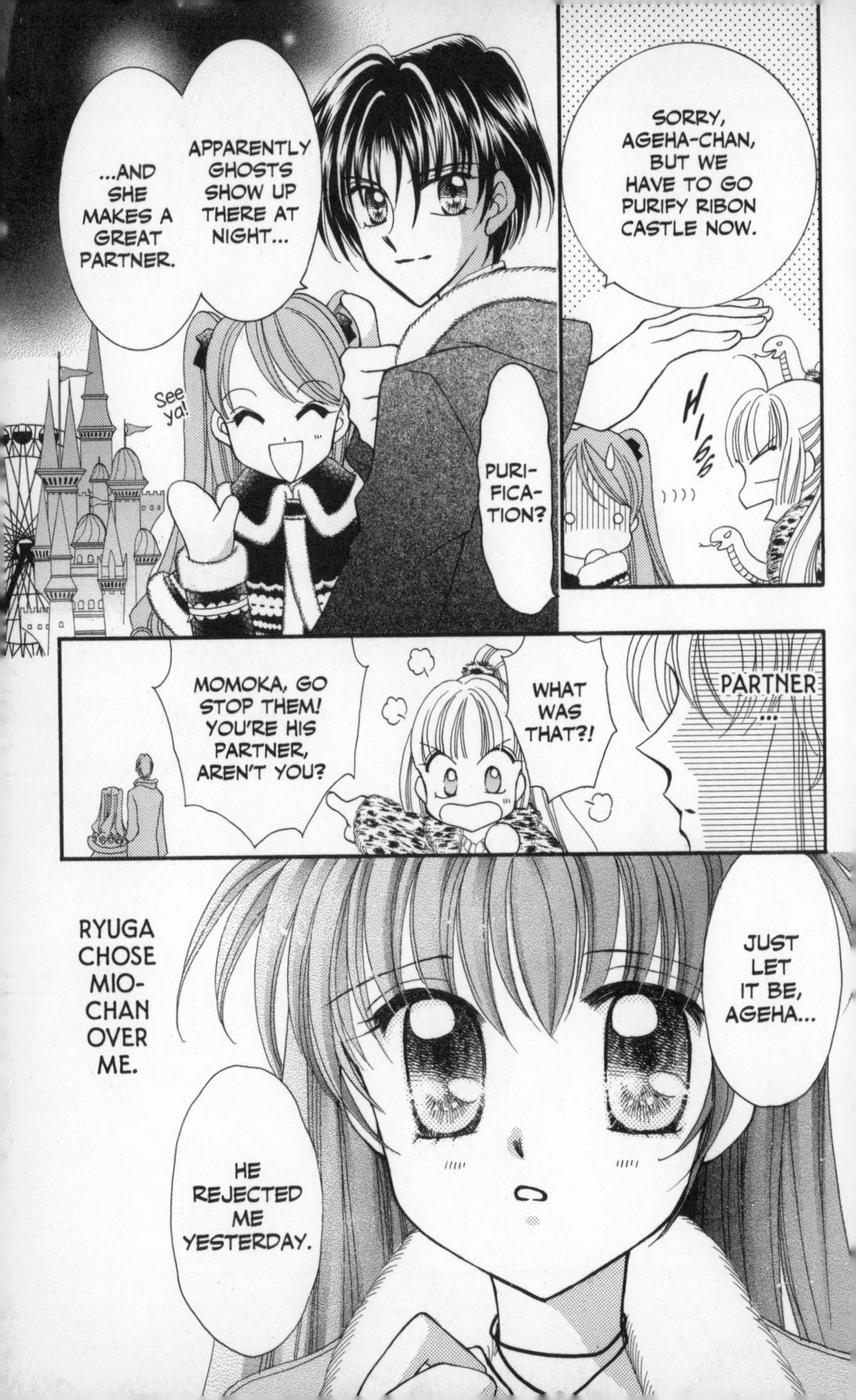
SORRY, AGEHA-CHAN, BUT WE HAVE TO GO PURIFY RIBON CASTLE NOW.
HISS
APPARENTLY GHOSTS SHOW UP THERE AT NIGHT...
...AND SHE MAKES A GREAT PARTNER.
See ya!
PURI-FICA-TION?
PARTNER...
WHAT WAS THAT?!
MOMOKA, GO STOP THEM! YOU'RE HIS PARTNER, AREN'T YOU?
JUST LET IT BE, AGEHA...
RYUGA CHOSE MIO-CHAN OVER ME.
HE REJECTED ME YESTERDAY.

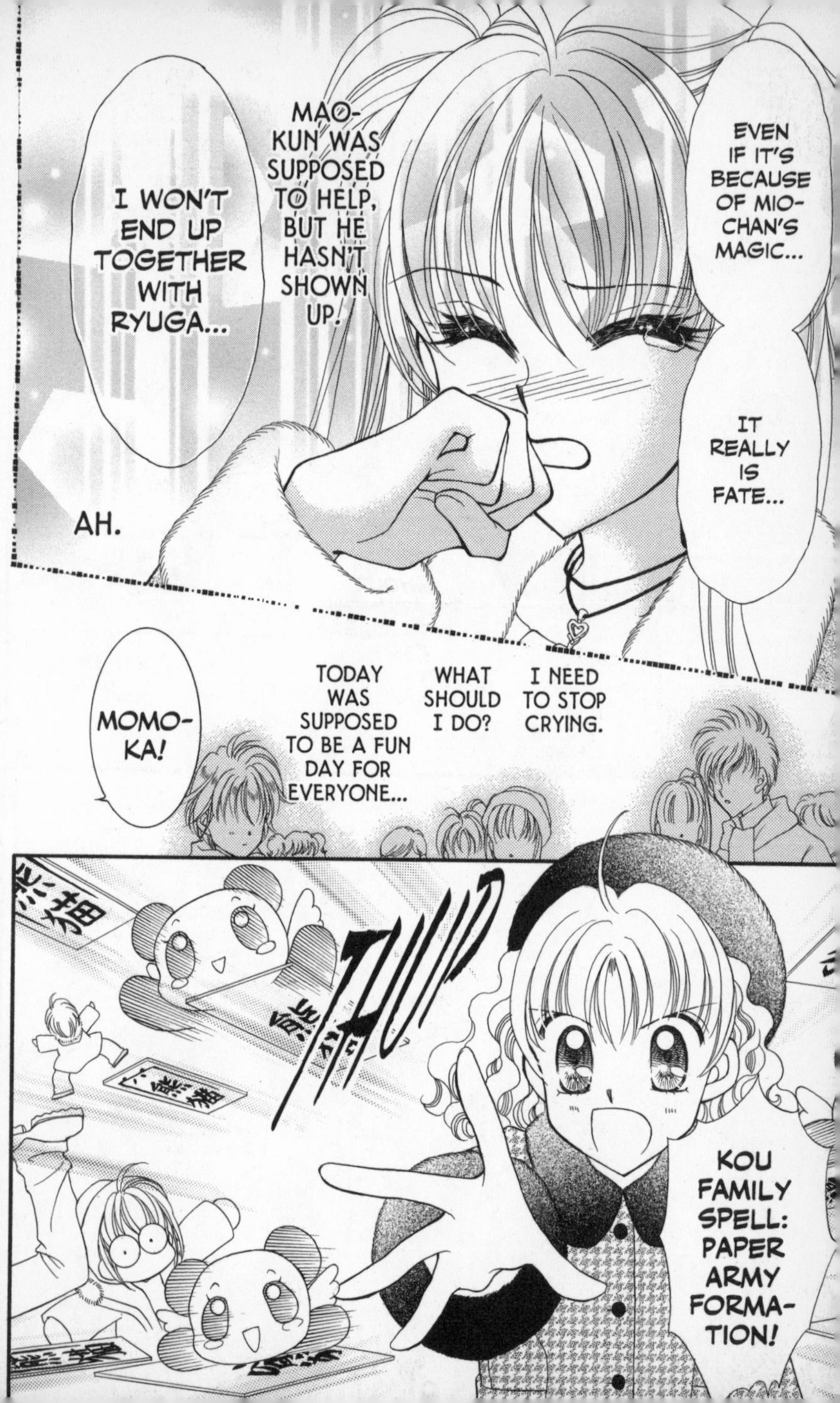
EVEN IF IT'S BECAUSE OF MIO-CHAN'S MAGIC...
IT REALLY IS FATE...
MAO-KUN WAS SUPPOSED TO HELP, BUT HE HASN'T SHOWN UP.
I WON'T END UP TOGETHER WITH RYUGA...
AH.
I NEED TO STOP CRYING.
WHAT SHOULD I DO?
TODAY WAS SUPPOSED TO BE A FUN DAY FOR EVERYONE...
MOMO-KA!
KOU FAMILY SPELL: PAPER ARMY FORMATION!
THUP

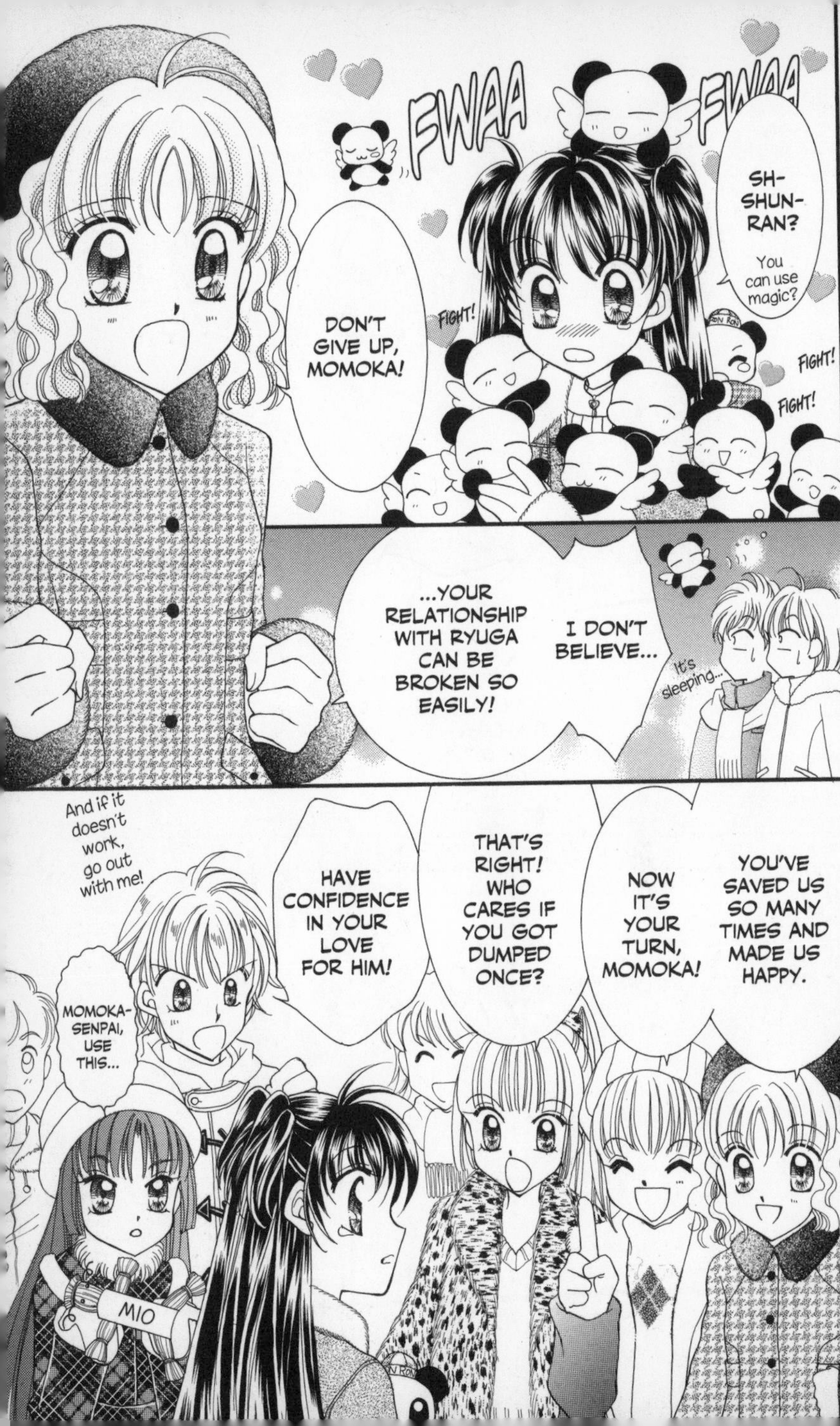
FWAA
FWAA
SH-SHUN-RAN?
You can use magic?
FIGHT!
FIGHT!
FIGHT!
DON'T GIVE UP, MOMOKA!
It's sleeping...
I DON'T BELIEVE...
...YOUR RELATIONSHIP WITH RYUGA CAN BE BROKEN SO EASILY!
YOU'VE SAVED US SO MANY TIMES AND MADE US HAPPY.
NOW IT'S YOUR TURN, MOMOKA!
THAT'S RIGHT! WHO CARES IF YOU GOT DUMPED ONCE?
HAVE CONFIDENCE IN YOUR LOVE FOR HIM!
And if it doesn't work, go out with me!
MOMOKA-SENPAI, USE THIS...
MIO

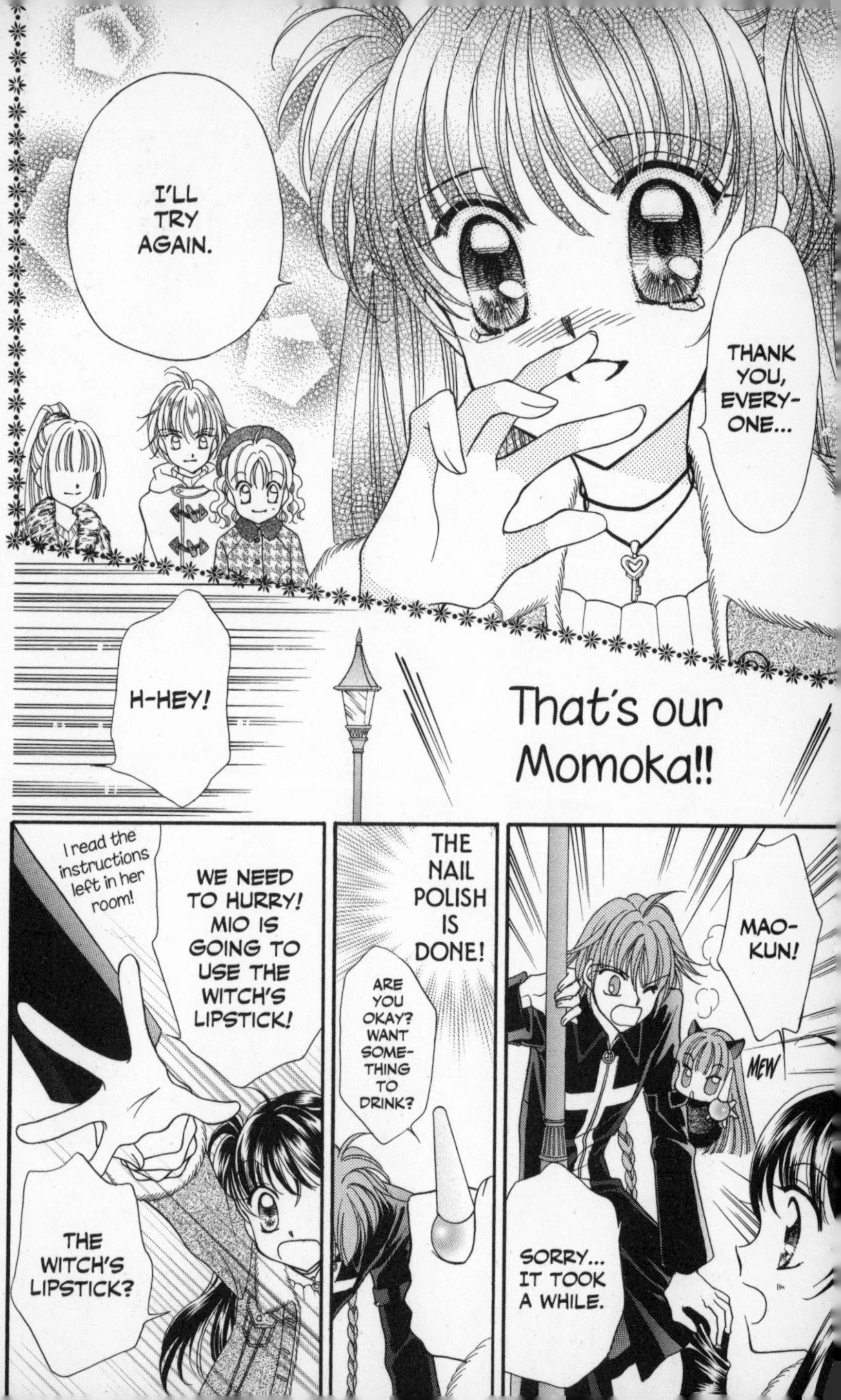
THANK YOU, EVERYONE...
I'LL TRY AGAIN.
That's our Momoka!!
H-HEY!
MAO-KUN!
MEW
SORRY... IT TOOK A WHILE.
THE NAIL POLISH IS DONE!
ARE YOU OKAY? WANT SOMETHING TO DRINK?
WE NEED TO HURRY! MIO IS GOING TO USE THE WITCH'S LIPSTICK!
I read the instructions left in her room!
THE WITCH'S LIPSTICK?

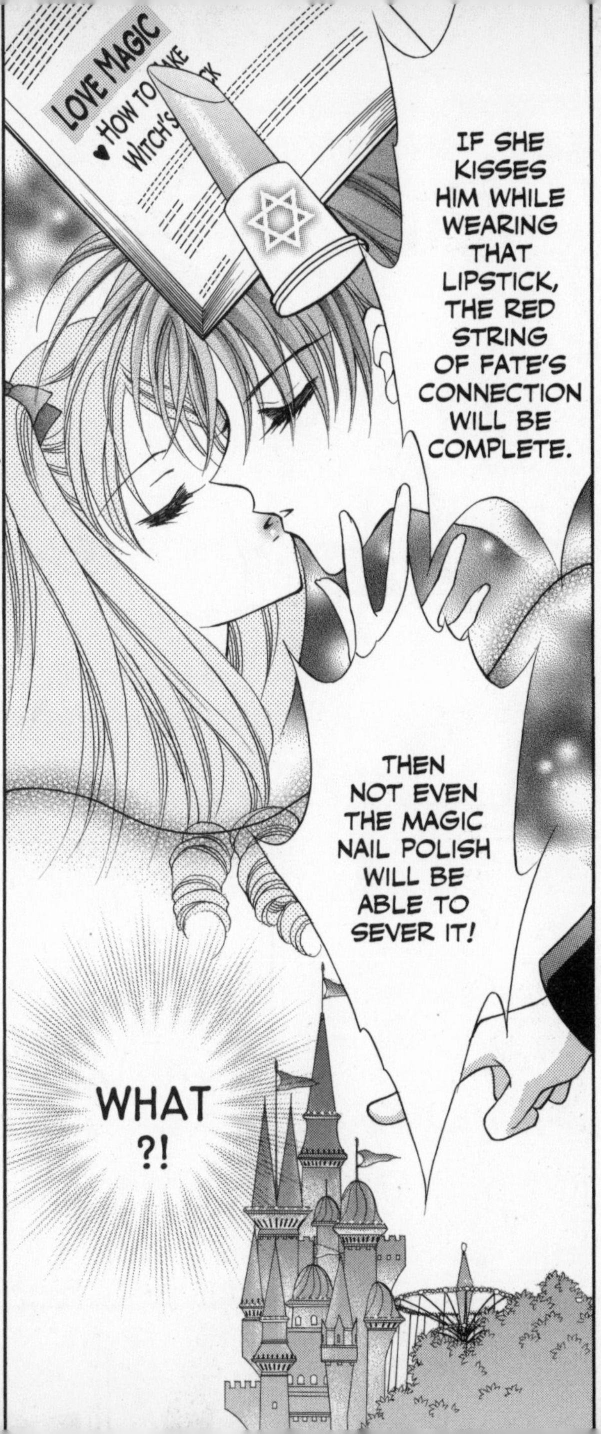
LOVE MAGIC
IF SHE KISSES HIM WHILE WEARING THAT LIPSTICK, THE RED STRING OF FATE'S CONNECTION WILL BE COMPLETE.
THEN NOT EVEN THE MAGIC NAIL POLISH WILL BE ABLE TO SEVER IT!
WHAT ?!

2

This manga will go on sale in September. But the story is set in winter. Since the seasons will be off, I used summery graphics in these sidebars.

I've made a lot of furoku for *Ribon*. Those are prepared many months beforehand.

In the boiling hot summer, I was making *St.♥Dragon Girl* Christmas cards! What a good memory...

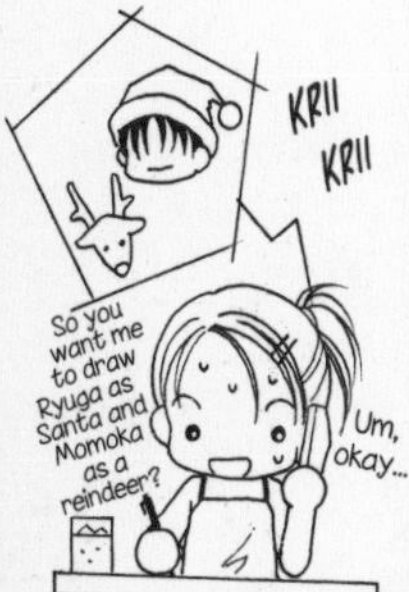
KRII
KRII
So you want me to draw Ryuga as Santa and Momoka as a reindeer?
Um, okay...

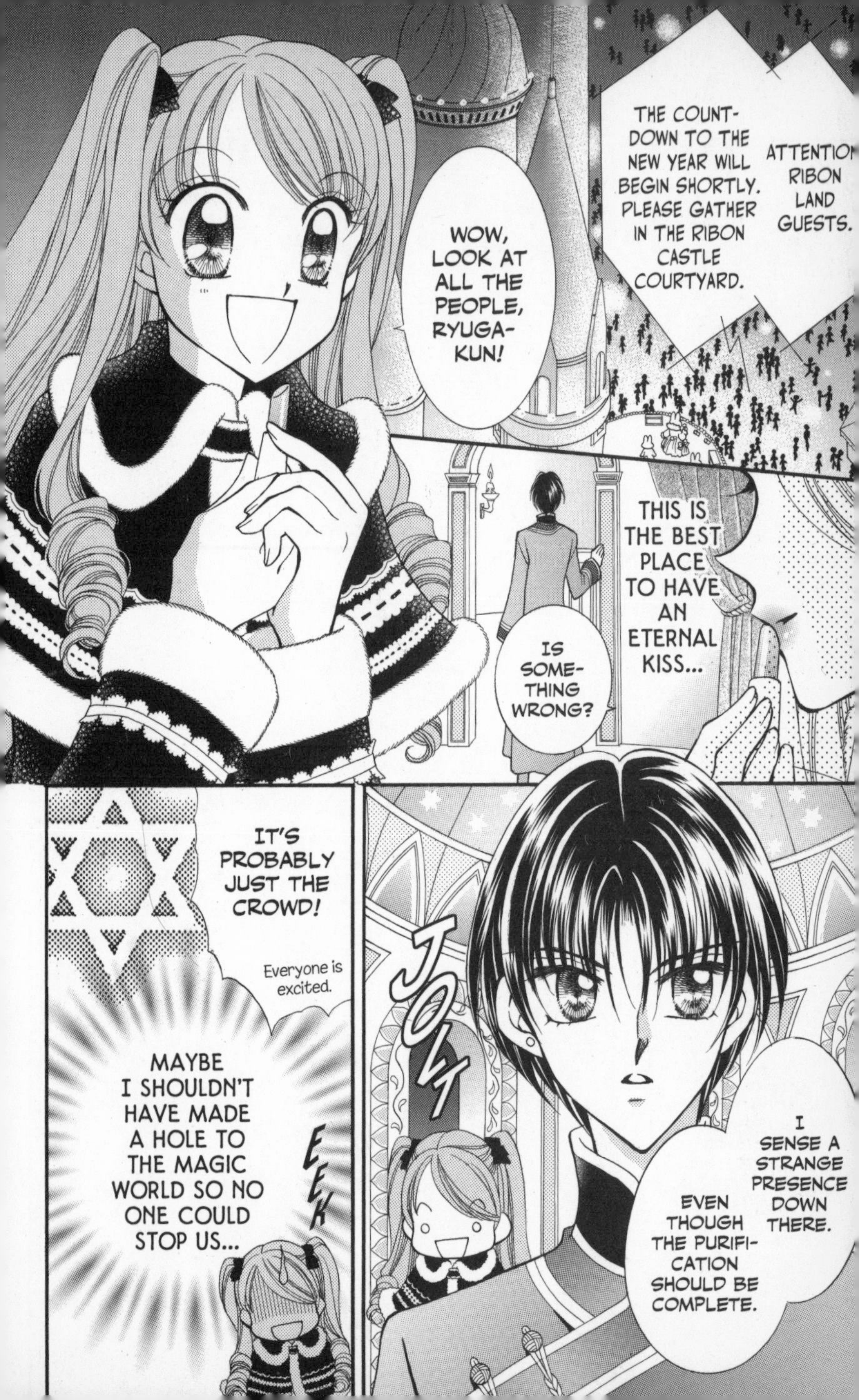
ATTENTION RIBON LAND GUESTS.
THE COUNTDOWN TO THE NEW YEAR WILL BEGIN SHORTLY. PLEASE GATHER IN THE RIBON CASTLE COURTYARD.
THIS IS THE BEST PLACE TO HAVE AN ETERNAL KISS...
IS SOMETHING WRONG?
WOW, LOOK AT ALL THE PEOPLE, RYUGA-KUN!
JOLT
I SENSE A STRANGE PRESENCE DOWN THERE.
EVEN THOUGH THE PURIFICATION SHOULD BE COMPLETE.
IT'S PROBABLY JUST THE CROWD!
Everyone is excited.
MAYBE I SHOULDN'T HAVE MADE A HOLE TO THE MAGIC WORLD SO NO ONE COULD STOP US...
EEK

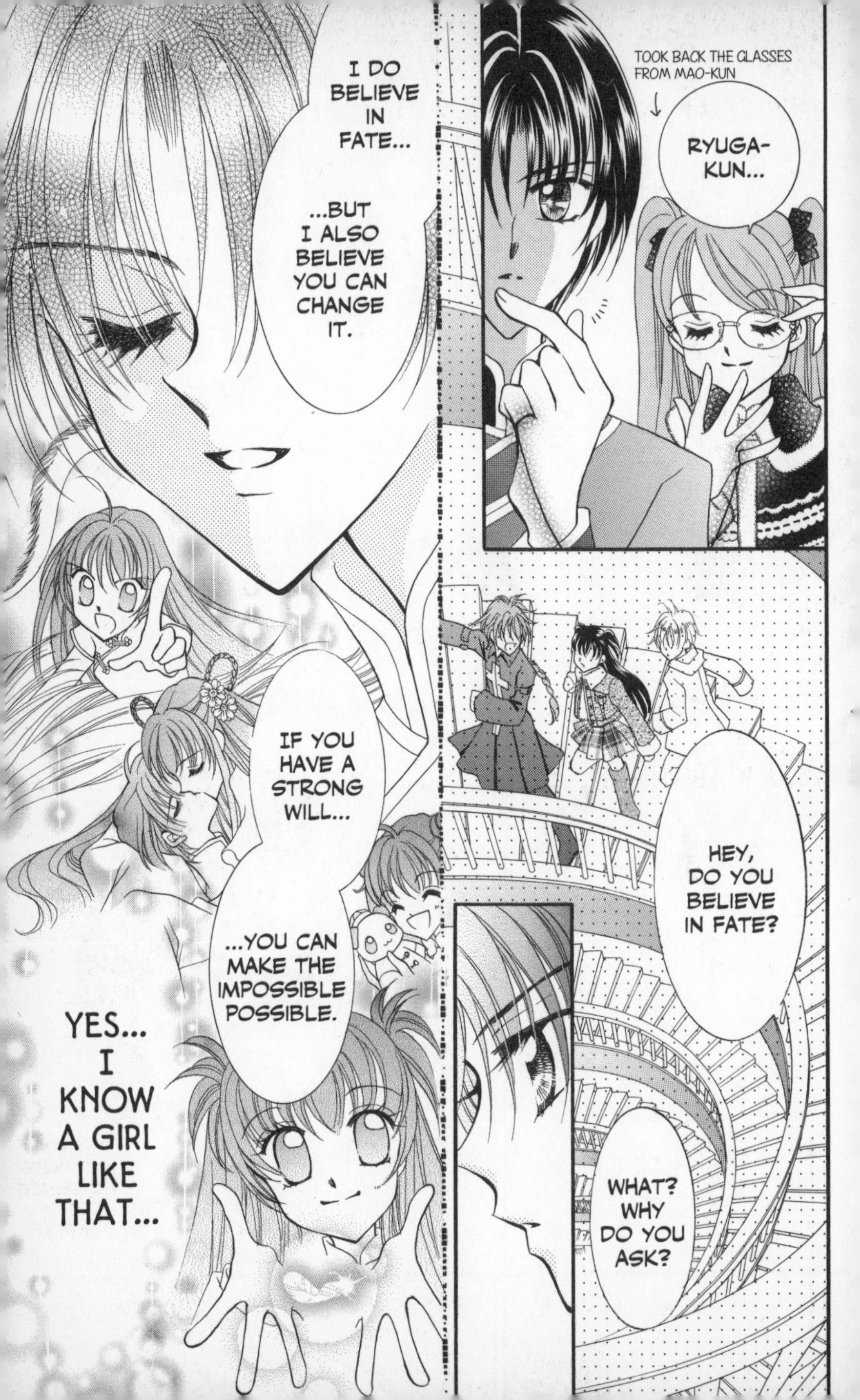
TOOK BACK THE GLASSES FROM MAO-KUN
RYUGA-KUN...
HEY, DO YOU BELIEVE IN FATE?
WHAT? WHY DO YOU ASK?
I DO BELIEVE IN FATE...
...BUT I ALSO BELIEVE YOU CAN CHANGE IT.
IF YOU HAVE A STRONG WILL...
...YOU CAN MAKE THE IMPOSSIBLE POSSIBLE.
YES... I KNOW A GIRL LIKE THAT...

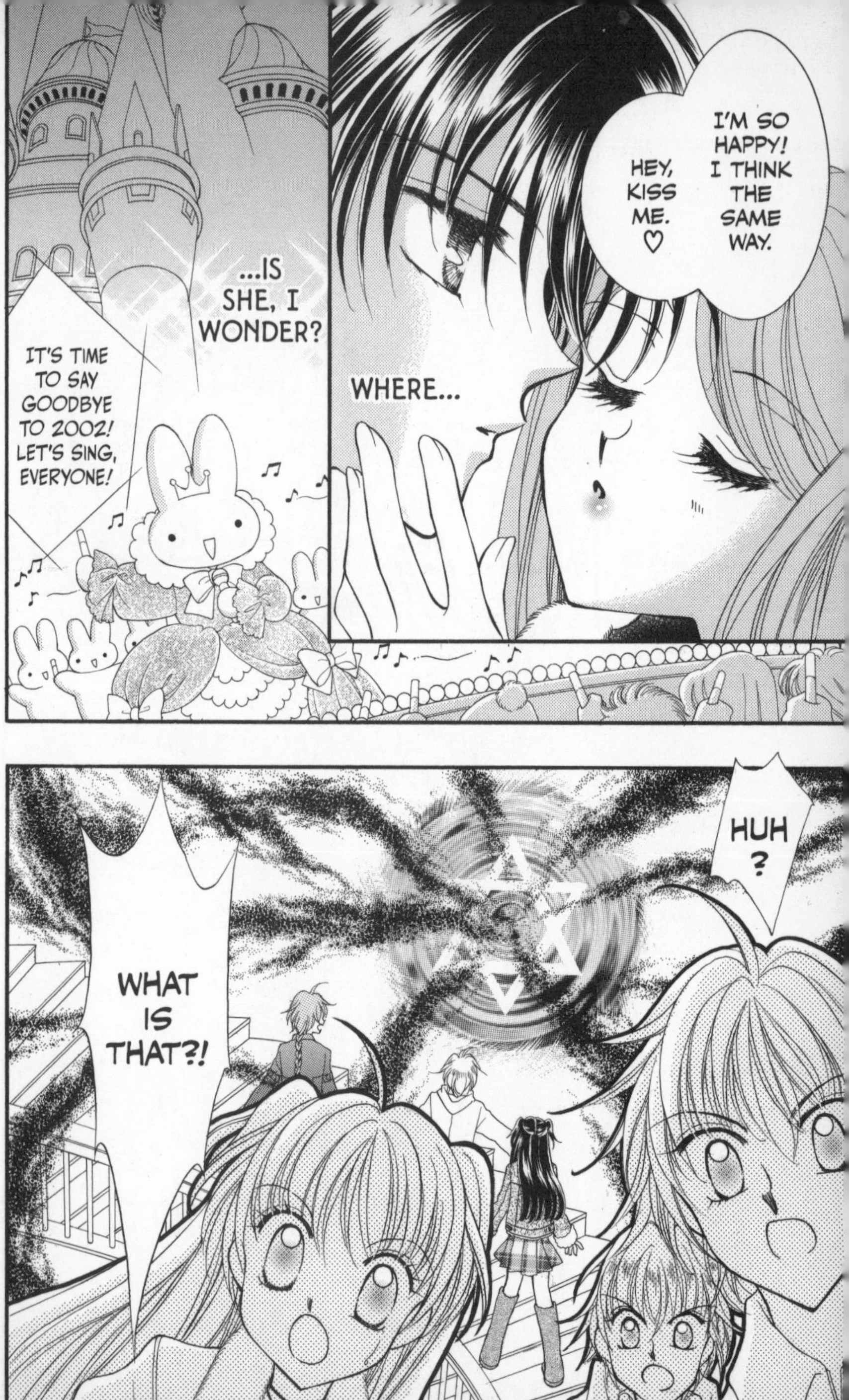
I'M SO HAPPY! I THINK THE SAME WAY.
HEY, KISS ME. ♡
WHERE...
...IS SHE, I WONDER?
IT'S TIME TO SAY GOODBYE TO 2002! LET'S SING, EVERYONE!
HUH?
WHAT IS THAT?!

3

In this story Shunran used magic! A lot of people were surprised by that. But just because she can conjure up pandas doesn't mean she can do any other sorcery! (laugh)

I wanted to write a story about Momoka's friends saving her. Even though they are just encouraging her, I'm glad I could write this story.

There were a lot of characters and they weren't wearing school uniforms, so it was a little difficult to draw, but since I was able to show everyone's individual styles, I enjoyed it.

I like drawing coats, but since there were a lot of action scenes with Momoka, I just put her in a denim jacket.

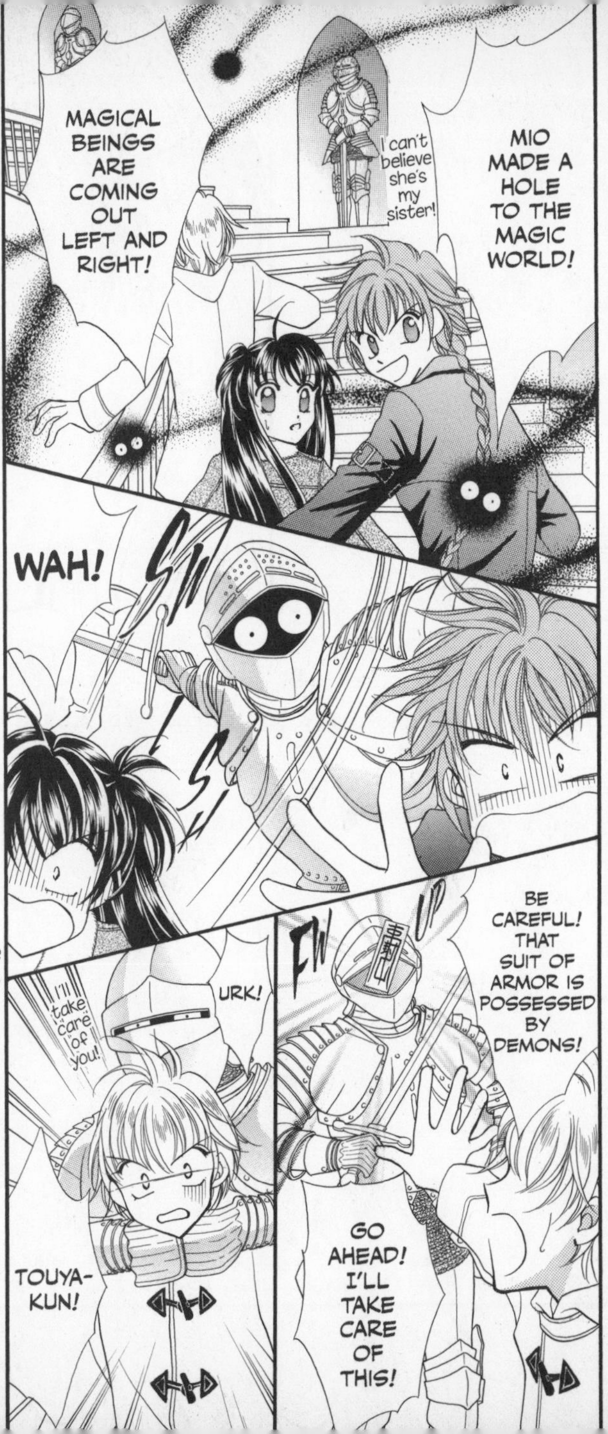
MIO MADE A HOLE TO THE MAGIC WORLD!
I can't believe she's my sister!
MAGICAL BEINGS ARE COMING OUT LEFT AND RIGHT!
WAH!
BE CAREFUL! THAT SUIT OF ARMOR IS POSSESSED BY DEMONS!
GO AHEAD! I'LL TAKE CARE OF THIS!
URK!
I'll take care of you!
TOUYA-KUN!

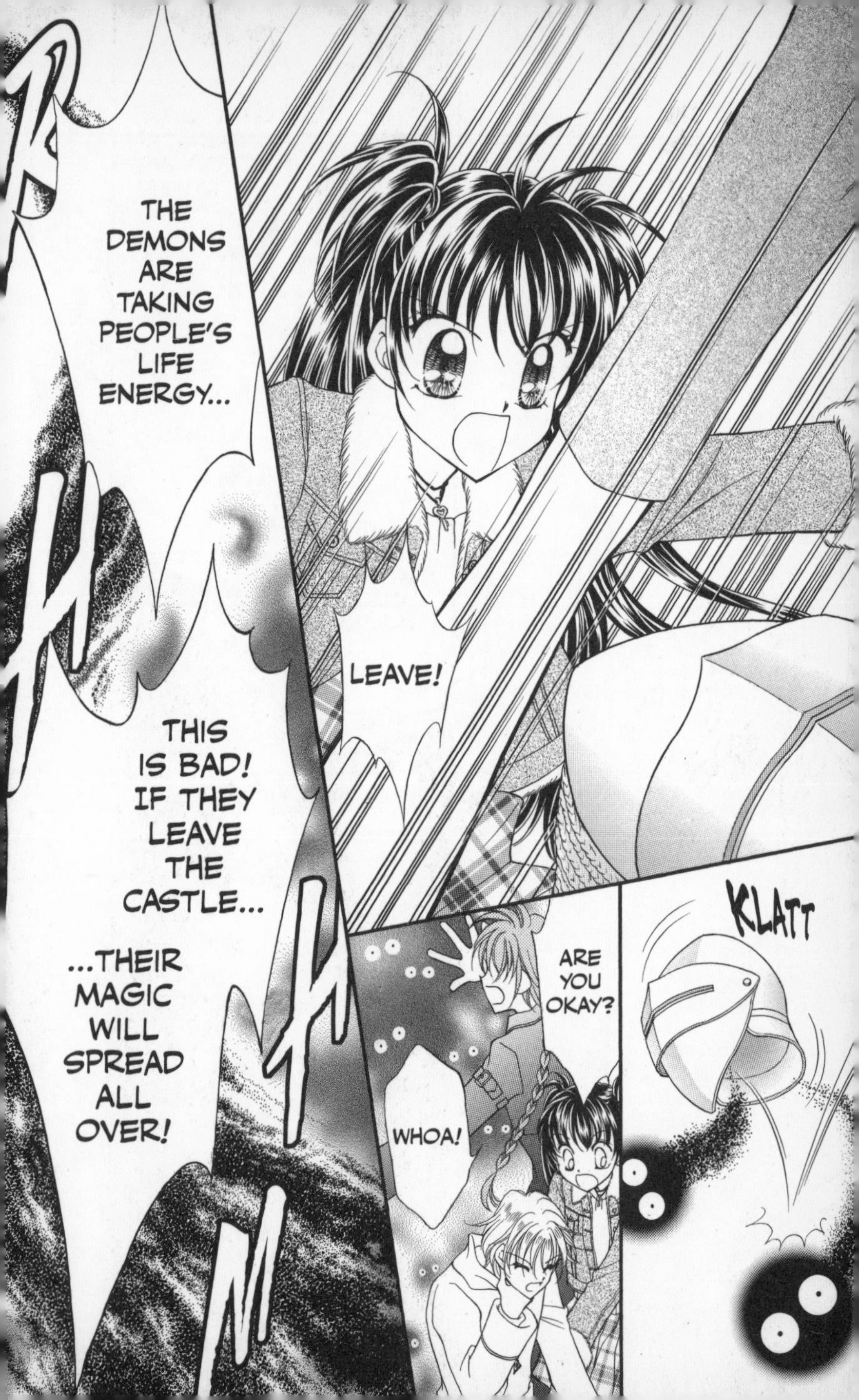
LEAVE!
KLATT
ARE YOU OKAY?
WHOA!
THE DEMONS ARE TAKING PEOPLE'S LIFE ENERGY...
THIS IS BAD! IF THEY LEAVE THE CASTLE...
...THEIR MAGIC WILL SPREAD ALL OVER!

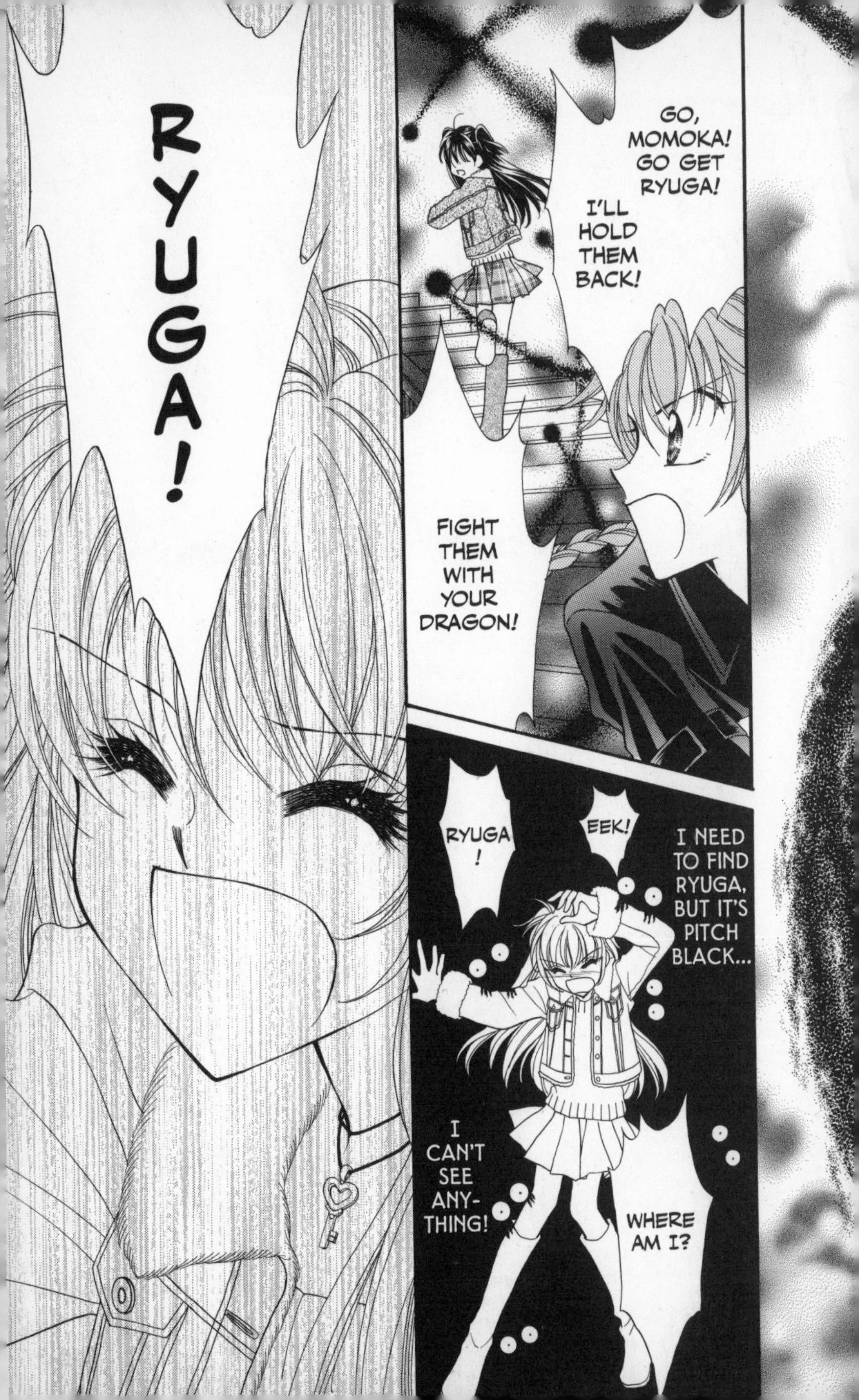
GO, MOMOKA! GO GET RYUGA!
I'LL HOLD THEM BACK!
FIGHT THEM WITH YOUR DRAGON!
I NEED TO FIND RYUGA, BUT IT'S PITCH BLACK...
EEK!
RYUGA!
WHERE AM I?
I CAN'T SEE ANY-THING!
RYUGA!

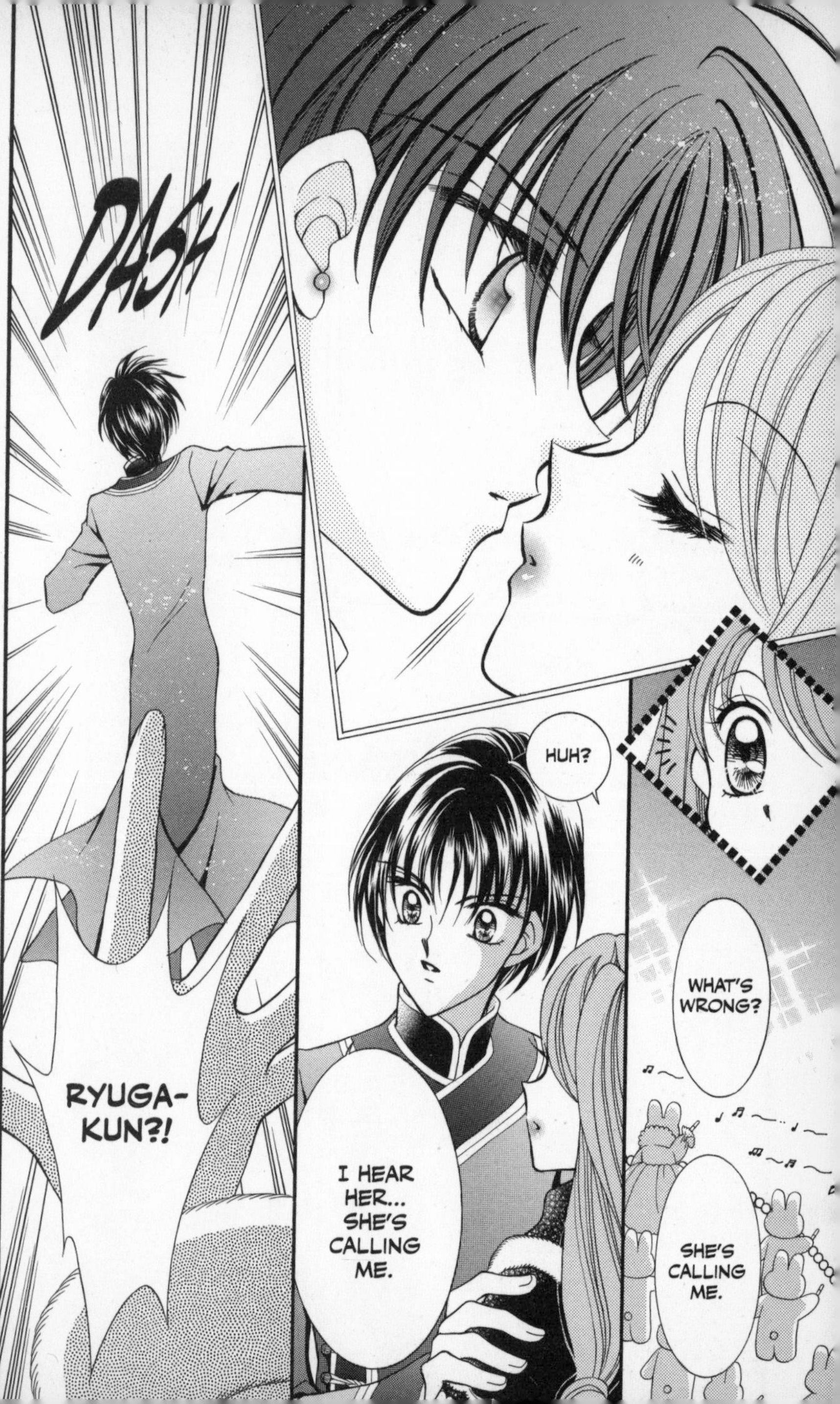
WHAT'S WRONG?
SHE'S CALLING ME.
HUH?
I HEAR HER... SHE'S CALLING ME.
DASH
RYUGA-KUN?!

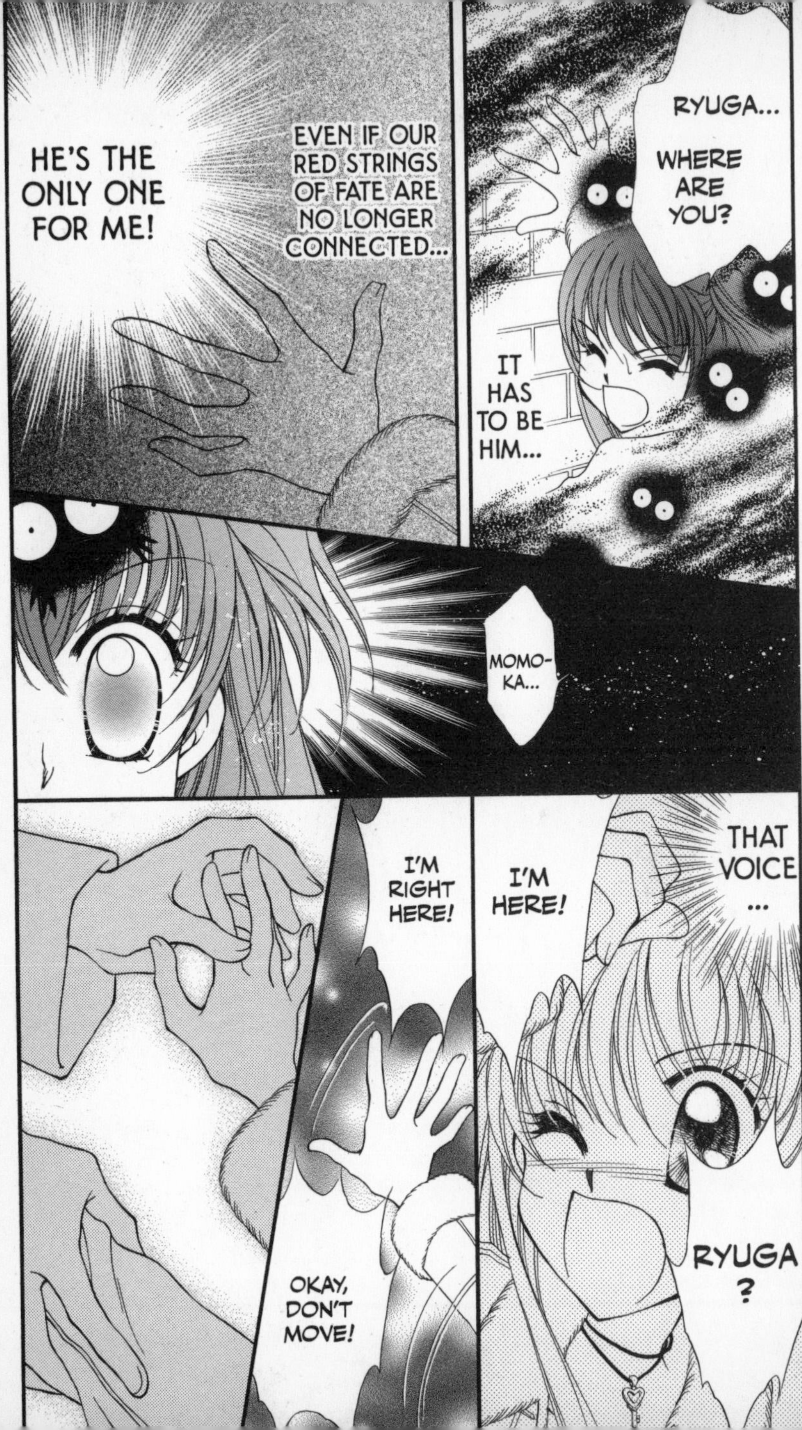
RYUGA...
WHERE ARE YOU?
IT HAS TO BE HIM...
EVEN IF OUR RED STRINGS OF FATE ARE NO LONGER CONNECTED...
HE'S THE ONLY ONE FOR ME!
MOMO-KA...
THAT VOICE ...
I'M HERE!
RYUGA ?
I'M RIGHT HERE!
OKAY, DON'T MOVE!

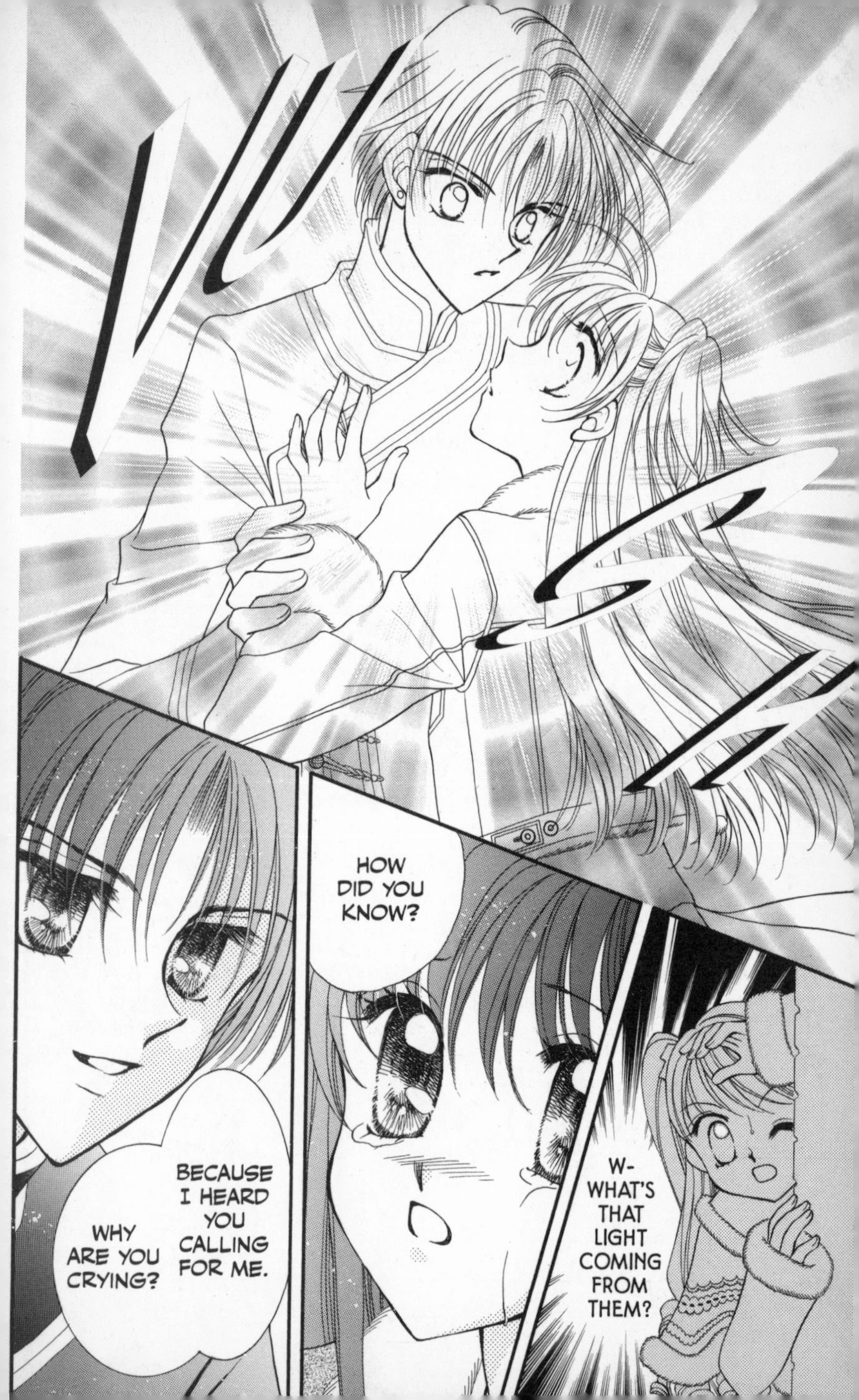
W- WHAT'S THAT LIGHT COMING FROM THEM?
HOW DID YOU KNOW?
BECAUSE I HEARD YOU CALLING FOR ME.
WHY ARE YOU CRYING?

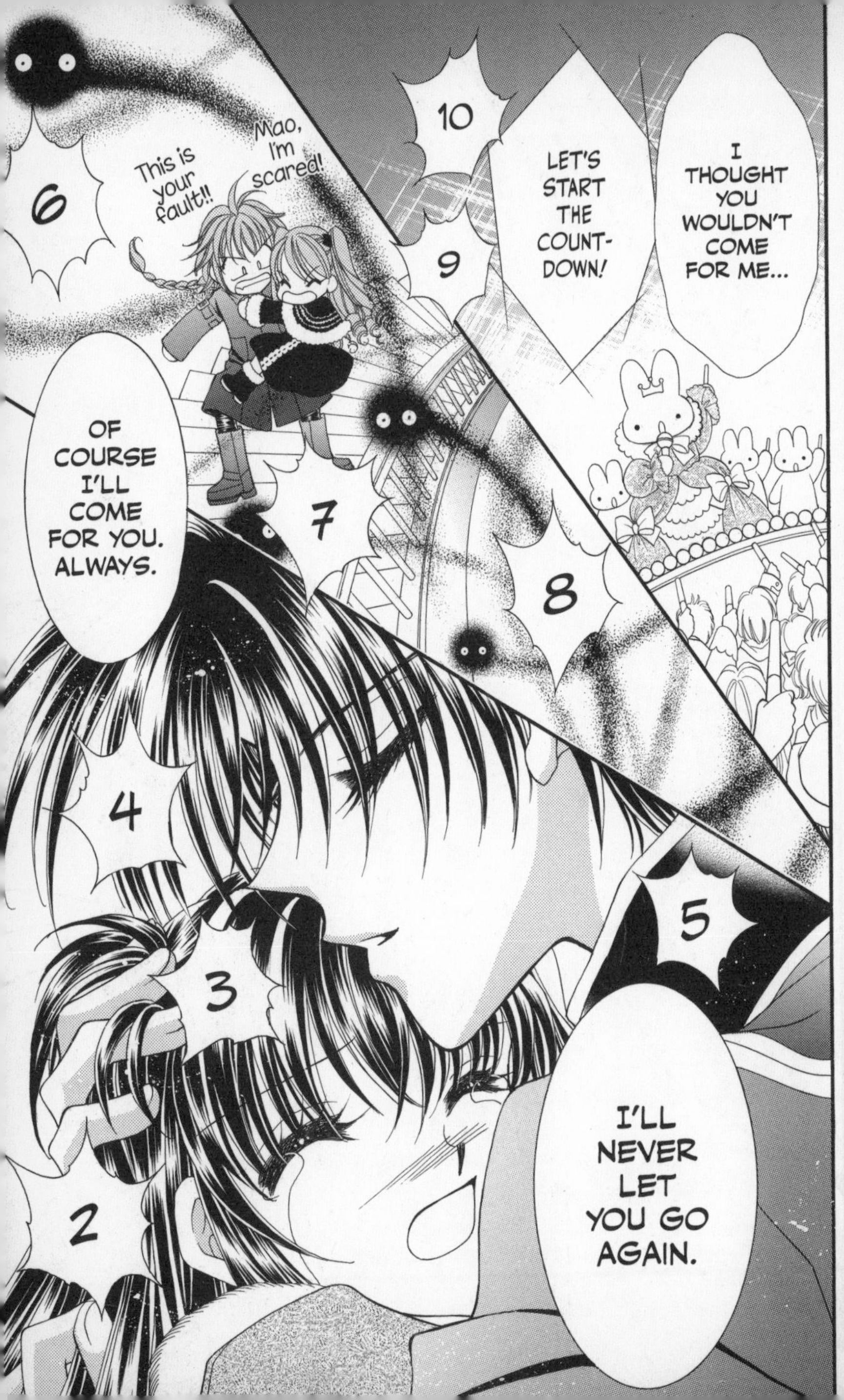
I THOUGHT YOU WOULDN'T COME FOR ME...
LET'S START THE COUNT-DOWN!
10
9
8
7
Mao, I'm scared!
This is your fault!!
6
5
OF COURSE I'LL COME FOR YOU. ALWAYS.
4
3
I'LL NEVER LET YOU GO AGAIN.
2

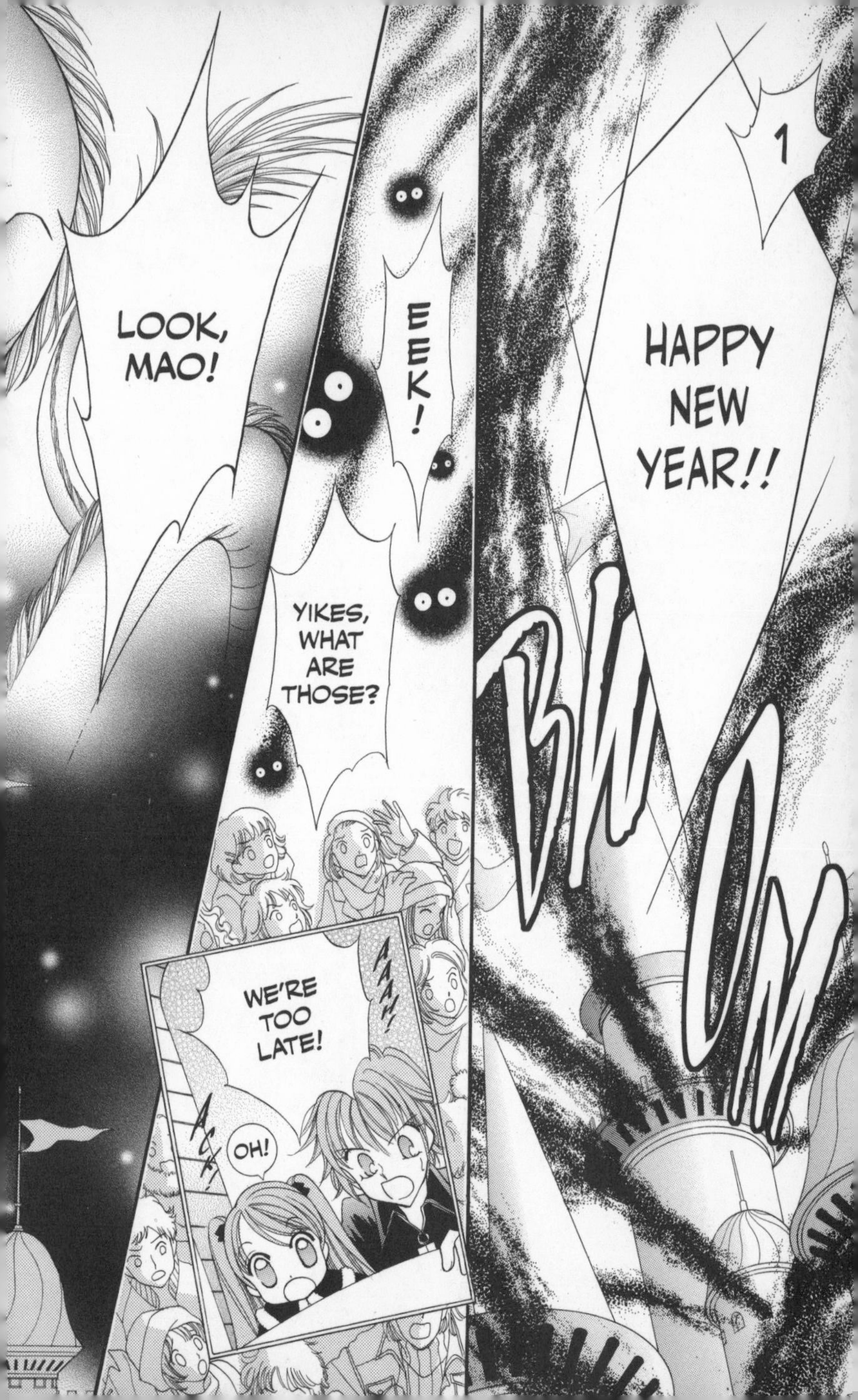
1
HAPPY NEW YEAR!!
EEK!
YIKES, WHAT ARE THOSE?
WE'RE TOO LATE!
AAAH!
ACK!
OH!
LOOK, MAO!

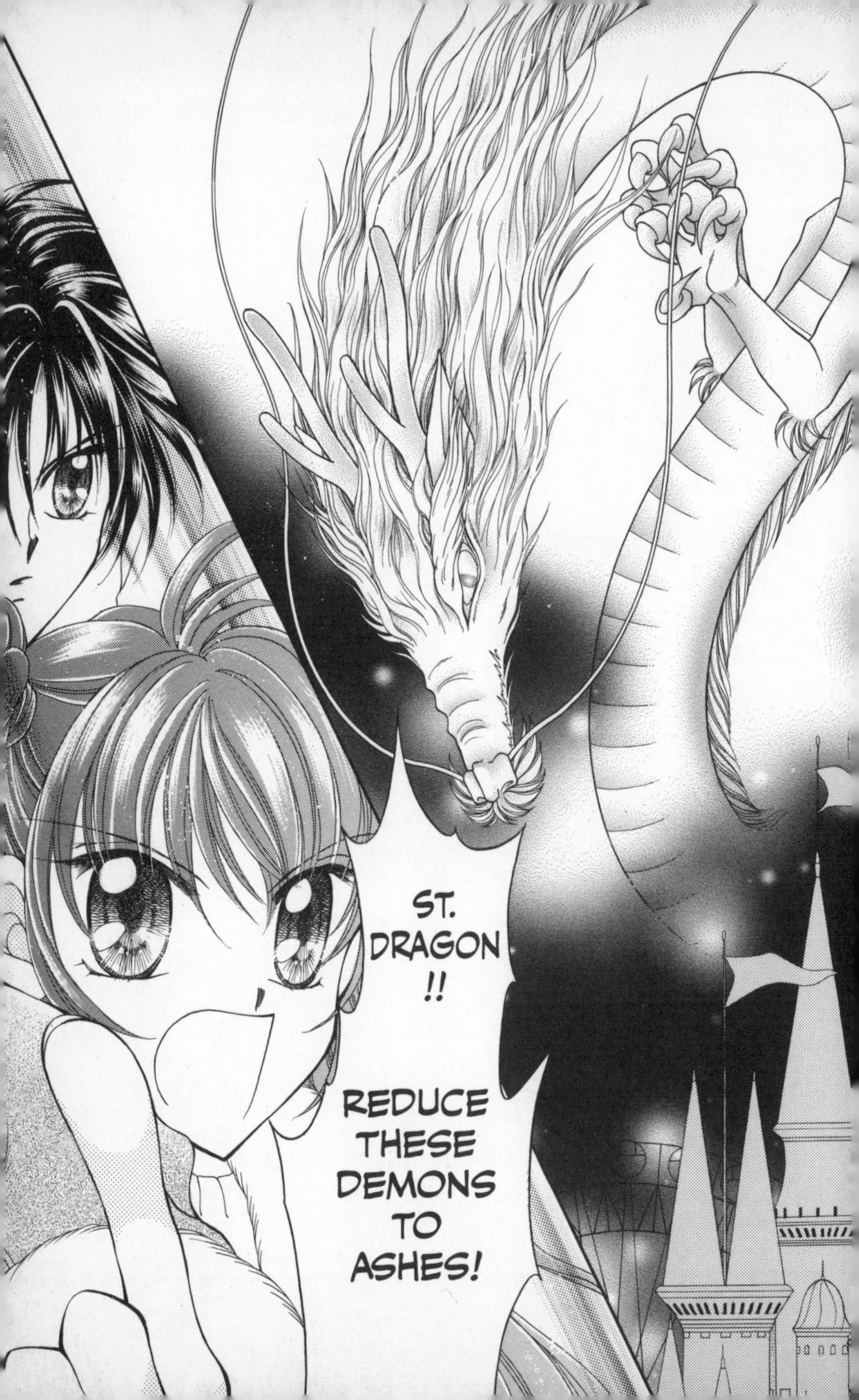
ST. DRAGON !!
REDUCE THESE DEMONS TO ASHES!

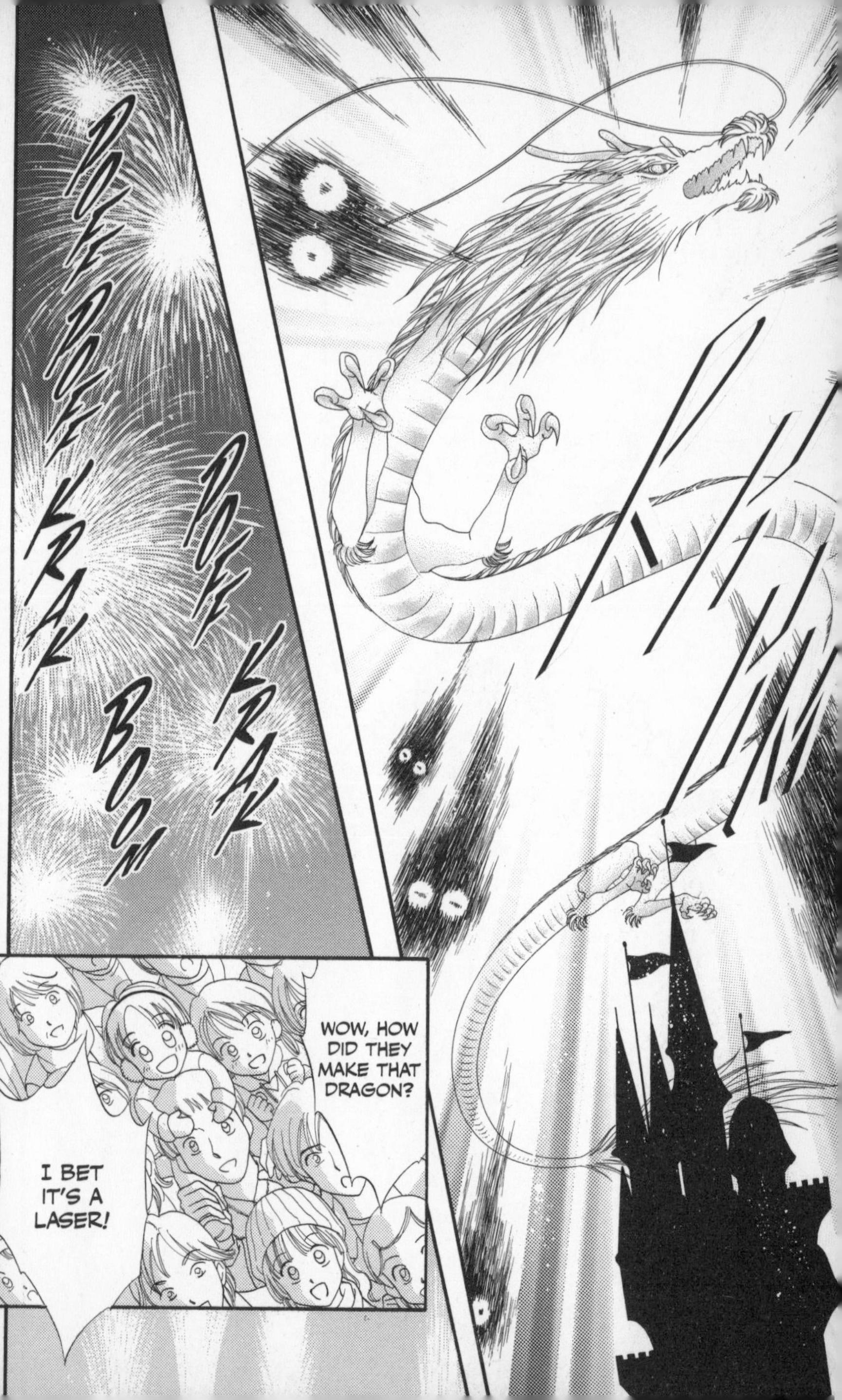
DOOOOOM KRAK
DOOM KRAK
BOOM
WOW, HOW DID THEY MAKE THAT DRAGON?
I BET IT'S A LASER!

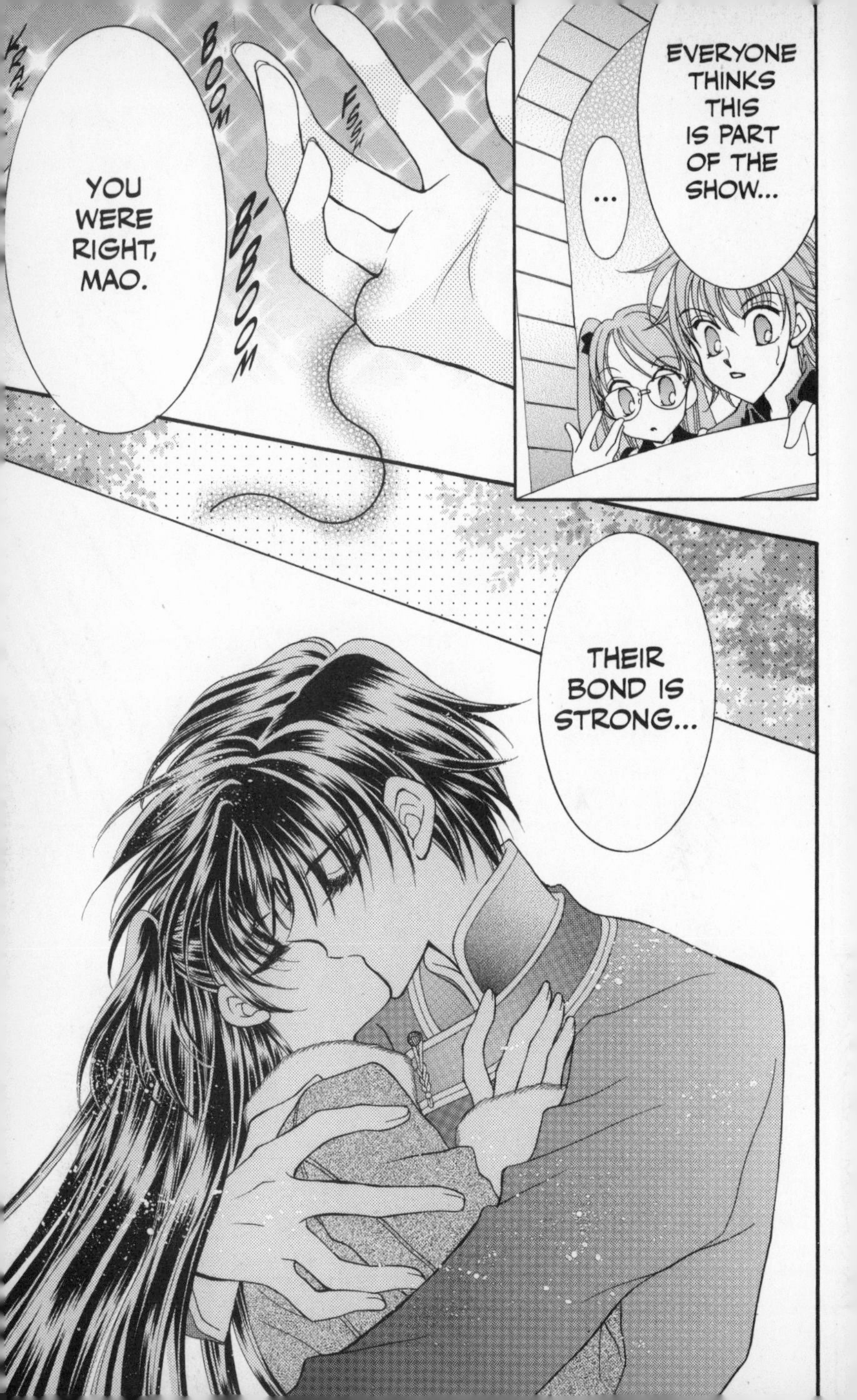
EVERYONE THINKS THIS IS PART OF THE SHOW...
...
FSSH
BOOM
B'BOOM
KRAK
YOU WERE RIGHT, MAO.
THEIR BOND IS STRONG...

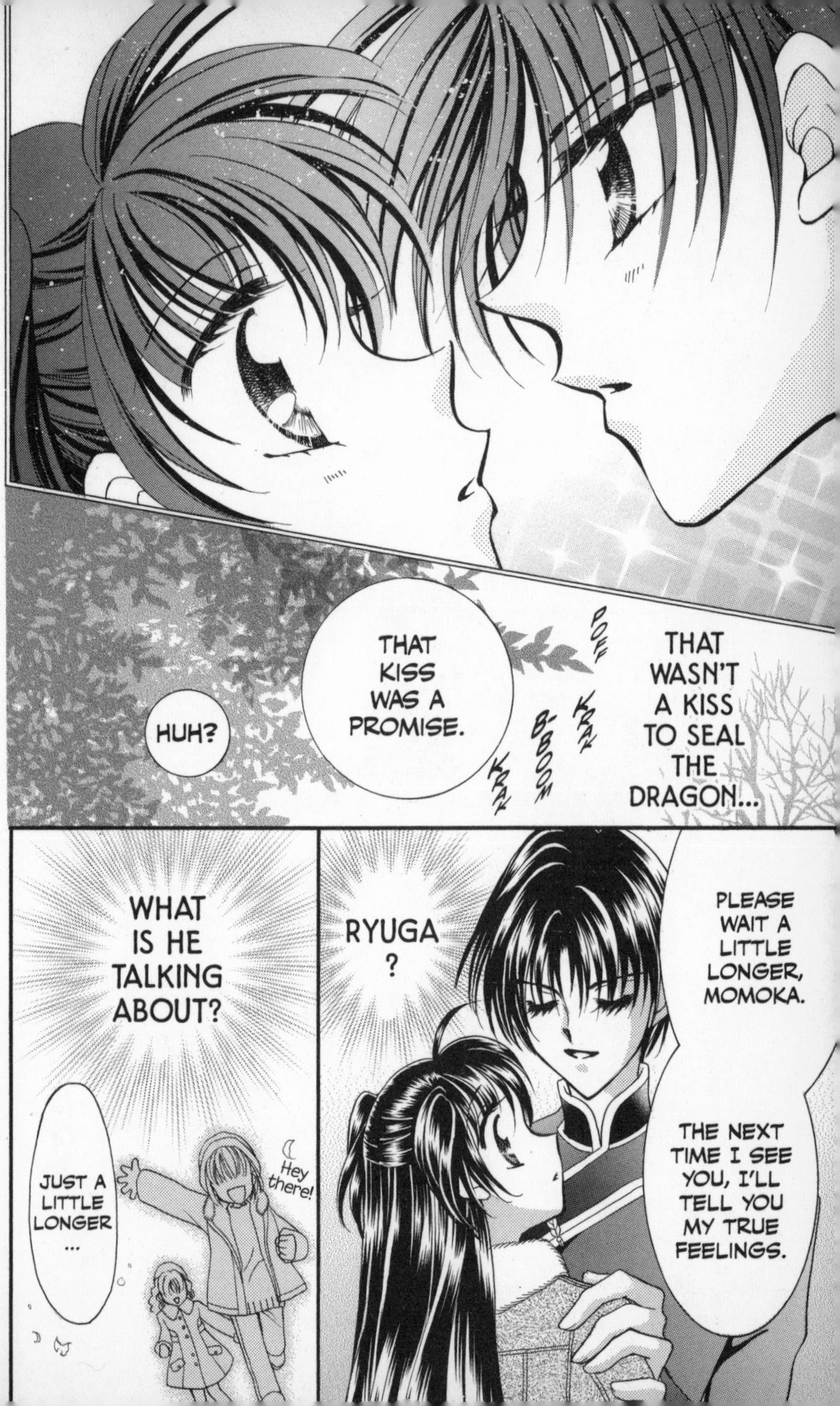
THAT WASN'T A KISS TO SEAL THE DRAGON...
POFF
KRAK
B-BOOM
KRAK
THAT KISS WAS A PROMISE.
HUH?
PLEASE WAIT A LITTLE LONGER, MOMOKA.
RYUGA?
THE NEXT TIME I SEE YOU, I'LL TELL YOU MY TRUE FEELINGS.
WHAT IS HE TALKING ABOUT?
Hey there!
JUST A LITTLE LONGER ...

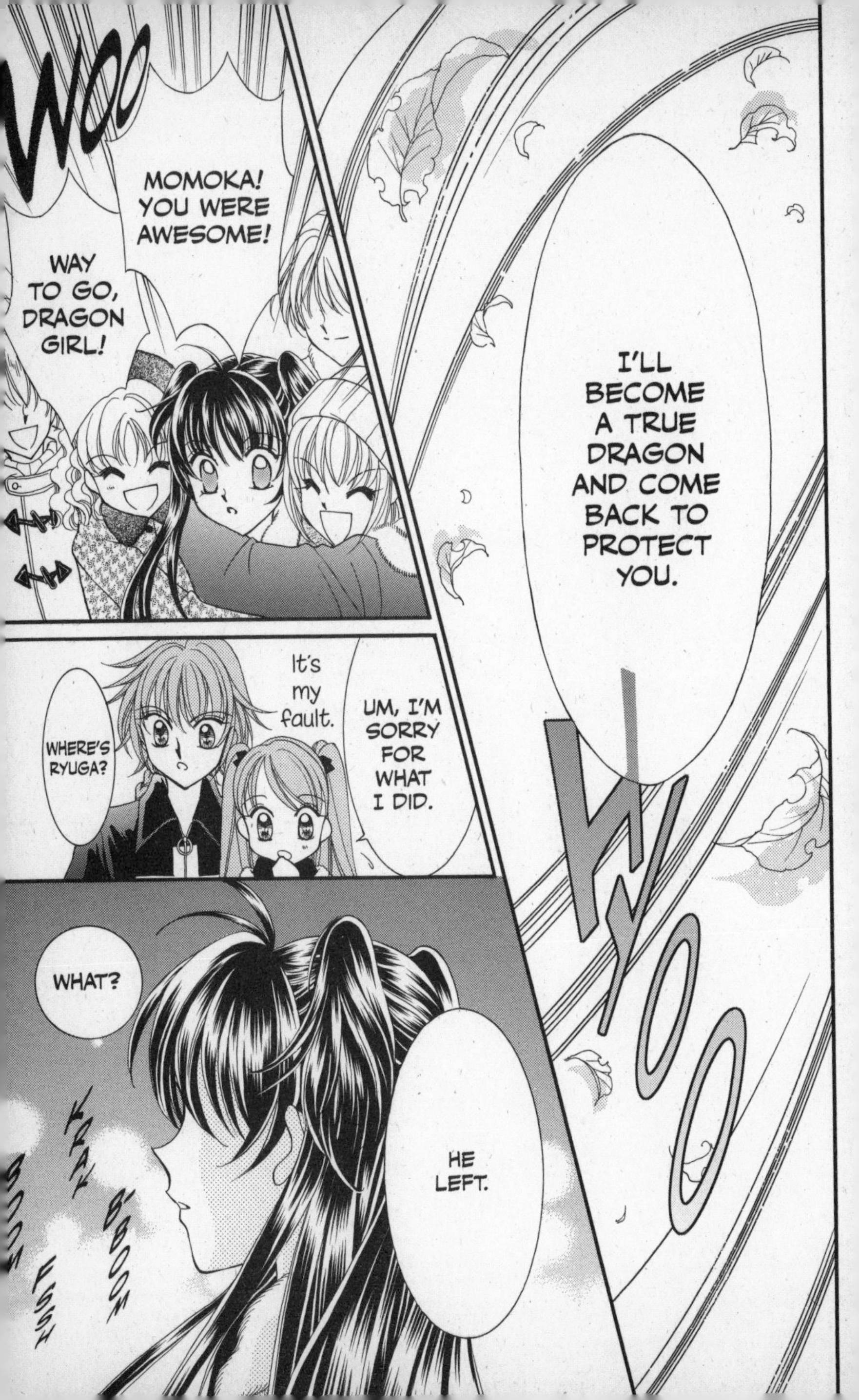
I'LL BECOME A TRUE DRAGON AND COME BACK TO PROTECT YOU.
WOO
MOMOKA! YOU WERE AWESOME!
WAY TO GO, DRAGON GIRL!
UM, I'M SORRY FOR WHAT I DID.
It's my fault.
WHERE'S RYUGA?
HE LEFT.
WHAT?

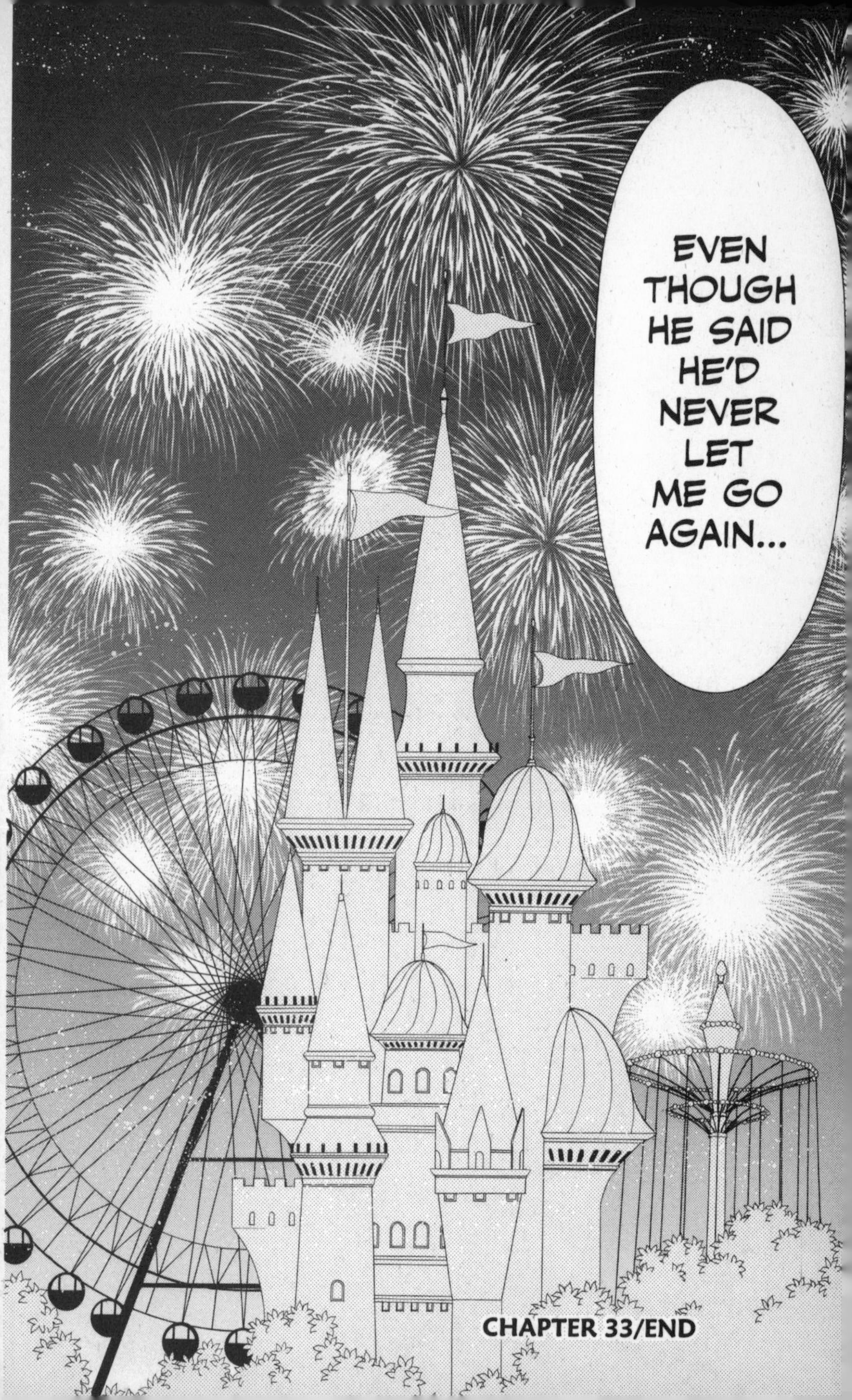
EVEN THOUGH HE SAID HE'D NEVER LET ME GO AGAIN...
CHAPTER 33/END

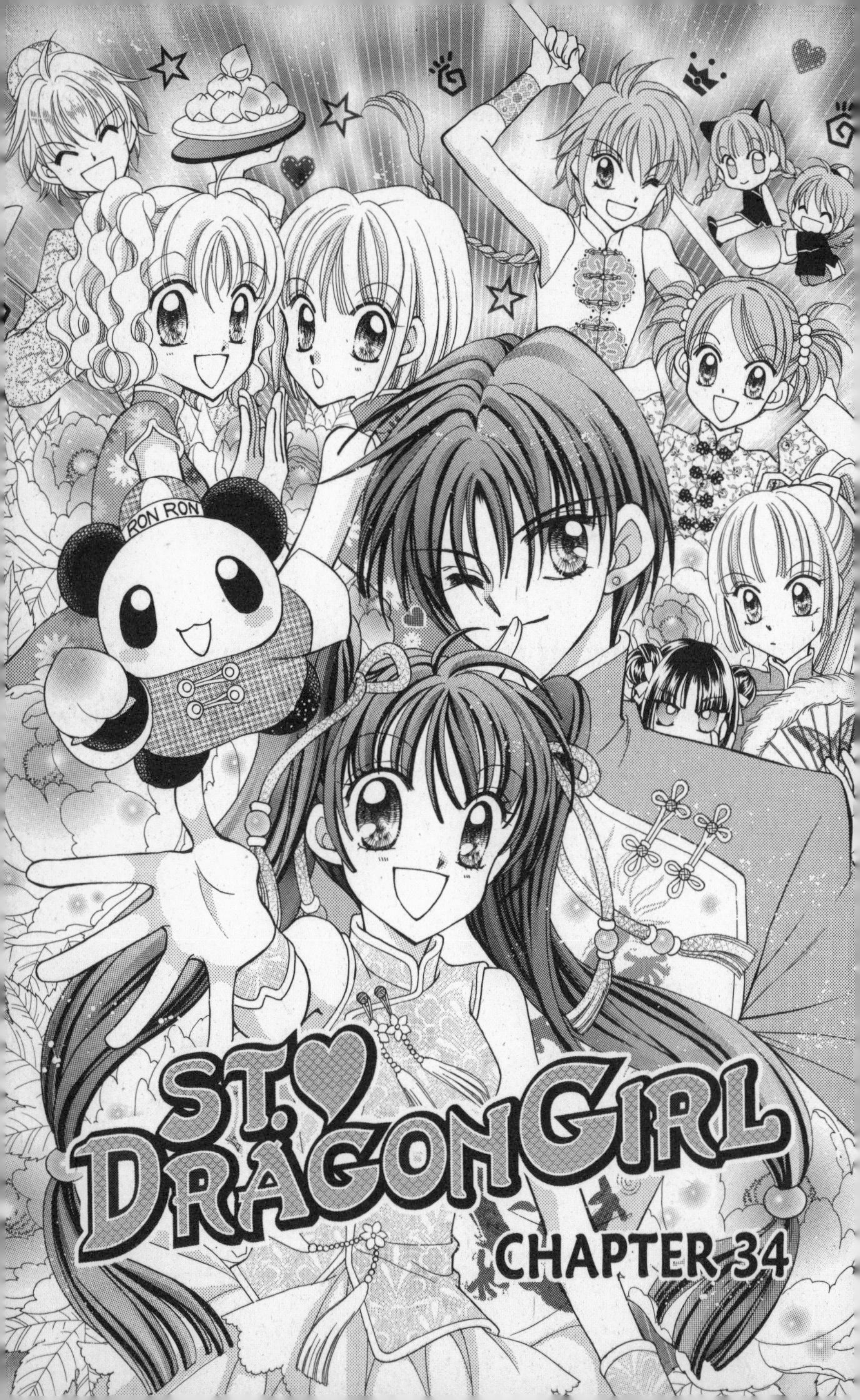
RON RON
ST.♥DRAGON GIRL
CHAPTER 34

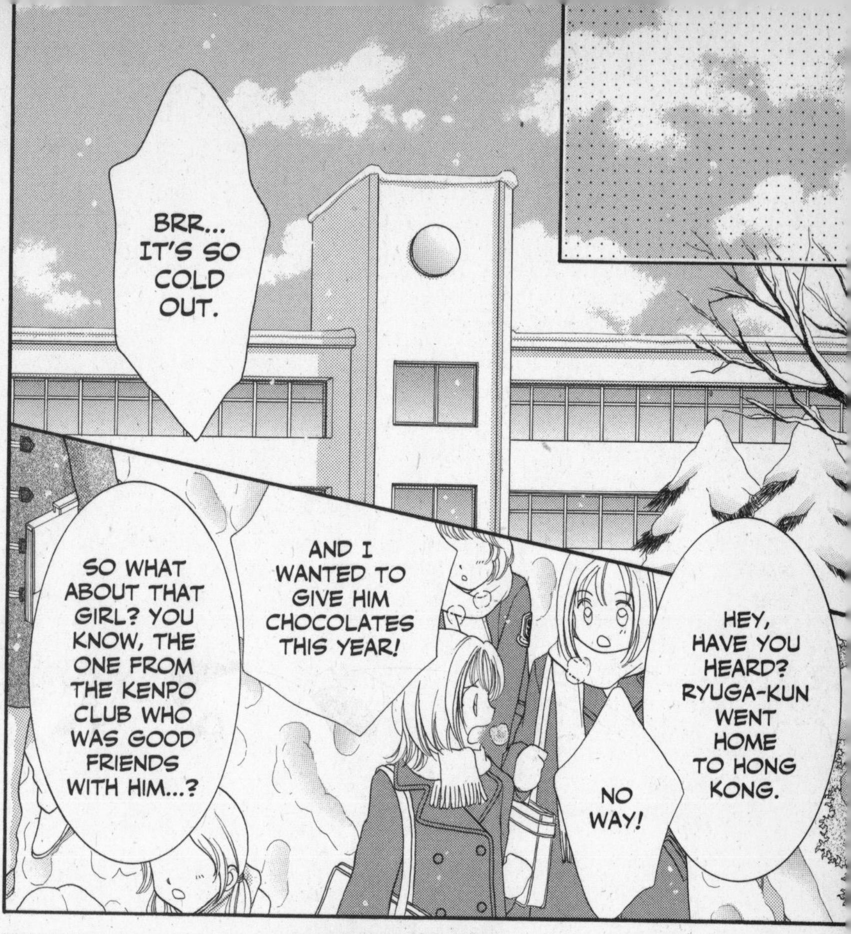
BRR... IT'S SO COLD OUT.
HEY, HAVE YOU HEARD? RYUGA-KUN WENT HOME TO HONG KONG.
NO WAY!
AND I WANTED TO GIVE HIM CHOCOLATES THIS YEAR!
SO WHAT ABOUT THAT GIRL? YOU KNOW, THE ONE FROM THE KENPO CLUB WHO WAS GOOD FRIENDS WITH HIM...?

Kouju

Ryuga's dragon. Female. A golden dragon with immense power who appears in China once every decade or so. Her human form has blond hair and golden eyes. She and Momoka's dragon fall in love at first sight. Normally she is sealed inside Ryuga.

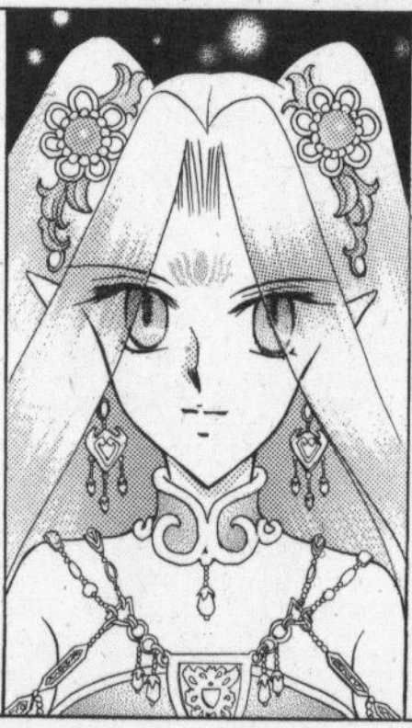

She's about 5,000 years old, older than Shiou. When she gets mad, it's really scary! 💧 Wears more accessories than Shiou. Apparently dragons love being flashy. After Ryuga breaks the seal, his hair shines with a golden sheen.

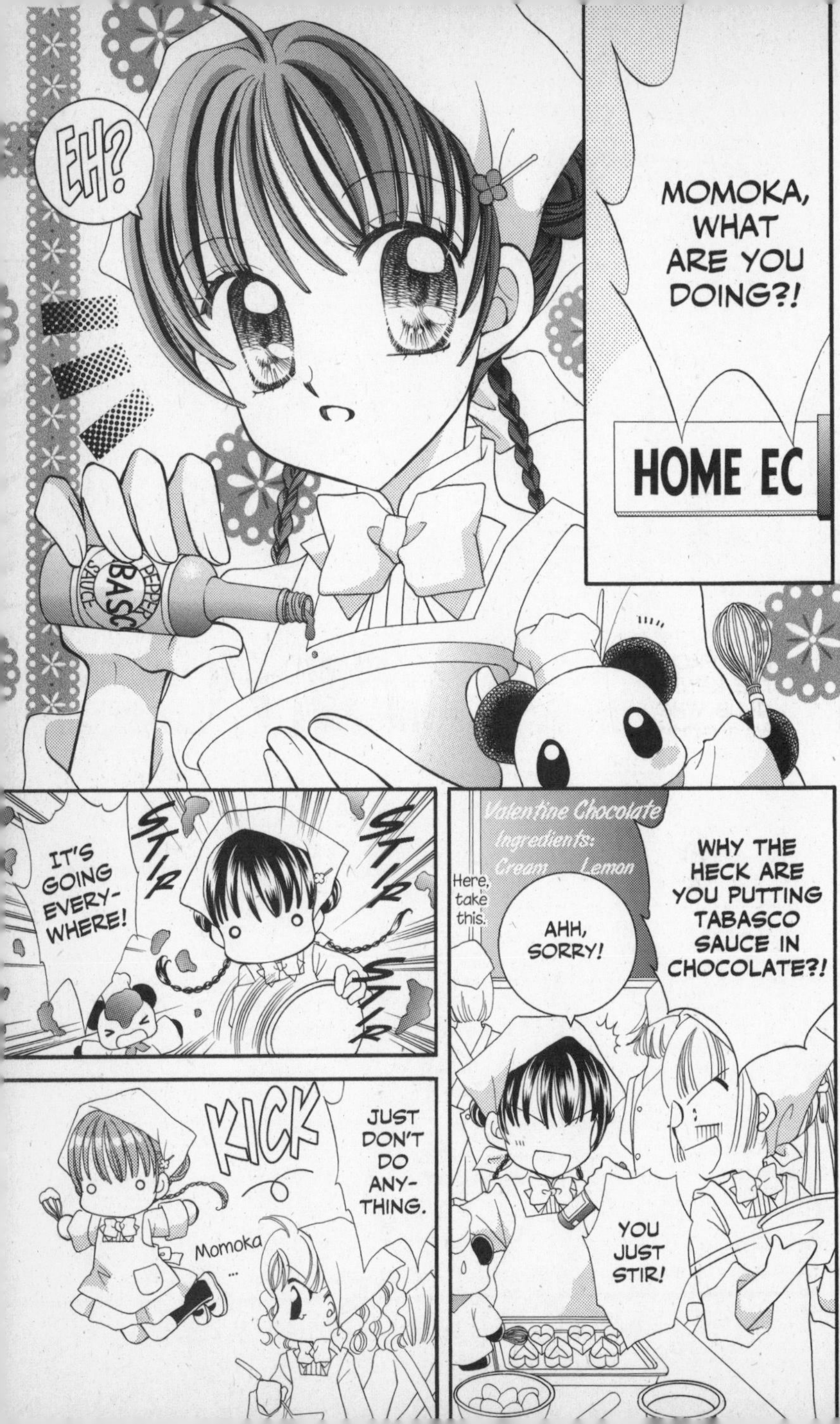
HOME EC
MOMOKA, WHAT ARE YOU DOING?!
EH?
Valentine Chocolate
Ingredients:
Cream Lemon
WHY THE HECK ARE YOU PUTTING TABASCO SAUCE IN CHOCOLATE?!
Here, take this.
AHH, SORRY!
YOU JUST STIR!
STIR
STIR
STIR
STIR
IT'S GOING EVERY-WHERE!
KICK
JUST DON'T DO ANY-THING.
Momoka ...

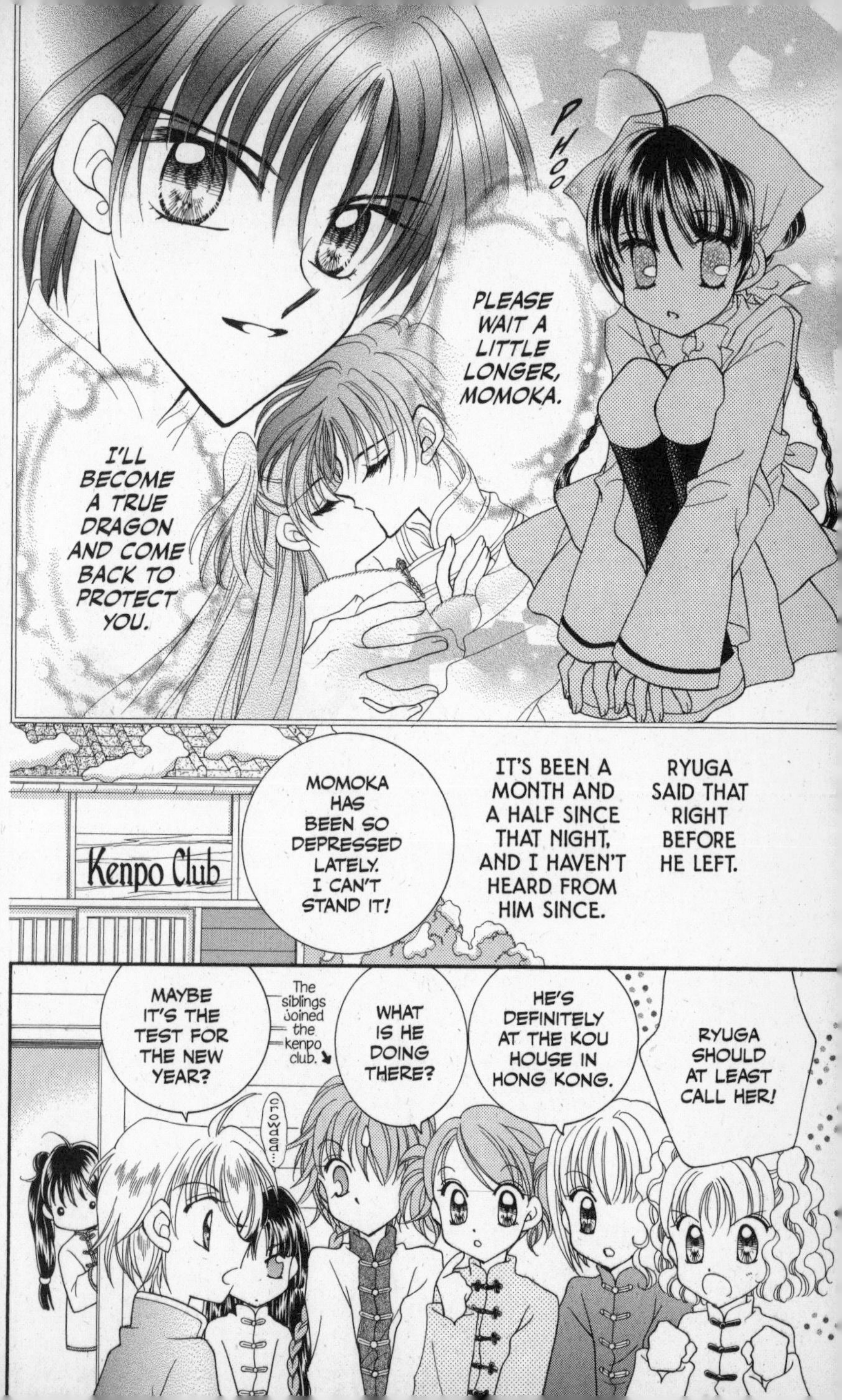
PHOO
PLEASE WAIT A LITTLE LONGER, MOMOKA.
I'LL BECOME A TRUE DRAGON AND COME BACK TO PROTECT YOU.
RYUGA SAID THAT RIGHT BEFORE HE LEFT.
IT'S BEEN A MONTH AND A HALF SINCE THAT NIGHT, AND I HAVEN'T HEARD FROM HIM SINCE.
MOMOKA HAS BEEN SO DEPRESSED LATELY. I CAN'T STAND IT!
Kenpo Club
RYUGA SHOULD AT LEAST CALL HER!
HE'S DEFINITELY AT THE KOU HOUSE IN HONG KONG.
WHAT IS HE DOING THERE?
The siblings joined the kenpo club.
MAYBE IT'S THE TEST FOR THE NEW YEAR?
Crowded...

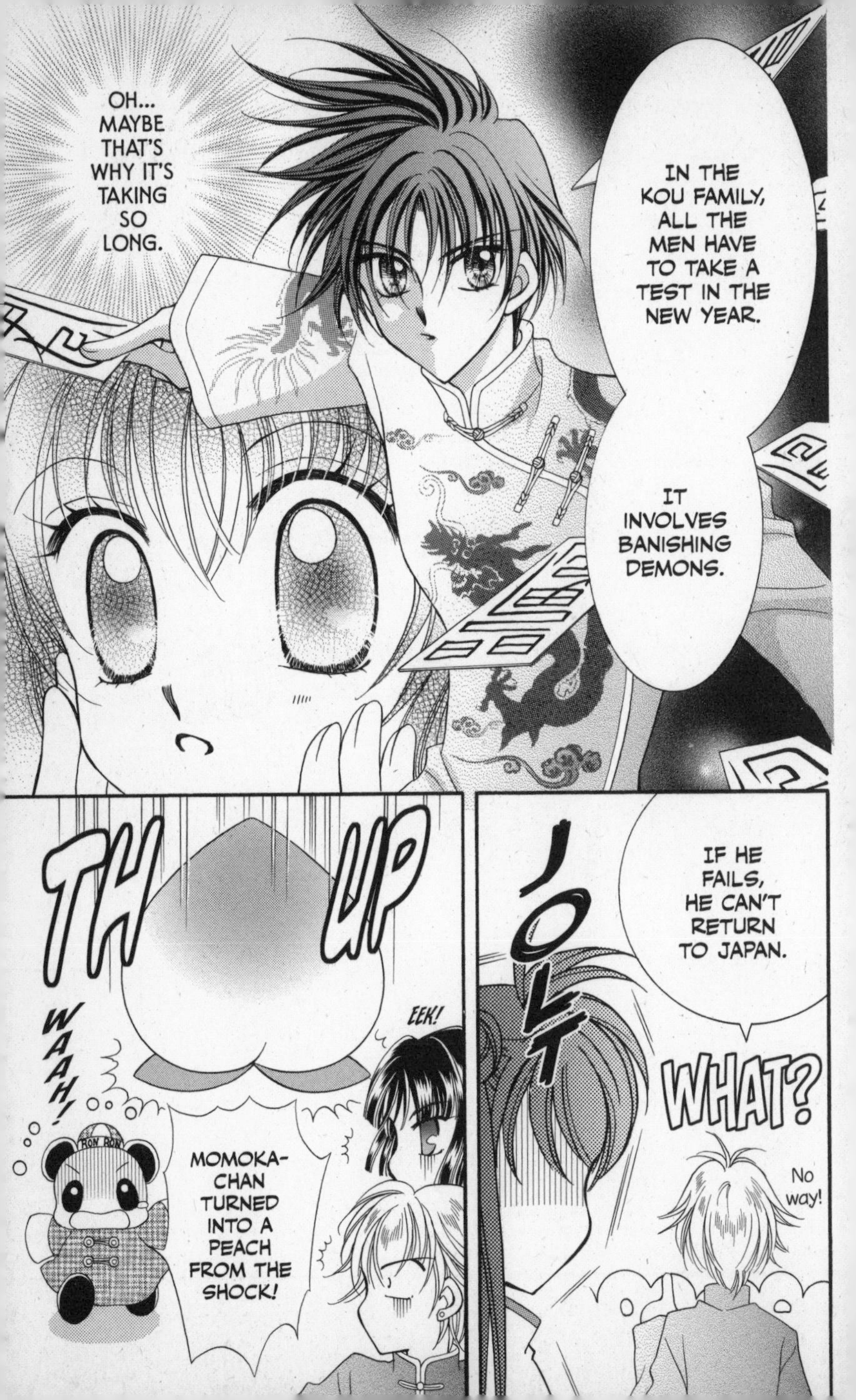
IN THE KOU FAMILY, ALL THE MEN HAVE TO TAKE A TEST IN THE NEW YEAR.
IT INVOLVES BANISHING DEMONS.
OH... MAYBE THAT'S WHY IT'S TAKING SO LONG.
JOLT
IF HE FAILS, HE CAN'T RETURN TO JAPAN.
WHAT?
No way!
TH UP
EEK!
WAAAH!
RON RON
MOMOKA-CHAN TURNED INTO A PEACH FROM THE SHOCK!

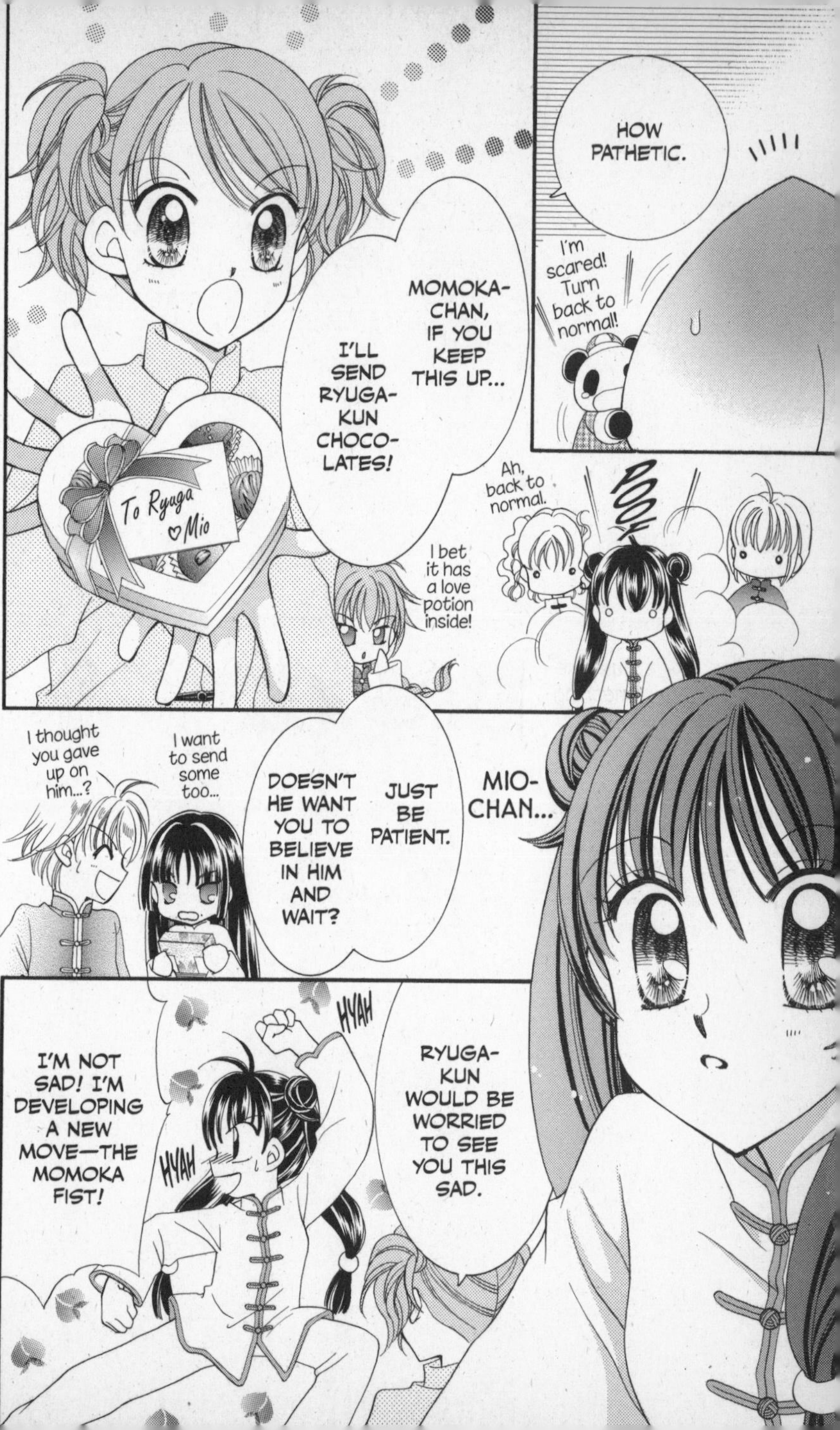
HOW PATHETIC.
I'm scared! Turn back to normal!
MOMOKA-CHAN, IF YOU KEEP THIS UP...
I'LL SEND RYUGA-KUN CHOCOLATES!
To Ryuga ♡ Mio
I bet it has a love potion inside!
POOF
Ah, back to normal.
MIO-CHAN...
JUST BE PATIENT.
DOESN'T HE WANT YOU TO BELIEVE IN HIM AND WAIT?
I want to send some too...
I thought you gave up on him...?
RYUGA-KUN WOULD BE WORRIED TO SEE YOU THIS SAD.
HYAH
I'M NOT SAD! I'M DEVELOPING A NEW MOVE—THE MOMOKA FIST!
HYAH

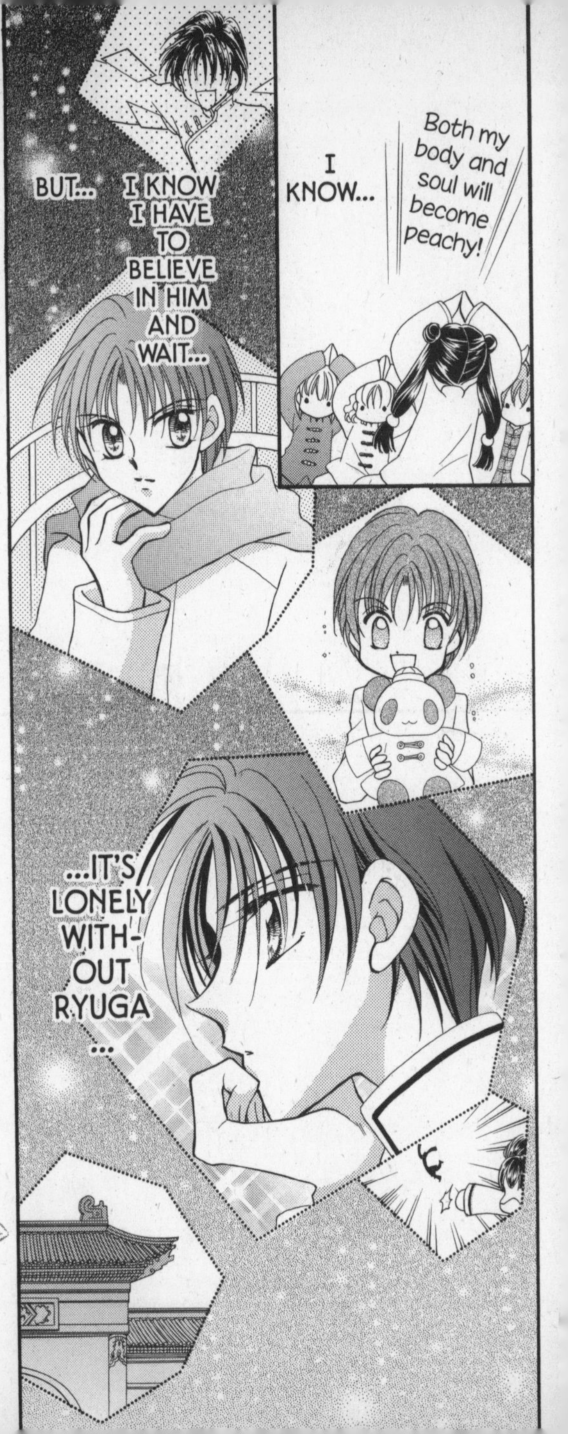
Both my body and soul will become peachy!
I KNOW...
BUT...
I KNOW I HAVE TO BELIEVE IN HIM AND WAIT...
...IT'S LONELY WITH-OUT RYUGA...

4

This is the final chapter of this series. A long time ago I decided what Ryuga does in this chapter (I won't spoil it for those of you who haven't read it yet), but there were a lot of people who were shocked. They said things like it was too early because they were in high school, or that it was just like Ryuga to do something like that.

The ending was just as I had imagined it, but I wish I could have written a little more about Mio and Reiji.

Since I wanted to write more about the individual characters, the publishers allowed me to write extra bonus at the end—even with Kouryu!

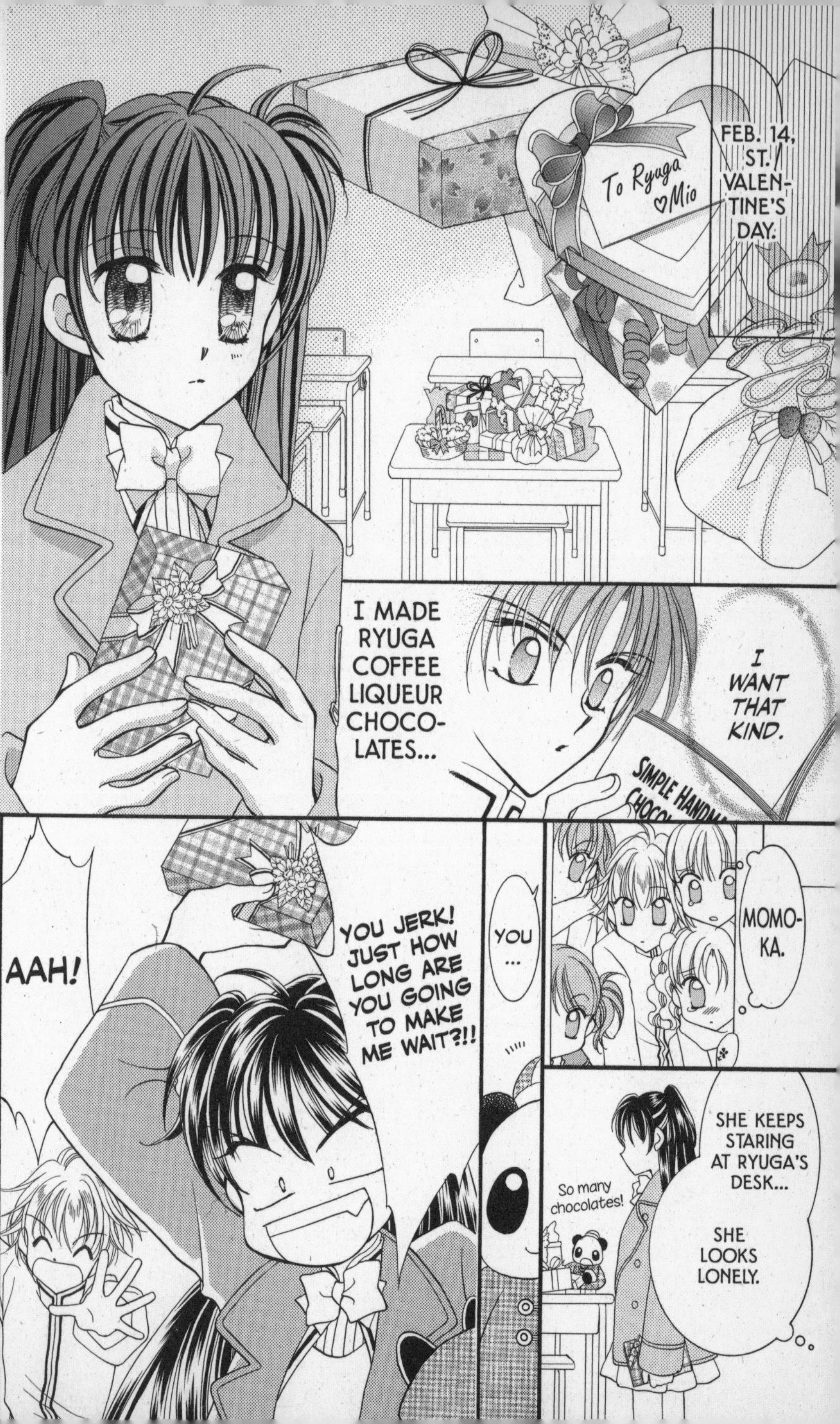
FEB. 14, ST. VALENTINE'S DAY.
To Ryuga ♡Mio
I WANT THAT KIND.
I MADE RYUGA COFFEE LIQUEUR CHOCOLATES...
MOMOKA.
SHE KEEPS STARING AT RYUGA'S DESK...
SHE LOOKS LONELY.
So many chocolates!
YOU ...
YOU JERK! JUST HOW LONG ARE YOU GOING TO MAKE ME WAIT?!!
AAH!

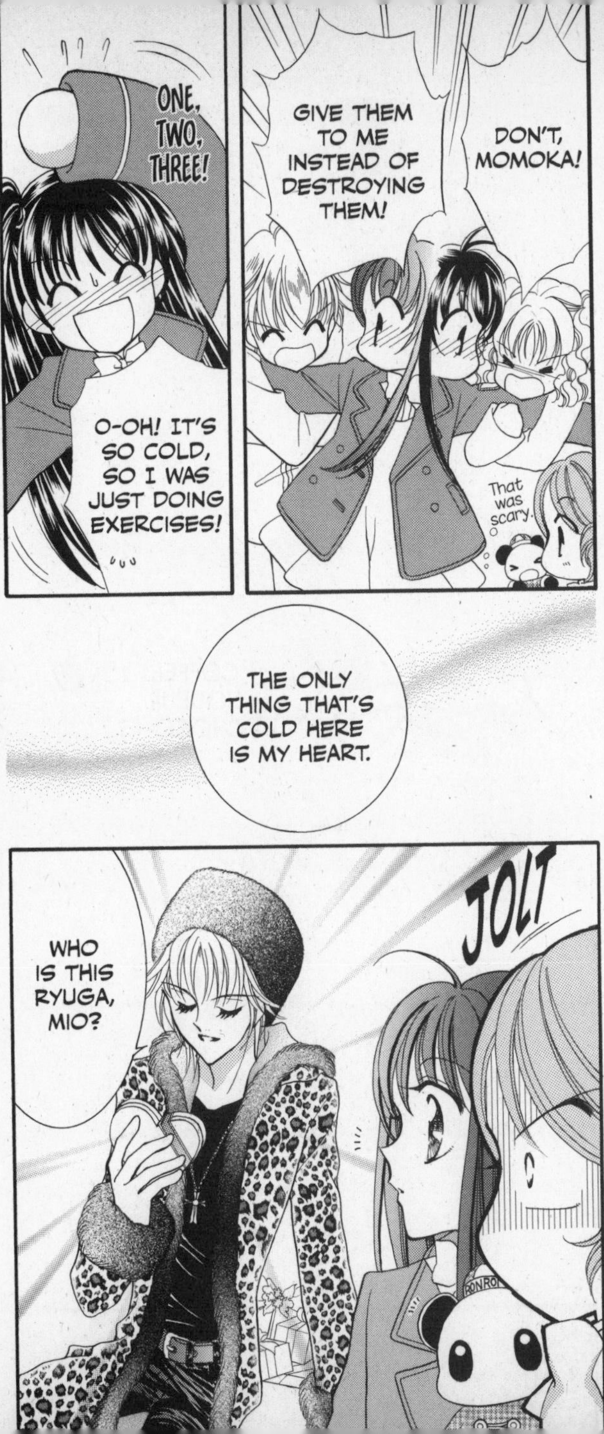
DON'T, MOMOKA!
GIVE THEM TO ME INSTEAD OF DESTROYING THEM!
That was scary.
ONE, TWO, THREE!
O-OH! IT'S SO COLD, SO I WAS JUST DOING EXERCISES!
THE ONLY THING THAT'S COLD HERE IS MY HEART.
JOLT
WHO IS THIS RYUGA, MIO?
RONRON

5

I've been sending out comic strips on dragon stationery to respond to letters. When I asked what the names of Ryuga's and Momoka's dragons should be, I received a lot of wonderful ideas. Thanks! But in the end I thought them up myself. Momoka's dragon is "Shiou" (Purple King) and Ryuga's is "Kouju" (Yellow Pearl). But everyone's ideas helped me a lot, and I sent everyone who suggested names a signed manga.

The most popular suggestions were "Shiryu" (Purple Dragon) and "Touga" (Peach Horn). Many of them had to do with the colors of the dragon.

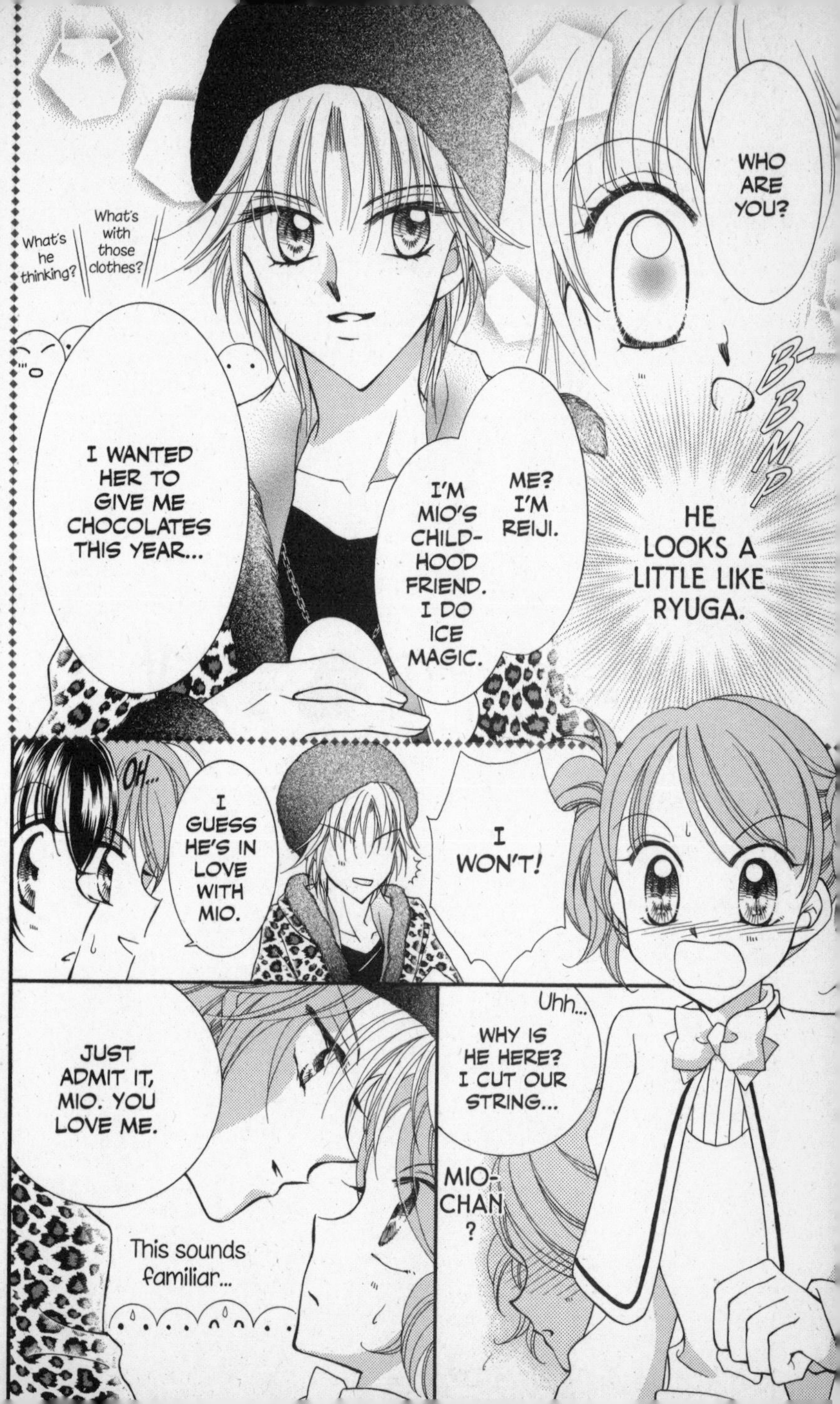
WHO ARE YOU?
B-BMP
HE LOOKS A LITTLE LIKE RYUGA.
What's with those clothes?
What's he thinking?
ME? I'M REIJI.
I'M MIO'S CHILD-HOOD FRIEND. I DO ICE MAGIC.
I WANTED HER TO GIVE ME CHOCOLATES THIS YEAR...
I WON'T!
OH...
I GUESS HE'S IN LOVE WITH MIO.
Uhh...
WHY IS HE HERE? I CUT OUR STRING...
MIO-CHAN?
JUST ADMIT IT, MIO. YOU LOVE ME.
This sounds familiar...

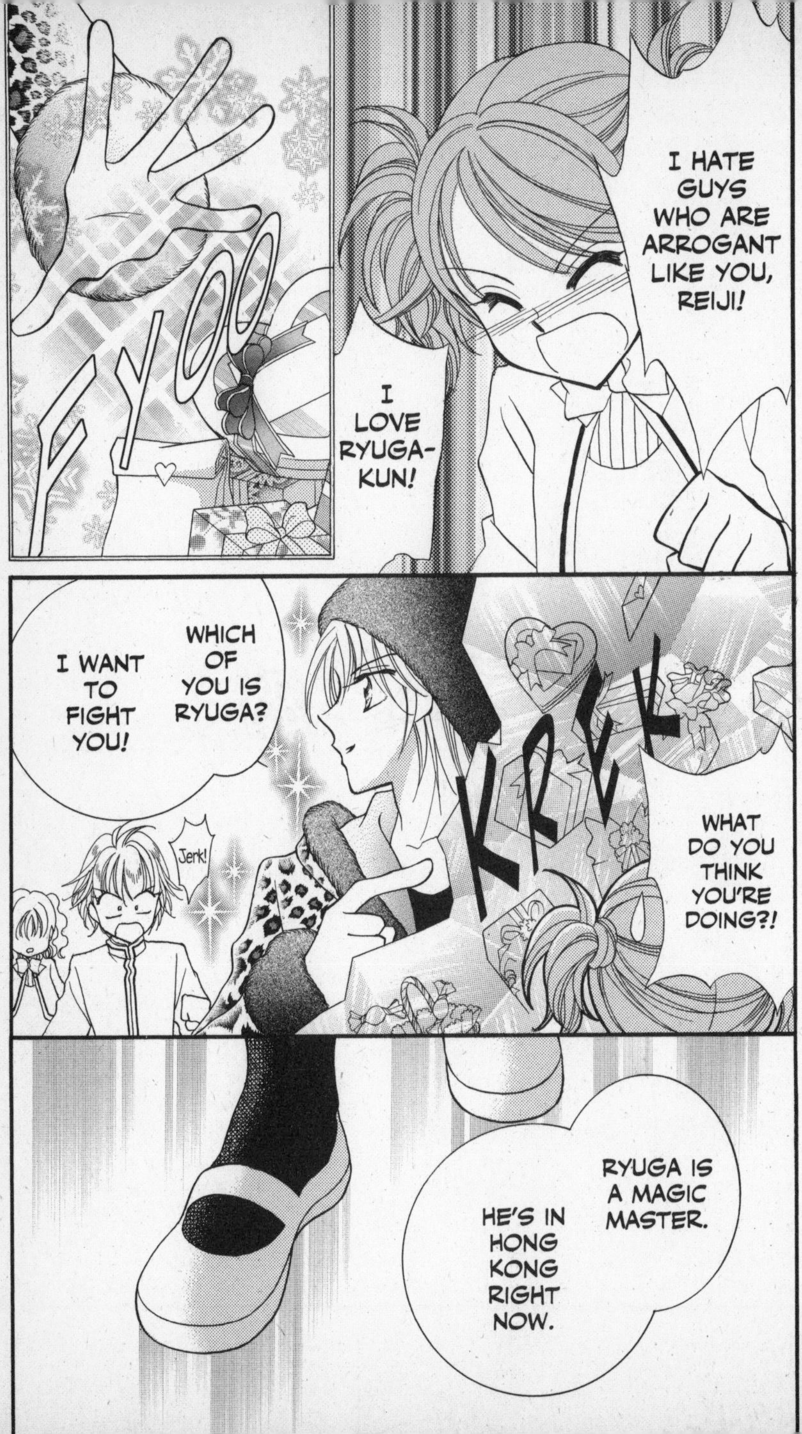
I HATE GUYS WHO ARE ARROGANT LIKE YOU, REIJI!
I LOVE RYUGA-KUN!
FYOO
WHAT DO YOU THINK YOU'RE DOING?!
KREK
WHICH OF YOU IS RYUGA?
I WANT TO FIGHT YOU!
Jerk!
RYUGA IS A MAGIC MASTER.
HE'S IN HONG KONG RIGHT NOW.

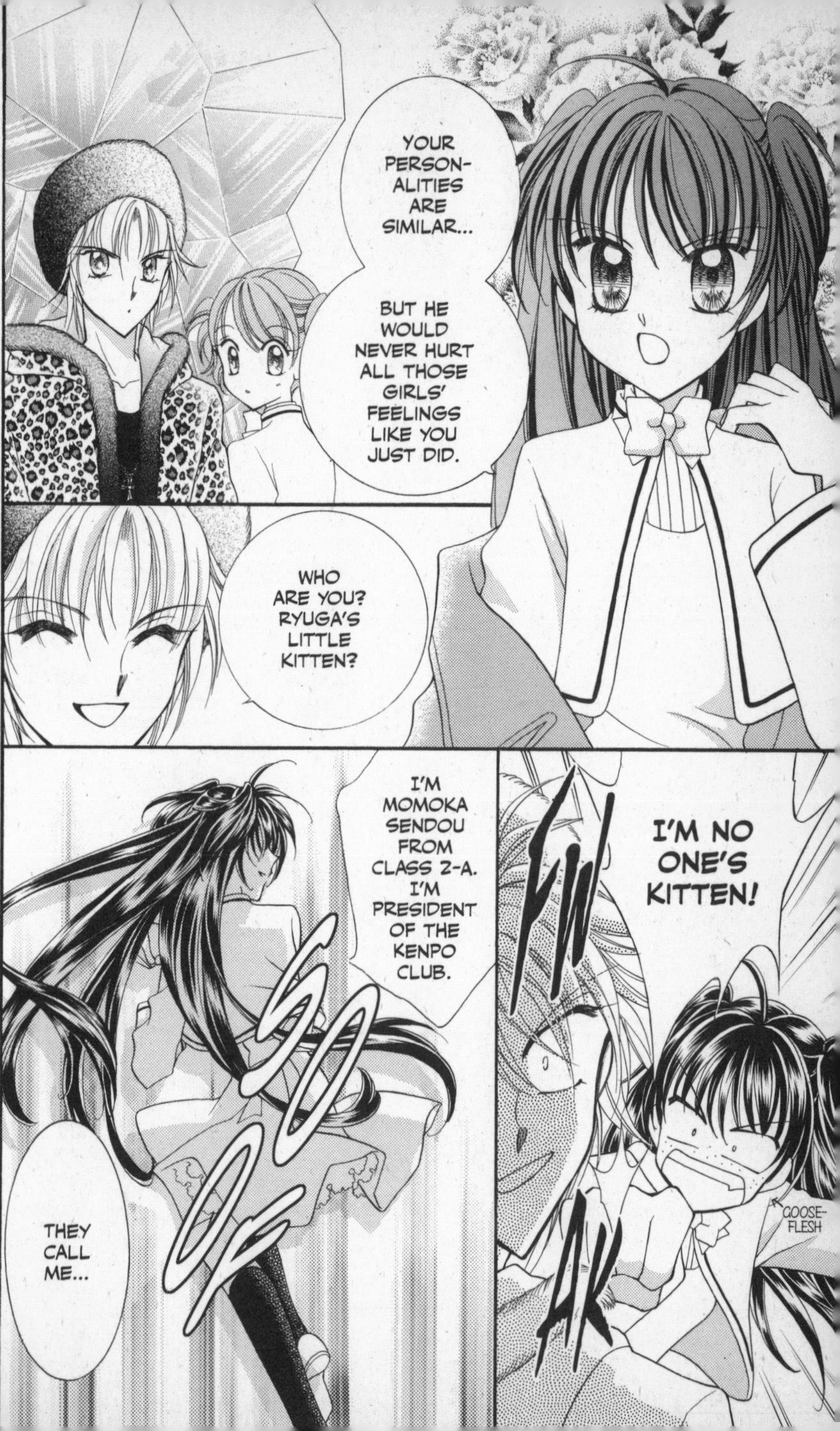
YOUR PERSON-ALITIES ARE SIMILAR...
BUT HE WOULD NEVER HURT ALL THOSE GIRLS' FEELINGS LIKE YOU JUST DID.
WHO ARE YOU? RYUGA'S LITTLE KITTEN?
I'M NO ONE'S KITTEN!
GOOSE-FLESH
I'M MOMOKA SENDOU FROM CLASS 2-A. I'M PRESIDENT OF THE KENPO CLUB.
THEY CALL ME...

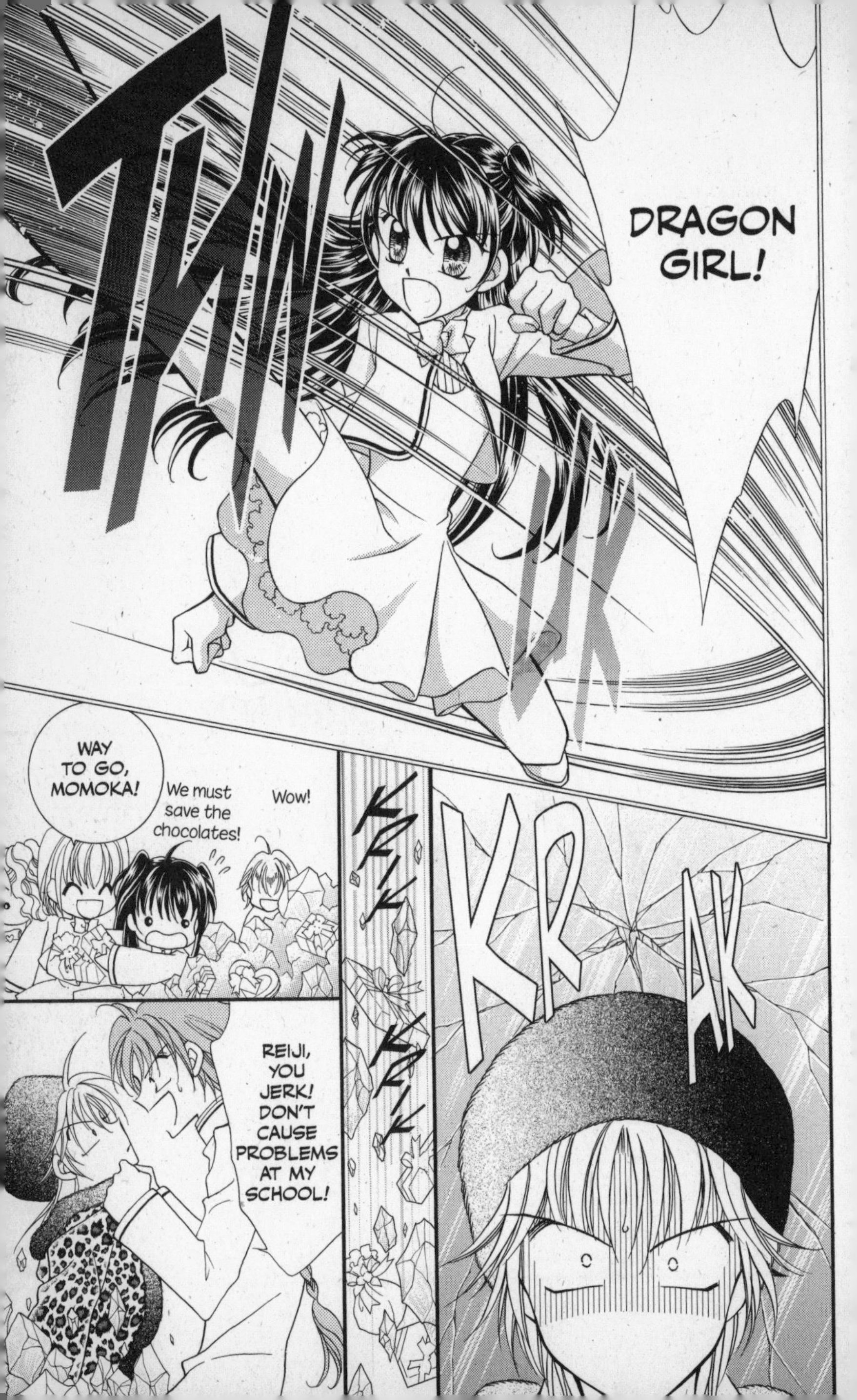
DRAGON GIRL!
KRAK
Wow!
We must save the chocolates!
WAY TO GO, MOMOKA!
REIJI, YOU JERK! DON'T CAUSE PROBLEMS AT MY SCHOOL!

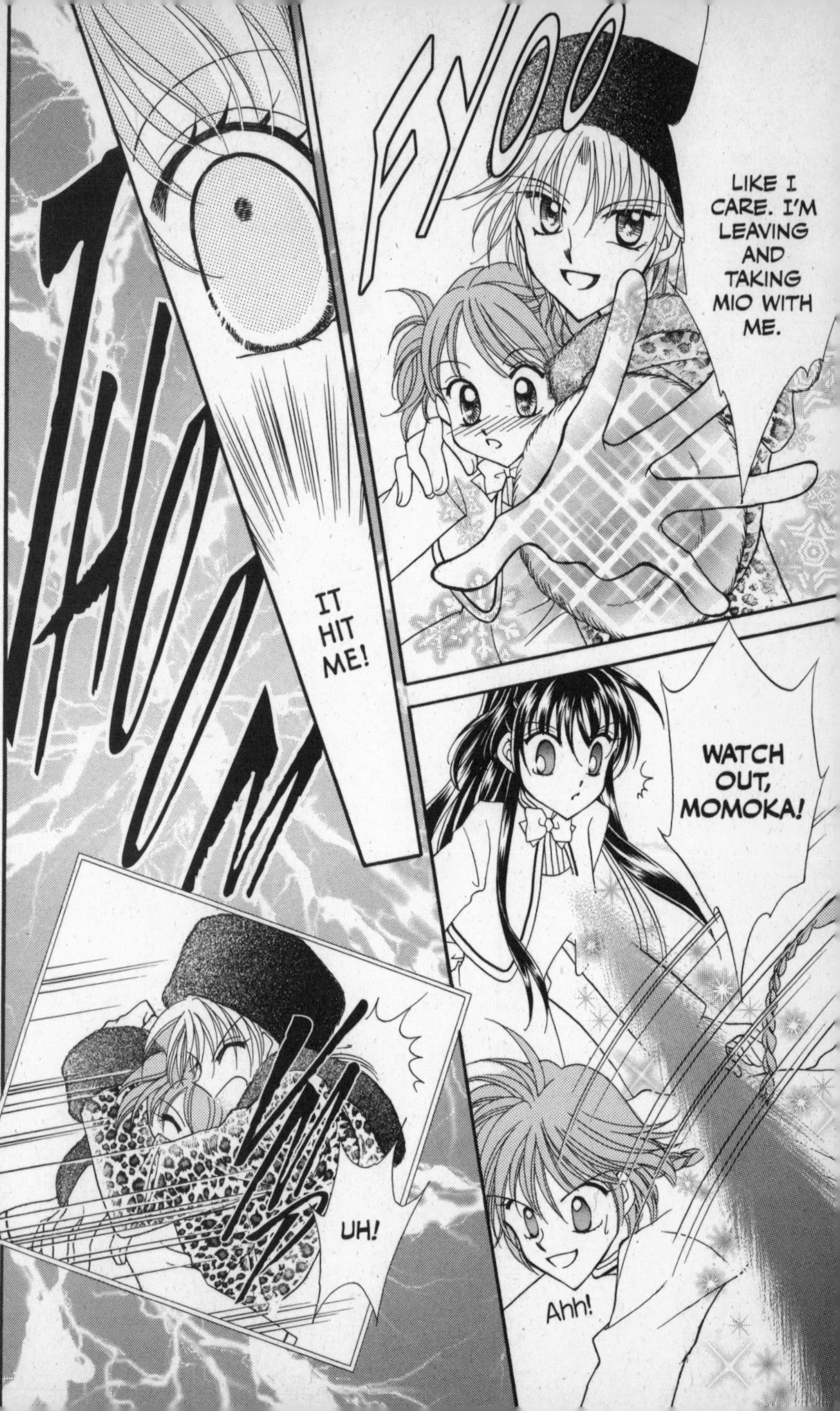
FYOO
LIKE I CARE. I'M LEAVING AND TAKING MIO WITH ME.
WATCH OUT, MOMOKA!
Ahh!
THUMM
IT HIT ME!
UH!

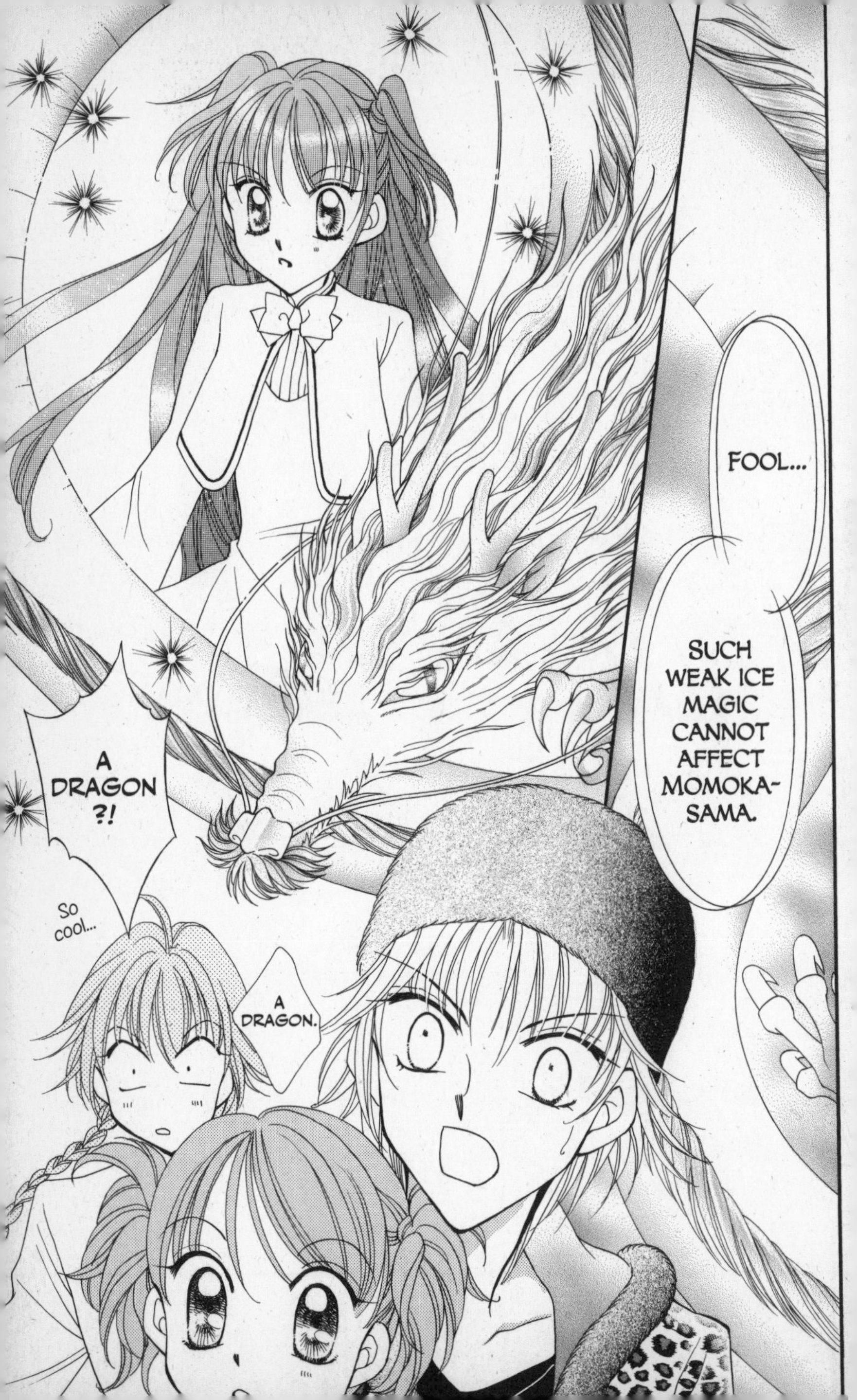
FOOL...
SUCH WEAK ICE MAGIC CANNOT AFFECT MOMOKA-SAMA.
A DRAGON?!
A DRAGON.
So cool...

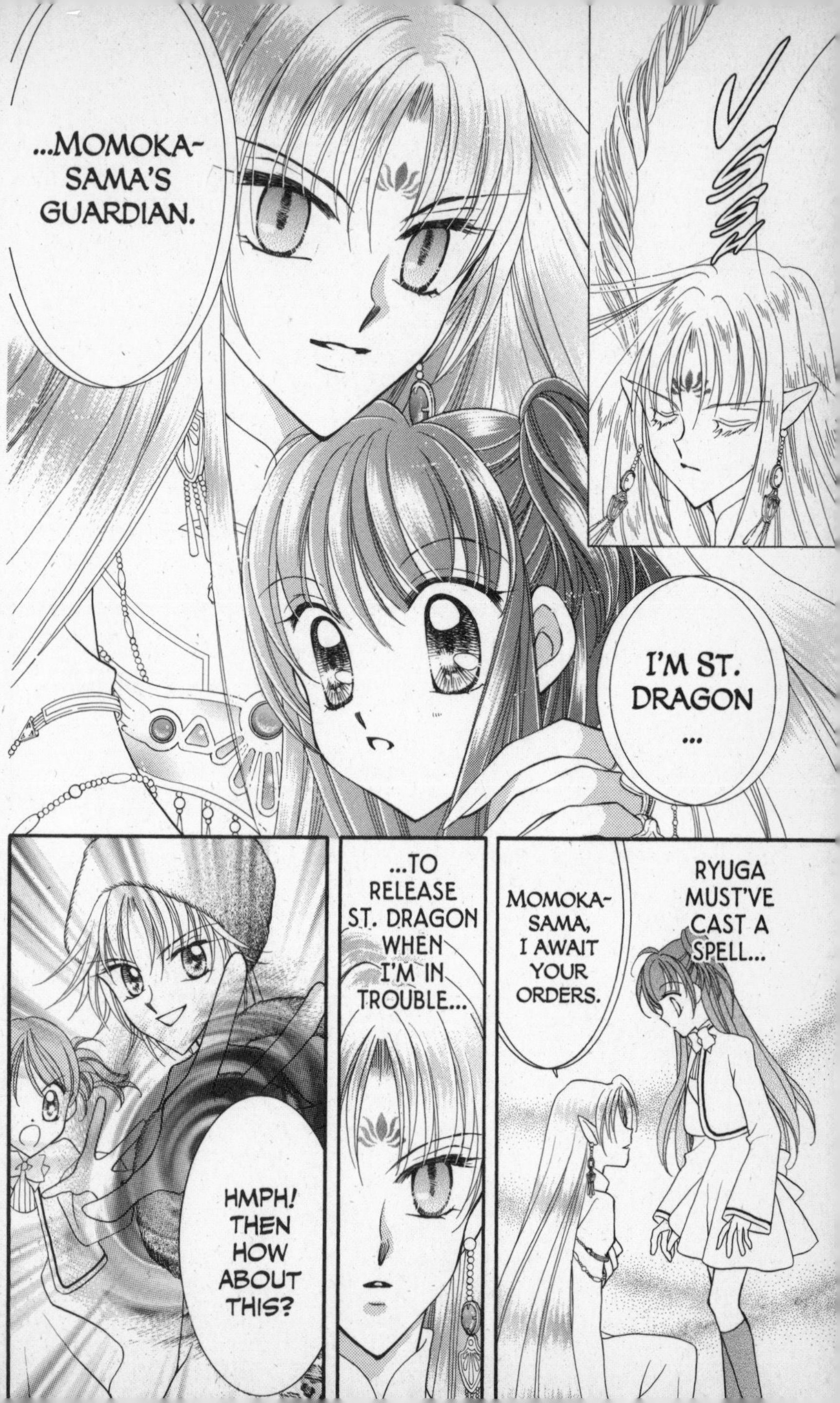
I'M ST. DRAGON ...
...MOMOKA-SAMA'S GUARDIAN.
RYUGA MUST'VE CAST A SPELL...
MOMOKA-SAMA, I AWAIT YOUR ORDERS.
...TO RELEASE ST. DRAGON WHEN I'M IN TROUBLE...
HMPH! THEN HOW ABOUT THIS?

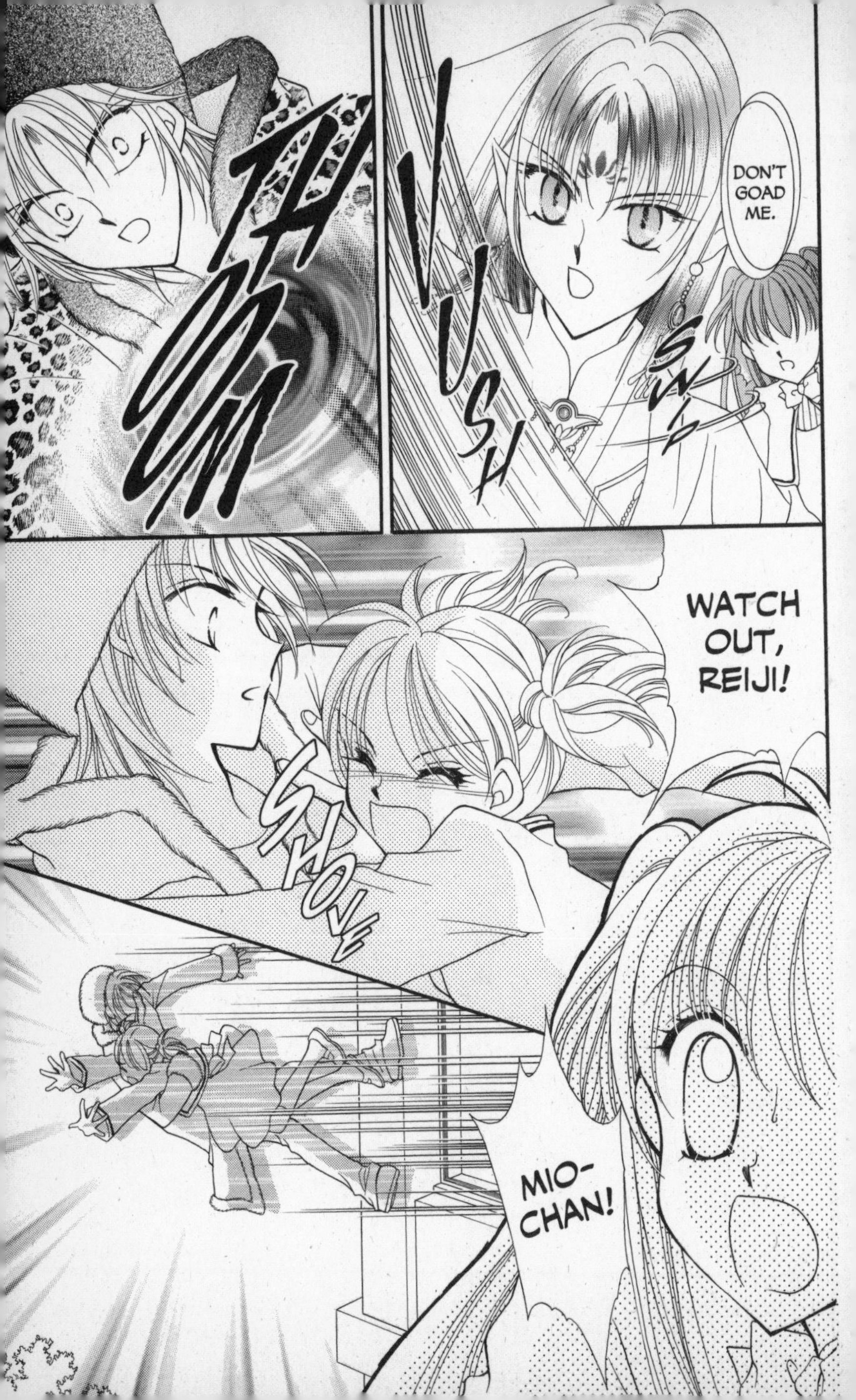
DON'T GOAD ME.
VUSH
SWIP
THOOM
WATCH OUT, REIJI!
SHOVE
MIO-CHAN!

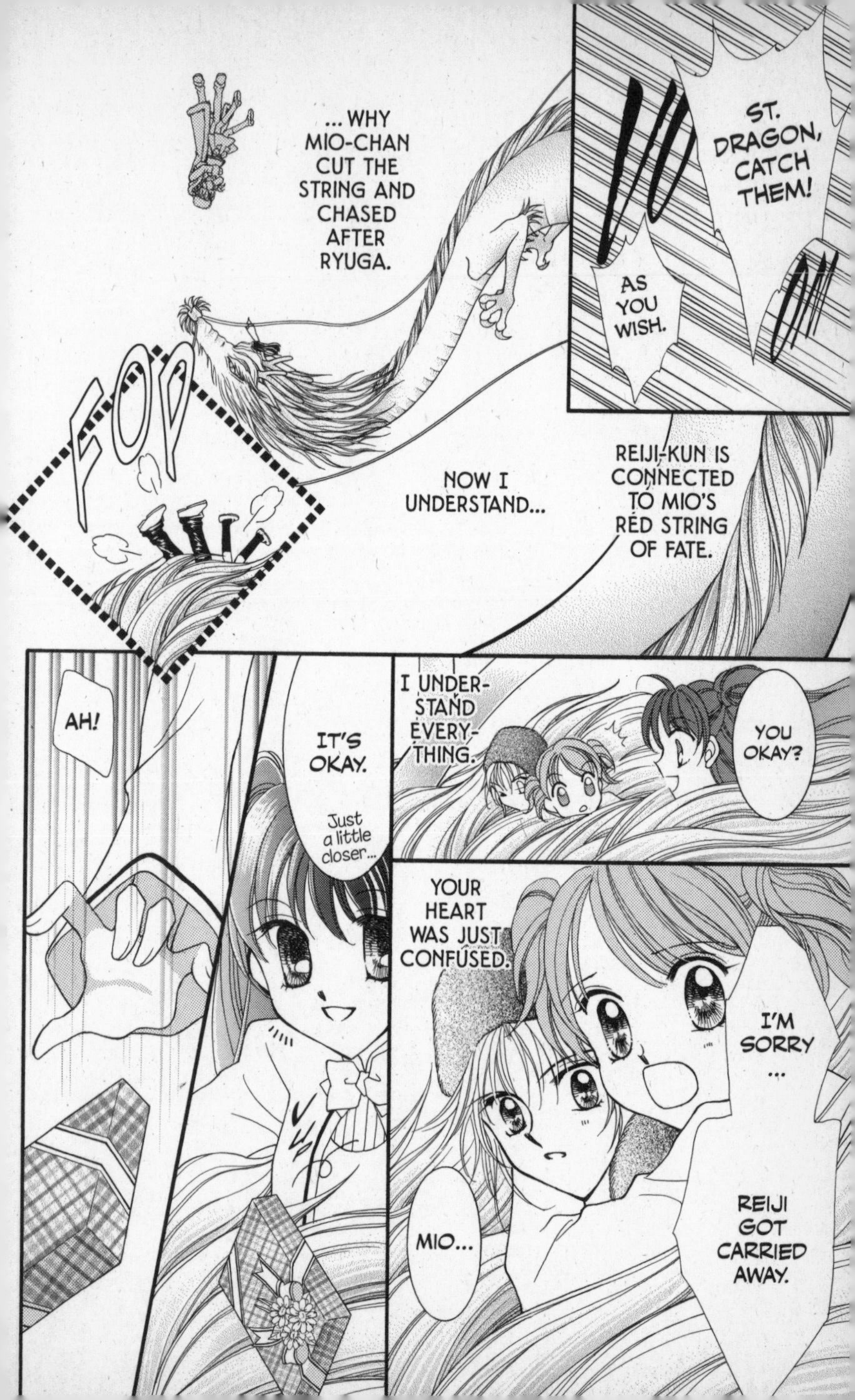
ST. DRAGON, CATCH THEM!
AS YOU WISH.
FOP
REIJI-KUN IS CONNECTED TO MIO'S RED STRING OF FATE.
NOW I UNDERSTAND...
... WHY MIO-CHAN CUT THE STRING AND CHASED AFTER RYUGA.
YOU OKAY?
I UNDER-STAND EVERY-THING.
I'M SORRY ...
REIJI GOT CARRIED AWAY.
YOUR HEART WAS JUST CONFUSED.
MIO...
IT'S OKAY.
Just a little closer...
AH!

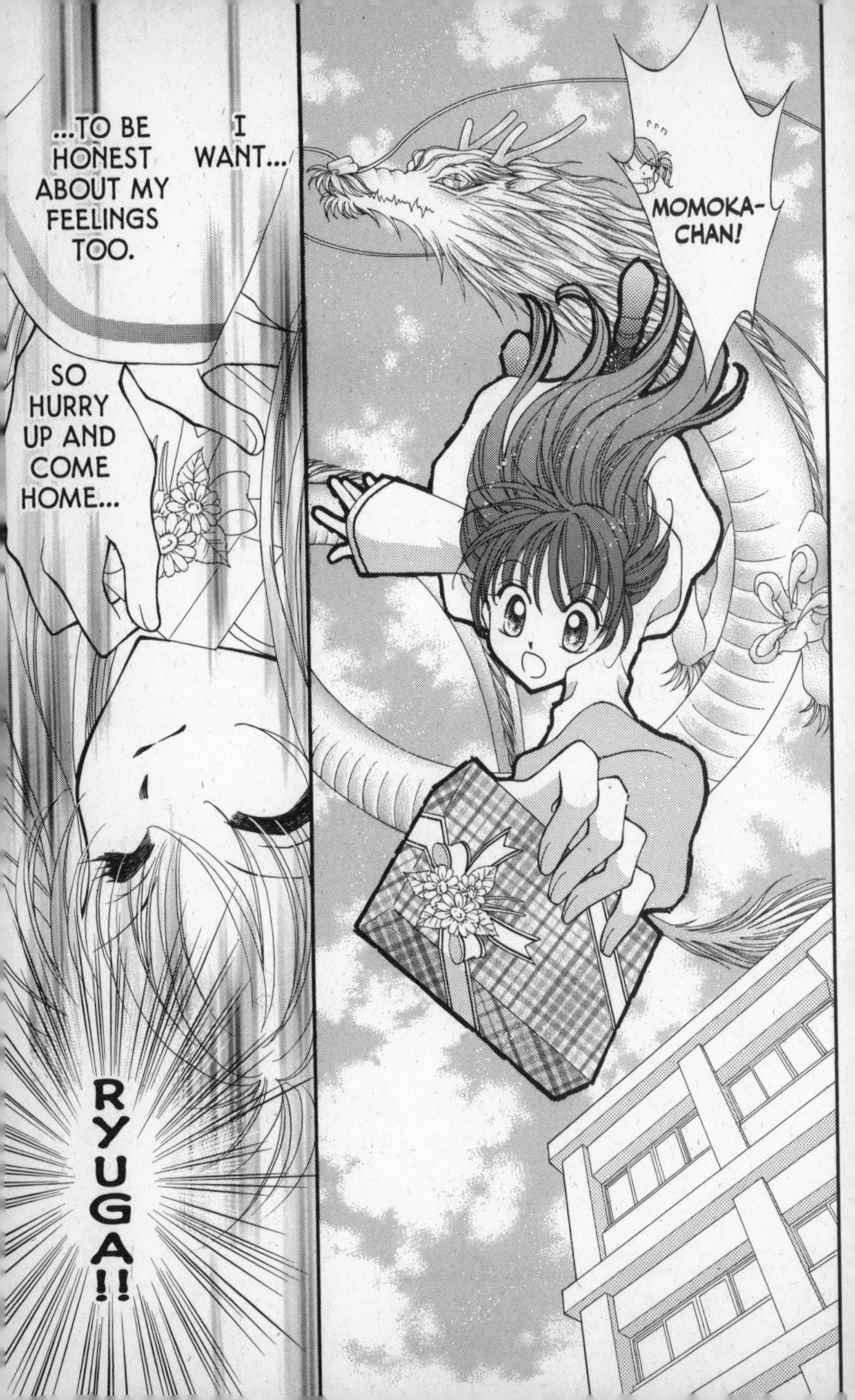
MOMOKA-CHAN!
I WANT...
...TO BE HONEST ABOUT MY FEELINGS TOO.
SO HURRY UP AND COME HOME...
RYUGA!!

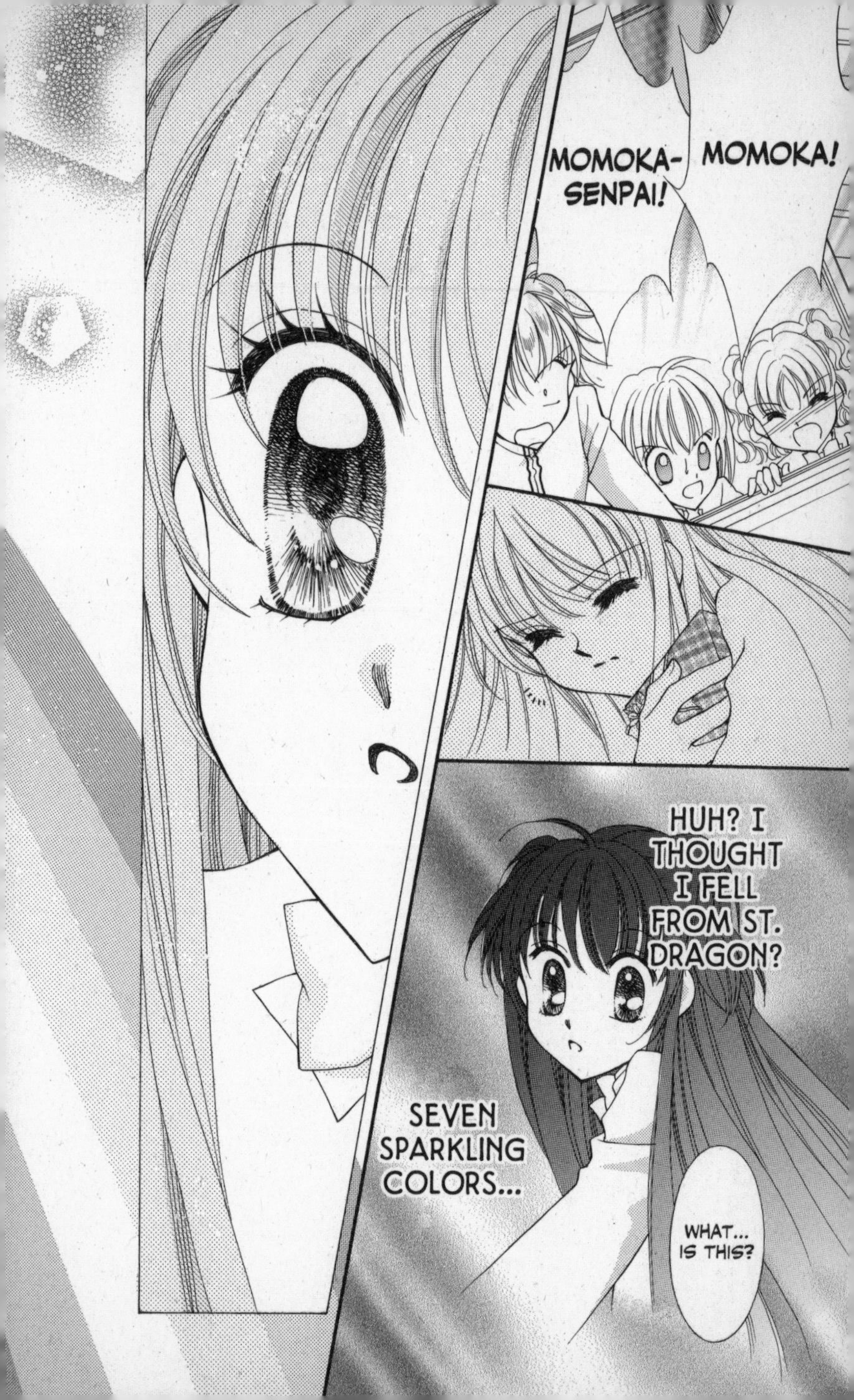
MOMOKA!
MOMOKA-SENPAI!
HUH? I THOUGHT I FELL FROM ST. DRAGON?
WHAT... IS THIS?
SEVEN SPARKLING COLORS...

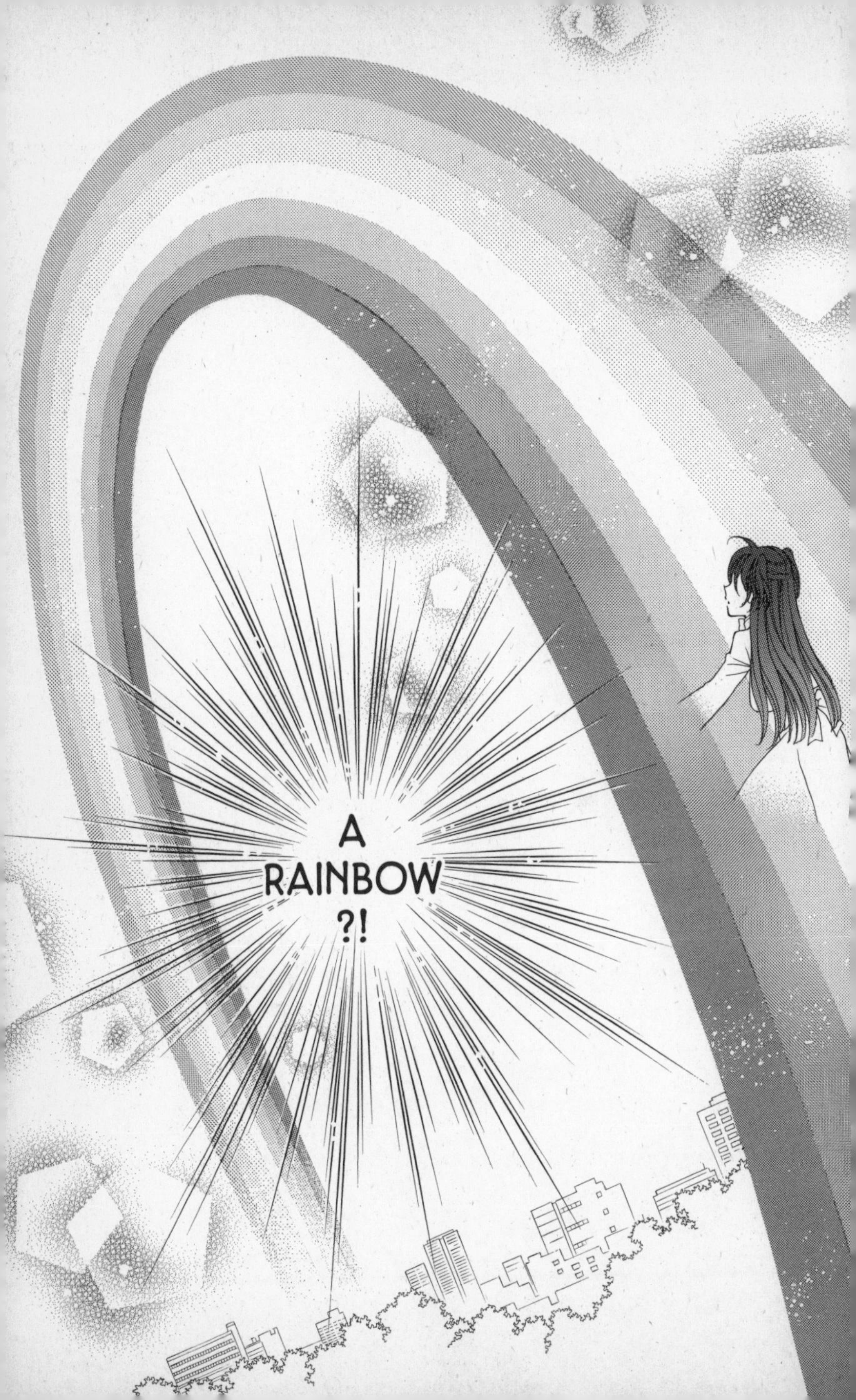
A RAINBOW ?!

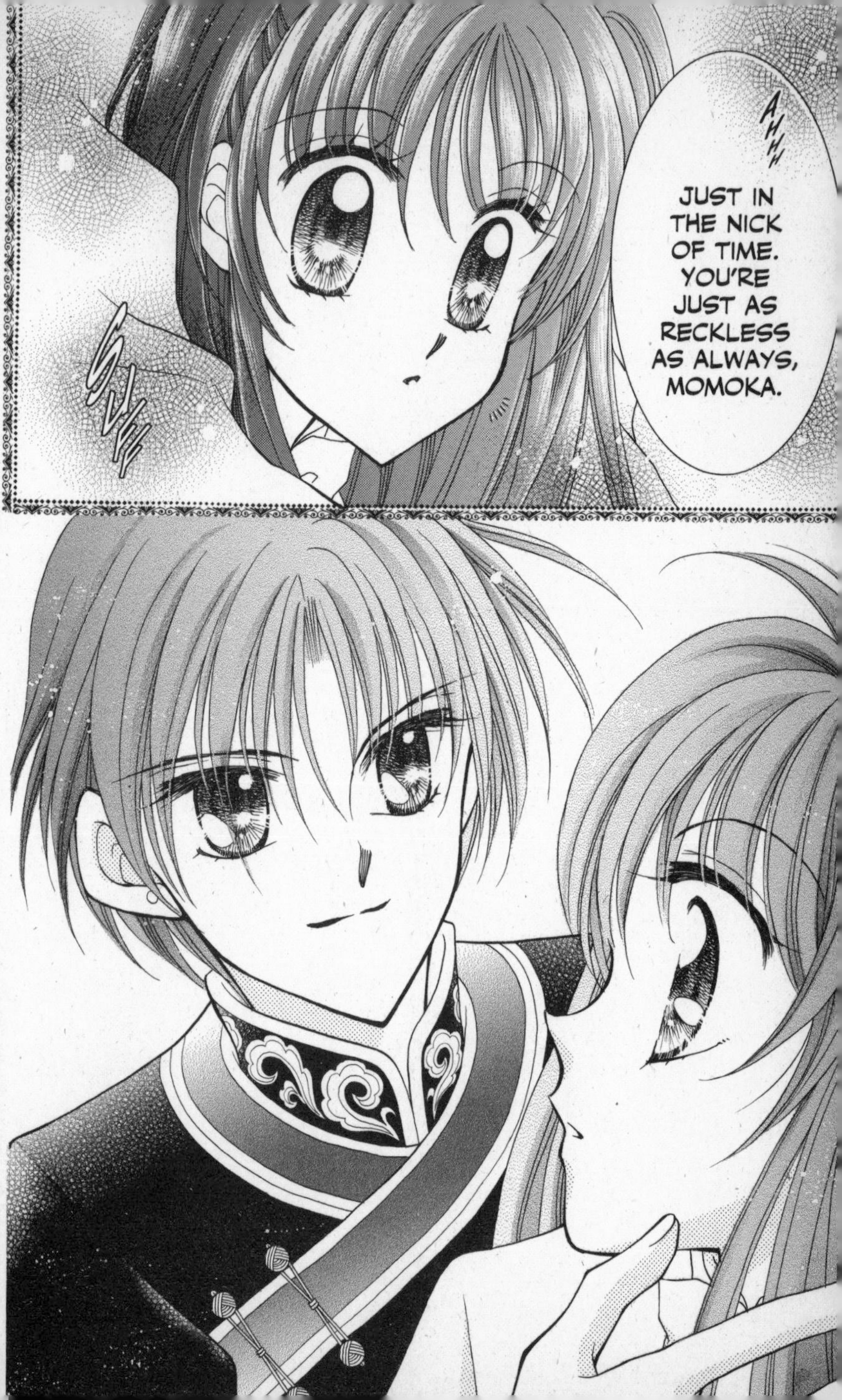
AHHH
JUST IN THE NICK OF TIME. YOU'RE JUST AS RECKLESS AS ALWAYS, MOMOKA.

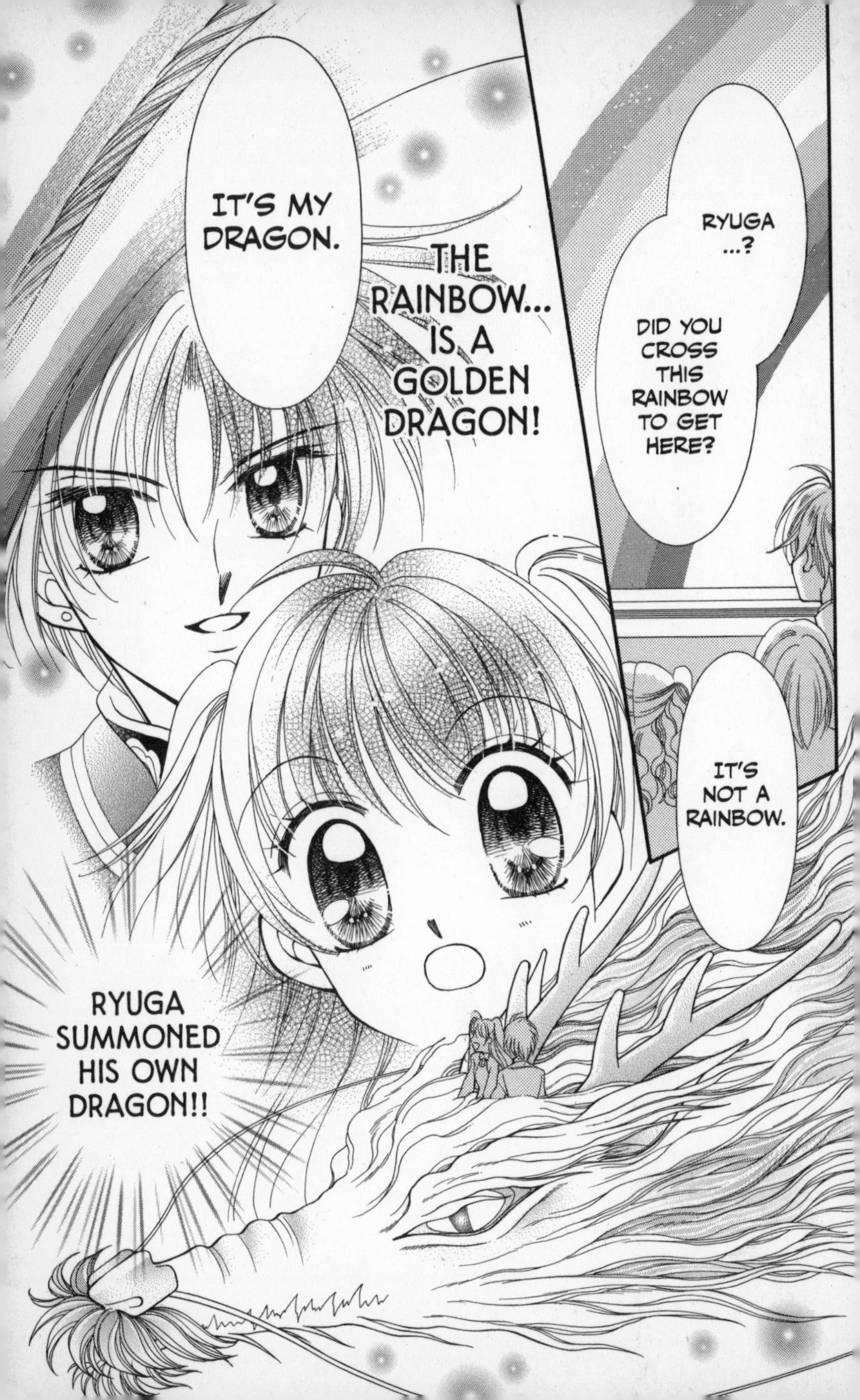
RYUGA ...?
DID YOU CROSS THIS RAINBOW TO GET HERE?
IT'S NOT A RAINBOW.
IT'S MY DRAGON.
THE RAINBOW... IS A GOLDEN DRAGON!
RYUGA SUMMONED HIS OWN DRAGON!!

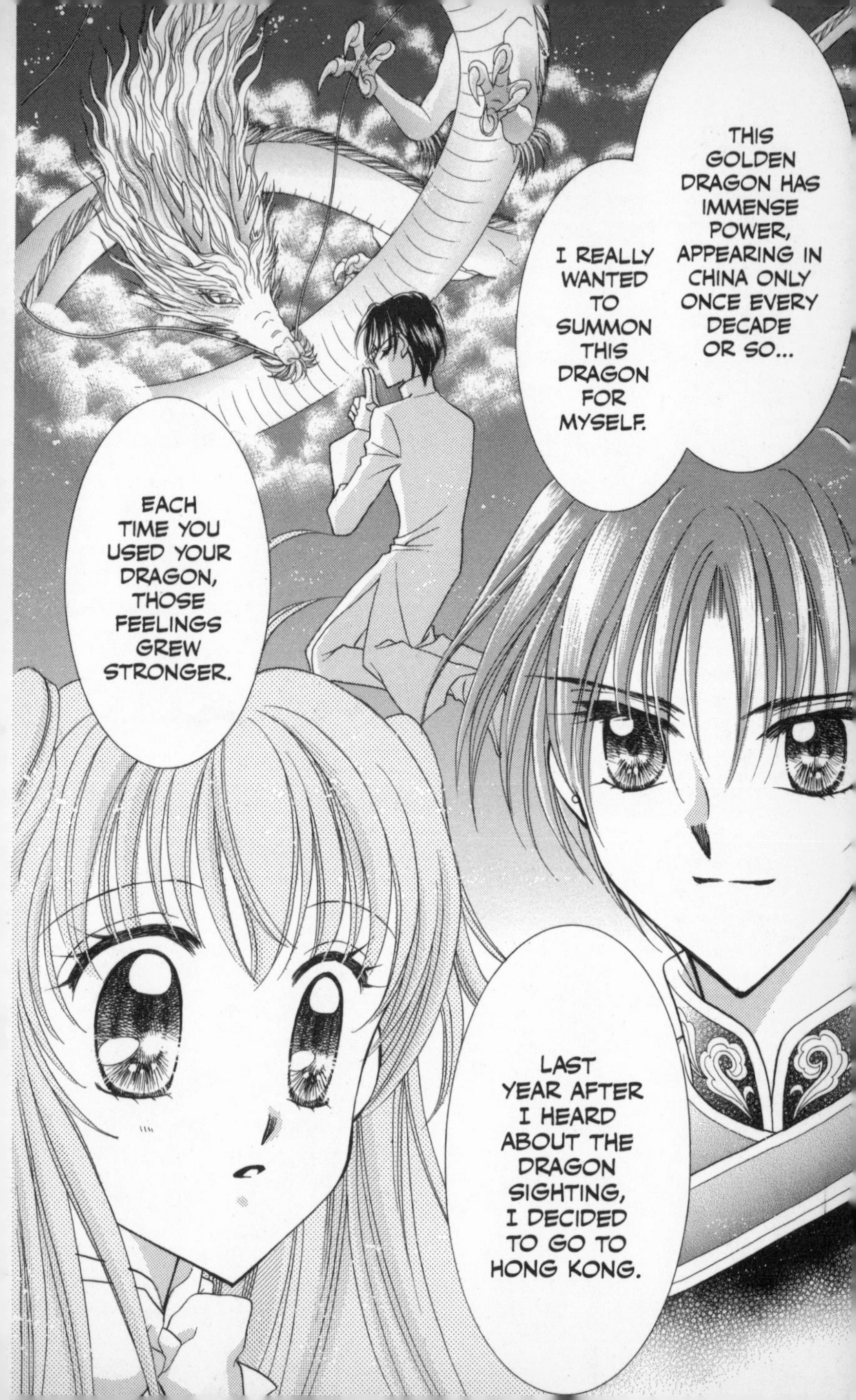
THIS GOLDEN DRAGON HAS IMMENSE POWER, APPEARING IN CHINA ONLY ONCE EVERY DECADE OR SO...
I REALLY WANTED TO SUMMON THIS DRAGON FOR MYSELF.
EACH TIME YOU USED YOUR DRAGON, THOSE FEELINGS GREW STRONGER.
LAST YEAR AFTER I HEARD ABOUT THE DRAGON SIGHTING, I DECIDED TO GO TO HONG KONG.

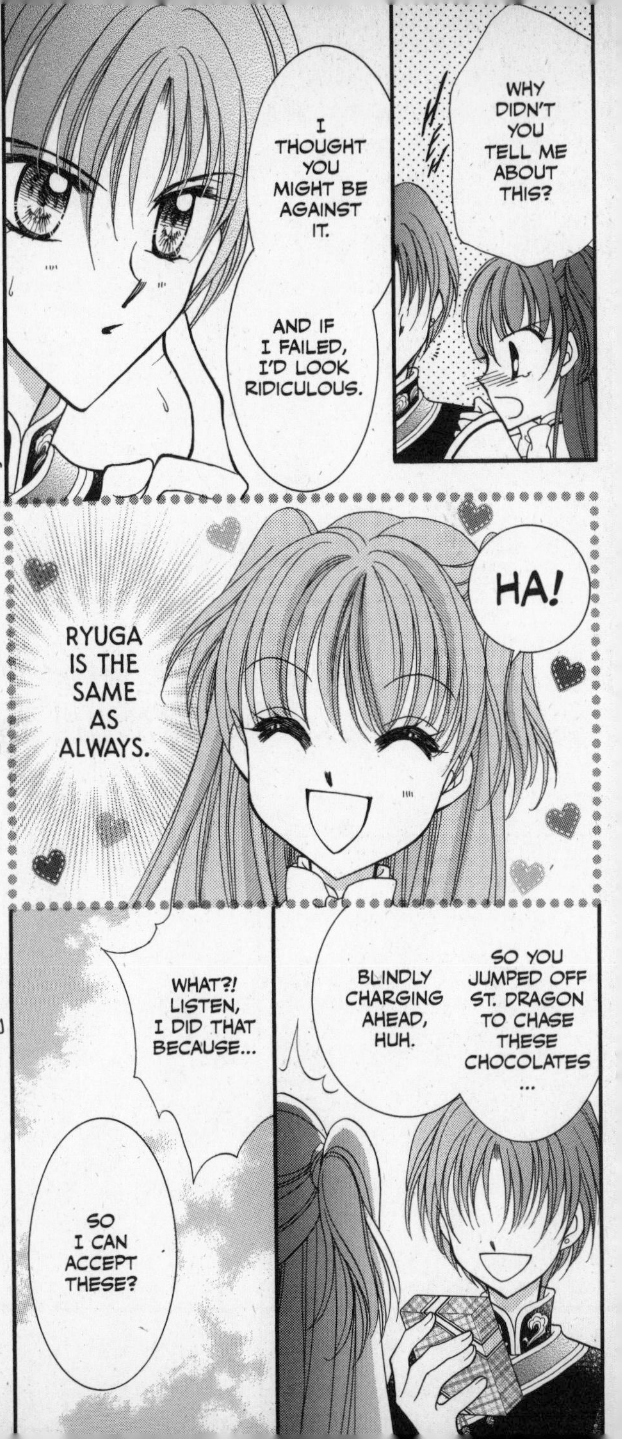
WHY DIDN'T YOU TELL ME ABOUT THIS?
I THOUGHT YOU MIGHT BE AGAINST IT.
AND IF I FAILED, I'D LOOK RIDICULOUS.
HA!
RYUGA IS THE SAME AS ALWAYS.
SO YOU JUMPED OFF ST. DRAGON TO CHASE THESE CHOCOLATES...
BLINDLY CHARGING AHEAD, HUH.
WHAT?! LISTEN, I DID THAT BECAUSE...
SO I CAN ACCEPT THESE?

6

There was one name someone suggested that I really thought about using: "Ginga" (Galaxy) for Momoka's dragon. It's so pretty and cool. But it sounded too much like Ryuga, so that's why I decided on Shiou. But I had so many great suggestions from so many people. Thanks so much!!

I haven't had much time to travel lately, so I wasn't able to buy any souvenirs to give away with this volume!

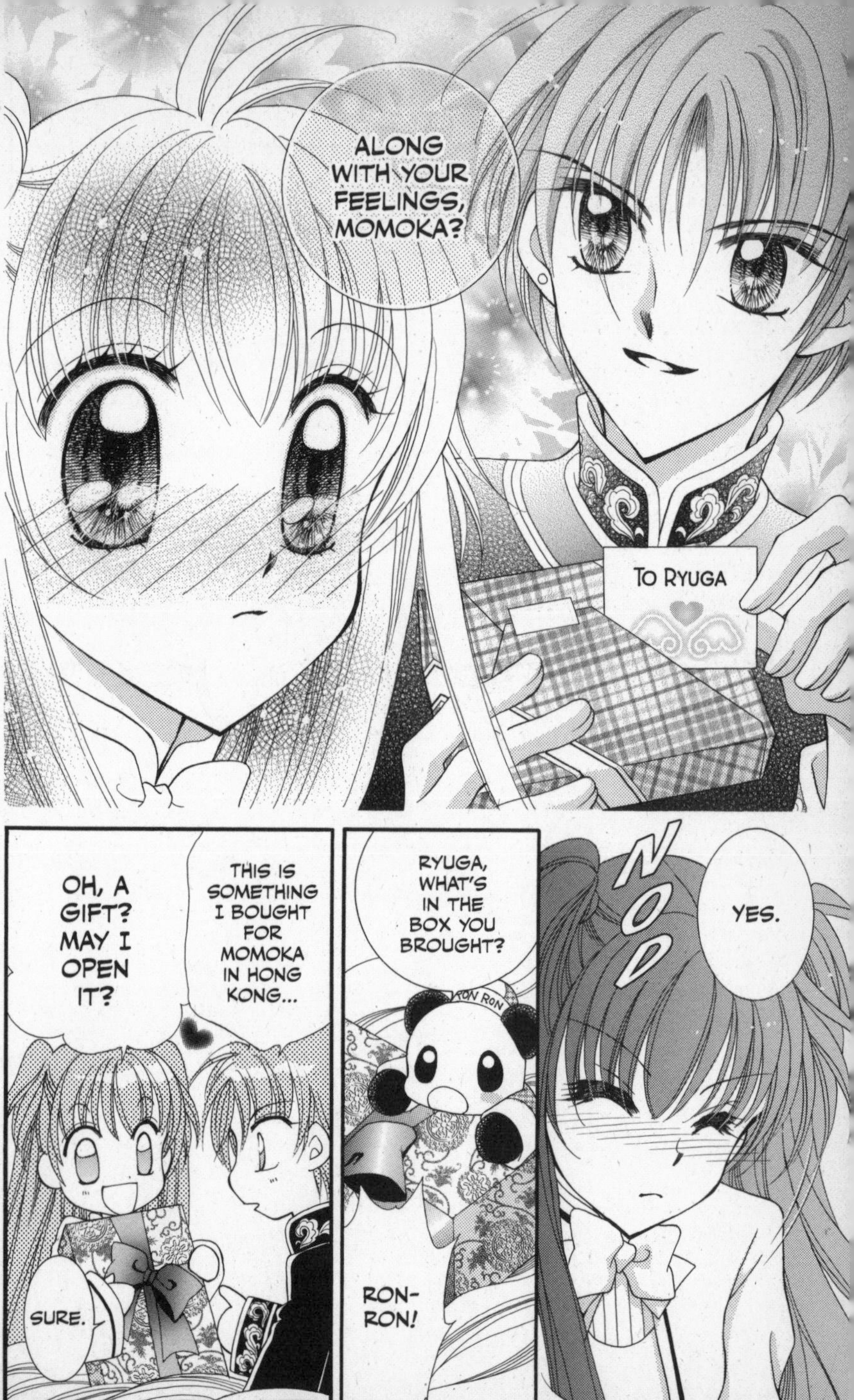
ALONG WITH YOUR FEELINGS, MOMOKA?
TO RYUGA
NOD
YES.
RYUGA, WHAT'S IN THE BOX YOU BROUGHT?
RON RON
RON-RON!
THIS IS SOMETHING I BOUGHT FOR MOMOKA IN HONG KONG...
OH, A GIFT? MAY I OPEN IT?
SURE.

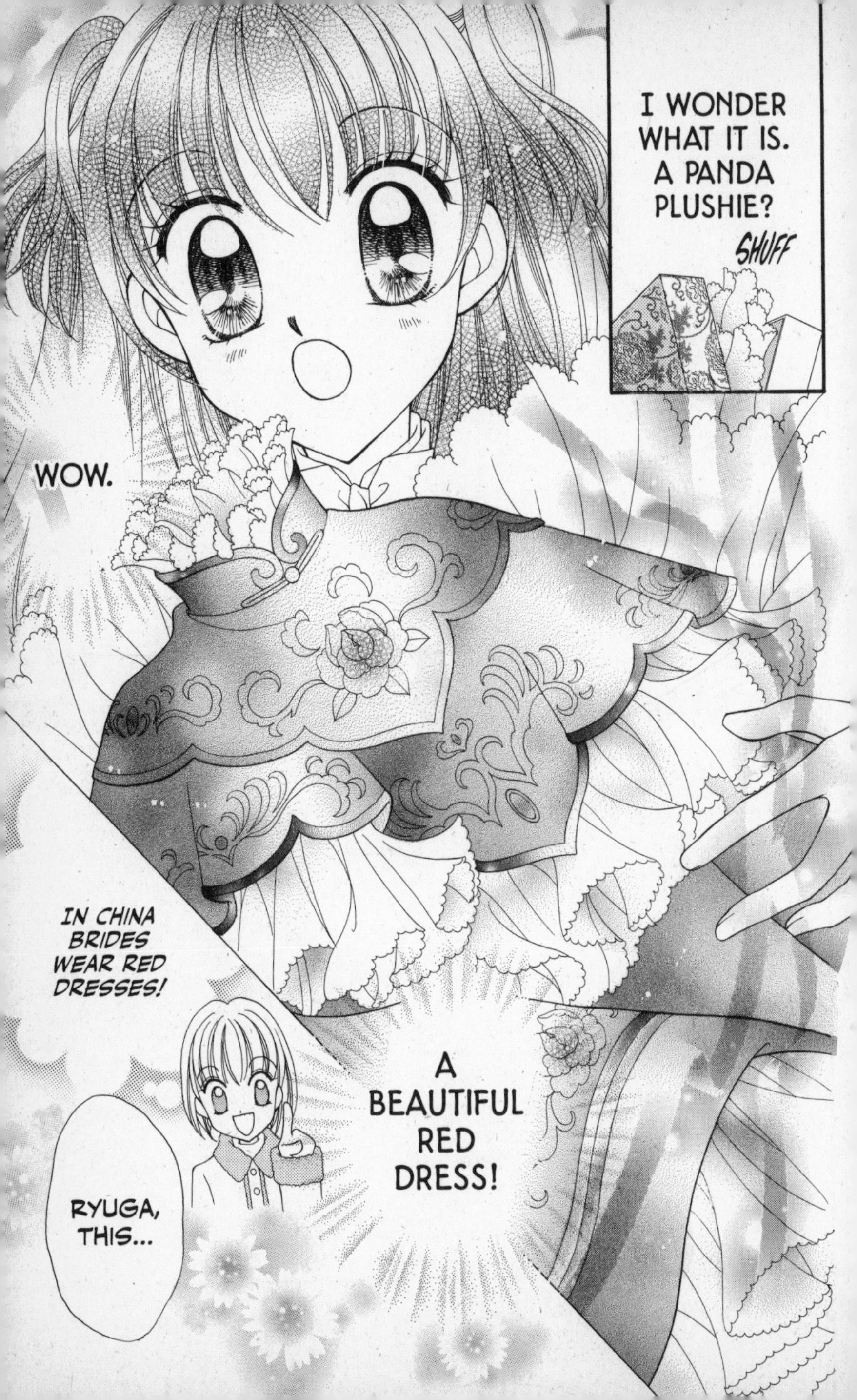
I WONDER WHAT IT IS. A PANDA PLUSHIE?
SHUFF
WOW.
A BEAUTIFUL RED DRESS!
IN CHINA BRIDES WEAR RED DRESSES!
RYUGA, THIS...

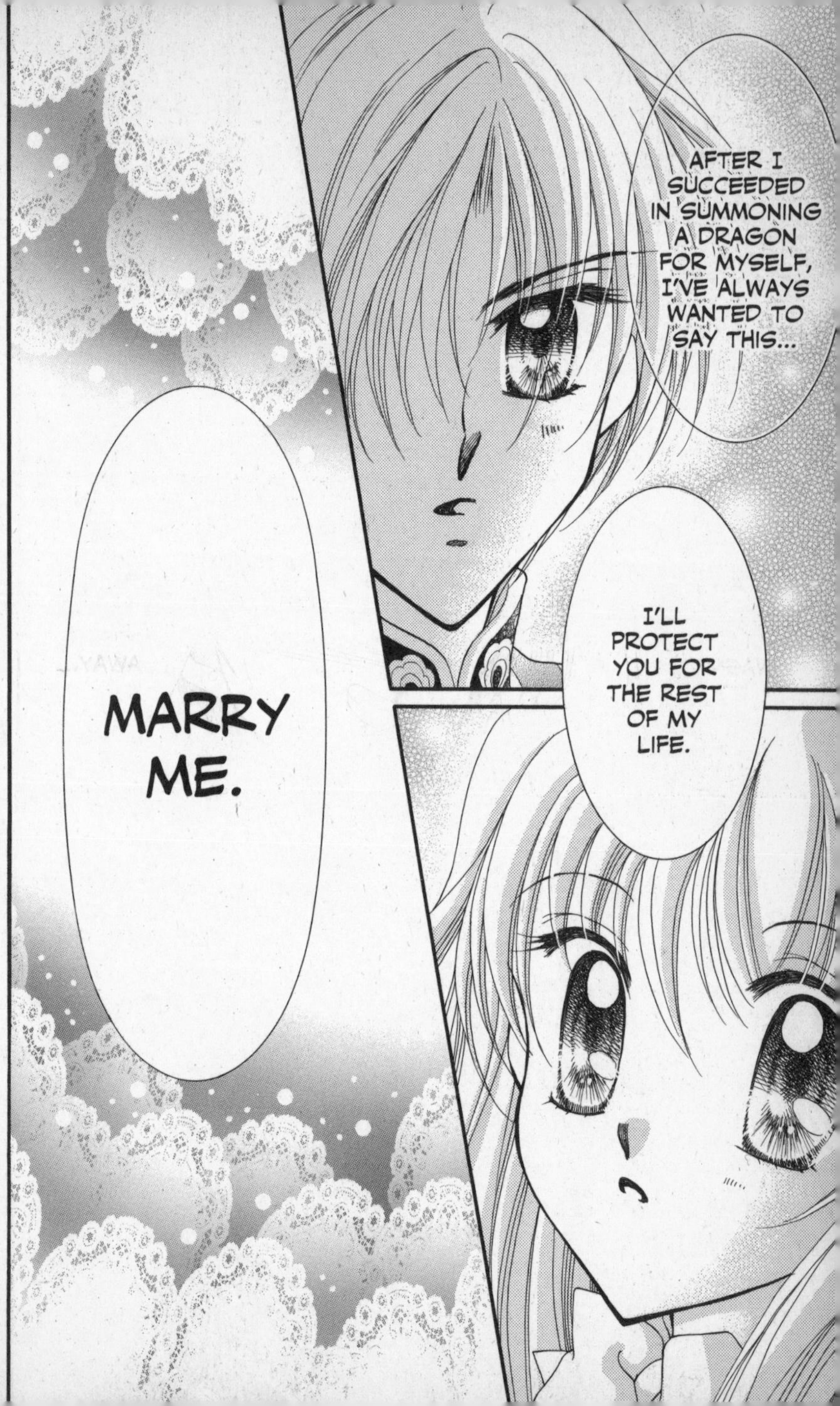
AFTER I SUCCEEDED IN SUMMONING A DRAGON FOR MYSELF, I'VE ALWAYS WANTED TO SAY THIS...
I'LL PROTECT YOU FOR THE REST OF MY LIFE.
MARRY ME.

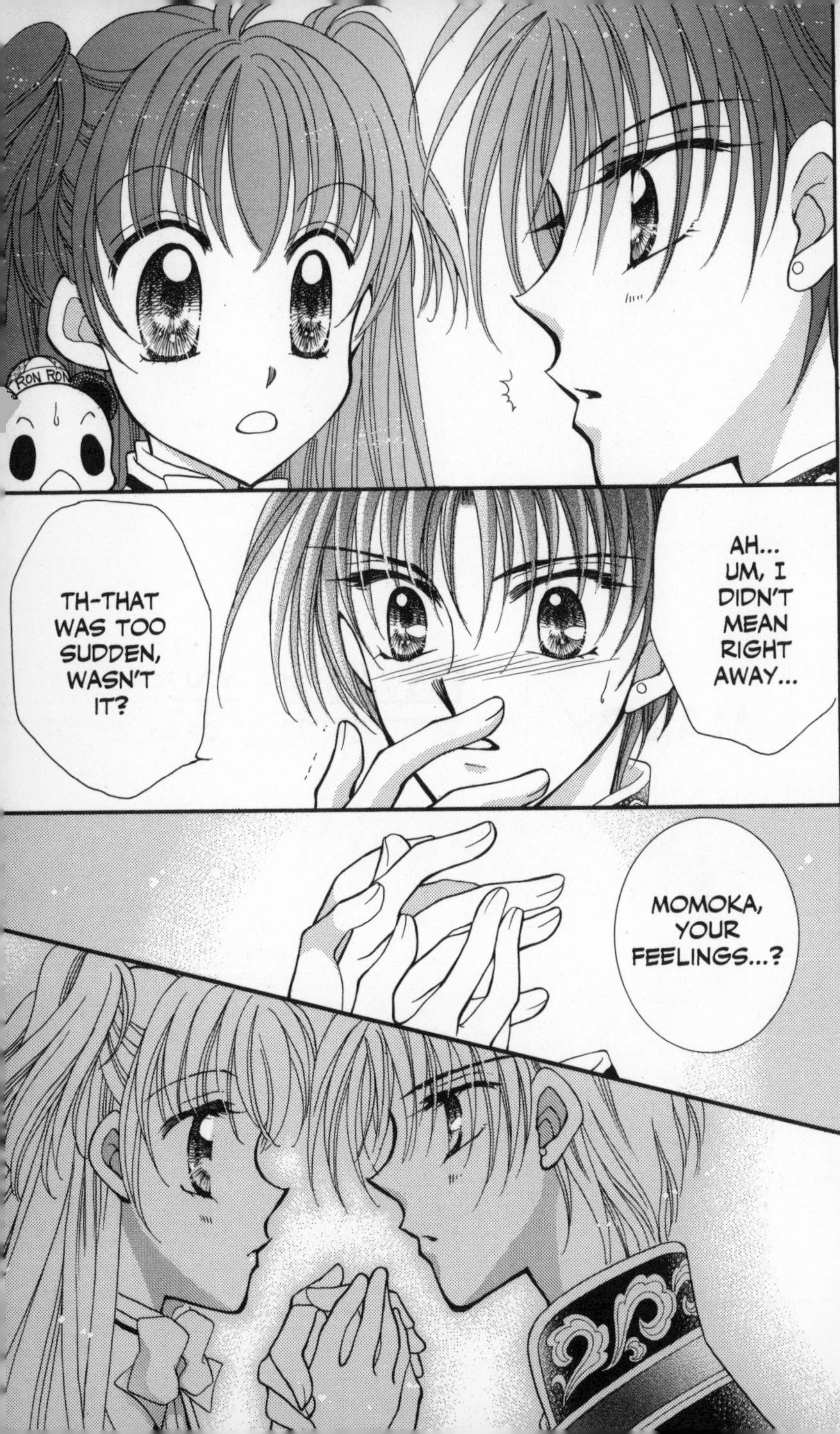
RON RON
AH... UM, I DIDN'T MEAN RIGHT AWAY...
TH-THAT WAS TOO SUDDEN, WASN'T IT?
MOMOKA, YOUR FEELINGS...?

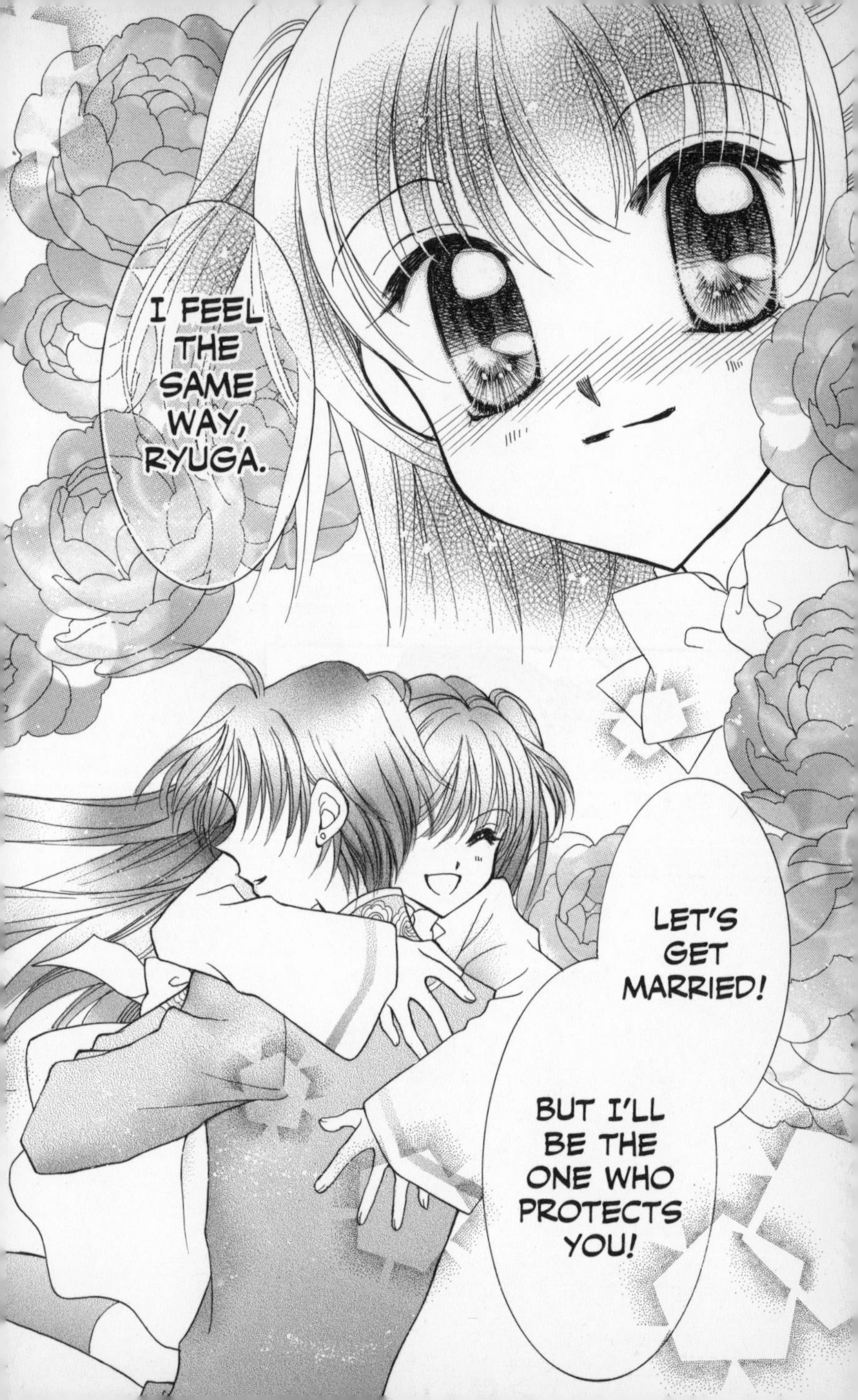
I FEEL THE SAME WAY, RYUGA.
LET'S GET MARRIED!
BUT I'LL BE THE ONE WHO PROTECTS YOU!

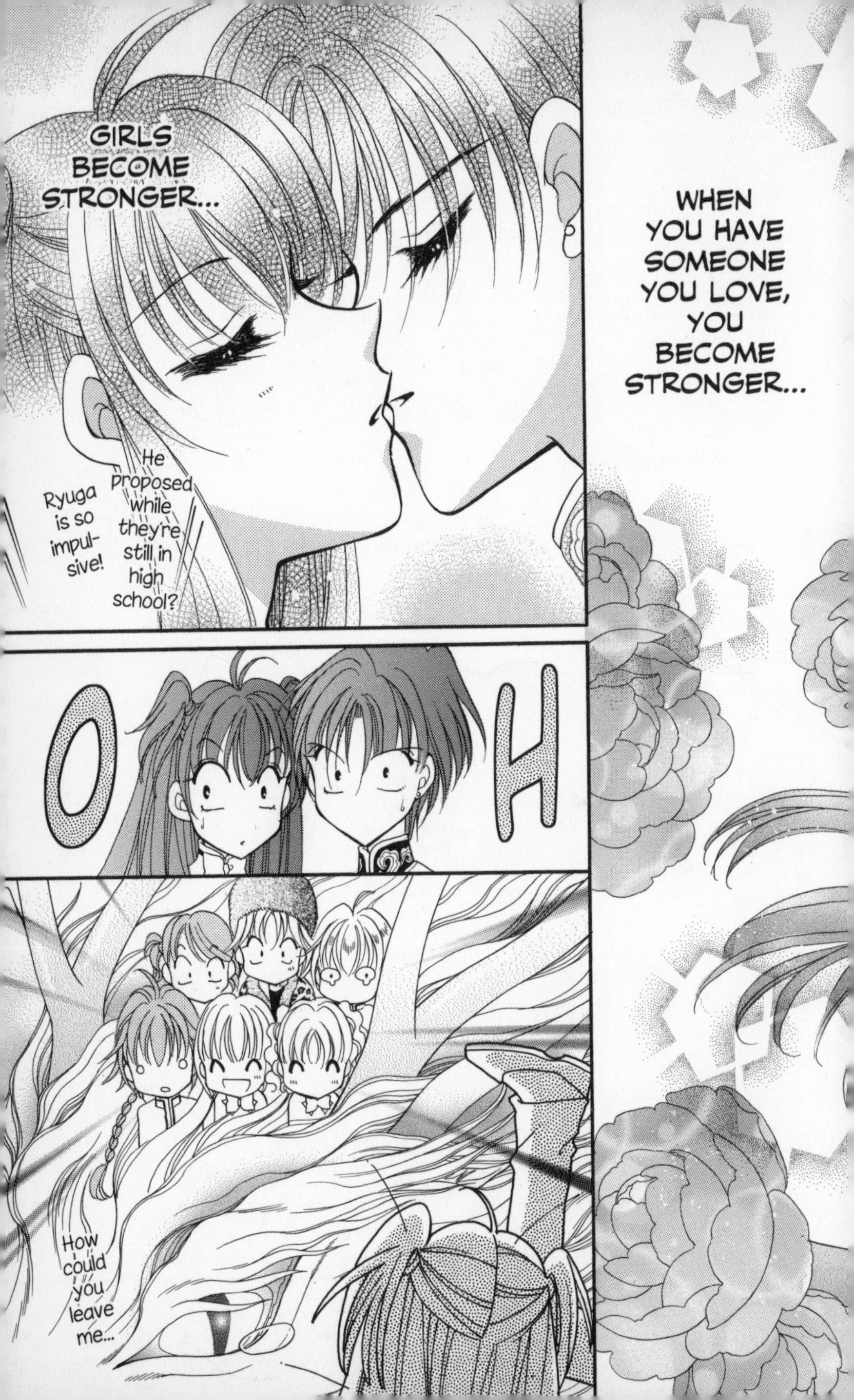
WHEN YOU HAVE SOMEONE YOU LOVE, YOU BECOME STRONGER...
GIRLS BECOME STRONGER...
He proposed while they're still in high school?
Ryuga is so impul-sive!
O H
How could you leave me...

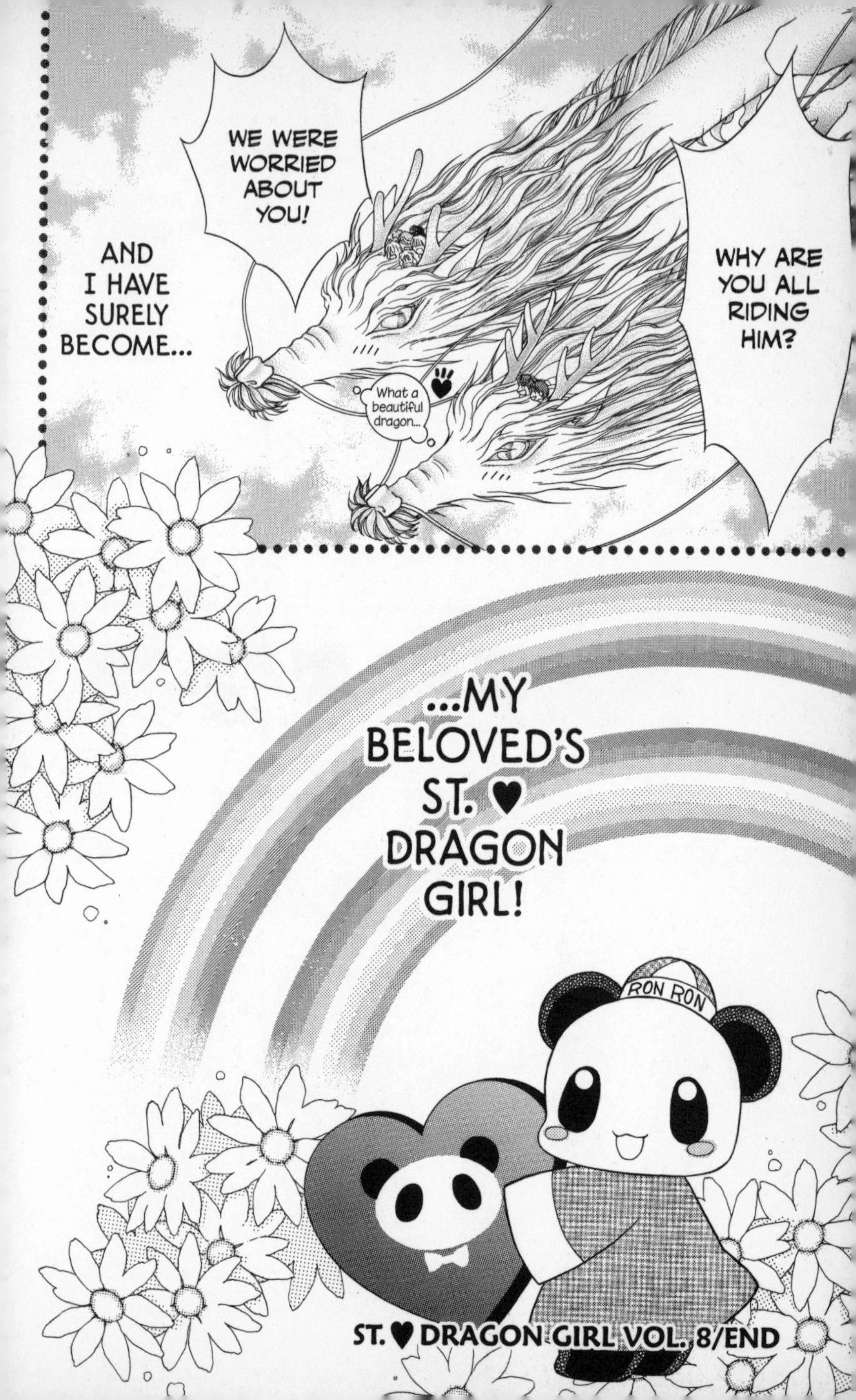
WHY ARE YOU ALL RIDING HIM?
WE WERE WORRIED ABOUT YOU!
What a beautiful dragon...
AND I HAVE SURELY BECOME...
...MY BELOVED'S ST. ♥ DRAGON GIRL!
RON RON
ST. ♥ DRAGON GIRL VOL. 8/END

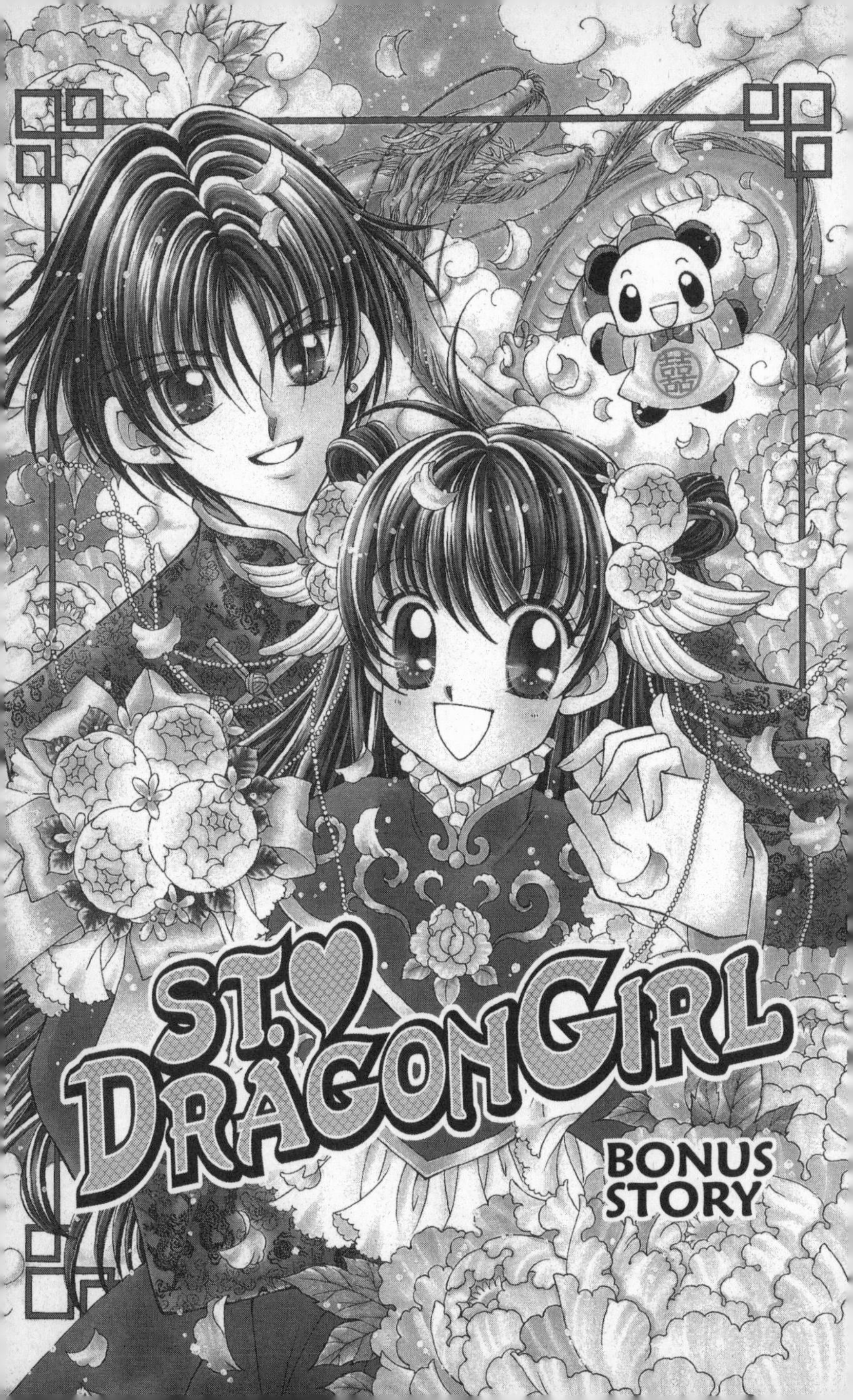
ST.♥DRAGON GIRL
BONUS STORY

HELLO! RYUGA?!

IDEA BY MIKA ISHIGAKI

I also thought of this while I was drawing the story! I thought it was so funny that I included it here. (laugh) Thanks, Mika!

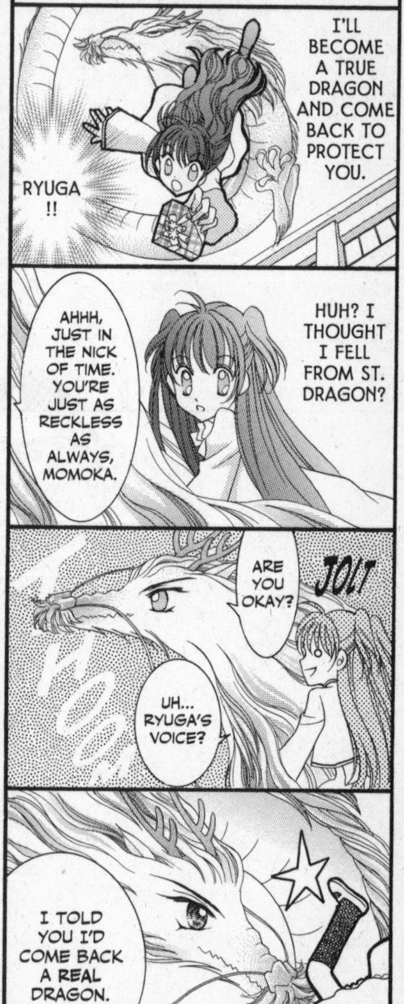
I'LL BECOME A TRUE DRAGON AND COME BACK TO PROTECT YOU.
RYUGA !!
HUH? I THOUGHT I FELL FROM ST. DRAGON?
AHHH, JUST IN THE NICK OF TIME. YOU'RE JUST AS RECKLESS AS ALWAYS, MOMOKA.
JOLT
ARE YOU OKAY?
UH... RYUGA'S VOICE?
I TOLD YOU I'D COME BACK A REAL DRAGON.

RON-RON'S DREAM

IDEA BY MIYU OHASHI

I have no idea where Ron-Ron would have gotten this idea.♪ Maybe he was sitting around in Momoka's room watching TV? The clothes of a company president strangely suit him...

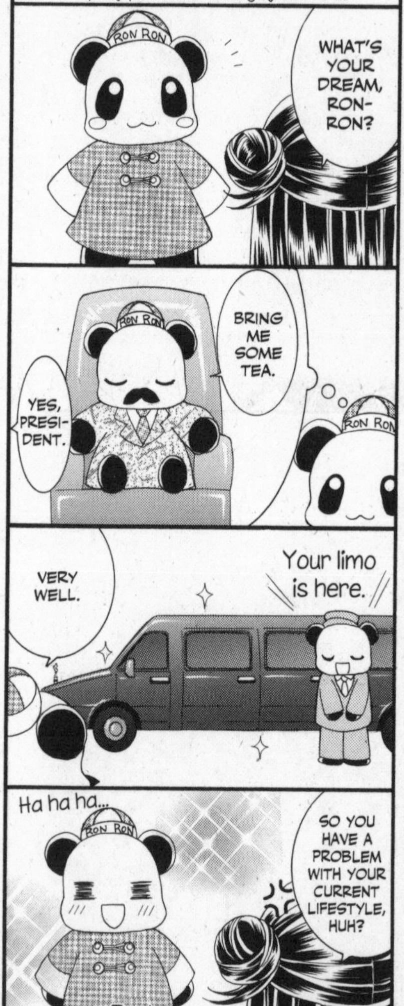
WHAT'S YOUR DREAM, RON-RON?
RON RON
BRING ME SOME TEA.
YES, PRESIDENT.
Your limo is here.
VERY WELL.
SO YOU HAVE A PROBLEM WITH YOUR CURRENT LIFESTYLE, HUH?
Ha ha ha...
Tee hee...

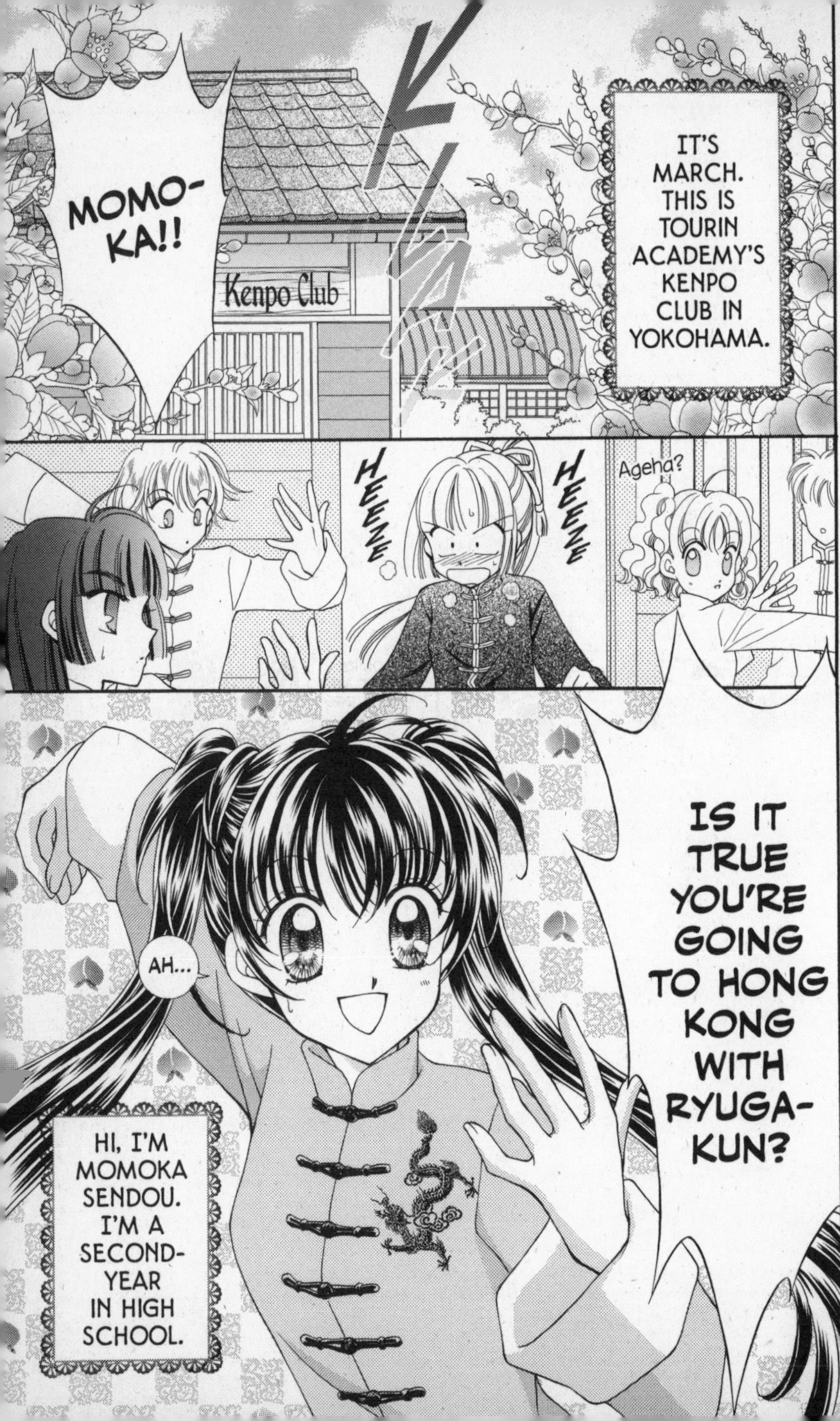
IT'S MARCH. THIS IS TOURIN ACADEMY'S KENPO CLUB IN YOKOHAMA.
Kenpo Club
MOMO-KA!!
Ageha?
HEEZE
HEEZE
IS IT TRUE YOU'RE GOING TO HONG KONG WITH RYUGA-KUN?
AH...
HI, I'M MOMOKA SENDOU. I'M A SECOND-YEAR IN HIGH SCHOOL.

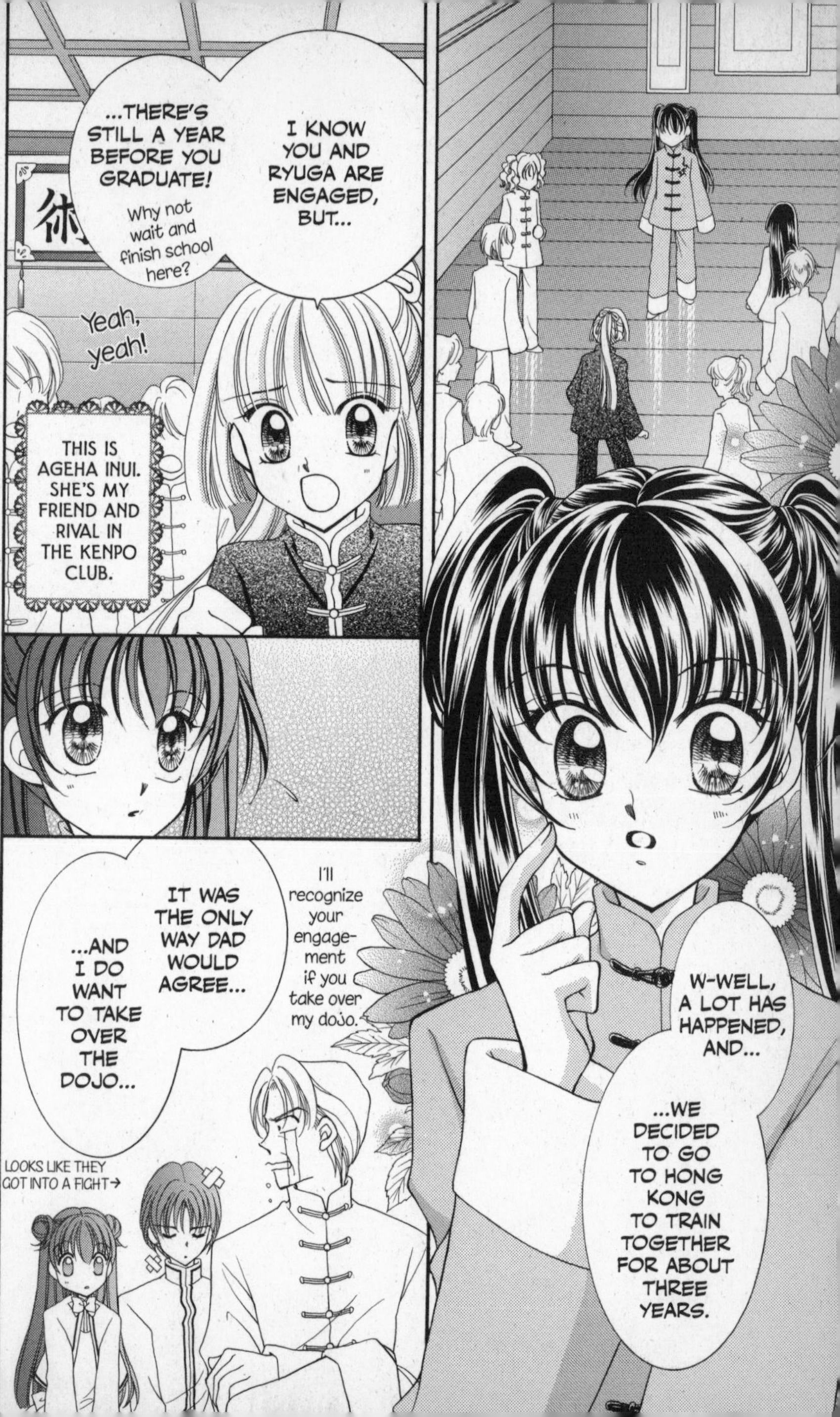
W-WELL, A LOT HAS HAPPENED, AND...
...WE DECIDED TO GO TO HONG KONG TO TRAIN TOGETHER FOR ABOUT THREE YEARS.
I KNOW YOU AND RYUGA ARE ENGAGED, BUT...
...THERE'S STILL A YEAR BEFORE YOU GRADUATE!
Why not wait and finish school here?
Yeah, yeah!
THIS IS AGEHA INUI. SHE'S MY FRIEND AND RIVAL IN THE KENPO CLUB.
IT WAS THE ONLY WAY DAD WOULD AGREE...
I'll recognize your engage-ment if you take over my dojo.
...AND I DO WANT TO TAKE OVER THE DOJO...
LOOKS LIKE THEY GOT INTO A FIGHT→

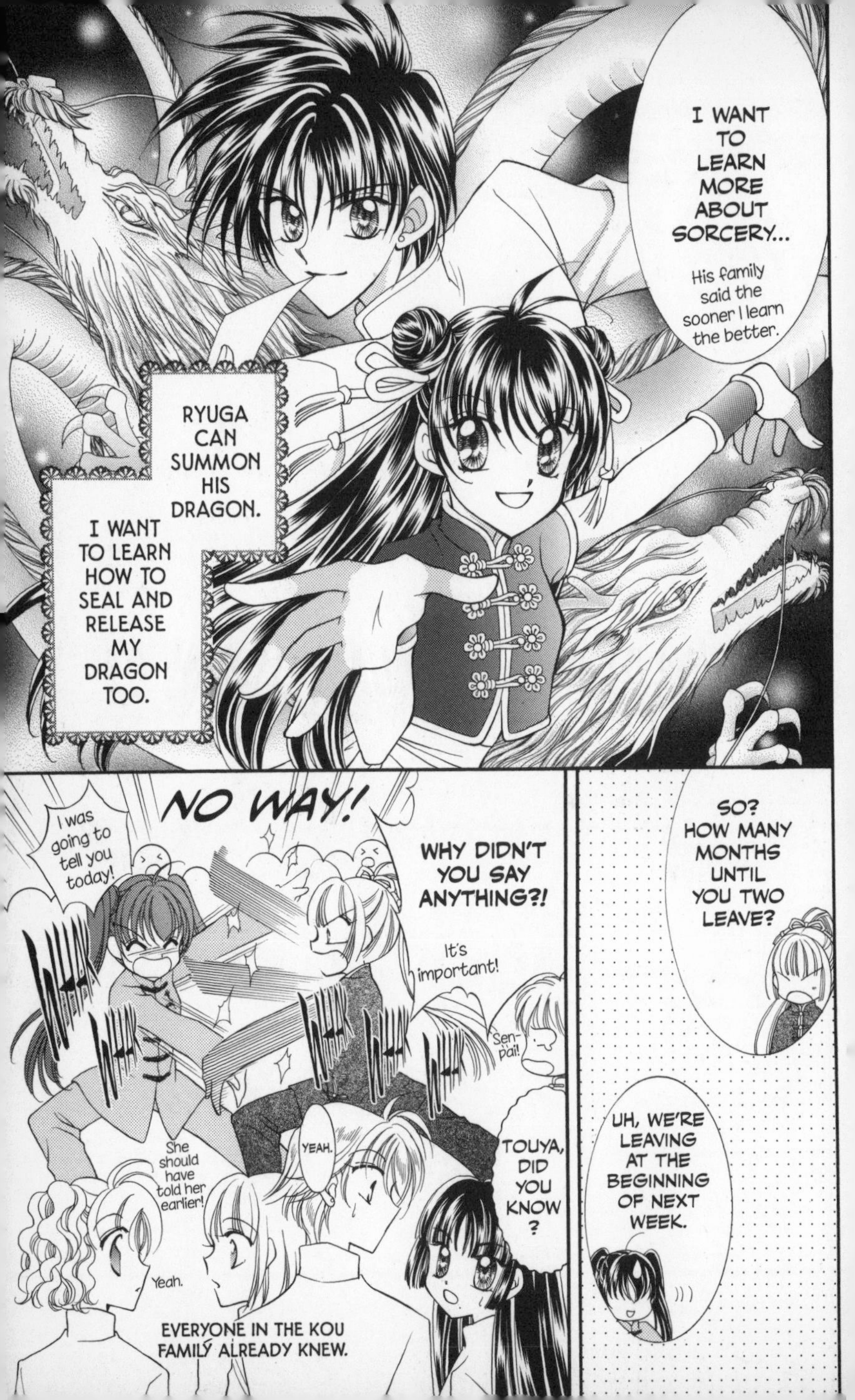
I WANT TO LEARN MORE ABOUT SORCERY...
His family said the sooner I learn the better.
RYUGA CAN SUMMON HIS DRAGON.
I WANT TO LEARN HOW TO SEAL AND RELEASE MY DRAGON TOO.
SO? HOW MANY MONTHS UNTIL YOU TWO LEAVE?
UH, WE'RE LEAVING AT THE BEGINNING OF NEXT WEEK.
WHY DIDN'T YOU SAY ANYTHING?!
It's important!
NO WAY!
I was going to tell you today!
Sen-pai!
TOUYA, DID YOU KNOW?
YEAH.
She should have told her earlier!
Yeah.
EVERYONE IN THE KOU FAMILY ALREADY KNEW.

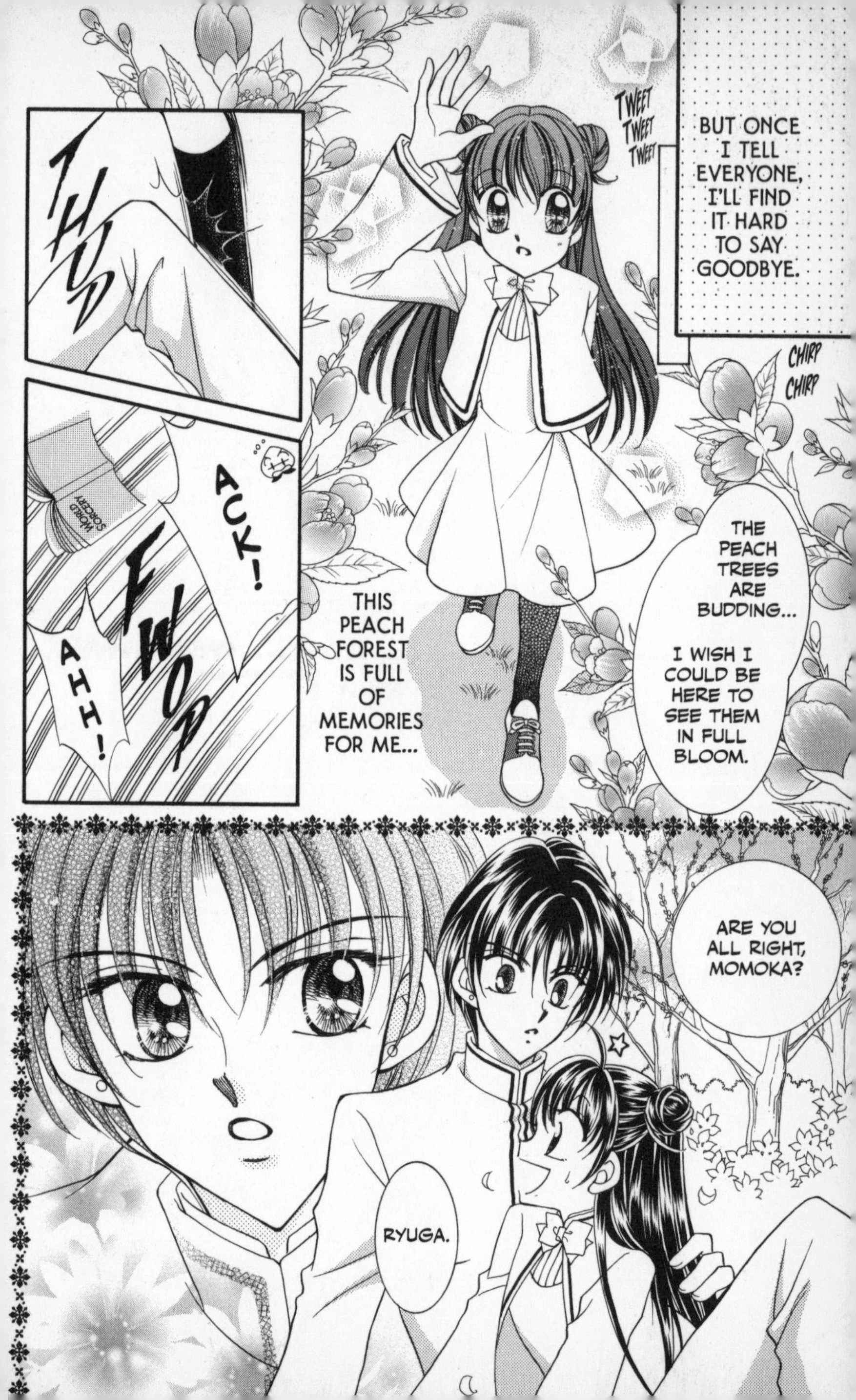
BUT ONCE I TELL EVERYONE, I'LL FIND IT HARD TO SAY GOODBYE.
TWEET TWEET TWEET
CHIRP CHIRP
THE PEACH TREES ARE BUDDING...
I WISH I COULD BE HERE TO SEE THEM IN FULL BLOOM.
THIS PEACH FOREST IS FULL OF MEMORIES FOR ME...
THUD
WORLD SORCERY
ACK!
FWOP
AHH!
ARE YOU ALL RIGHT, MOMOKA?
RYUGA.

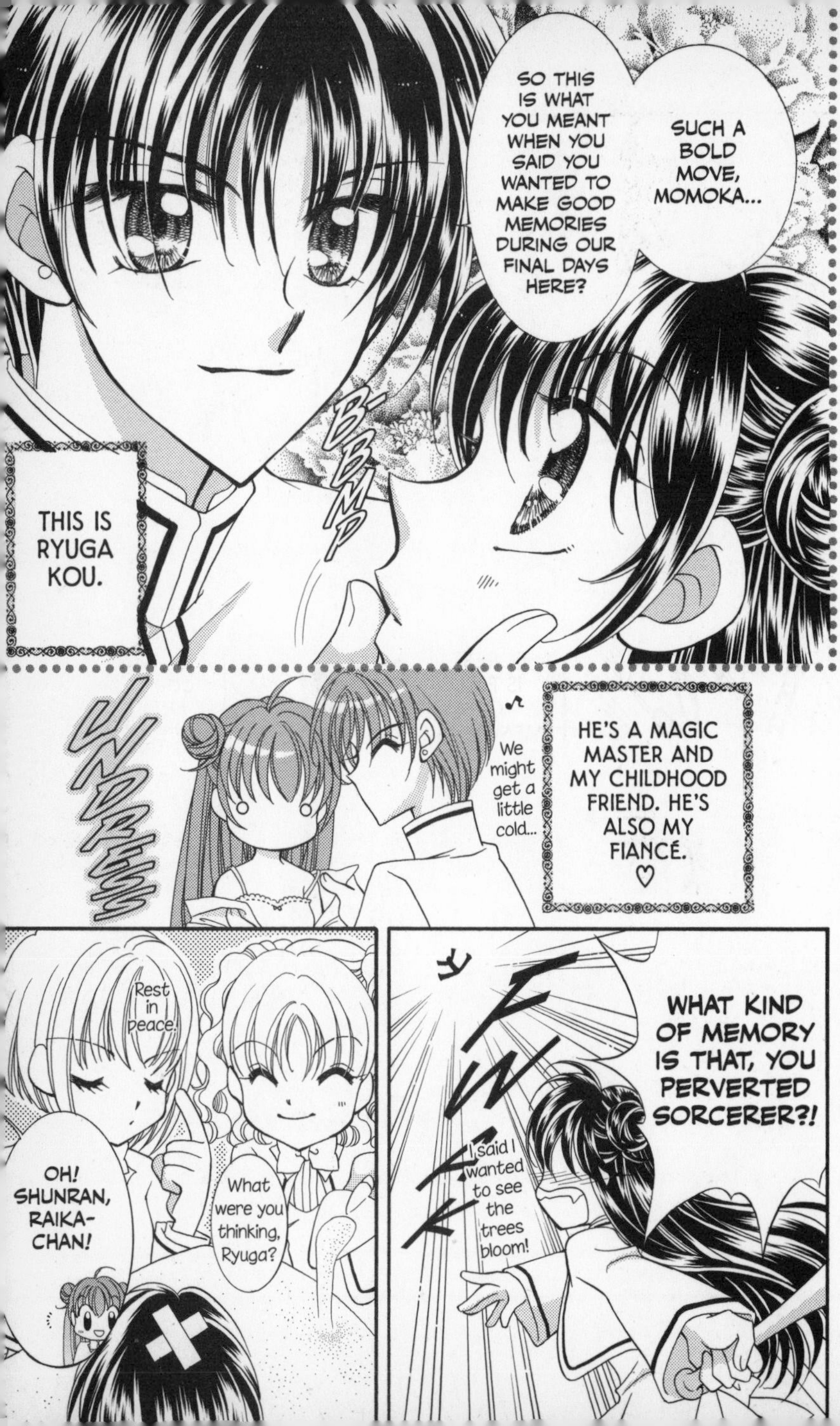
SUCH A BOLD MOVE, MOMOKA...
SO THIS IS WHAT YOU MEANT WHEN YOU SAID YOU WANTED TO MAKE GOOD MEMORIES DURING OUR FINAL DAYS HERE?
THIS IS RYUGA KOU.
HE'S A MAGIC MASTER AND MY CHILDHOOD FRIEND. HE'S ALSO MY FIANCÉ. ♡
We might get a little cold...
WHAT KIND OF MEMORY IS THAT, YOU PERVERTED SORCERER?!
I said I wanted to see the trees bloom!
Rest in peace.
What were you thinking, Ryuga?
OH! SHUNRAN, RAIKA-CHAN!

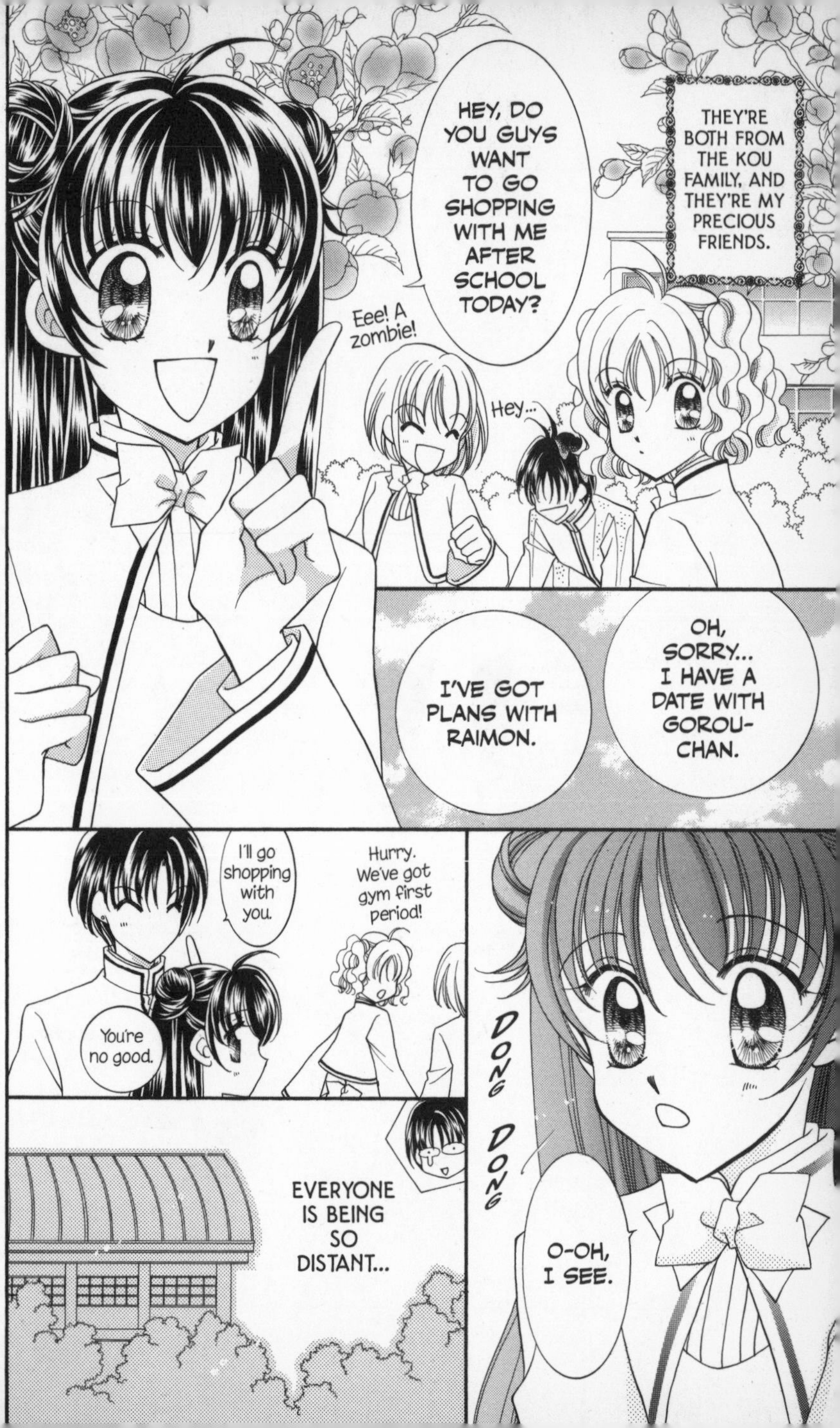
THEY'RE BOTH FROM THE KOU FAMILY, AND THEY'RE MY PRECIOUS FRIENDS.
HEY, DO YOU GUYS WANT TO GO SHOPPING WITH ME AFTER SCHOOL TODAY?
Eee! A zombie!
Hey...
OH, SORRY... I HAVE A DATE WITH GOROU-CHAN.
I'VE GOT PLANS WITH RAIMON.
DONG DONG
O-OH, I SEE.
Hurry. We've got gym first period!
I'll go shopping with you.
You're no good.
EVERYONE IS BEING SO DISTANT...

7

[Note: The following contest is already over. Sorry! -Ed.]

I'm going to give away 40 signed *St. Dragon Girl* manga (limit one per person).

It'll be 6 Taiwanese volumes, 3 Hong Kong volumes, 2 Chinese volumes and 29 Japanese volumes.

Those who want to apply, please send in a self-addressed, stamped envelope with a fan letter telling which volume you'd prefer.

It'll be first come, first served!
Good luck!

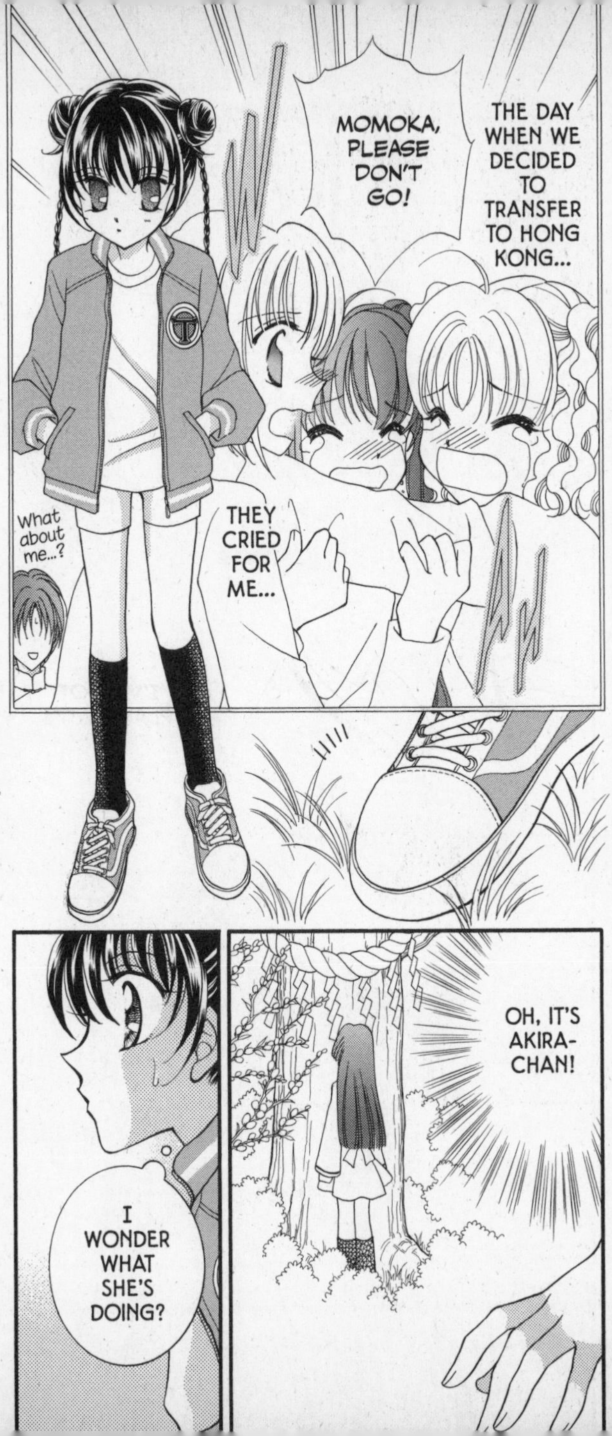
THE DAY WHEN WE DECIDED TO TRANSFER TO HONG KONG...
MOMOKA, PLEASE DON'T GO!
THEY CRIED FOR ME...
What about me...?
OH, IT'S AKIRA-CHAN!
I WONDER WHAT SHE'S DOING?

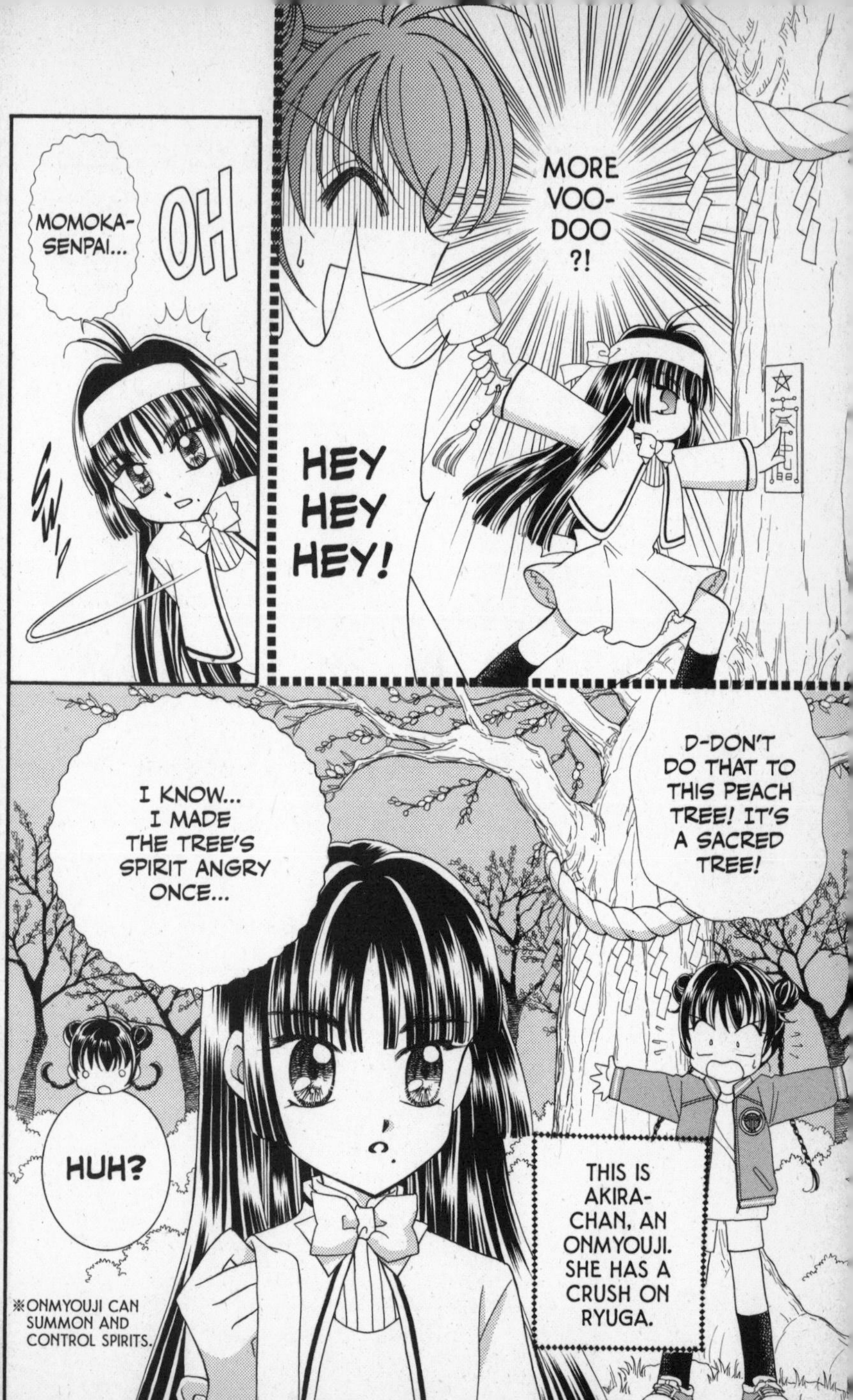
MORE VOO-DOO?!
HEY HEY HEY!
MOMOKA-SENPAI...
OH
D-DON'T DO THAT TO THIS PEACH TREE! IT'S A SACRED TREE!
I KNOW... I MADE THE TREE'S SPIRIT ANGRY ONCE...
THIS IS AKIRA-CHAN, AN ONMYOUJI. SHE HAS A CRUSH ON RYUGA.
HUH?
※ONMYOUJI CAN SUMMON AND CONTROL SPIRITS.

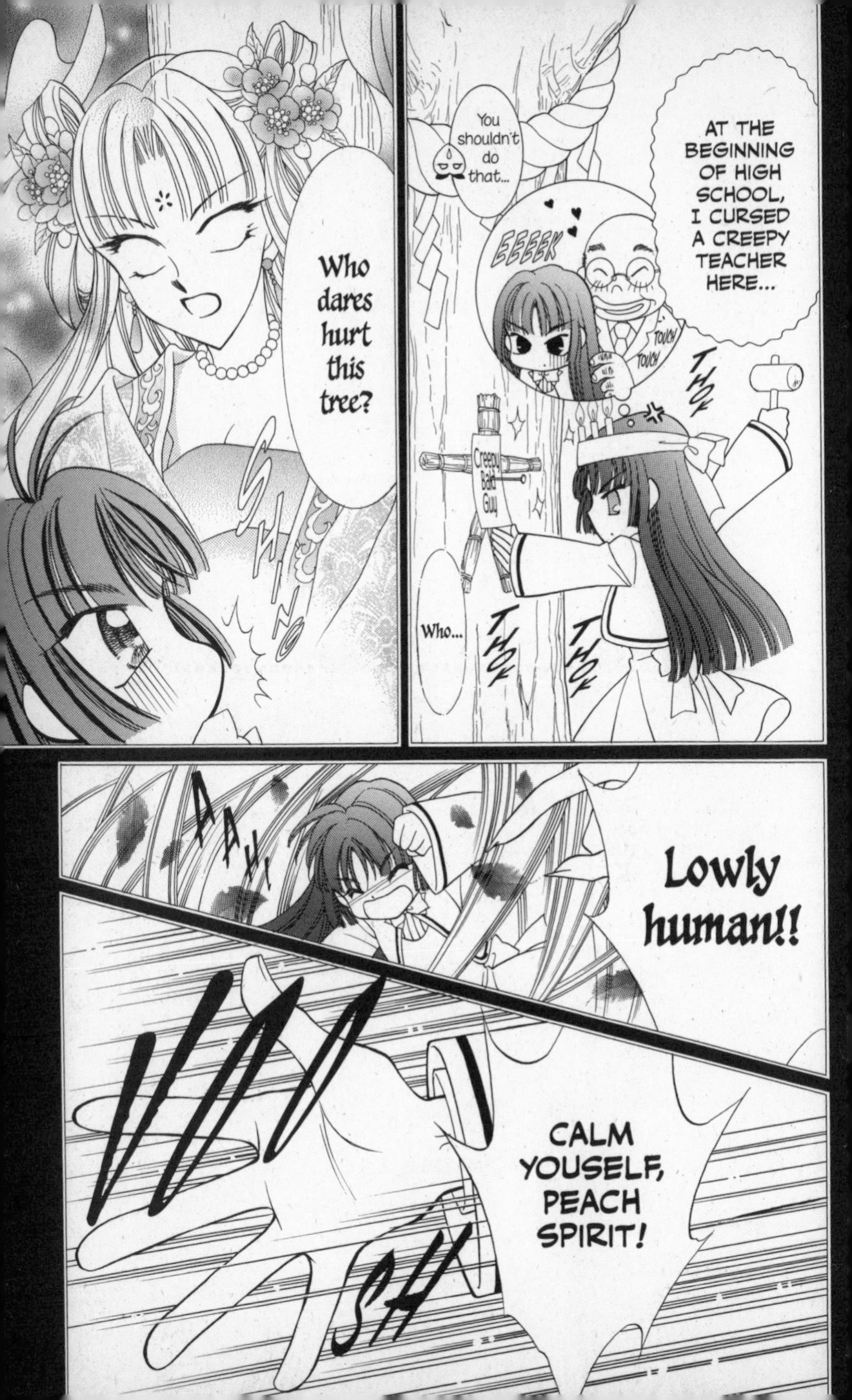
AT THE BEGINNING OF HIGH SCHOOL, I CURSED A CREEPY TEACHER HERE...
You shouldn't do that...
EEEEK
TOUCH TOUCH
THOK
Creepy Bald Guy
Who...
THOK THOK
Who dares hurt this tree?
SHING
Lowly human!!
AAH!
CALM YOUSELF, PEACH SPIRIT!
WOOSH

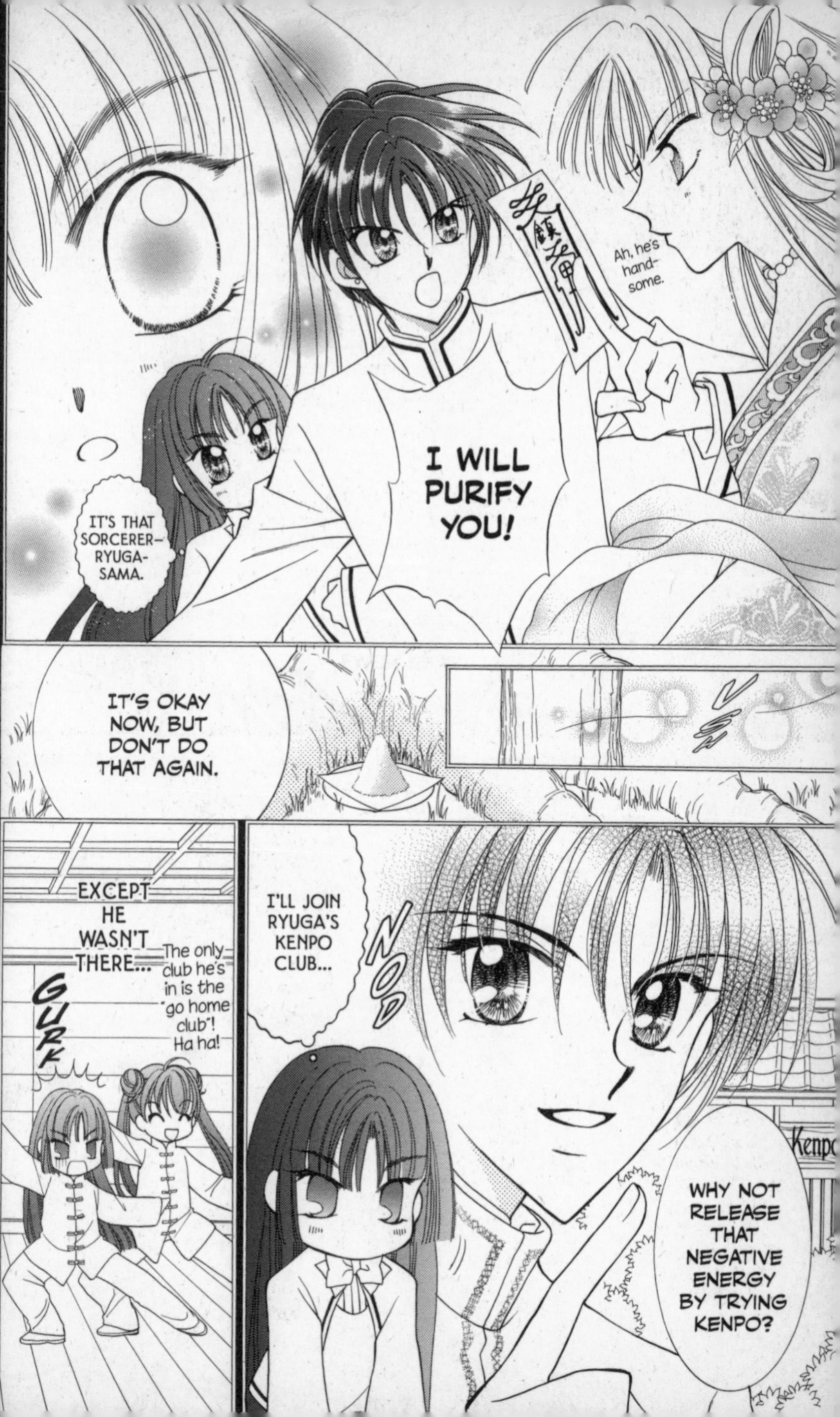
Ah, he's hand-some.
I WILL PURIFY YOU!
IT'S THAT SORCERER-RYUGA-SAMA.
VSH
IT'S OKAY NOW, BUT DON'T DO THAT AGAIN.
WHY NOT RELEASE THAT NEGATIVE ENERGY BY TRYING KENPO?
Kenpo
NOD
I'LL JOIN RYUGA'S KENPO CLUB...
EXCEPT HE WASN'T THERE...
The only club he's in is the "go home club"! Ha ha!
GURK

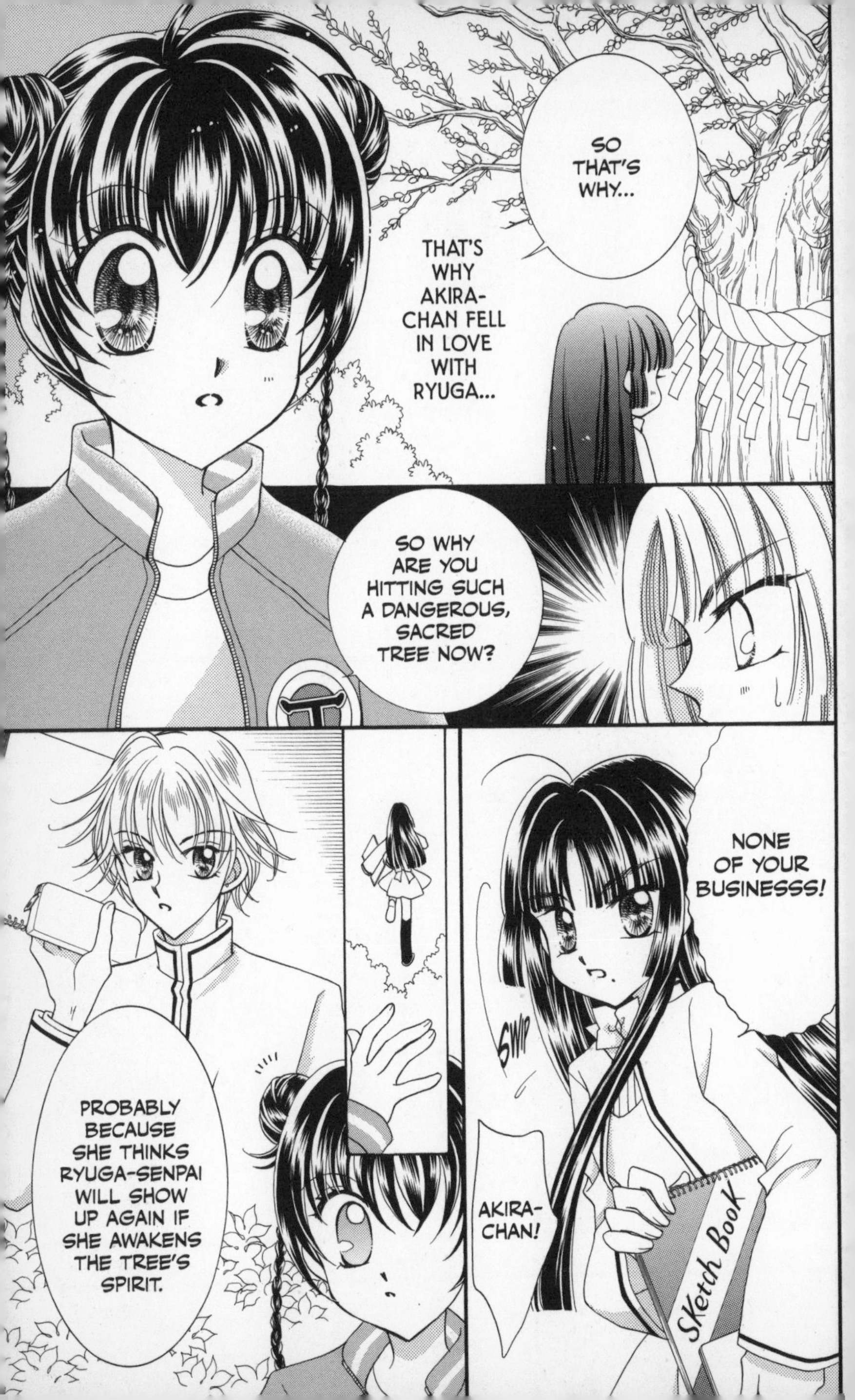
SO THAT'S WHY...
THAT'S WHY AKIRA-CHAN FELL IN LOVE WITH RYUGA...
SO WHY ARE YOU HITTING SUCH A DANGEROUS, SACRED TREE NOW?
NONE OF YOUR BUSINESSS!
SWIP
AKIRA-CHAN!
PROBABLY BECAUSE SHE THINKS RYUGA-SENPAI WILL SHOW UP AGAIN IF SHE AWAKENS THE TREE'S SPIRIT.
Sketch Book

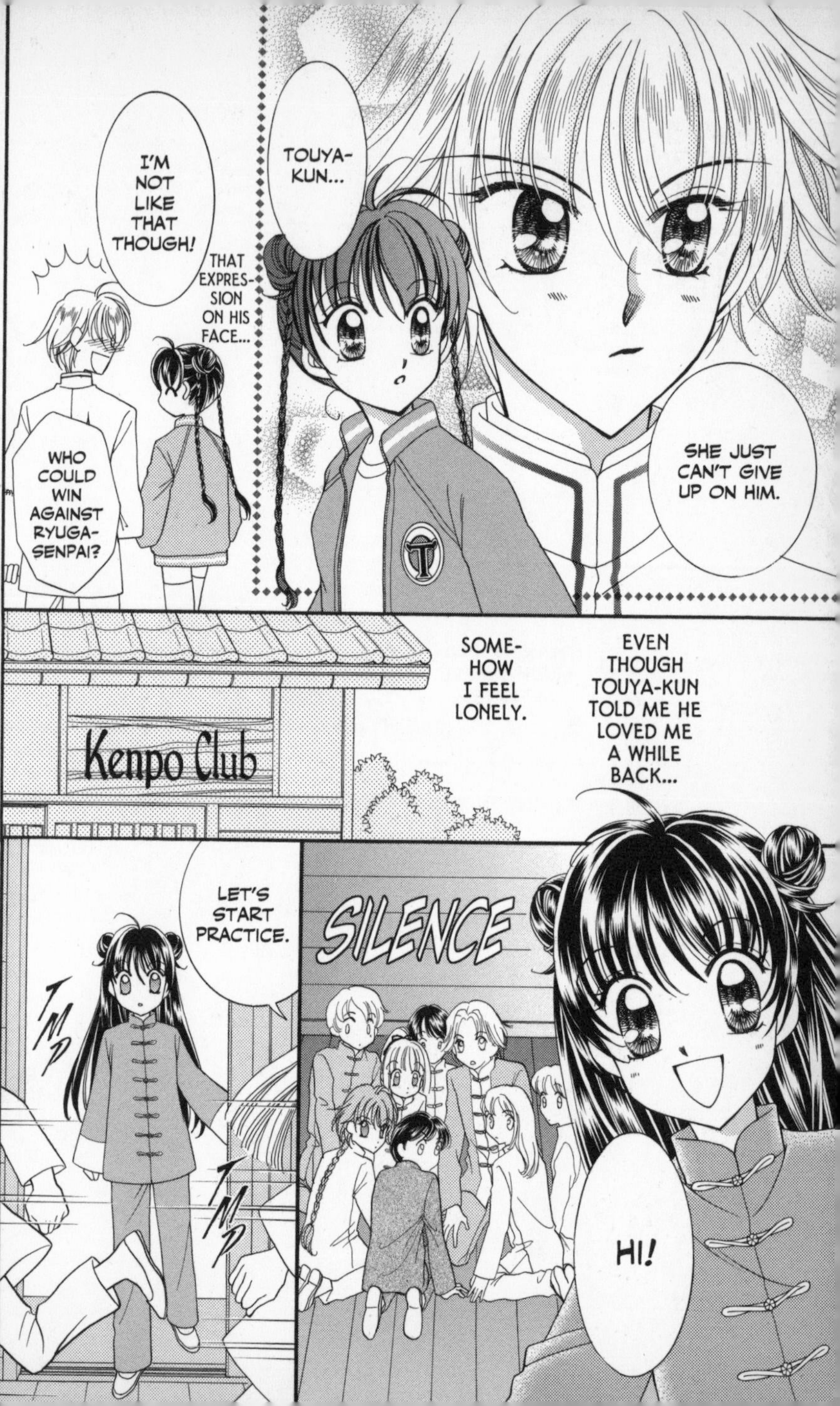
TOUYA-KUN...
THAT EXPRESSION ON HIS FACE...
SHE JUST CAN'T GIVE UP ON HIM.
I'M NOT LIKE THAT THOUGH!
WHO COULD WIN AGAINST RYUGA-SENPAI?
EVEN THOUGH TOUYA-KUN TOLD ME HE LOVED ME A WHILE BACK...
SOMEHOW I FEEL LONELY.
Kenpo Club
HI!
SILENCE
LET'S START PRACTICE.
TMP
TMP

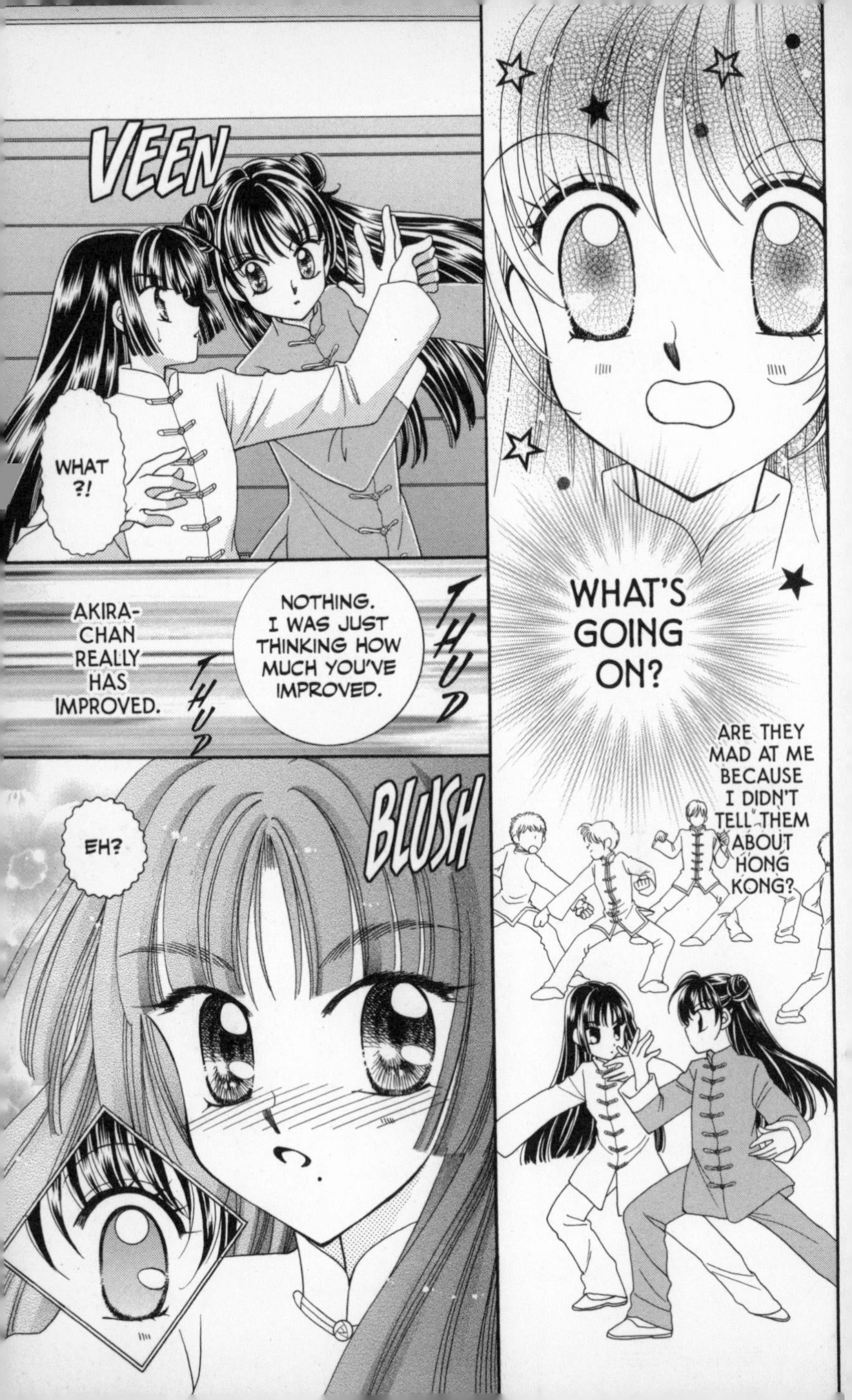
WHAT'S GOING ON?
ARE THEY MAD AT ME BECAUSE I DIDN'T TELL THEM ABOUT HONG KONG?
VEEN
WHAT ?!
THUD
NOTHING. I WAS JUST THINKING HOW MUCH YOU'VE IMPROVED.
THUD
AKIRA-CHAN REALLY HAS IMPROVED.
BLUSH
EH?

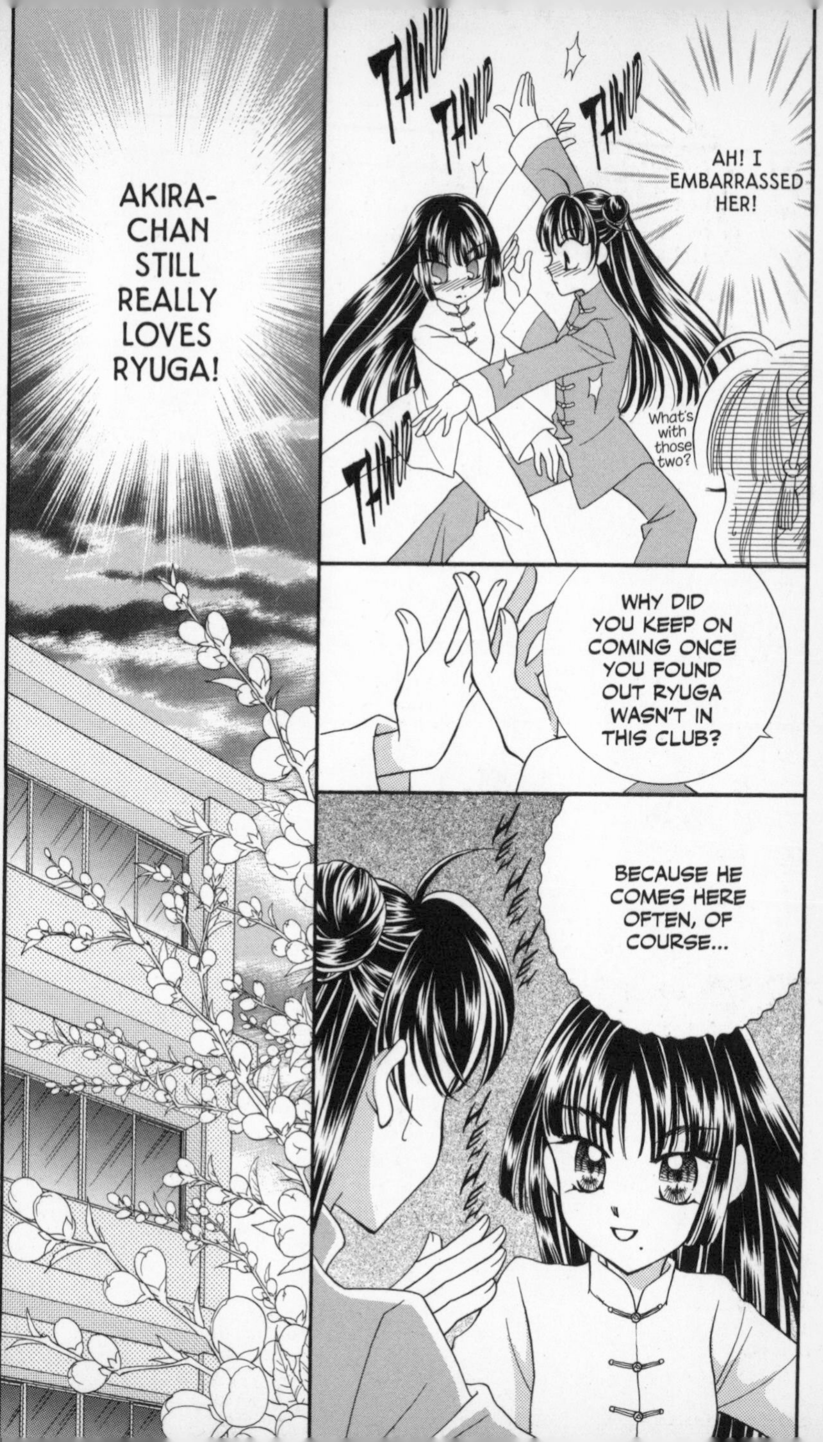
AH! I EMBARRASSED HER!
THWUP
THWUP
THWUP
What's with those two?
THWUP
WHY DID YOU KEEP ON COMING ONCE YOU FOUND OUT RYUGA WASN'T IN THIS CLUB?
BECAUSE HE COMES HERE OFTEN, OF COURSE...
AKIRA-CHAN STILL REALLY LOVES RYUGA!

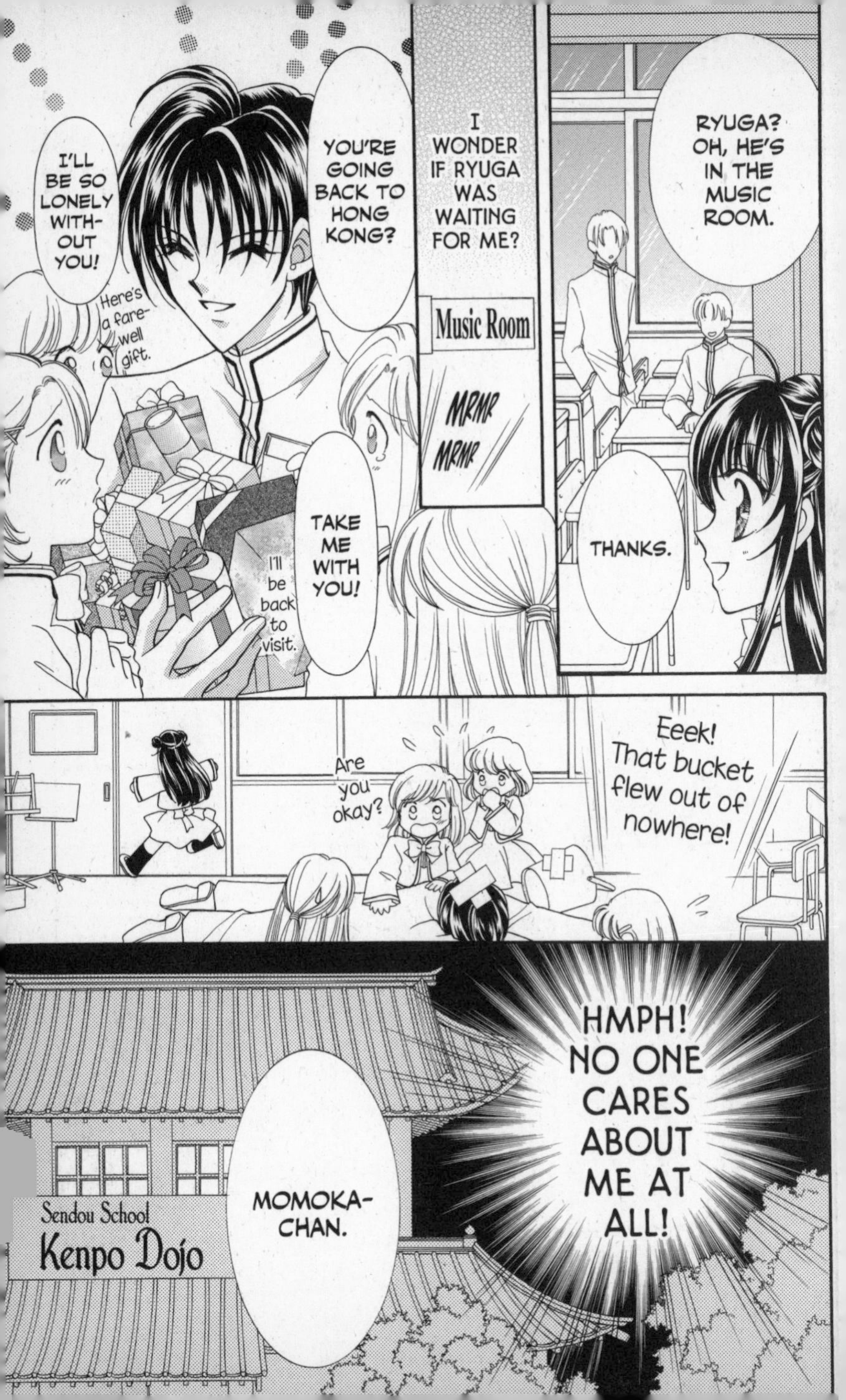
RYUGA? OH, HE'S IN THE MUSIC ROOM.
THANKS.
I WONDER IF RYUGA WAS WAITING FOR ME?
Music Room
MRMR MRMR
YOU'RE GOING BACK TO HONG KONG?
I'LL BE SO LONELY WITH-OUT YOU!
Here's a fare-well gift.
TAKE ME WITH YOU!
I'll be back to visit.
Eeek! That bucket flew out of nowhere!
Are you okay?
HMPH! NO ONE CARES ABOUT ME AT ALL!
MOMOKA-CHAN.
Sendou School
Kenpo Dojo

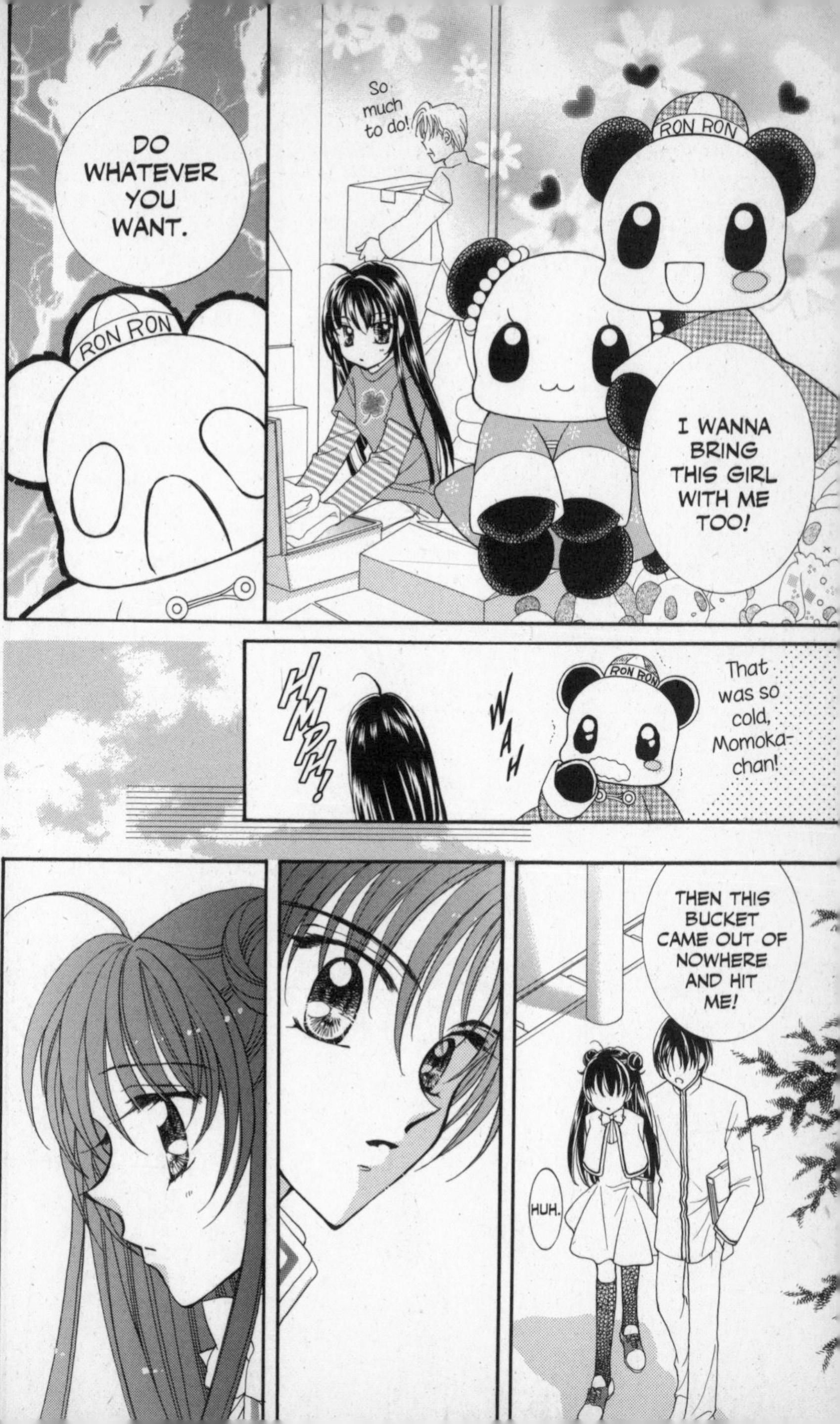
RON RON
I WANNA BRING THIS GIRL WITH ME TOO!
So much to do!
RON RON
DO WHATEVER YOU WANT.
RON RON
That was so cold, Momoka-chan!
WAH
HMPH!
THEN THIS BUCKET CAME OUT OF NOWHERE AND HIT ME!
HUH.

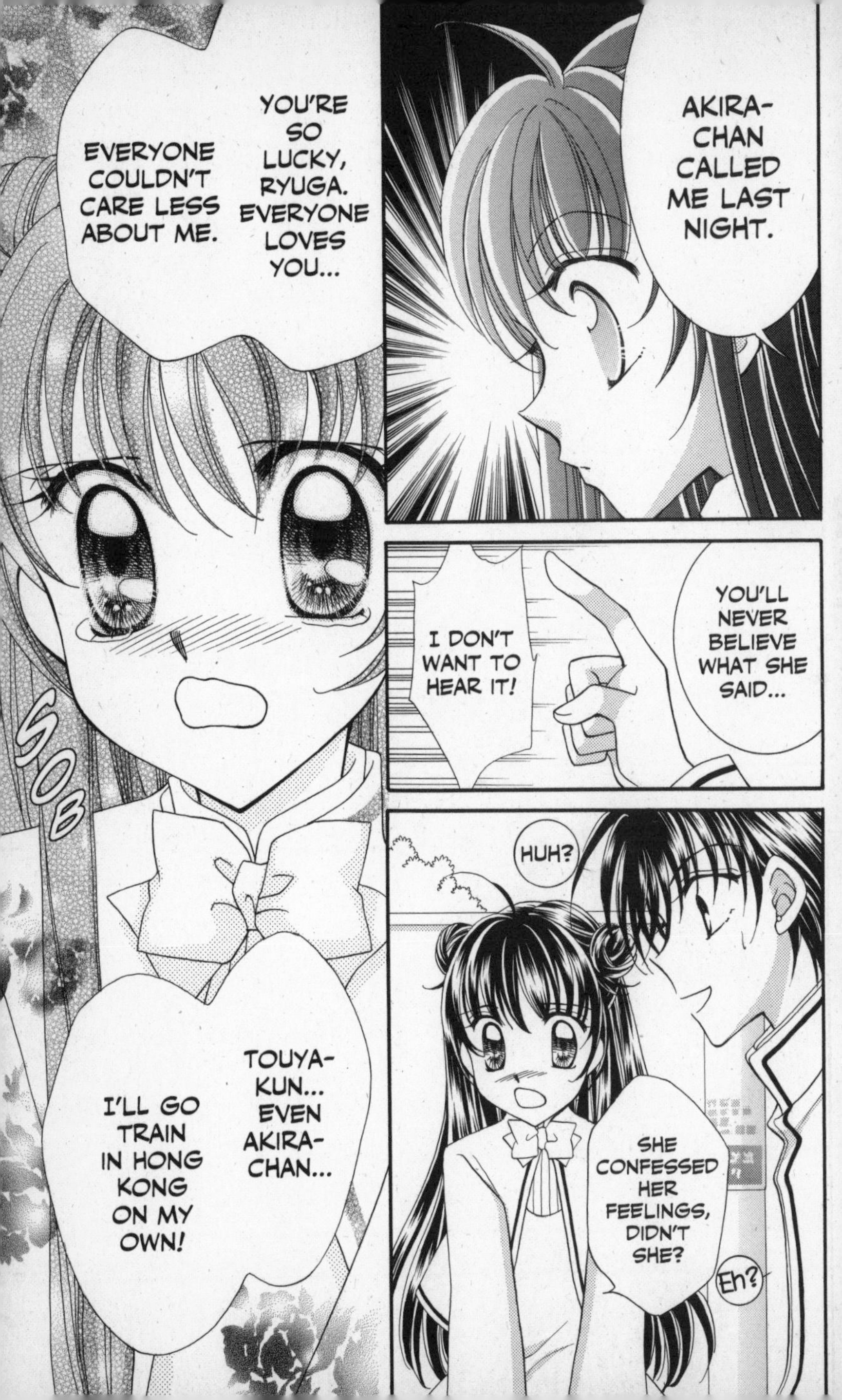
AKIRA-CHAN CALLED ME LAST NIGHT.
YOU'LL NEVER BELIEVE WHAT SHE SAID...
I DON'T WANT TO HEAR IT!
HUH?
SHE CONFESSED HER FEELINGS, DIDN'T SHE?
Eh?
YOU'RE SO LUCKY, RYUGA. EVERYONE LOVES YOU...
EVERYONE COULDN'T CARE LESS ABOUT ME.
SOB
TOUYA-KUN... EVEN AKIRA-CHAN...
I'LL GO TRAIN IN HONG KONG ON MY OWN!

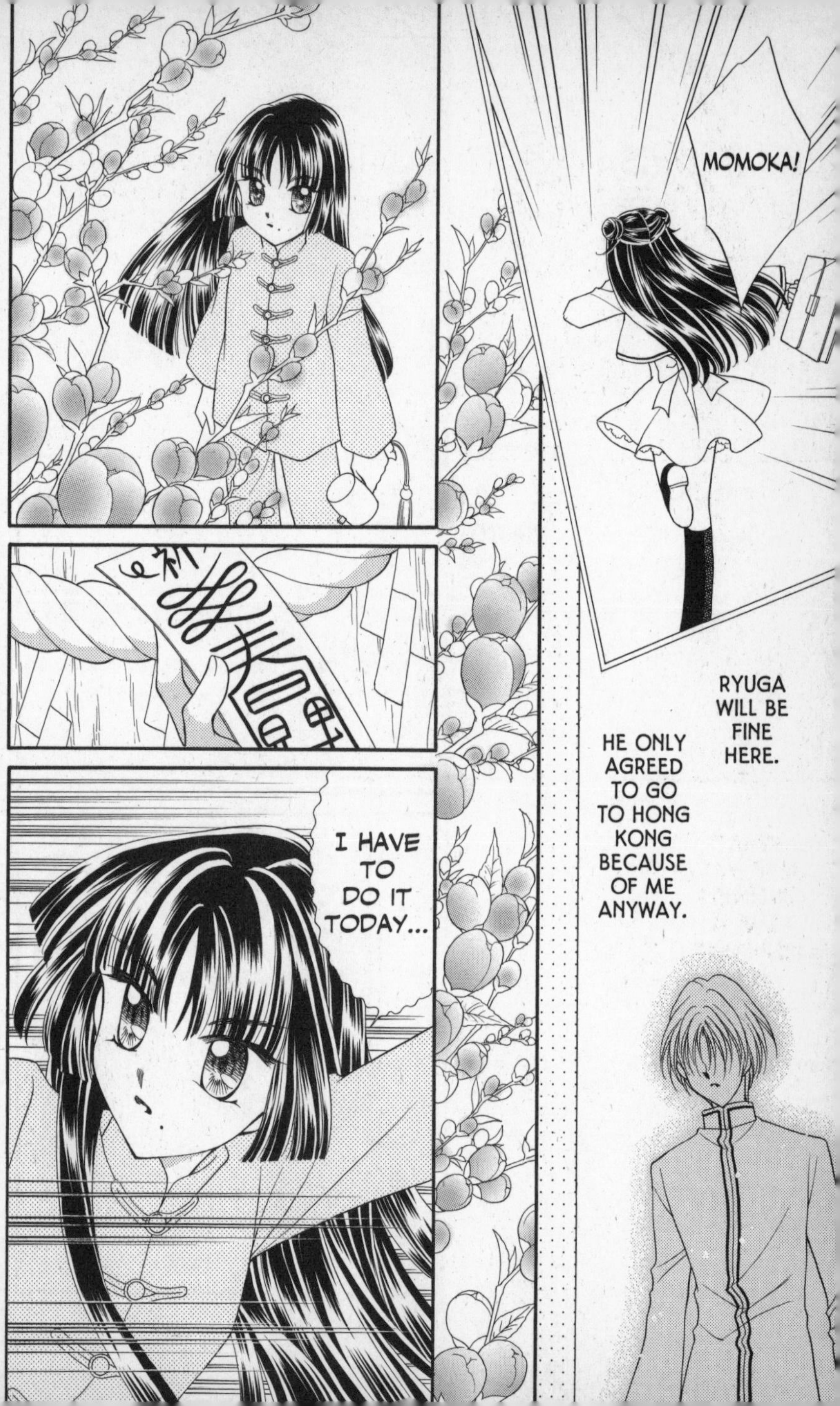
MOMOKA!
RYUGA WILL BE FINE HERE.
HE ONLY AGREED TO GO TO HONG KONG BECAUSE OF ME ANYWAY.
I HAVE TO DO IT TODAY...

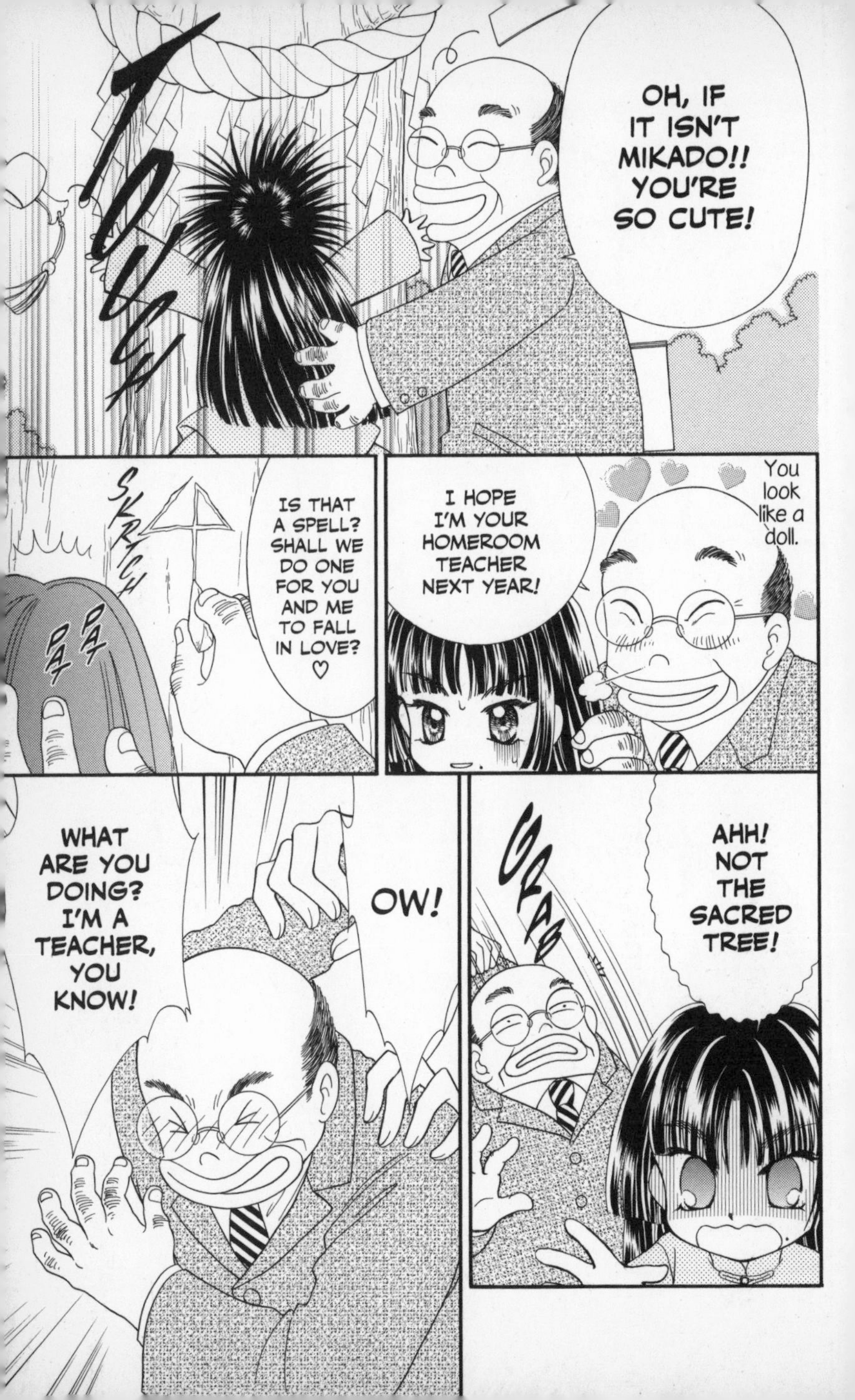
OH, IF IT ISN'T MIKADO!! YOU'RE SO CUTE!
I HOPE I'M YOUR HOMEROOM TEACHER NEXT YEAR!
You look like a doll.
IS THAT A SPELL? SHALL WE DO ONE FOR YOU AND ME TO FALL IN LOVE? ♡
SKRITCH
PAT PAT
AHH! NOT THE SACRED TREE!
OW!
WHAT ARE YOU DOING? I'M A TEACHER, YOU KNOW!

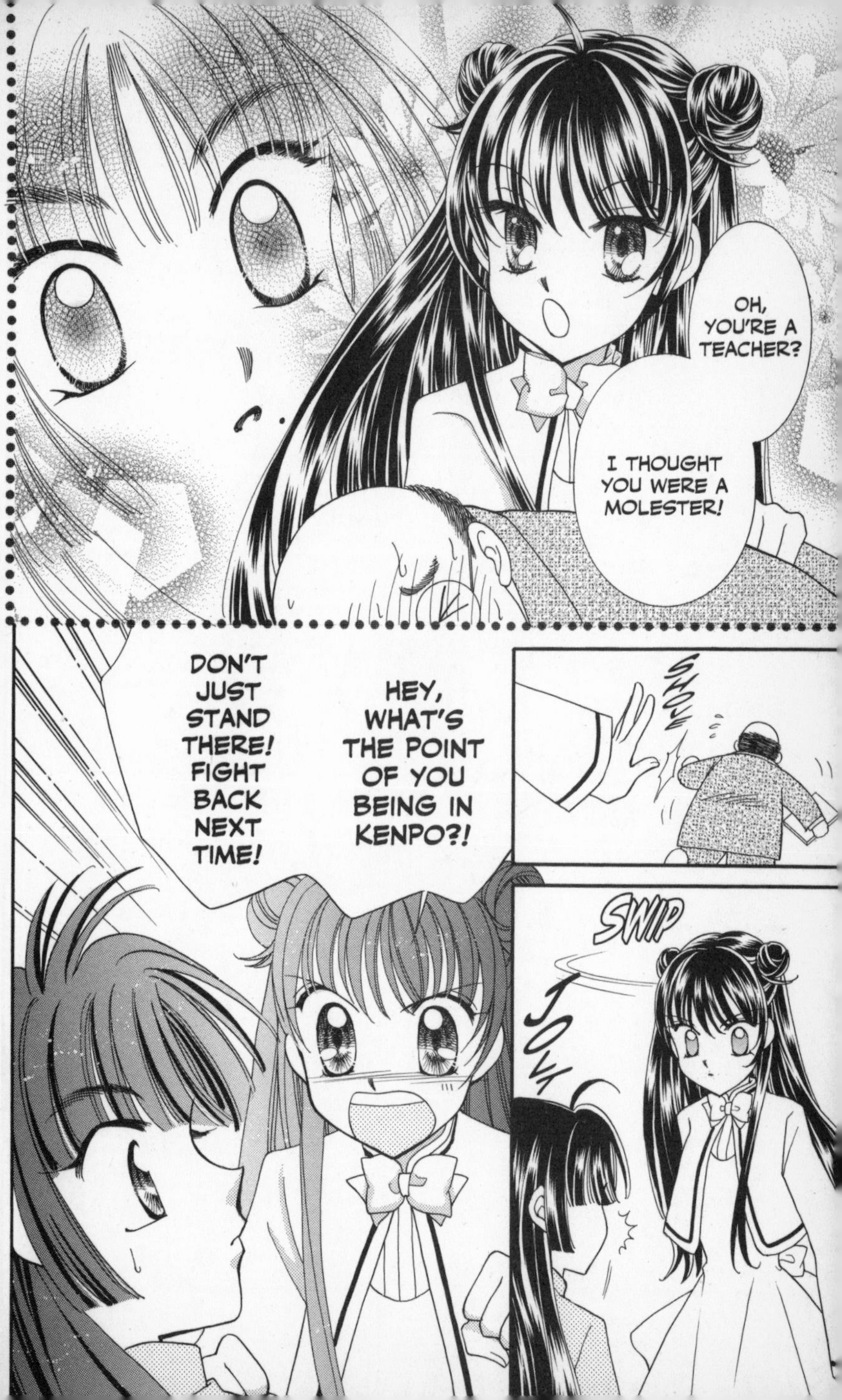
OH, YOU'RE A TEACHER?
I THOUGHT YOU WERE A MOLESTER!
SHOVE
SWIP
JOLT
HEY, WHAT'S THE POINT OF YOU BEING IN KENPO?!
DON'T JUST STAND THERE! FIGHT BACK NEXT TIME!

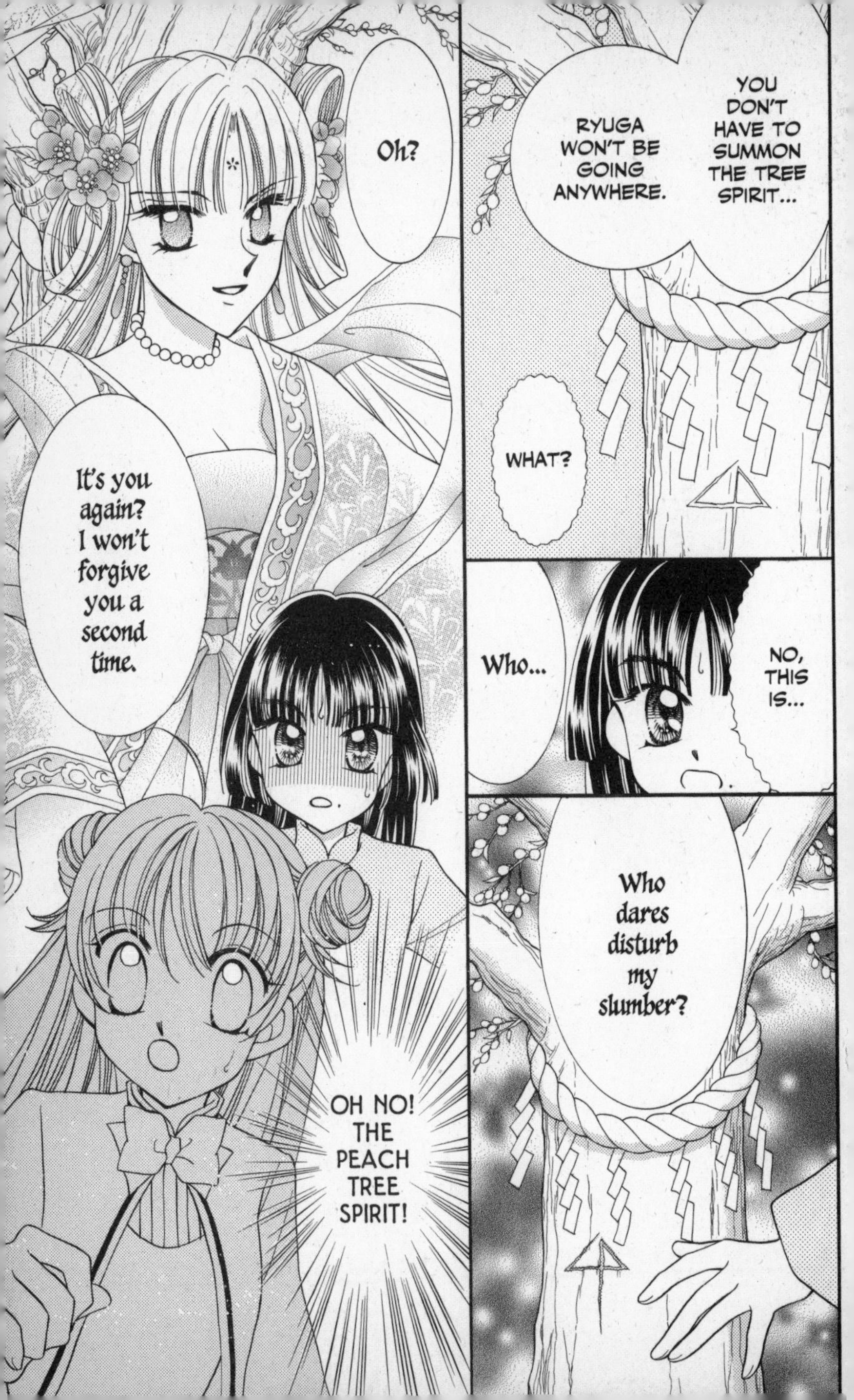
YOU DON'T HAVE TO SUMMON THE TREE SPIRIT...
RYUGA WON'T BE GOING ANYWHERE.
WHAT?
NO, THIS IS...
Who...
Who dares disturb my slumber?
Oh?
It's you again? I won't forgive you a second time.
OH NO! THE PEACH TREE SPIRIT!

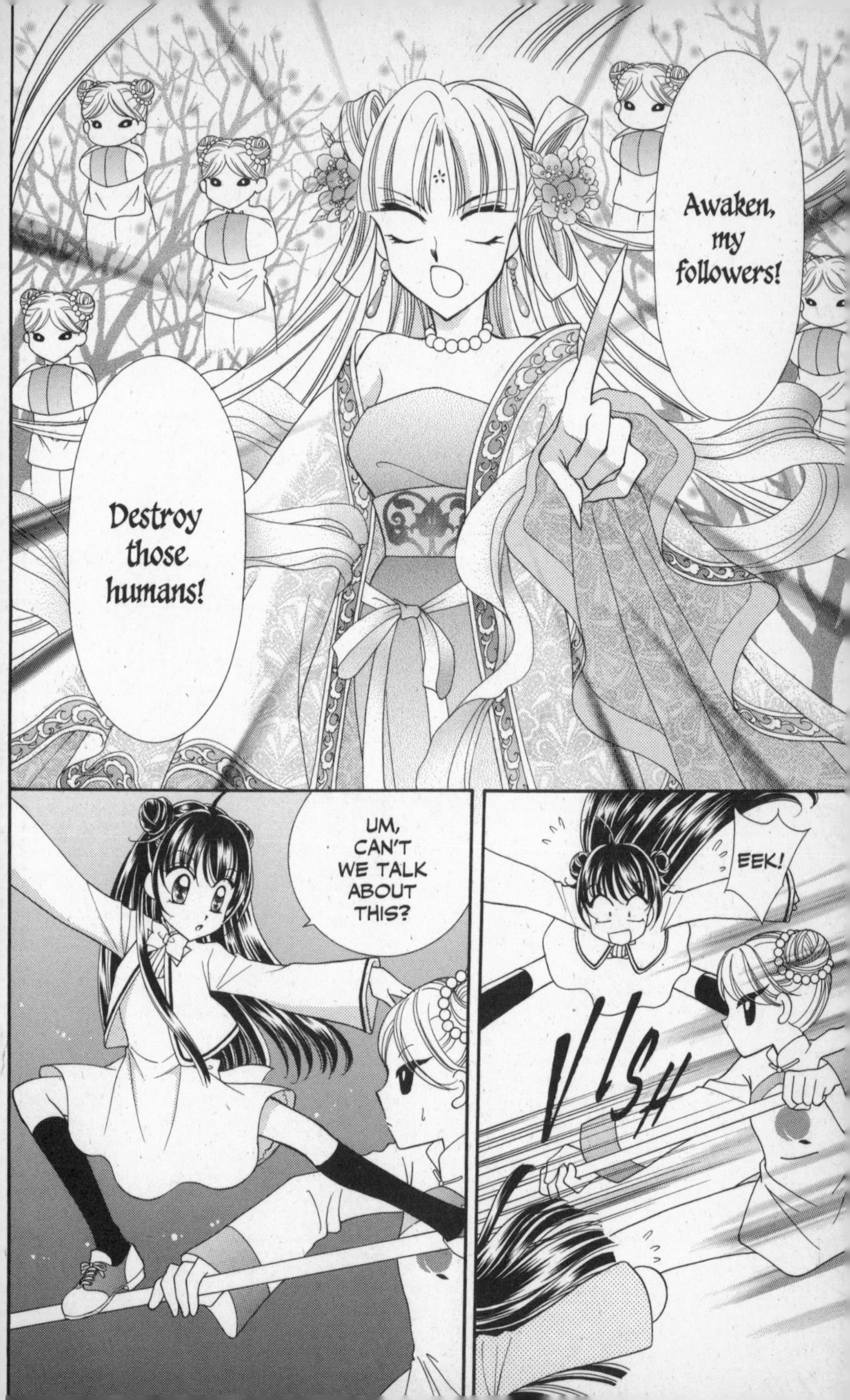
Awaken, my followers!
Destroy those humans!
EEK!
VISH
UM, CAN'T WE TALK ABOUT THIS?

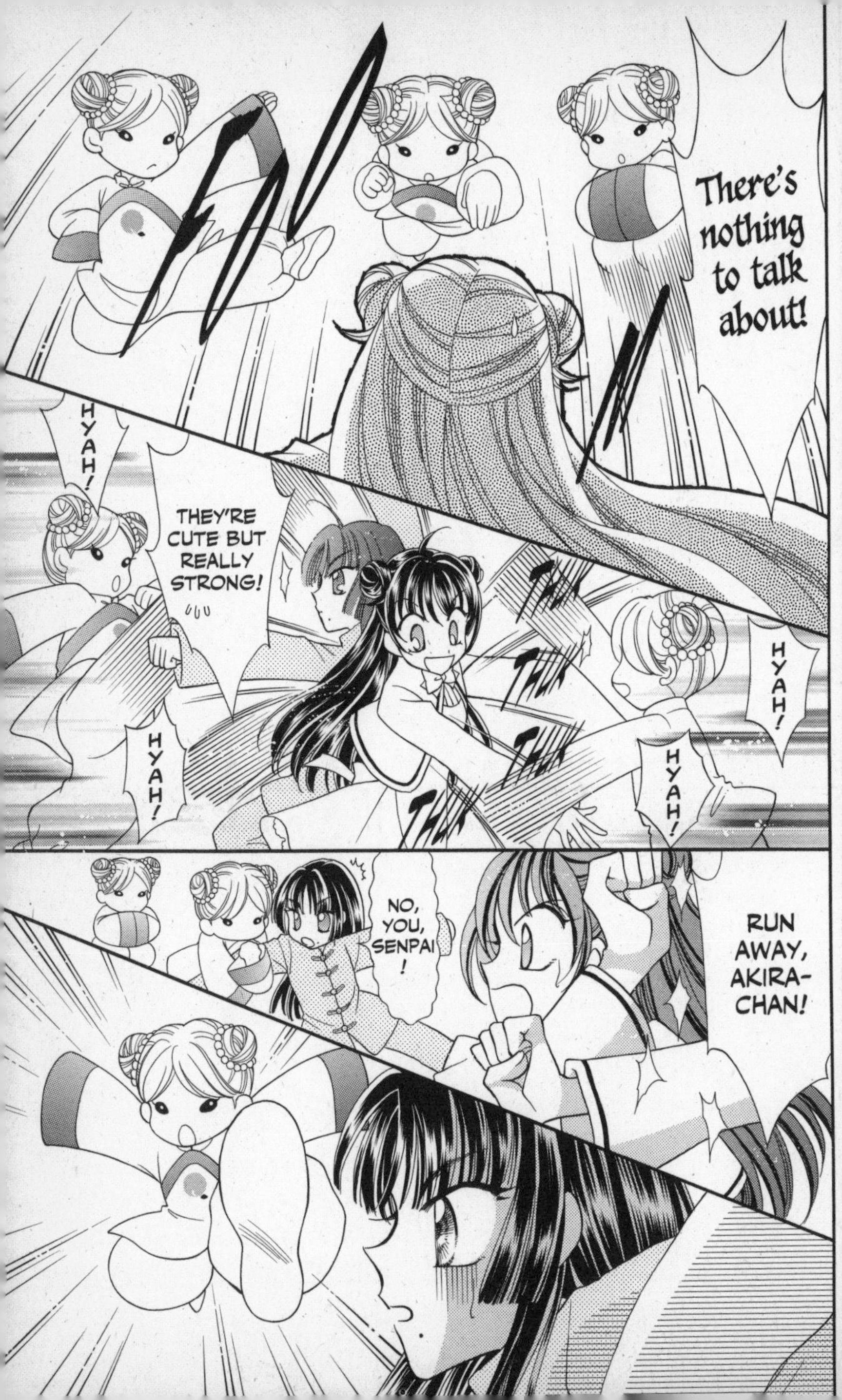
There's nothing to talk about!
HYAH!
HYAH!
THEY'RE CUTE BUT REALLY STRONG!
HYAH!
HYAH!
RUN AWAY, AKIRA-CHAN!
NO, YOU, SENPAI!

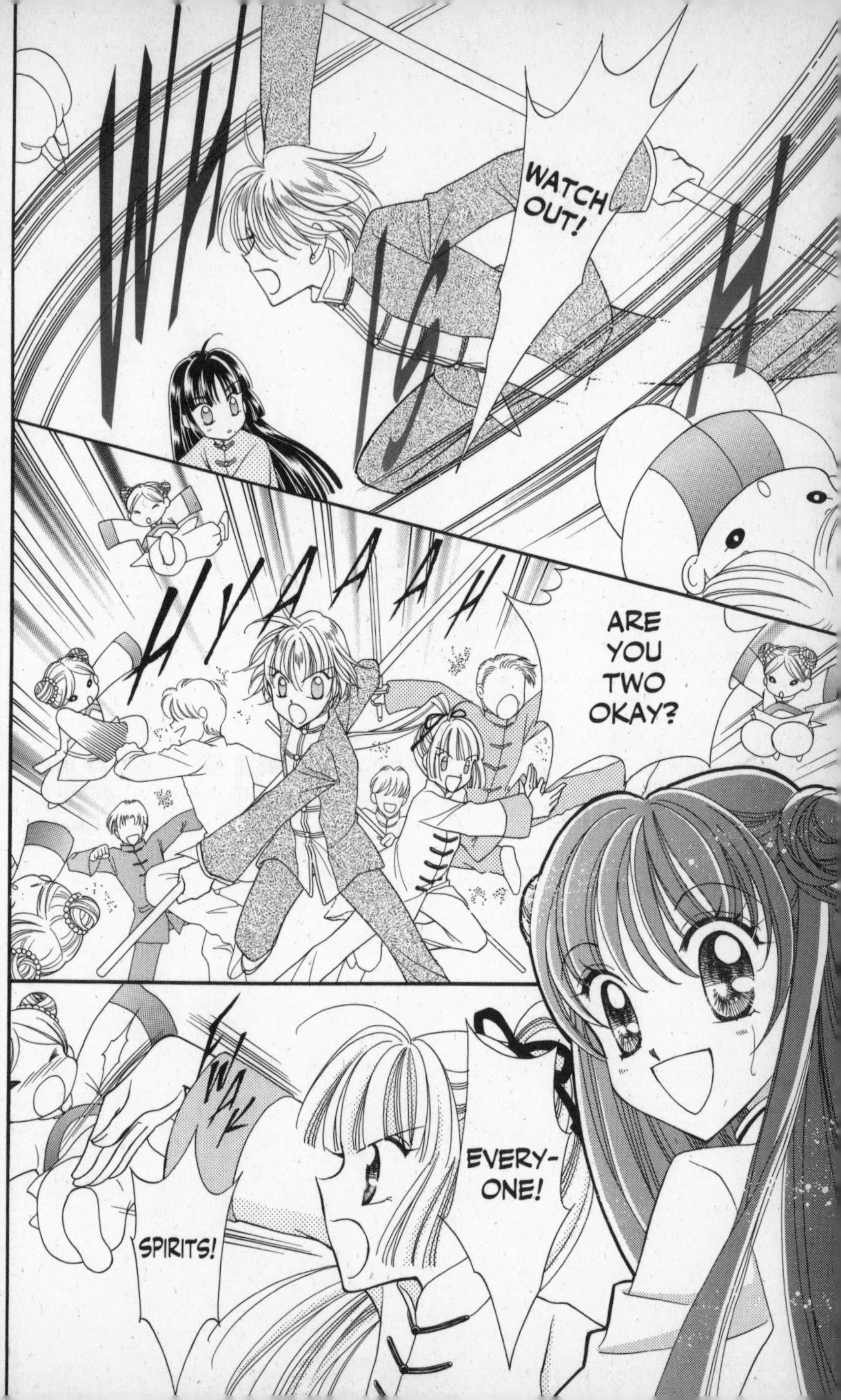
WATCH OUT!
ARE YOU TWO OKAY?
EVERY-ONE!
SPIRITS!

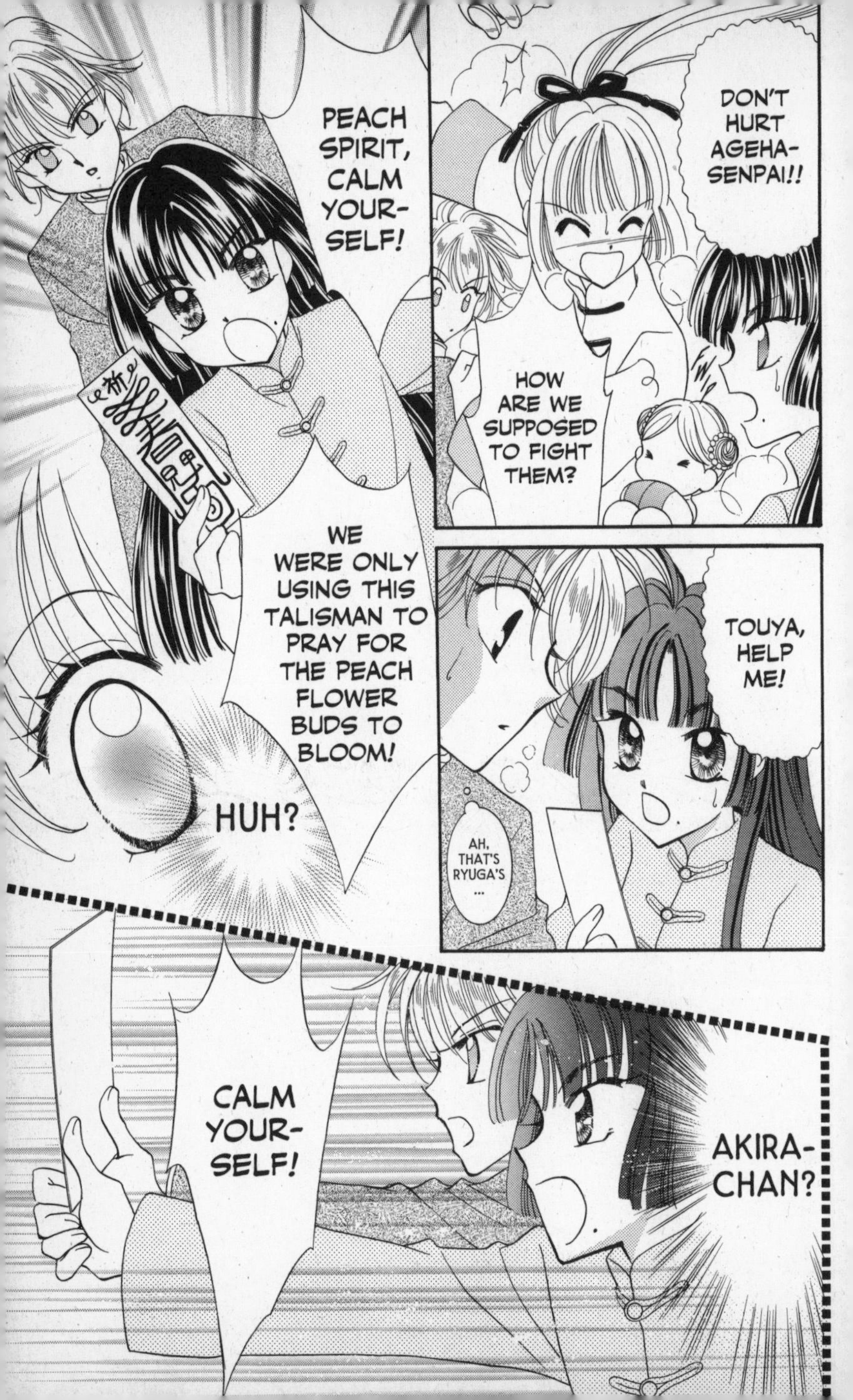
DON'T HURT AGEHA-SENPAI!!
HOW ARE WE SUPPOSED TO FIGHT THEM?
TOUYA, HELP ME!
AH, THAT'S RYUGA'S ...
PEACH SPIRIT, CALM YOUR-SELF!
WE WERE ONLY USING THIS TALISMAN TO PRAY FOR THE PEACH FLOWER BUDS TO BLOOM!
HUH?
AKIRA-CHAN?
CALM YOUR-SELF!

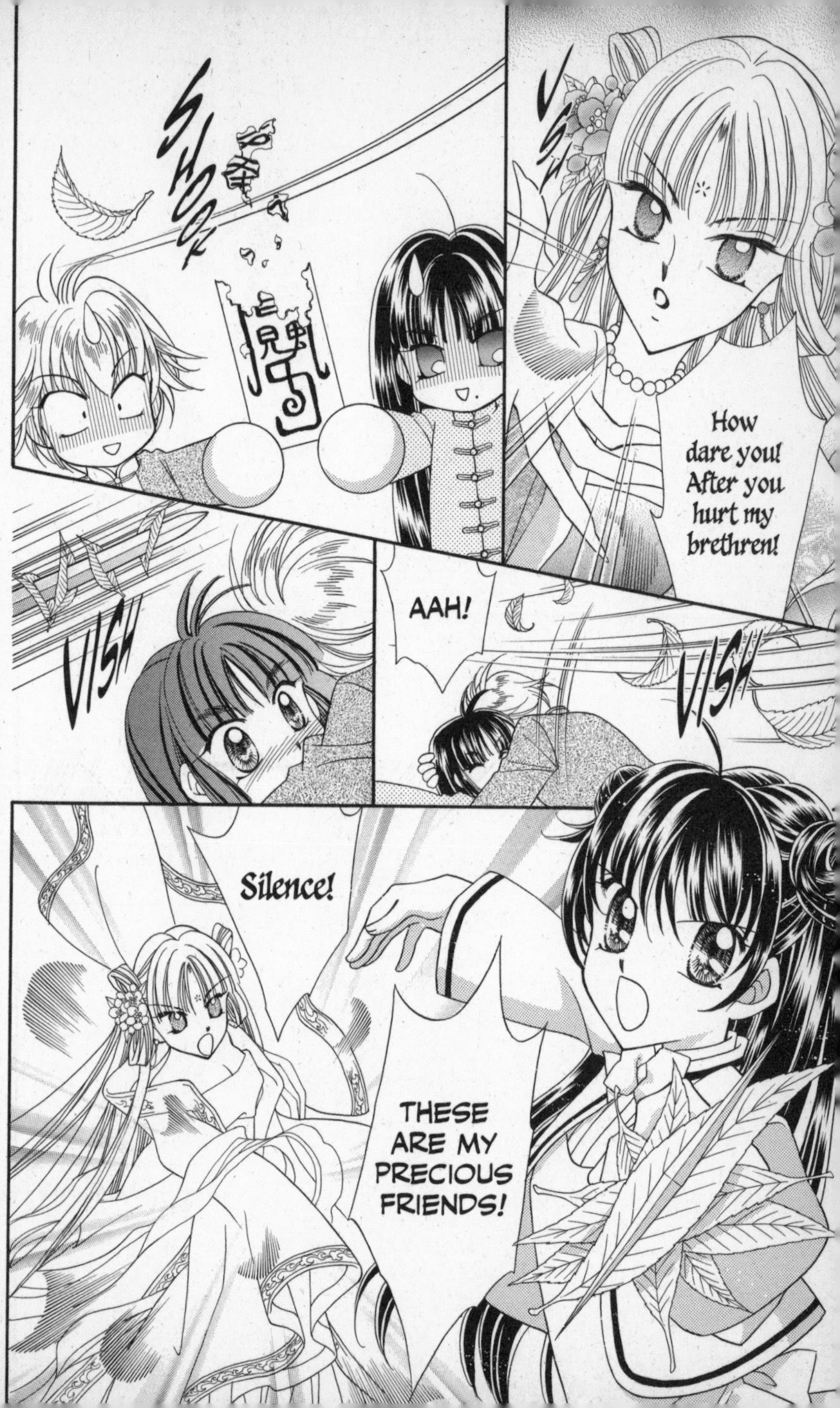
How dare you! After you hurt my brethren!
AAH!
VISH
VISH
Silence!
THESE ARE MY PRECIOUS FRIENDS!

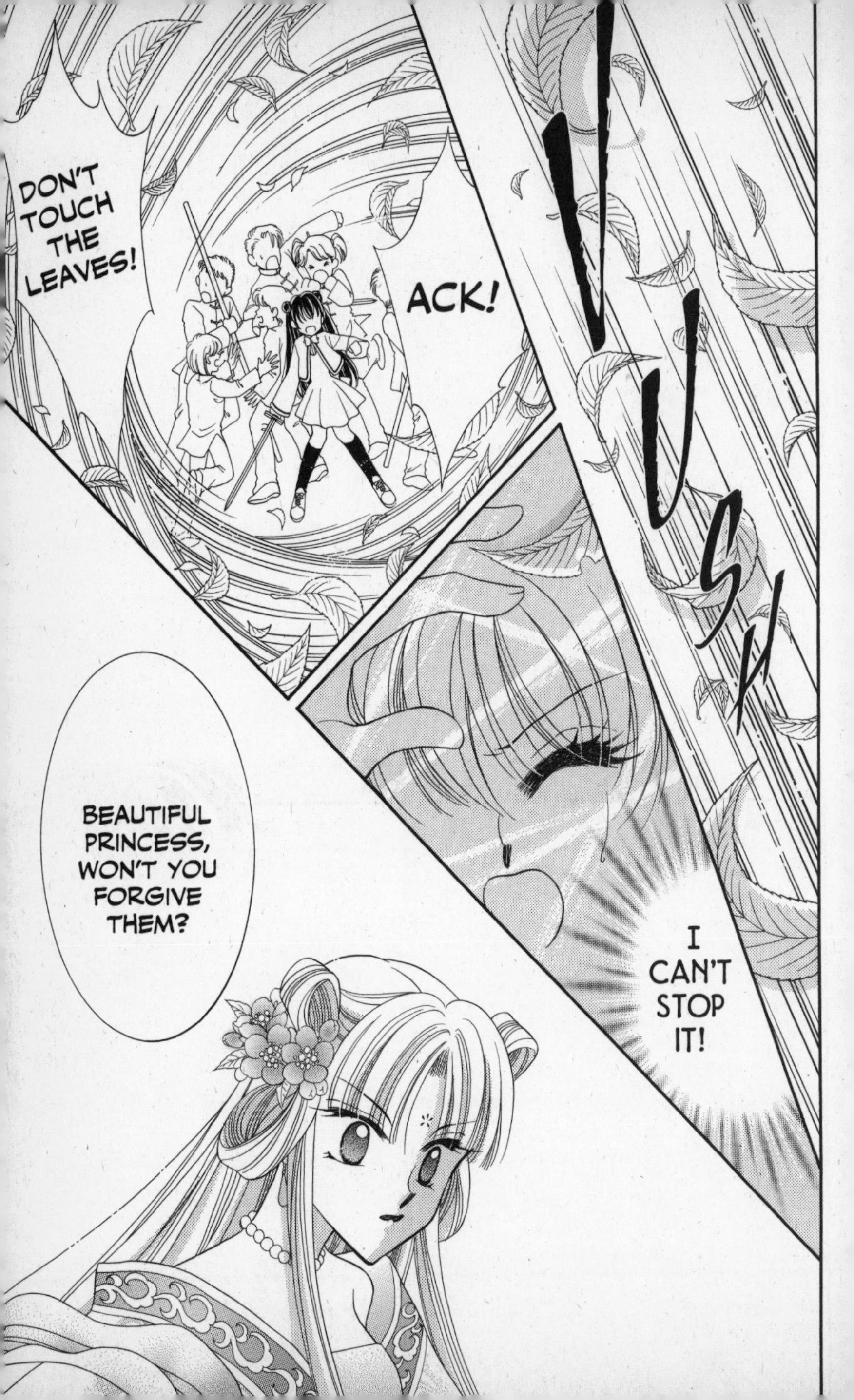
VUSH
ACK!
DON'T TOUCH THE LEAVES!
I CAN'T STOP IT!
BEAUTIFUL PRINCESS, WON'T YOU FORGIVE THEM?

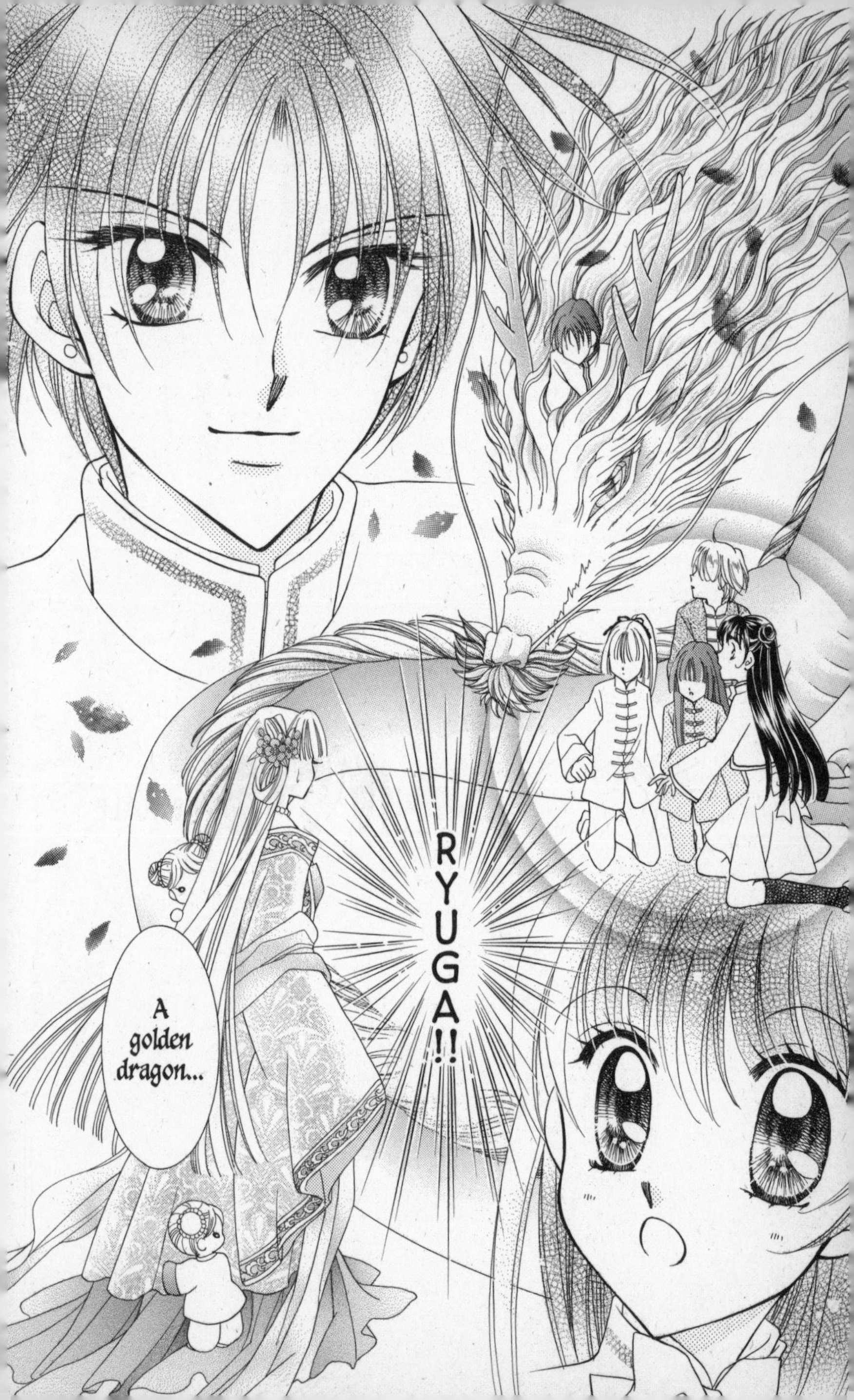
RYUGA!!
A golden dragon...

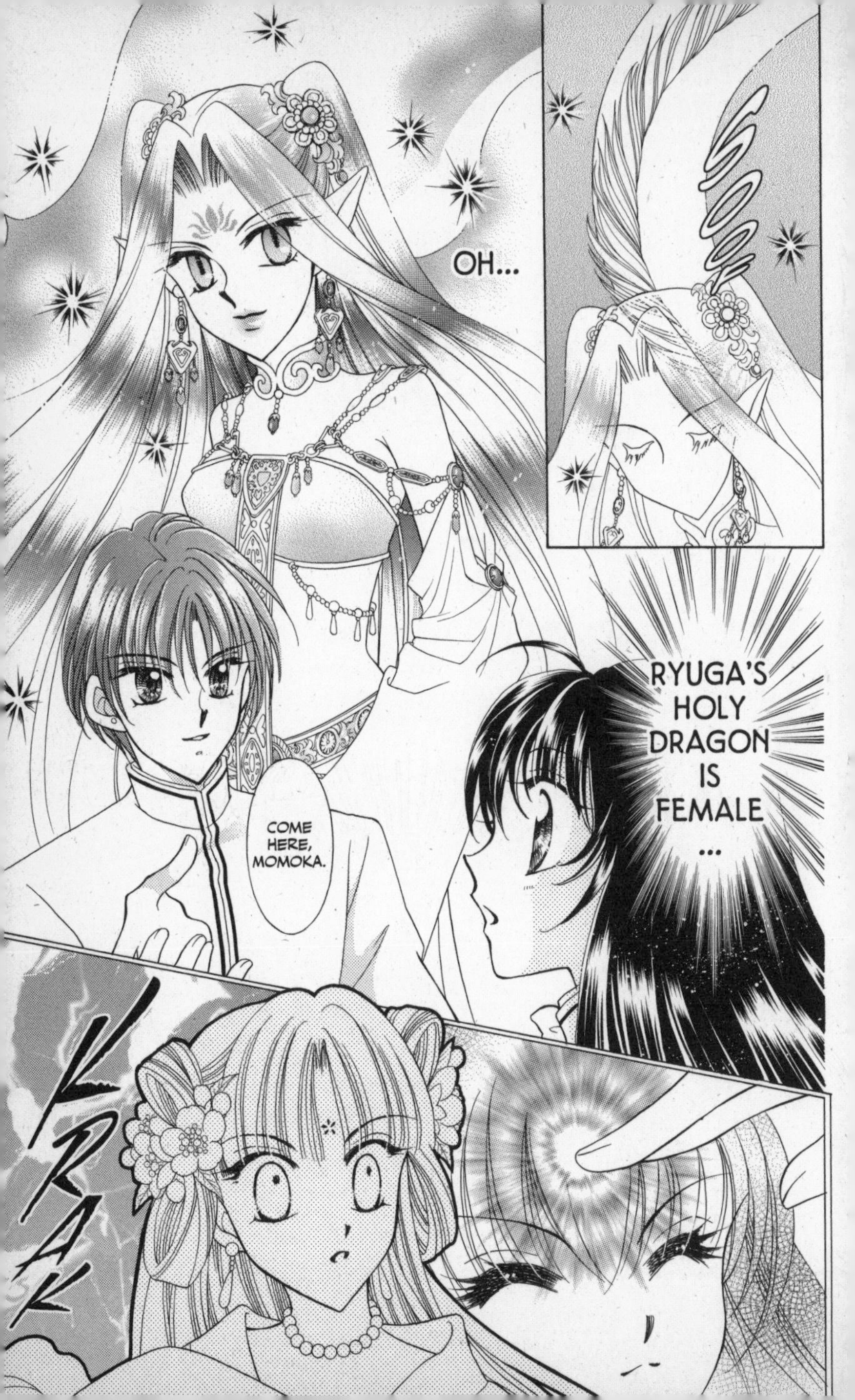
OH...
RYUGA'S HOLY DRAGON IS FEMALE ...
COME HERE, MOMOKA.
KRAK

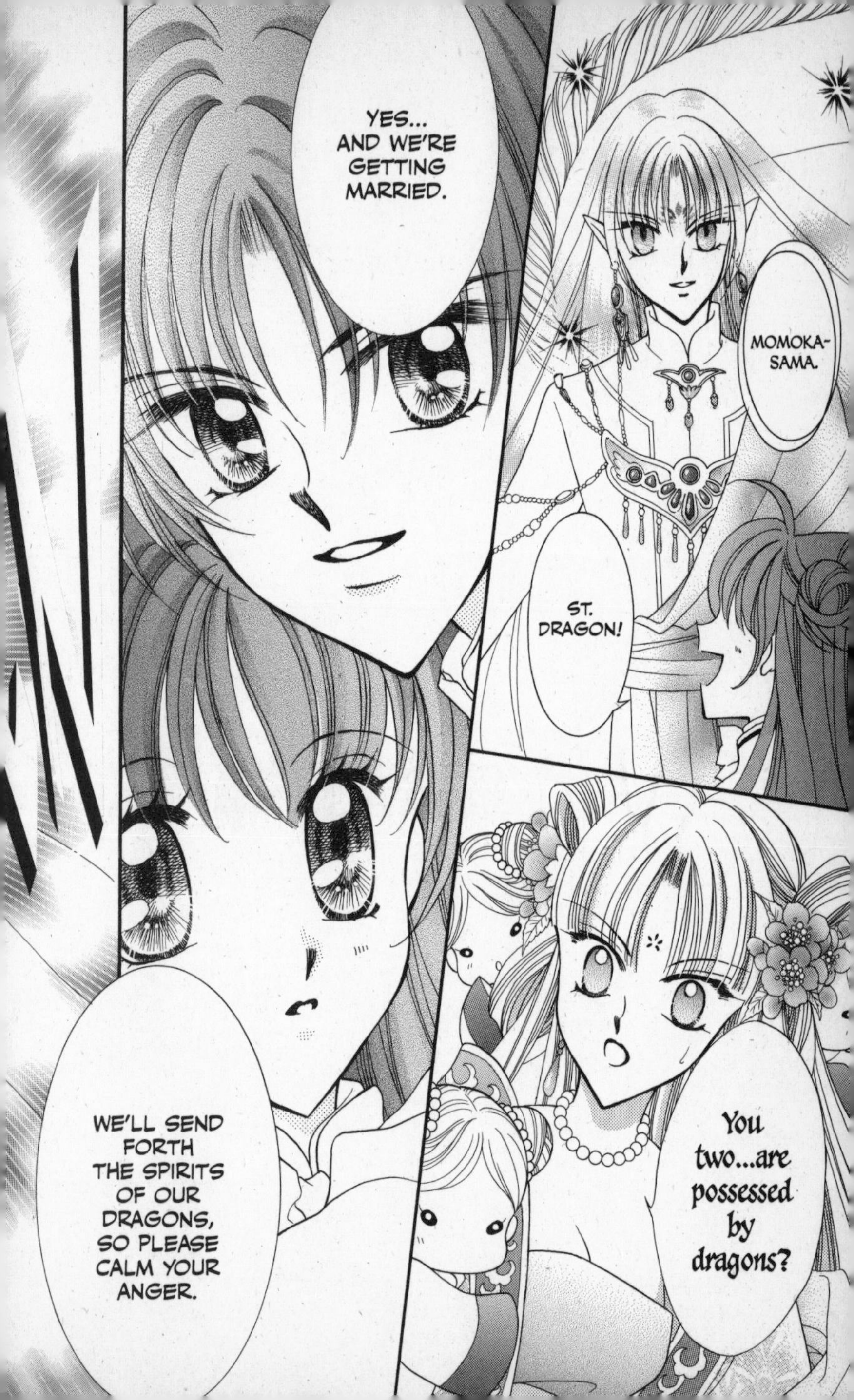
MOMOKA-SAMA.
ST. DRAGON!
You two...are possessed by dragons?
YES... AND WE'RE GETTING MARRIED.
WE'LL SEND FORTH THE SPIRITS OF OUR DRAGONS, SO PLEASE CALM YOUR ANGER.

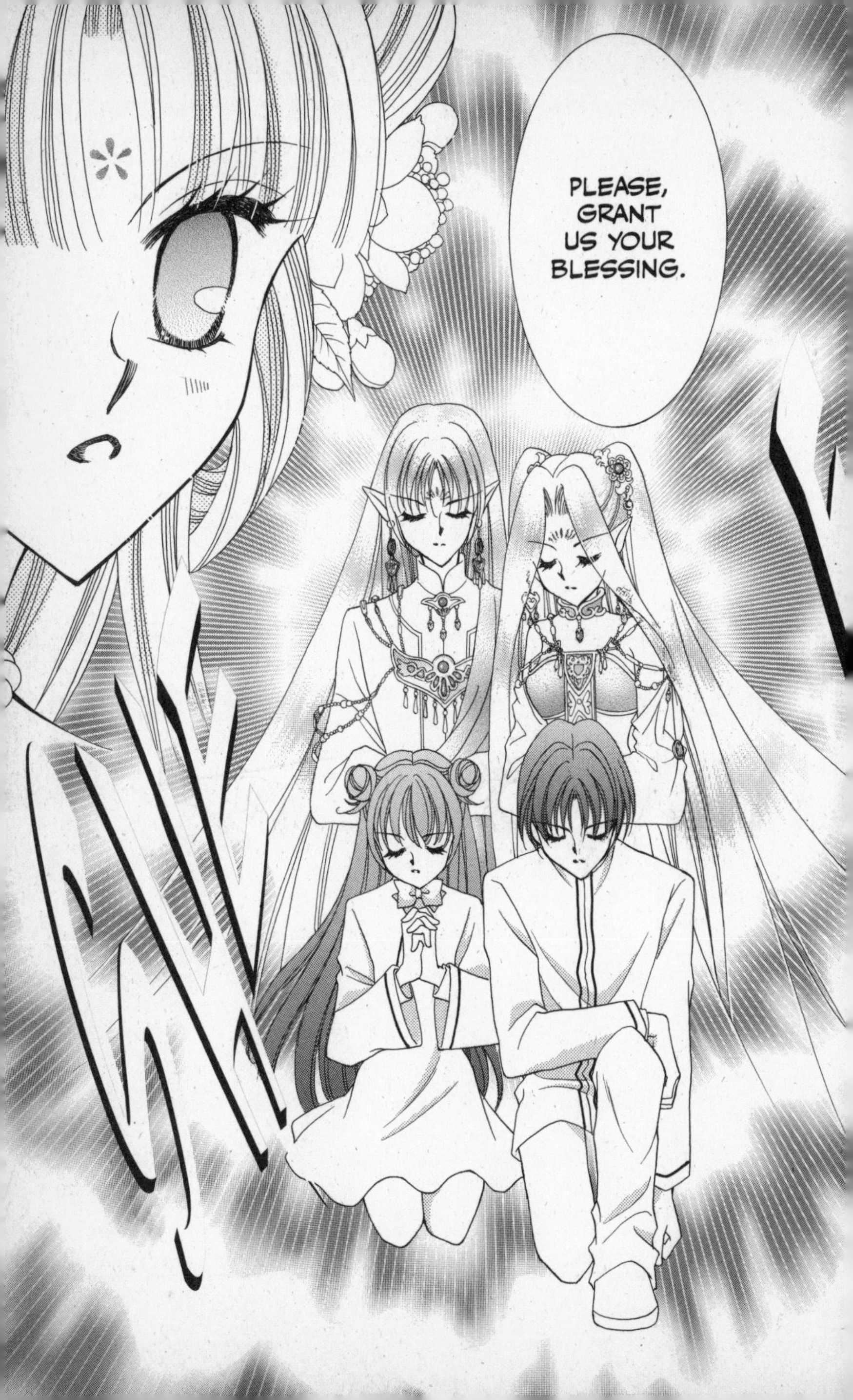
PLEASE, GRANT US YOUR BLESSING.

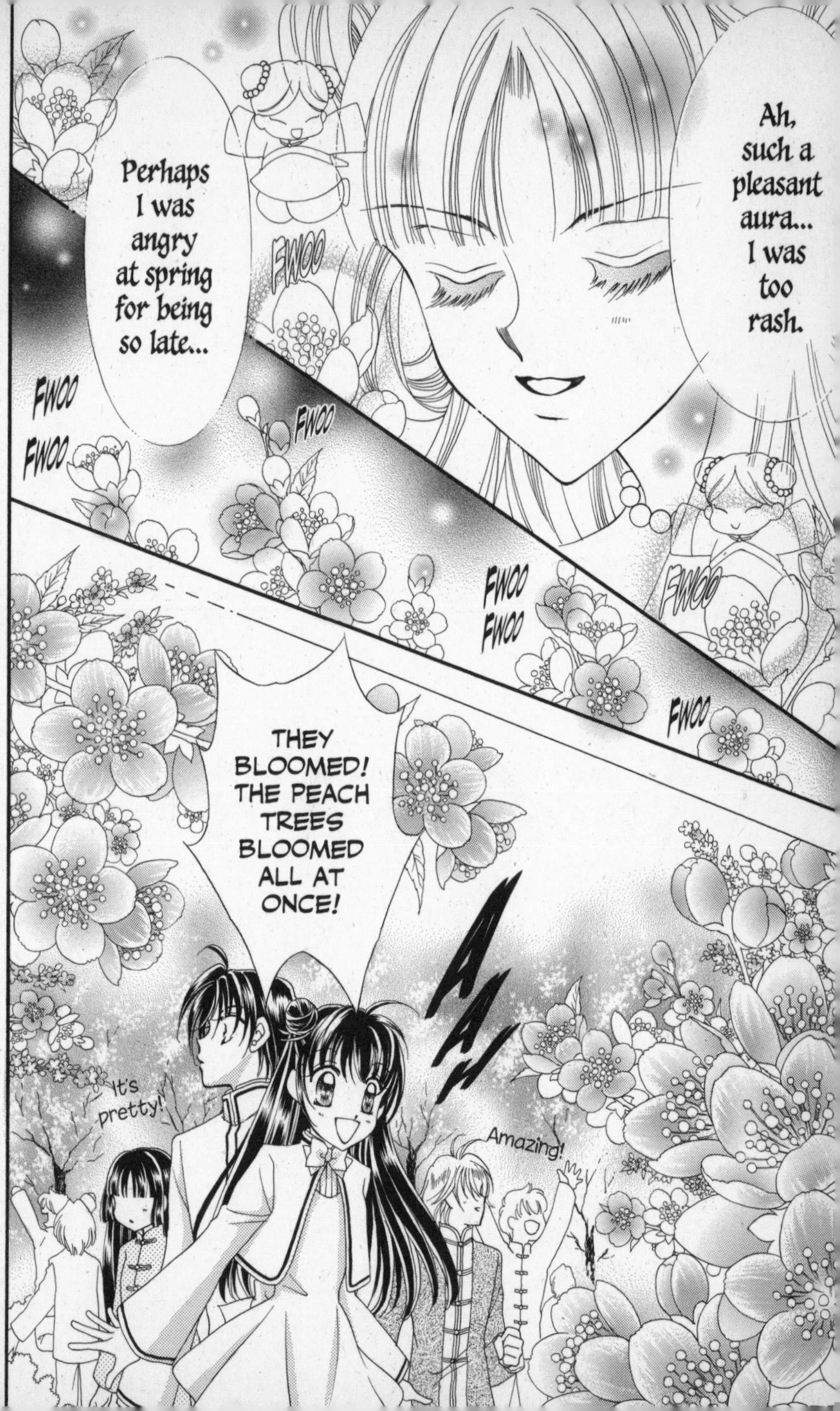
Ah, such a pleasant aura... I was too rash.
FWOO
Perhaps I was angry at spring for being so late...
FWOO
FWOO
FWOO
FWOO
FWOO
FWOO
FWOO
THEY BLOOMED! THE PEACH TREES BLOOMED ALL AT ONCE!
AAAH
Amazing!
It's pretty!

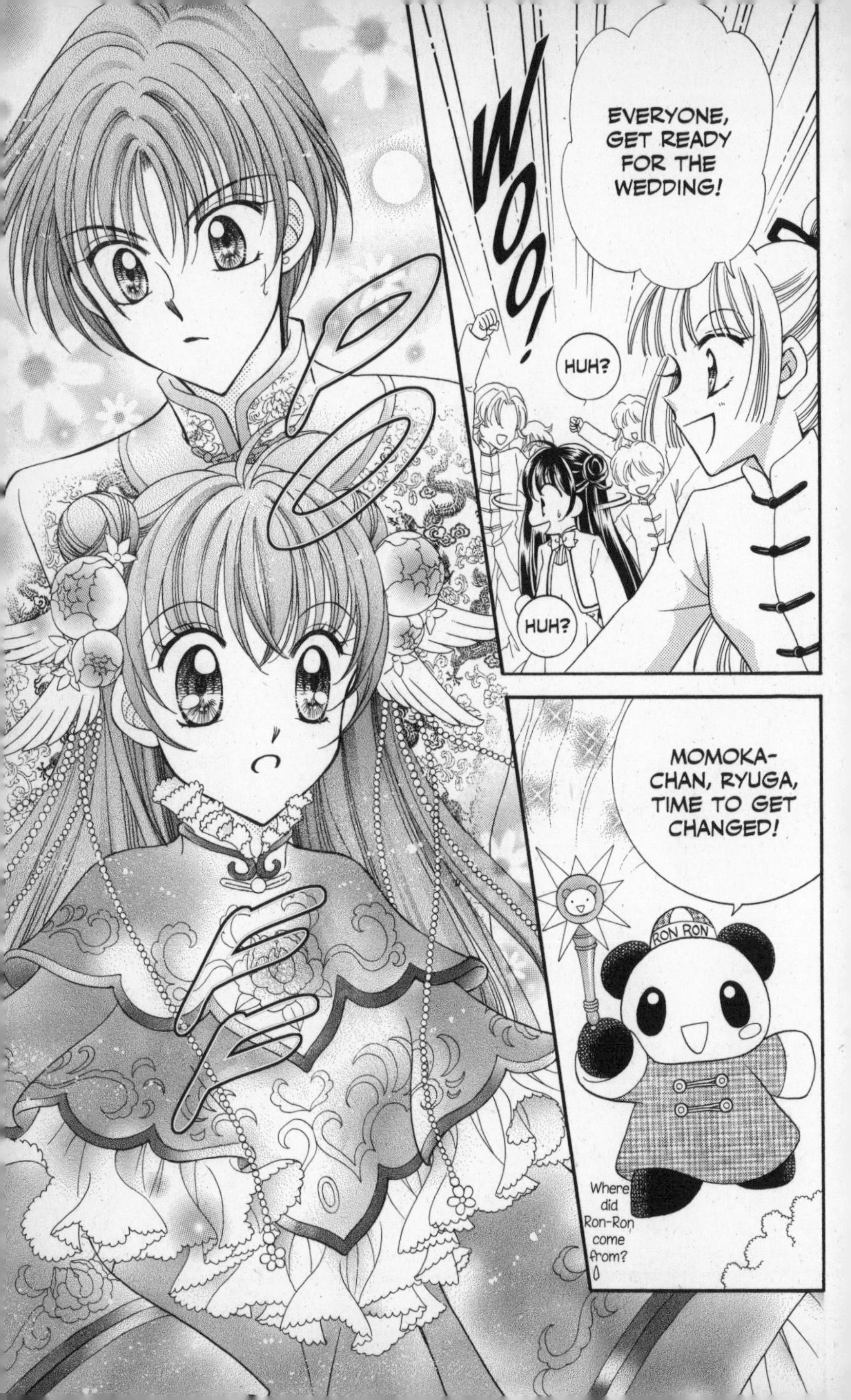
WOO!
EVERYONE, GET READY FOR THE WEDDING!
HUH?
HUH?
MOMOKA-CHAN, RYUGA, TIME TO GET CHANGED!
RON RON
Where did Ron-Ron come from?

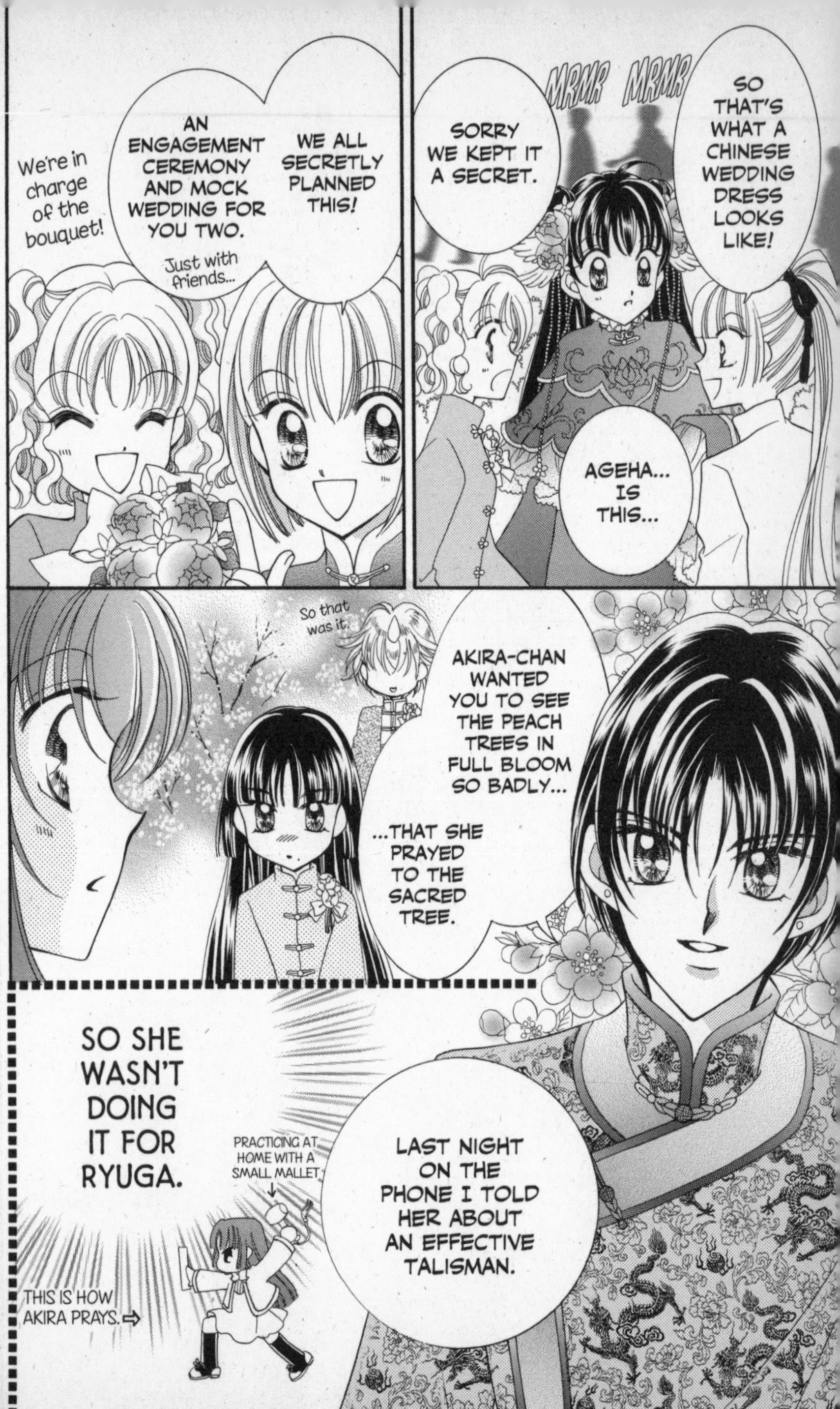
MRMR MRMR
SO THAT'S WHAT A CHINESE WEDDING DRESS LOOKS LIKE!
SORRY WE KEPT IT A SECRET.
AGEHA... IS THIS...
WE ALL SECRETLY PLANNED THIS!
AN ENGAGEMENT CEREMONY AND MOCK WEDDING FOR YOU TWO.
Just with friends...
We're in charge of the bouquet!
AKIRA-CHAN WANTED YOU TO SEE THE PEACH TREES IN FULL BLOOM SO BADLY...
...THAT SHE PRAYED TO THE SACRED TREE.
So that was it.
LAST NIGHT ON THE PHONE I TOLD HER ABOUT AN EFFECTIVE TALISMAN.
SO SHE WASN'T DOING IT FOR RYUGA.
PRACTICING AT HOME WITH A SMALL MALLET.
THIS IS HOW AKIRA PRAYS.

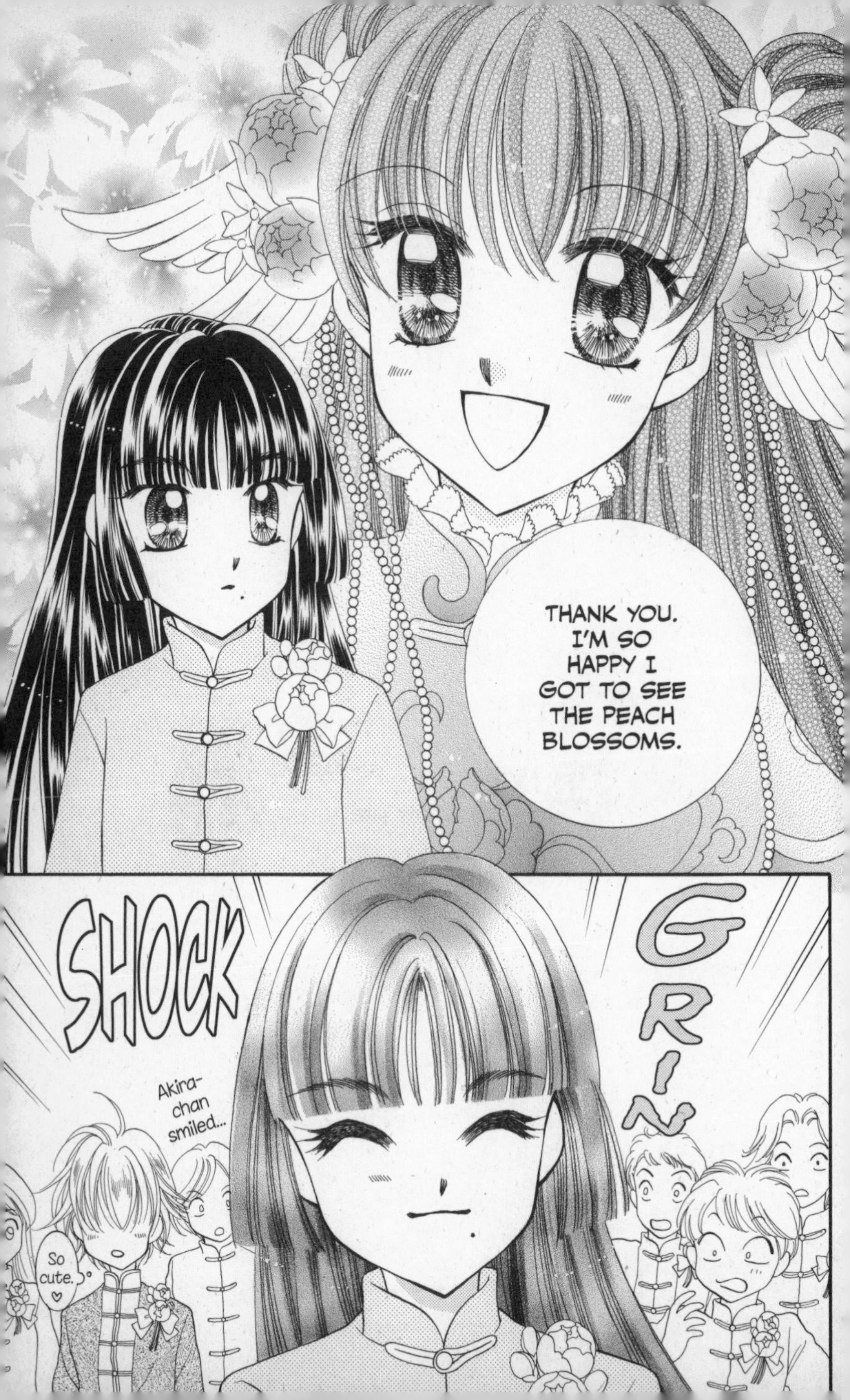
THANK YOU. I'M SO HAPPY I GOT TO SEE THE PEACH BLOSSOMS.
GRIN
SHOCK
Akira-chan smiled...
So cute.

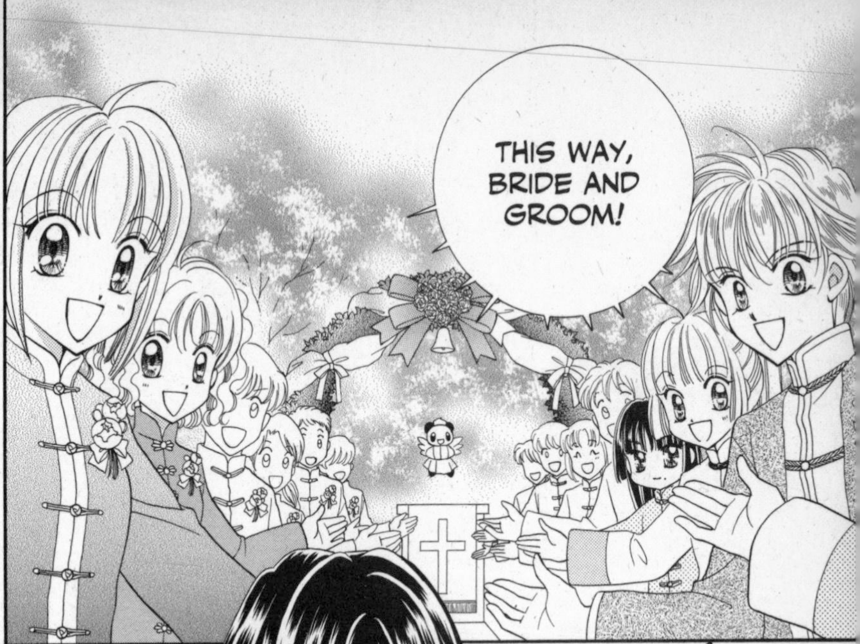
THIS WAY, BRIDE AND GROOM!
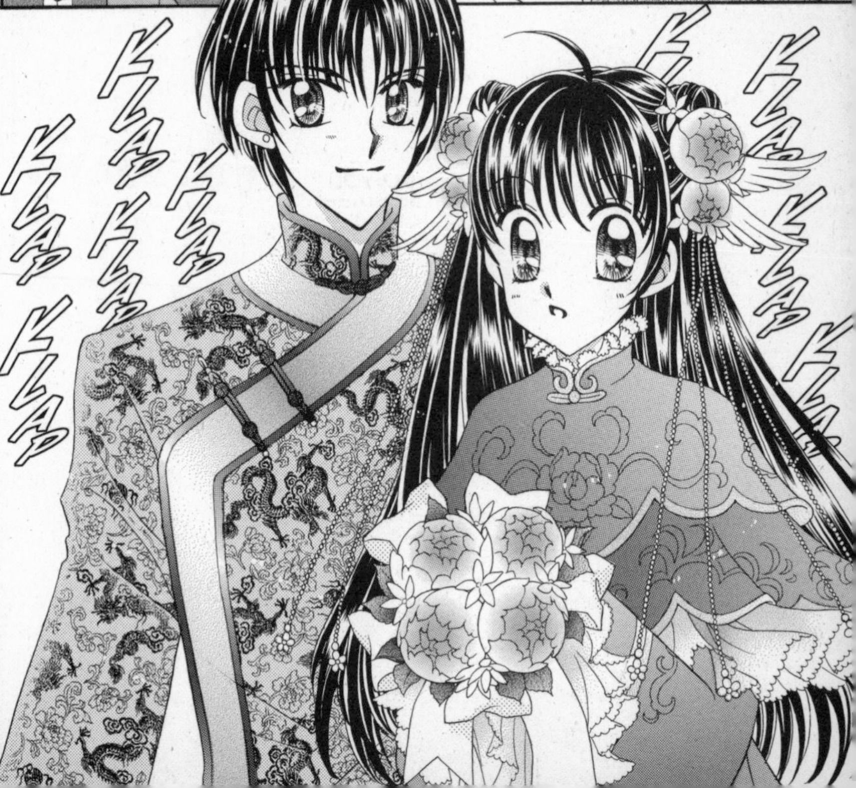
KLAP KLAP KLAP
KLAP KLAP
KLAP KLAP
KLAP KLAP

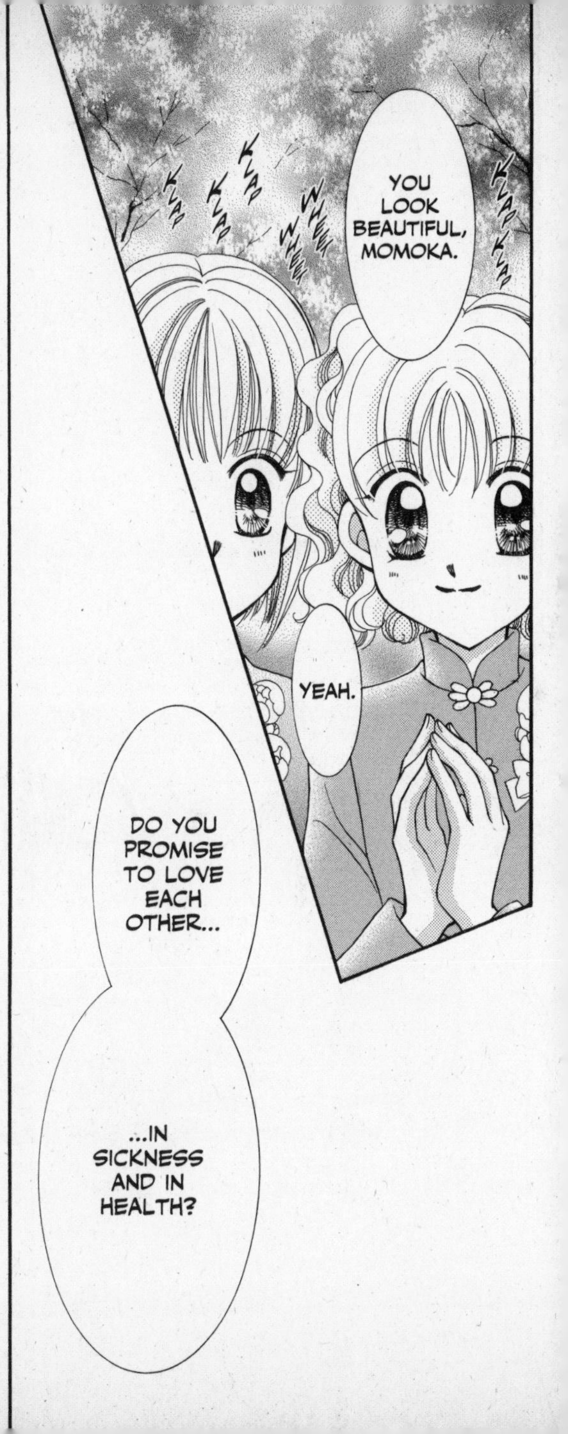
YOU LOOK BEAUTIFUL, MOMOKA.
YEAH.
DO YOU PROMISE TO LOVE EACH OTHER...
...IN SICKNESS AND IN HEALTH?

8

This is the final sidebar. Thanks to everyone who has supported me and *St.♥Dragon Girl.* This was my first long series, and I owe it all to you. Momoka and I and everyone are so, so happy...♥

You'll be parted from Momoka for now, but there are plans for her to appear in a new series called *St.♥Dragon Girl Miracle.* I hope to see you all again sometime!

Special Thanks:

- ♥ Satomi Kodaka
- ♥ Naomi Hiromasa
- ♥ Kinuko Sasaki
- ♥ Sanako Wakamatsu
- ♥ Chizuru Wakamatsu
- ♥ Naruto Kakegawa
- ♥ Michiyo Kushida
- ♥ Tomohiro Jibu

And you! ♥♥♥

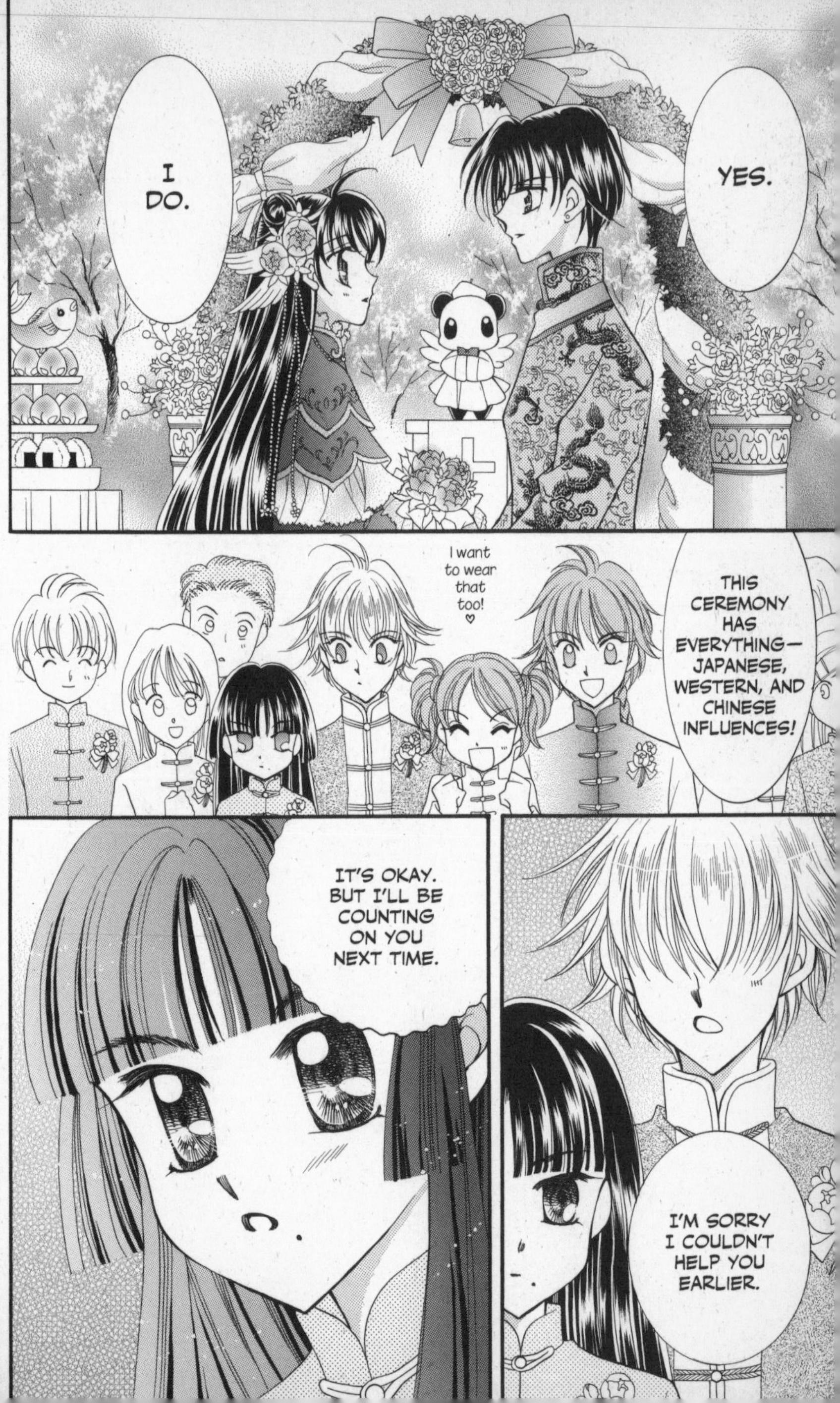
YES.
I DO.
THIS CEREMONY HAS EVERYTHING— JAPANESE, WESTERN, AND CHINESE INFLUENCES!
I want to wear that too! ♡
I'M SORRY I COULDN'T HELP YOU EARLIER.
IT'S OKAY. BUT I'LL BE COUNTING ON YOU NEXT TIME.

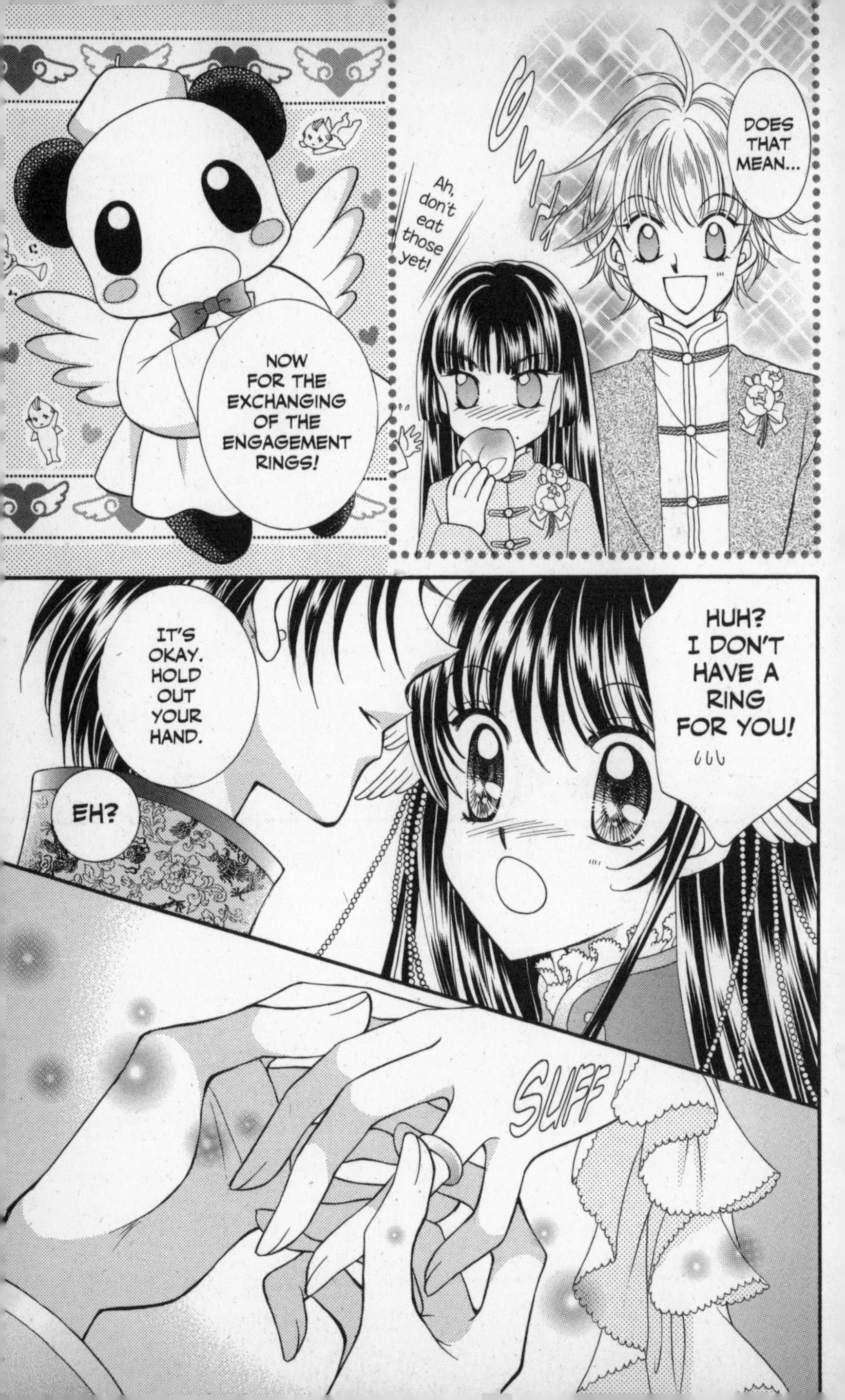
DOES THAT MEAN...
Ah, don't eat those yet!
NOW FOR THE EXCHANGING OF THE ENGAGEMENT RINGS!
HUH? I DON'T HAVE A RING FOR YOU!
IT'S OKAY. HOLD OUT YOUR HAND.
EH?
SUFF

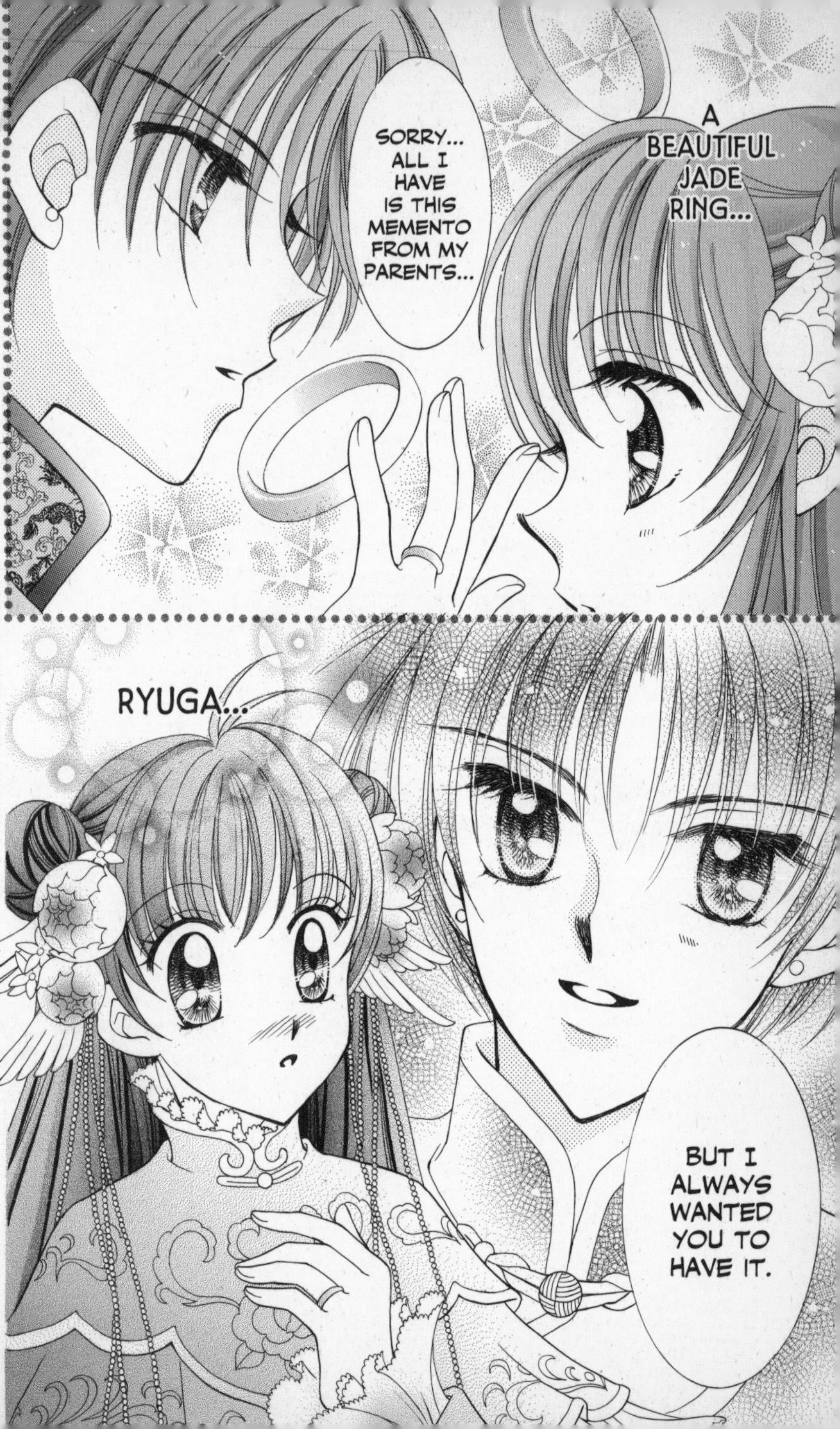
A BEAUTIFUL JADE RING...
SORRY... ALL I HAVE IS THIS MEMENTO FROM MY PARENTS...
BUT I ALWAYS WANTED YOU TO HAVE IT.
RYUGA...

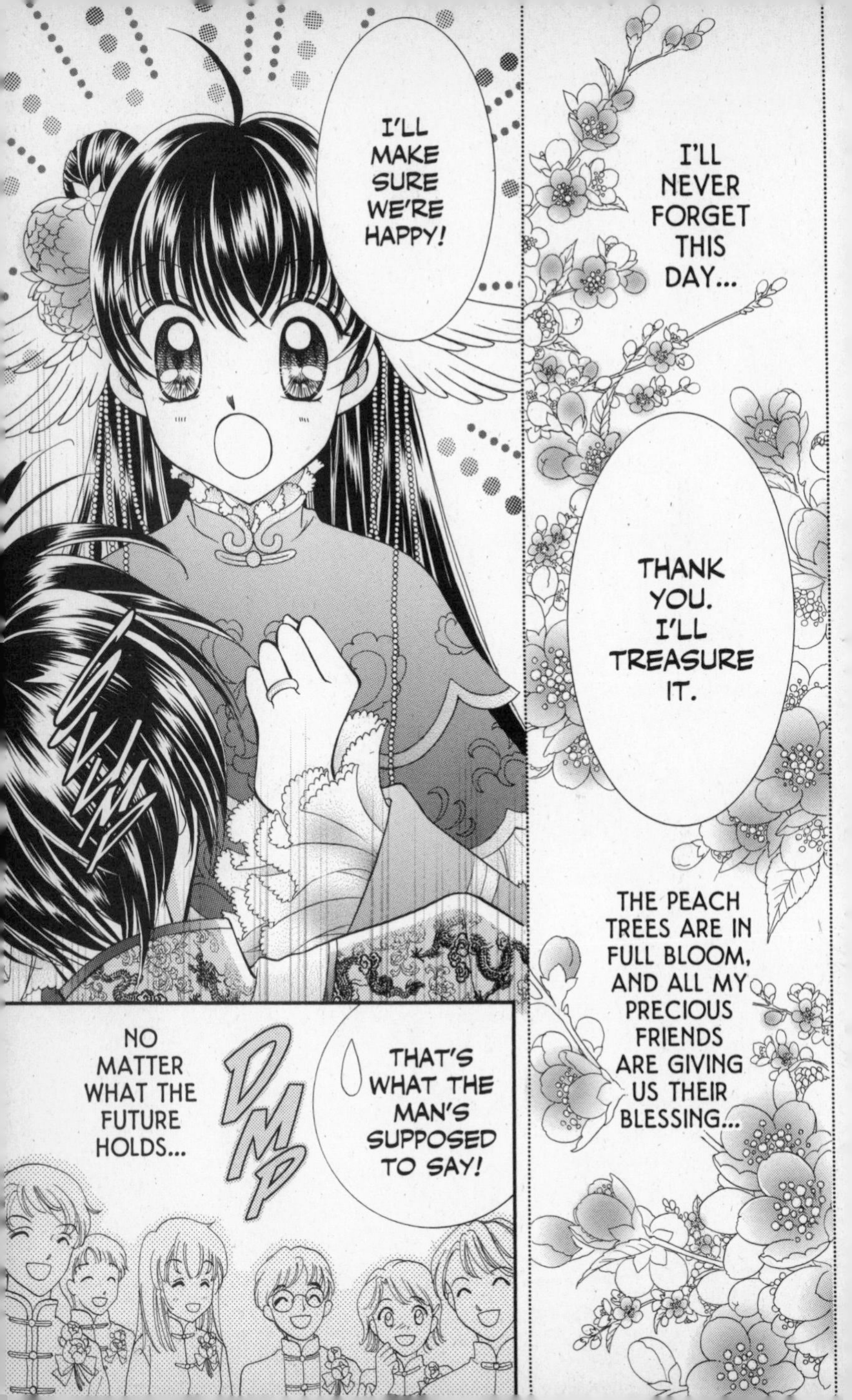
I'LL NEVER FORGET THIS DAY...
THANK YOU. I'LL TREASURE IT.
THE PEACH TREES ARE IN FULL BLOOM, AND ALL MY PRECIOUS FRIENDS ARE GIVING US THEIR BLESSING...
I'LL MAKE SURE WE'RE HAPPY!
THAT'S WHAT THE MAN'S SUPPOSED TO SAY!
DMP
NO MATTER WHAT THE FUTURE HOLDS...

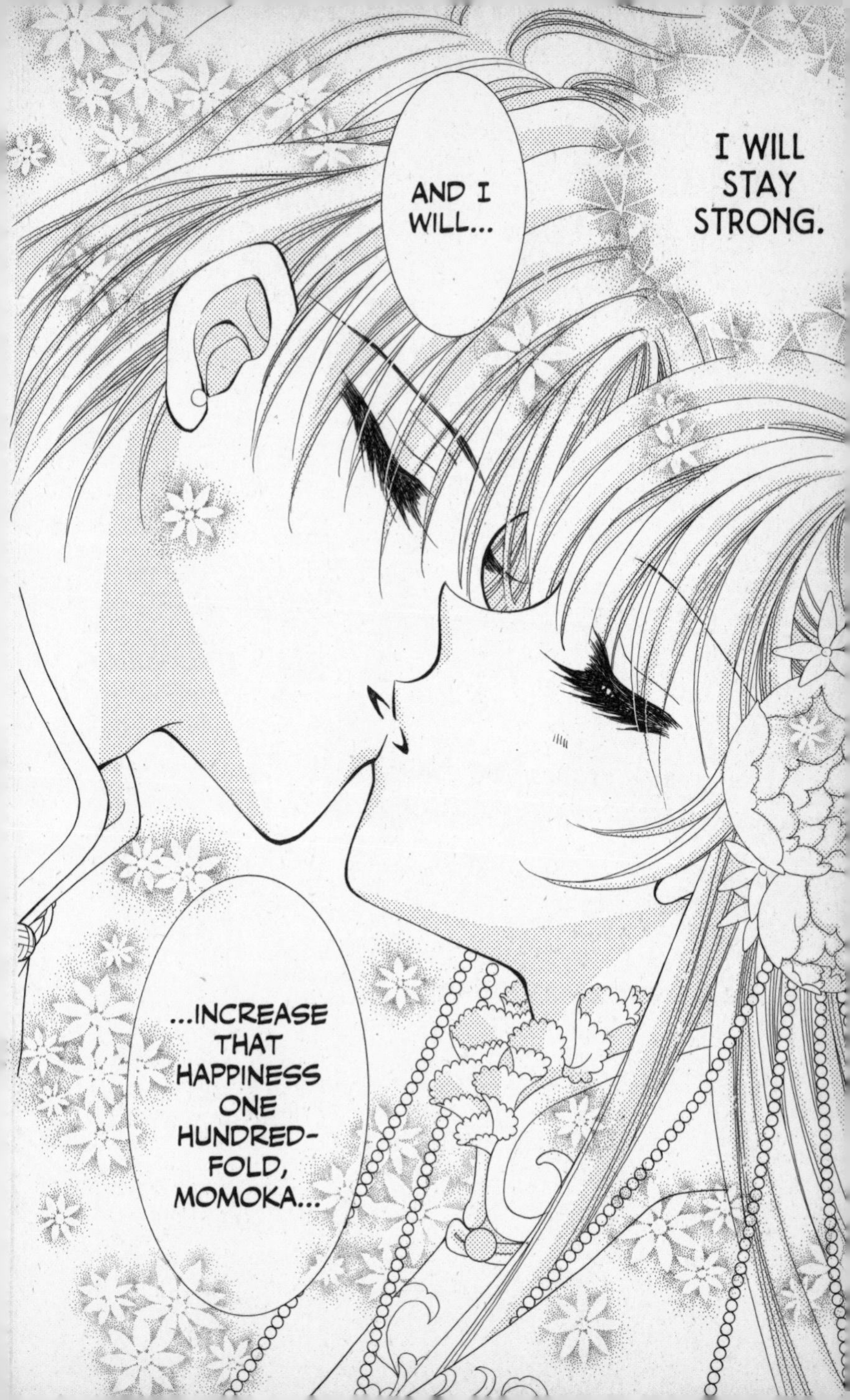
I WILL STAY STRONG.
AND I WILL...
...INCREASE THAT HAPPINESS ONE HUNDRED-FOLD, MOMOKA...

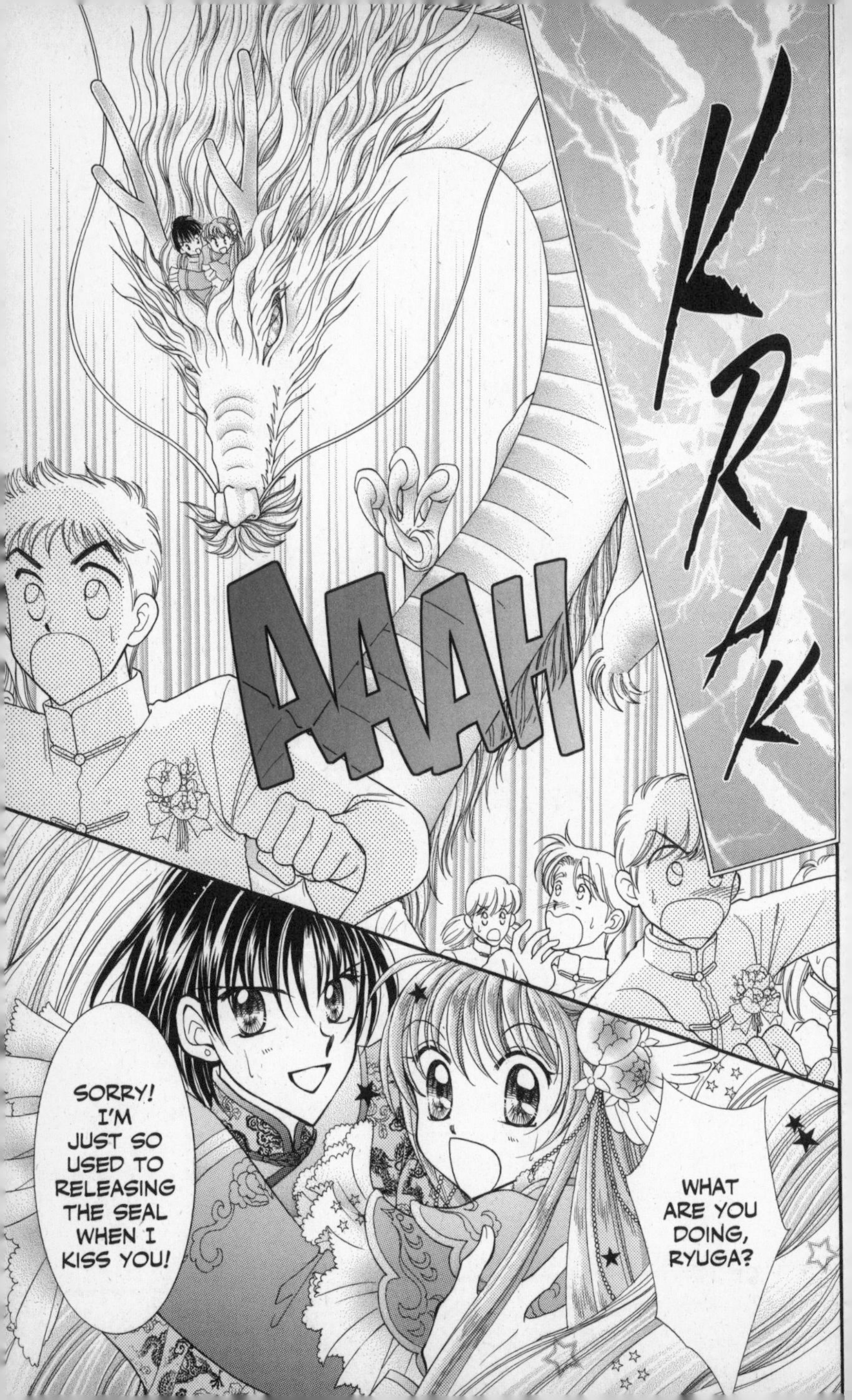
KRAK
AAAH
WHAT ARE YOU DOING, RYUGA?
SORRY! I'M JUST SO USED TO RELEASING THE SEAL WHEN I KISS YOU!

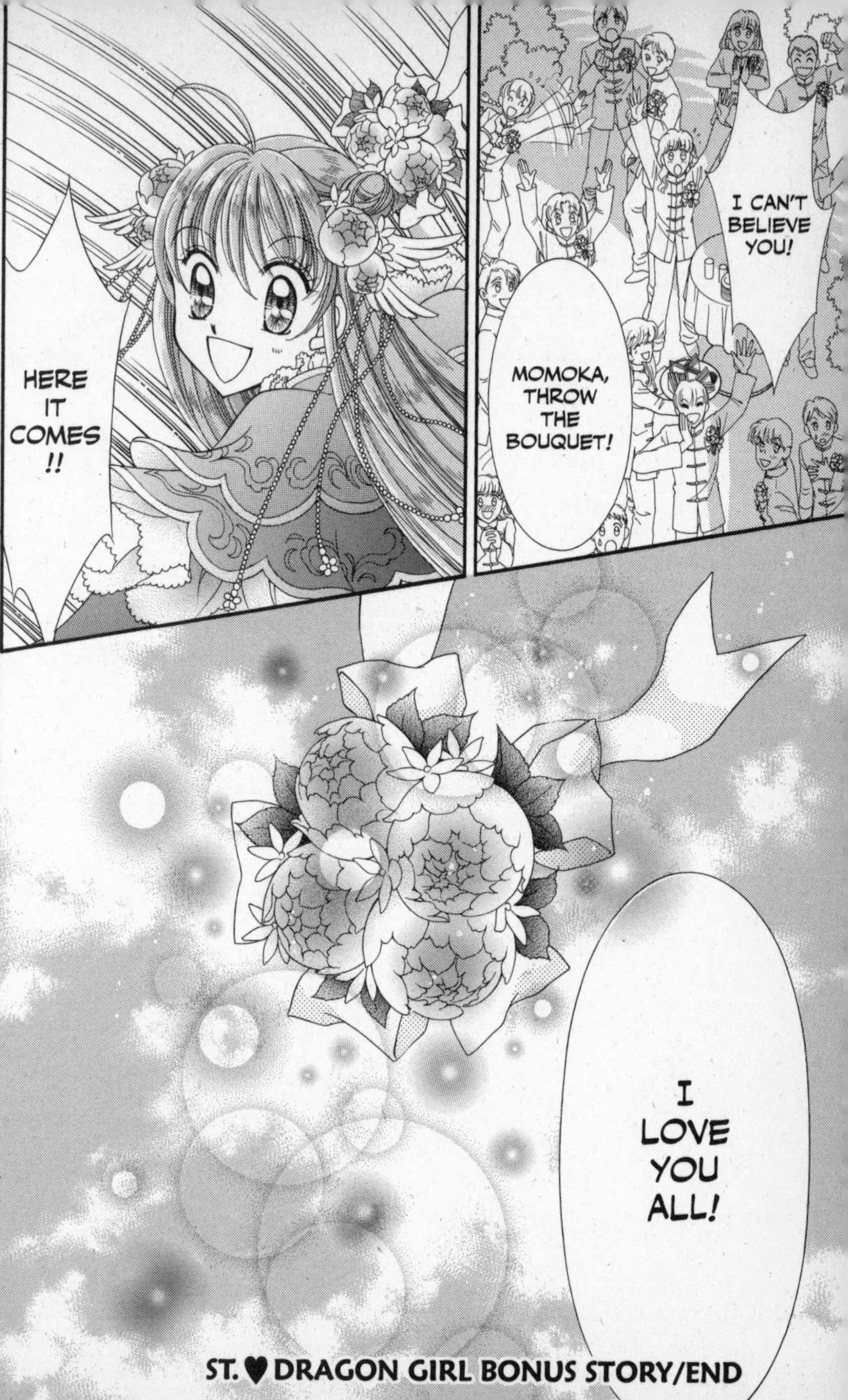
I CAN'T BELIEVE YOU!
MOMOKA, THROW THE BOUQUET!
HERE IT COMES!!
I LOVE YOU ALL!
ST.♥DRAGON GIRL BONUS STORY/END

Please, Momoka!

Idea by Kanae Funato

Kanae-chan's Ron-Ron is so cute that I had to use both of her ideas! ♡ Thanks, Kanae-chan!

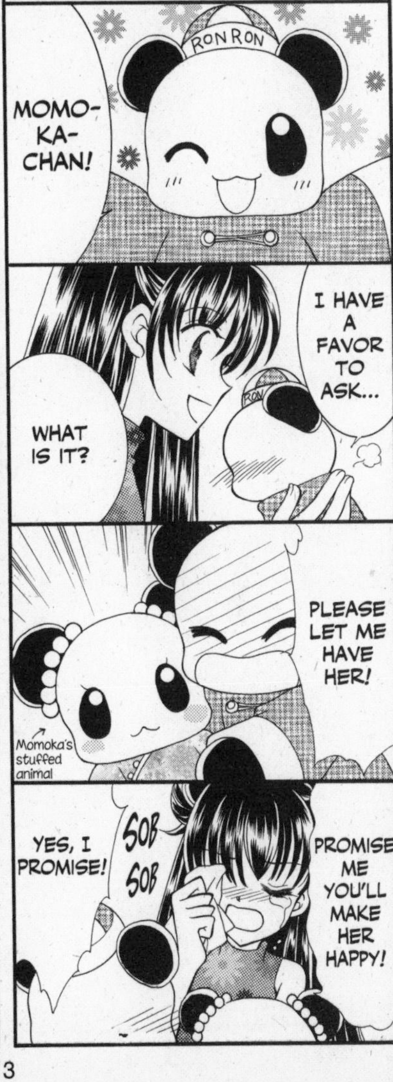
RON RON
MOMO-KA-CHAN!
I HAVE A FAVOR TO ASK...
WHAT IS IT?
PLEASE LET ME HAVE HER!
Momoka's stuffed animal
PROMISE ME YOU'LL MAKE HER HAPPY!
SOB SOB
YES, I PROMISE!

I Want to Marry ♡

Idea by Kanae Funato

I sent a signed manga to all the people who sent in the ideas I used.

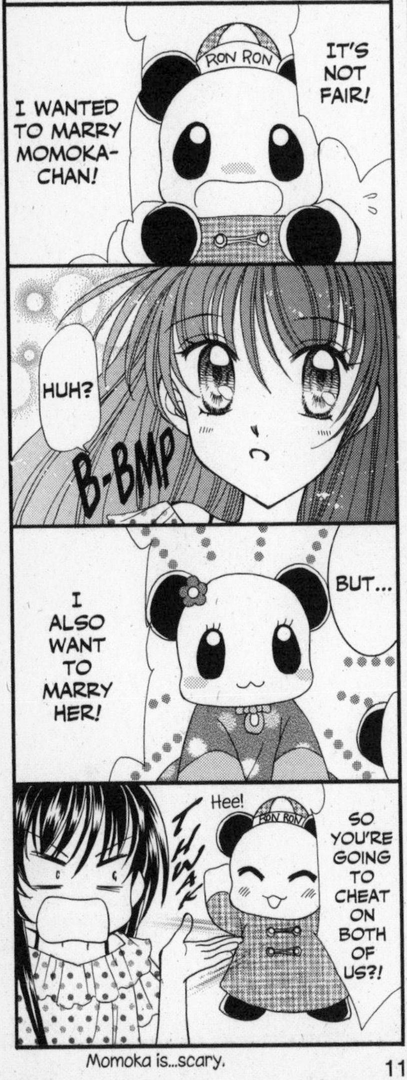
RON RON
IT'S NOT FAIR!
I WANTED TO MARRY MOMOKA-CHAN!
HUH?
B-BMP
BUT...
I ALSO WANT TO MARRY HER!
SO YOU'RE GOING TO CHEAT ON BOTH OF US?!
Hee!
THWAK

Momoka is...scary.

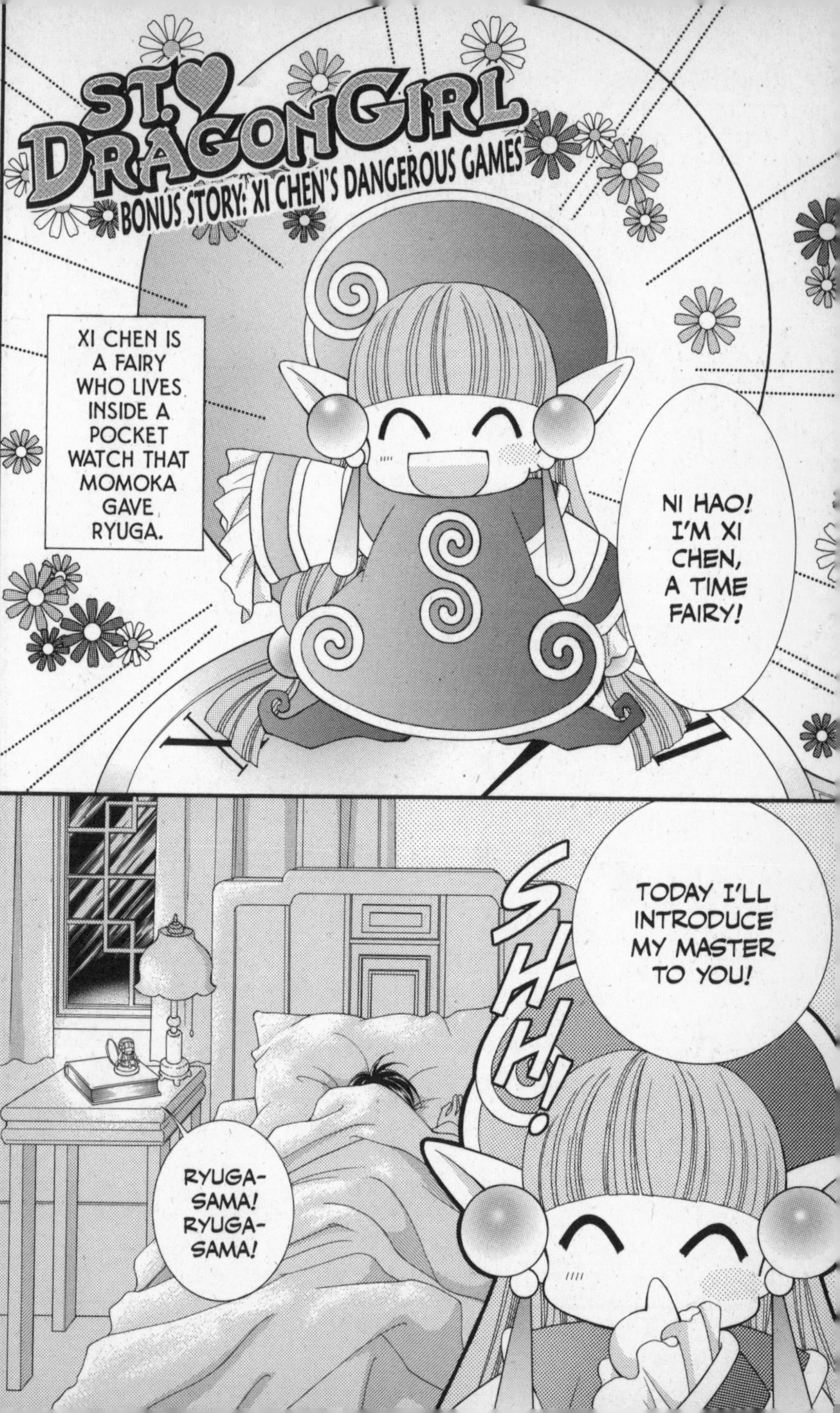
ST. ♥ DRAGON GIRL
BONUS STORY: XI CHEN'S DANGEROUS GAMES
XI CHEN IS A FAIRY WHO LIVES INSIDE A POCKET WATCH THAT MOMOKA GAVE RYUGA.
NI HAO! I'M XI CHEN, A TIME FAIRY!
TODAY I'LL INTRODUCE MY MASTER TO YOU!
SHURU!
RYUGA-SAMA! RYUGA-SAMA!

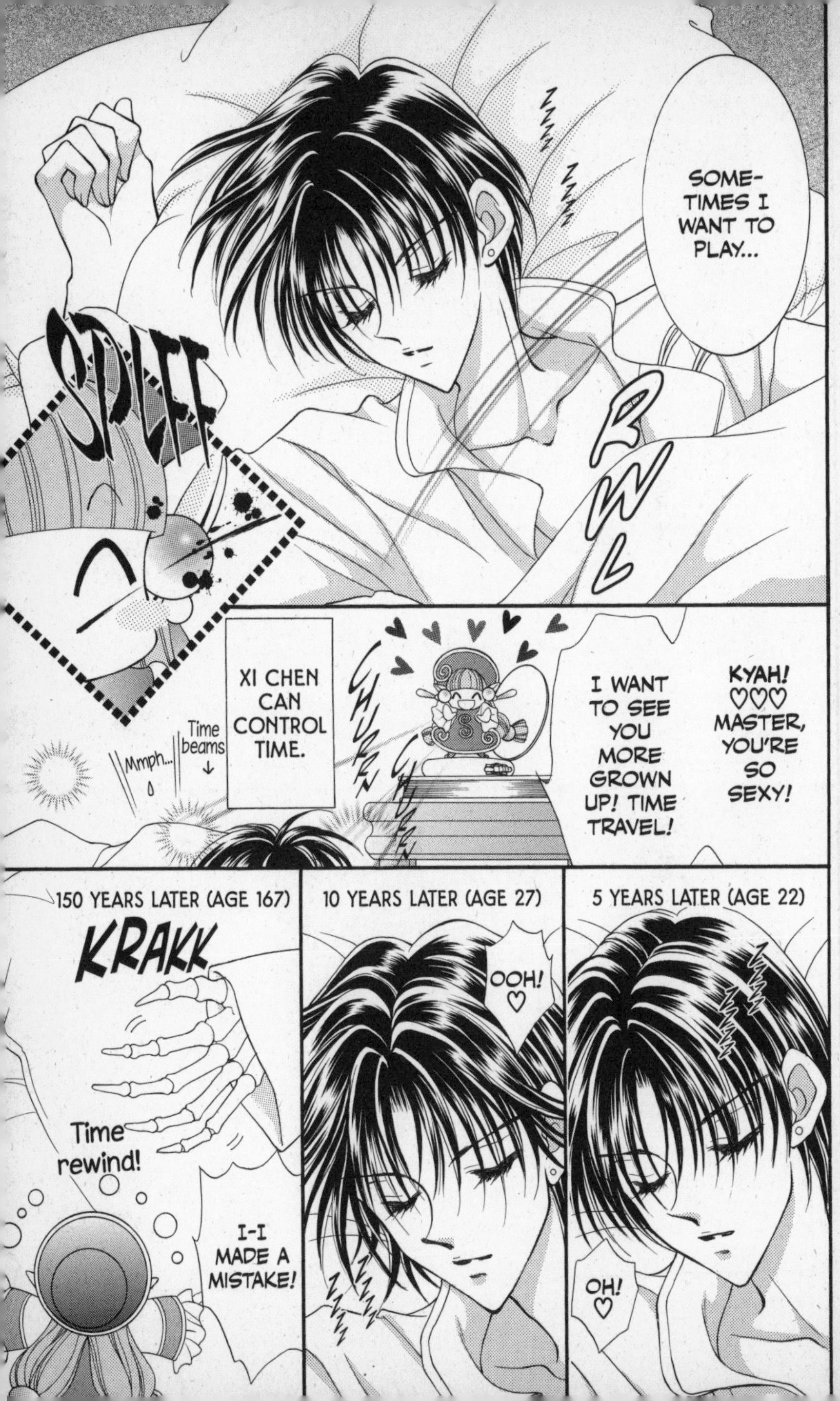
SOME-TIMES I WANT TO PLAY...
SPLFF
KYAH! ♡♡♡ MASTER, YOU'RE SO SEXY!
I WANT TO SEE YOU MORE GROWN UP! TIME TRAVEL!
XI CHEN CAN CONTROL TIME.
Time beams ↓
Mmph...
5 YEARS LATER (AGE 22)
OH! ♡
10 YEARS LATER (AGE 27)
OOH! ♡
150 YEARS LATER (AGE 167)
KRAKK
Time rewind!
I-I MADE A MISTAKE!

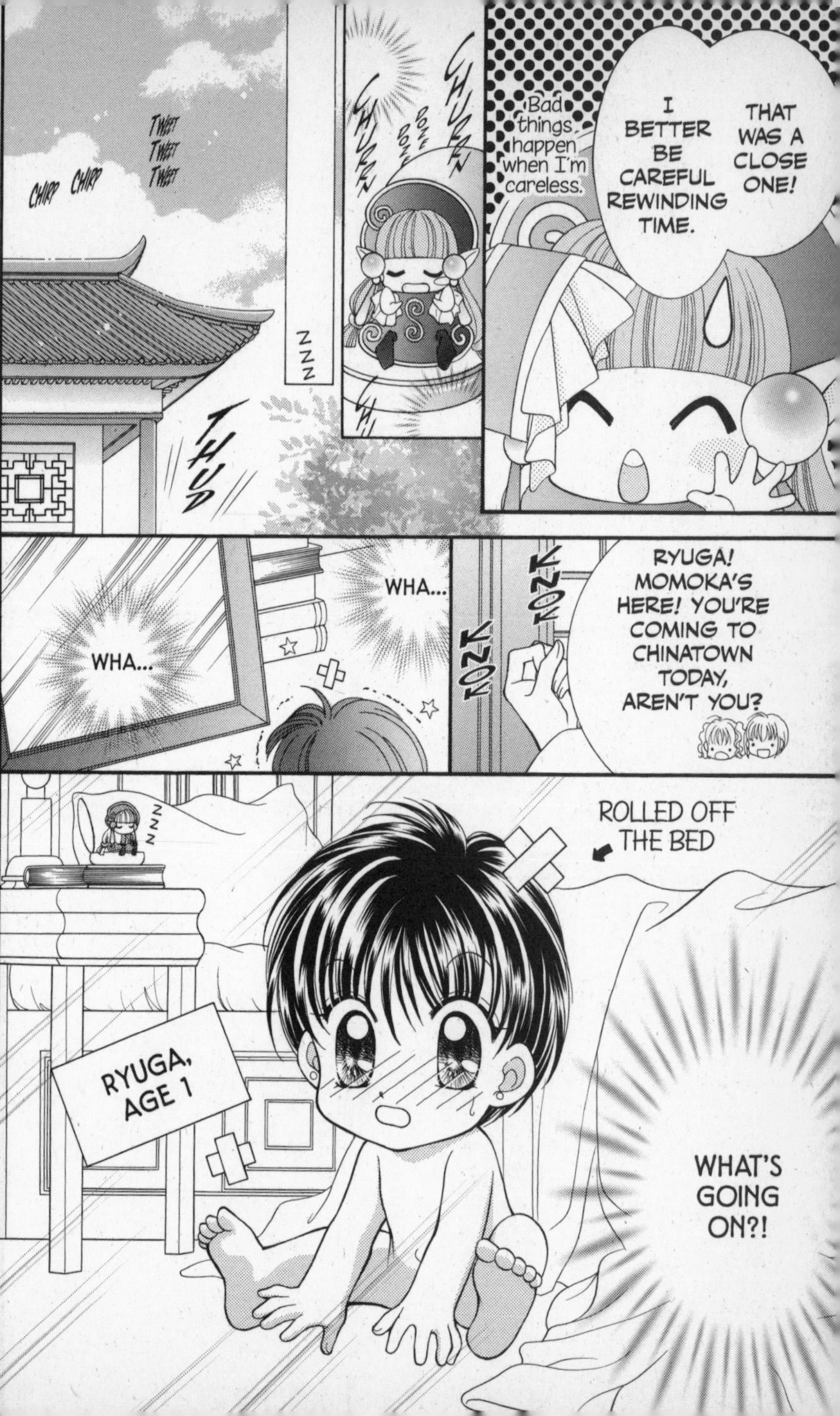
THAT WAS A CLOSE ONE!
I BETTER BE CAREFUL REWINDING TIME.
Bad things happen when I'm careless.
DOZE DOZE
ZZZ
TWEET TWEET TWEET
CHIRP CHIRP
THUD
KNOK KNOK
RYUGA! MOMOKA'S HERE! YOU'RE COMING TO CHINATOWN TODAY, AREN'T YOU?
WHA...
WHA...
ROLLED OFF THE BED
ZZZ
RYUGA, AGE 1
WHAT'S GOING ON?!

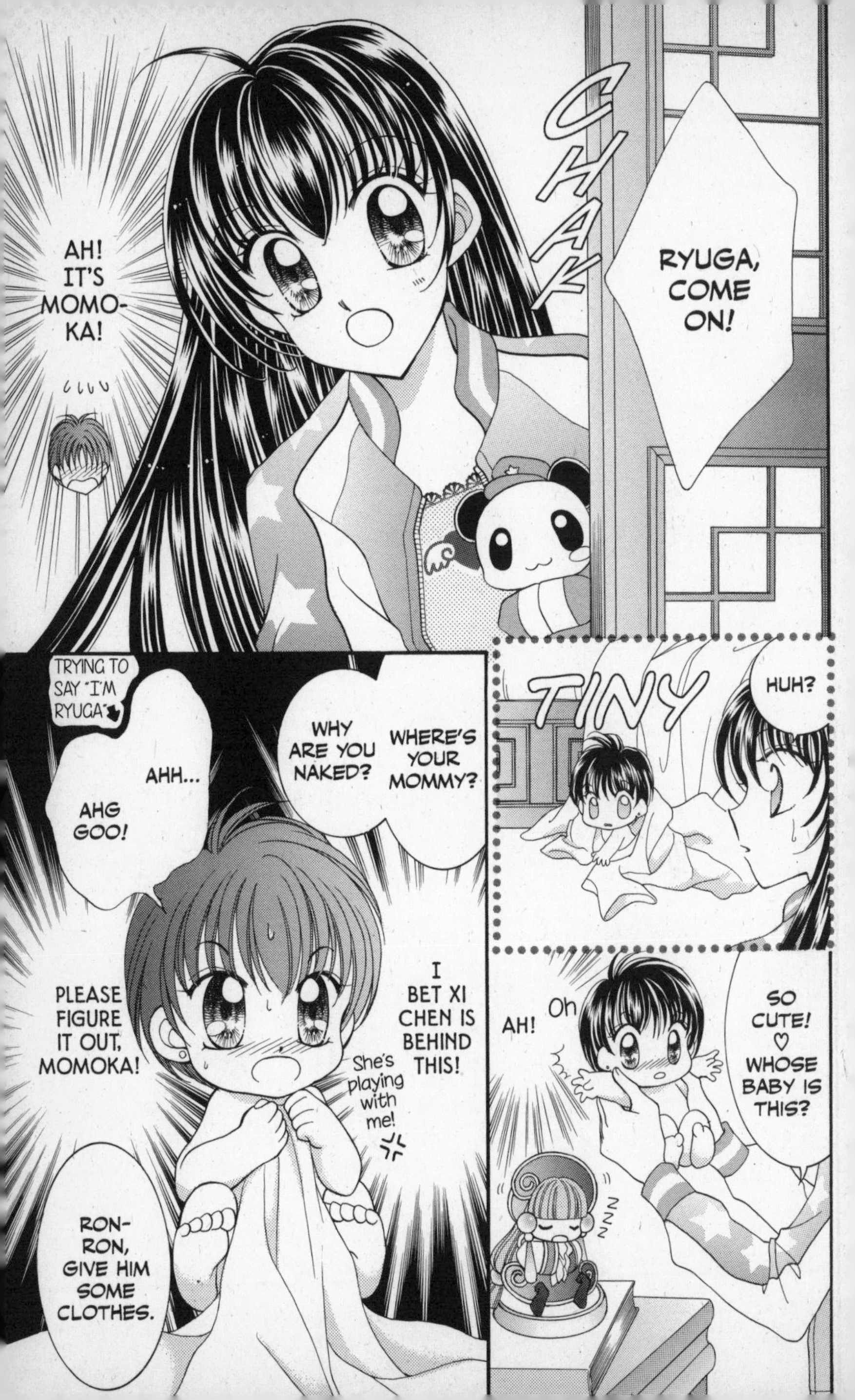
CHAK
RYUGA, COME ON!
AH! IT'S MOMO-KA!
TINY
HUH?
SO CUTE! ♡ WHOSE BABY IS THIS?
Oh
AH!
WHERE'S YOUR MOMMY?
WHY ARE YOU NAKED?
TRYING TO SAY "I'M RYUGA"
AHH...
AHG GOO!
I BET XI CHEN IS BEHIND THIS!
She's playing with me!
PLEASE FIGURE IT OUT, MOMOKA!
RON-RON, GIVE HIM SOME CLOTHES.

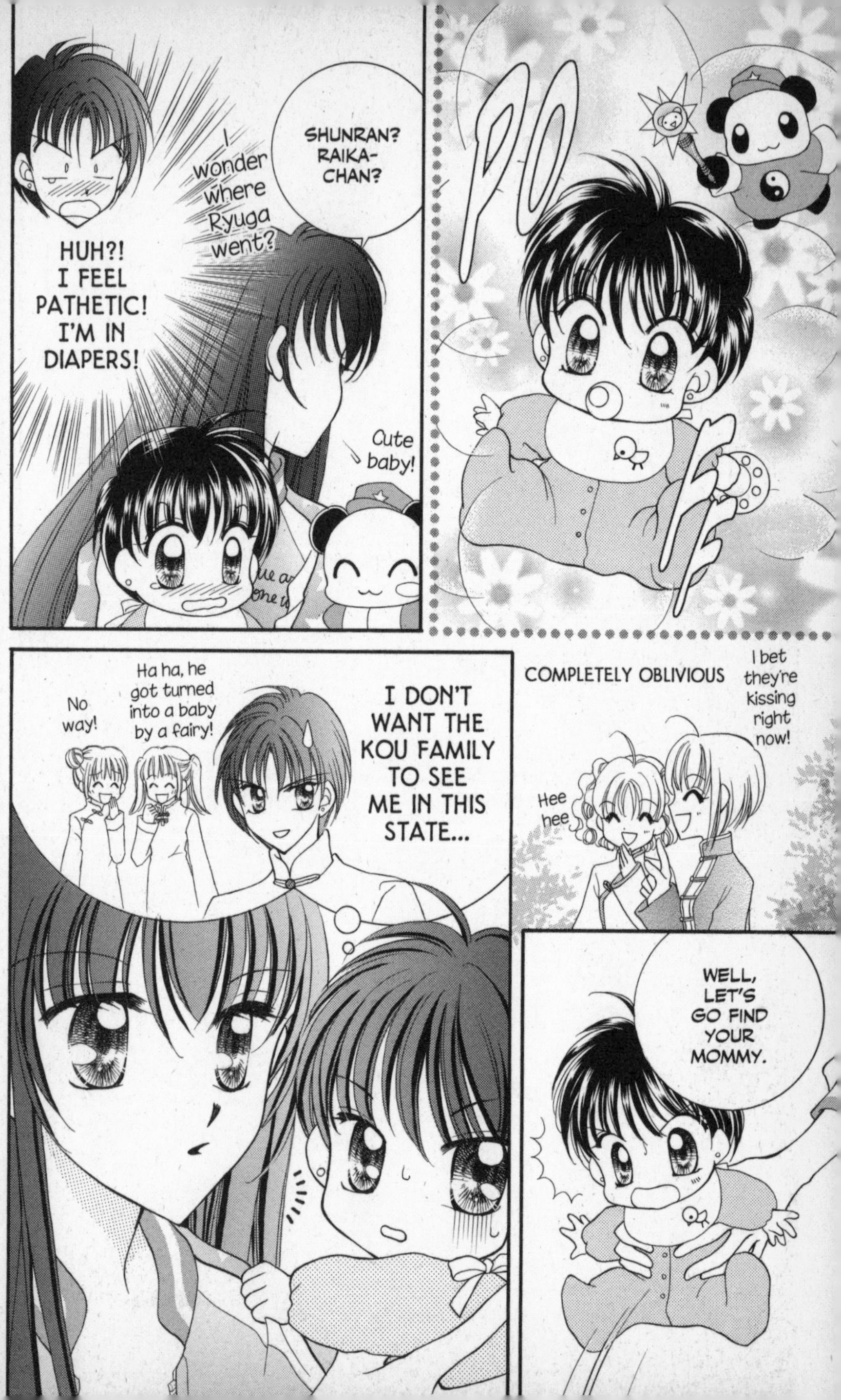
PO
SHUNRAN? RAIKA-CHAN?
I wonder where Ryuga went?
HUH?! I FEEL PATHETIC! I'M IN DIAPERS!
Cute baby!
COMPLETELY OBLIVIOUS
I bet they're kissing right now!
Hee hee
WELL, LET'S GO FIND YOUR MOMMY.
I DON'T WANT THE KOU FAMILY TO SEE ME IN THIS STATE...
Ha ha, he got turned into a baby by a fairy!
No way!

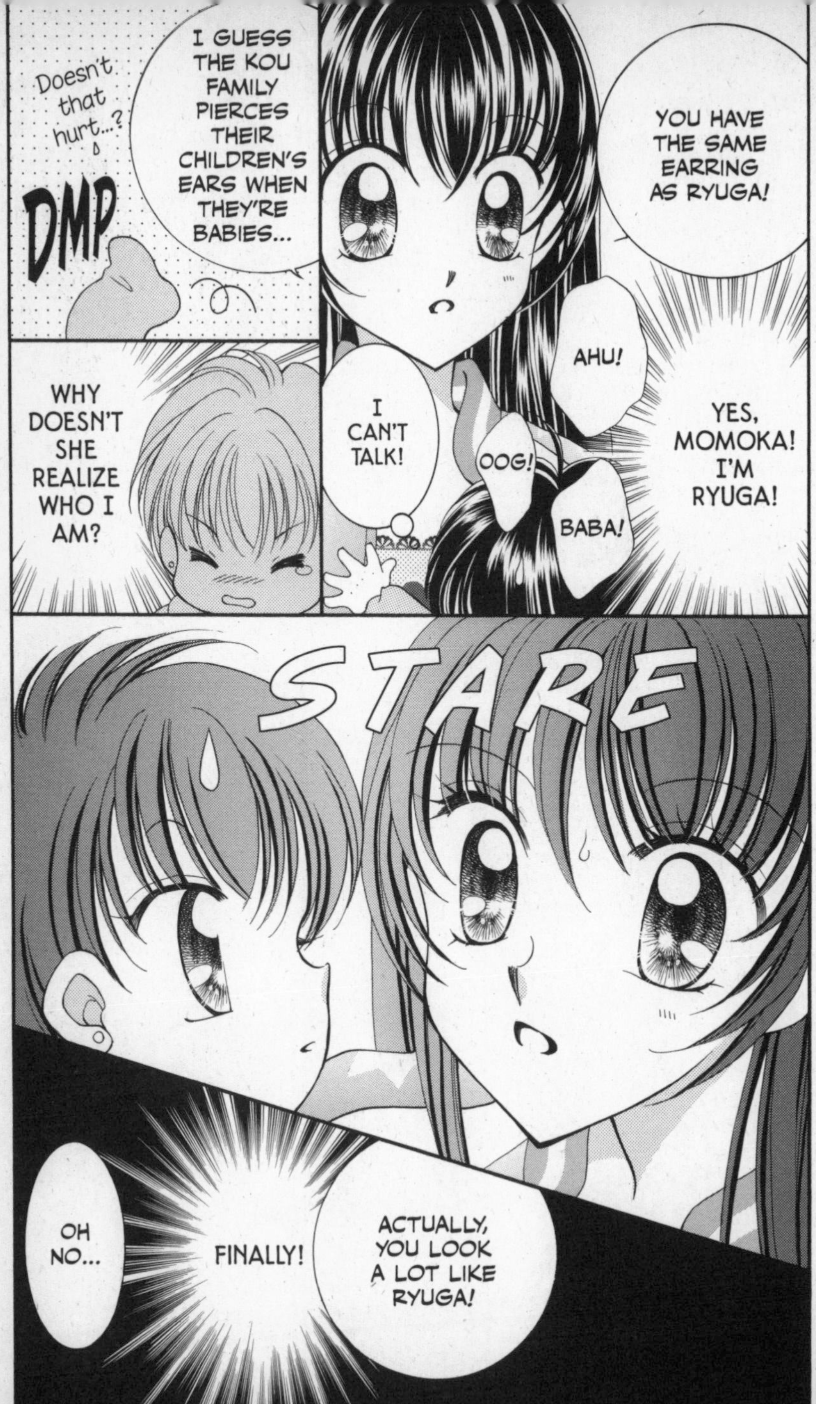
YOU HAVE THE SAME EARRING AS RYUGA!
I GUESS THE KOU FAMILY PIERCES THEIR CHILDREN'S EARS WHEN THEY'RE BABIES...
Doesn't that hurt...?
DMP
YES, MOMOKA! I'M RYUGA!
AHU!
BABA!
OOG!
I CAN'T TALK!
WHY DOESN'T SHE REALIZE WHO I AM?
STARE
ACTUALLY, YOU LOOK A LOT LIKE RYUGA!
FINALLY!
OH NO...

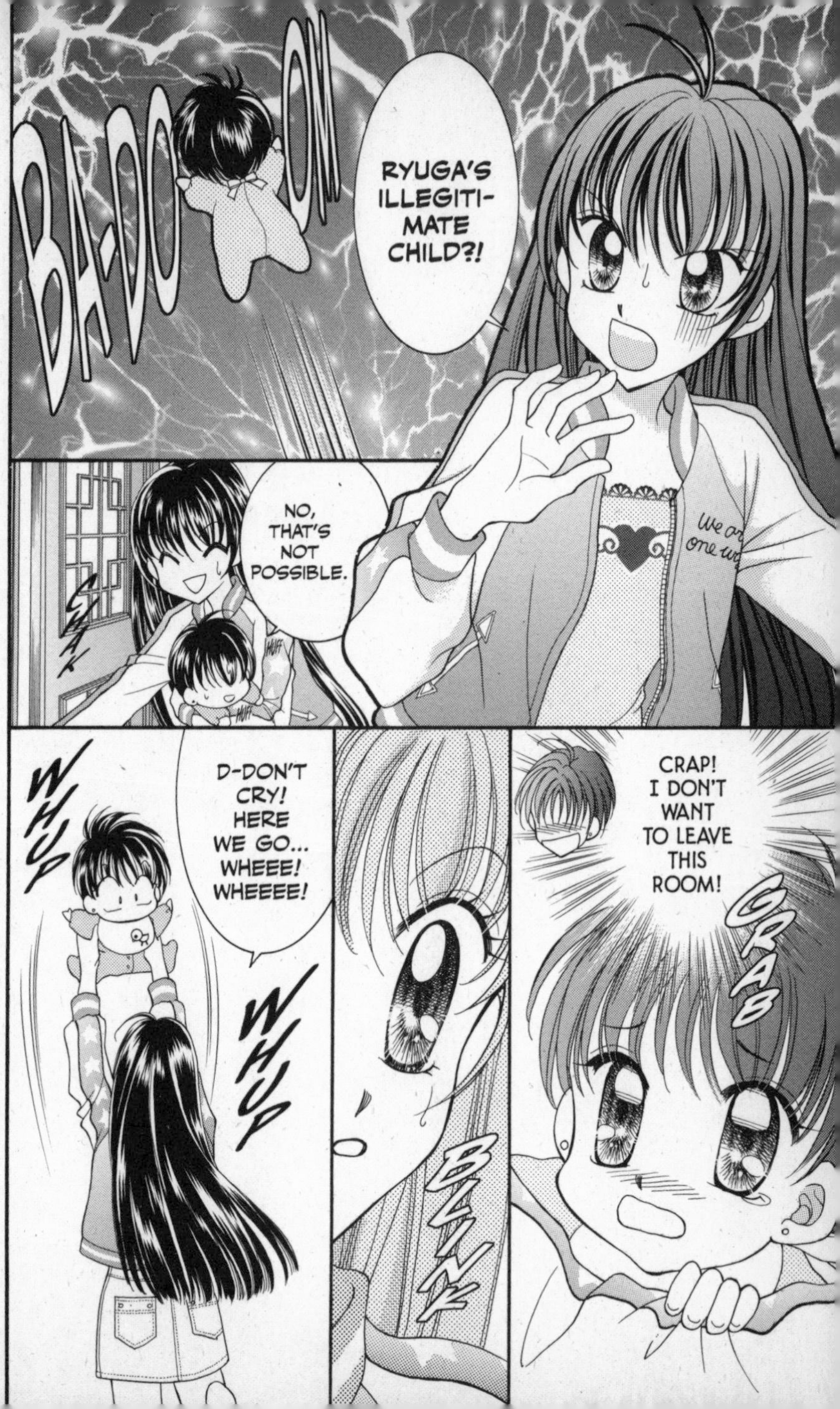
RYUGA'S ILLEGITI-MATE CHILD?!
BA-DOOM
NO, THAT'S NOT POSSIBLE.
HUFF
HUFF
CRAP! I DON'T WANT TO LEAVE THIS ROOM!
GRAB
BLINK
D-DON'T CRY! HERE WE GO... WHEEE! WHEEEE!
WHUP
WHUP

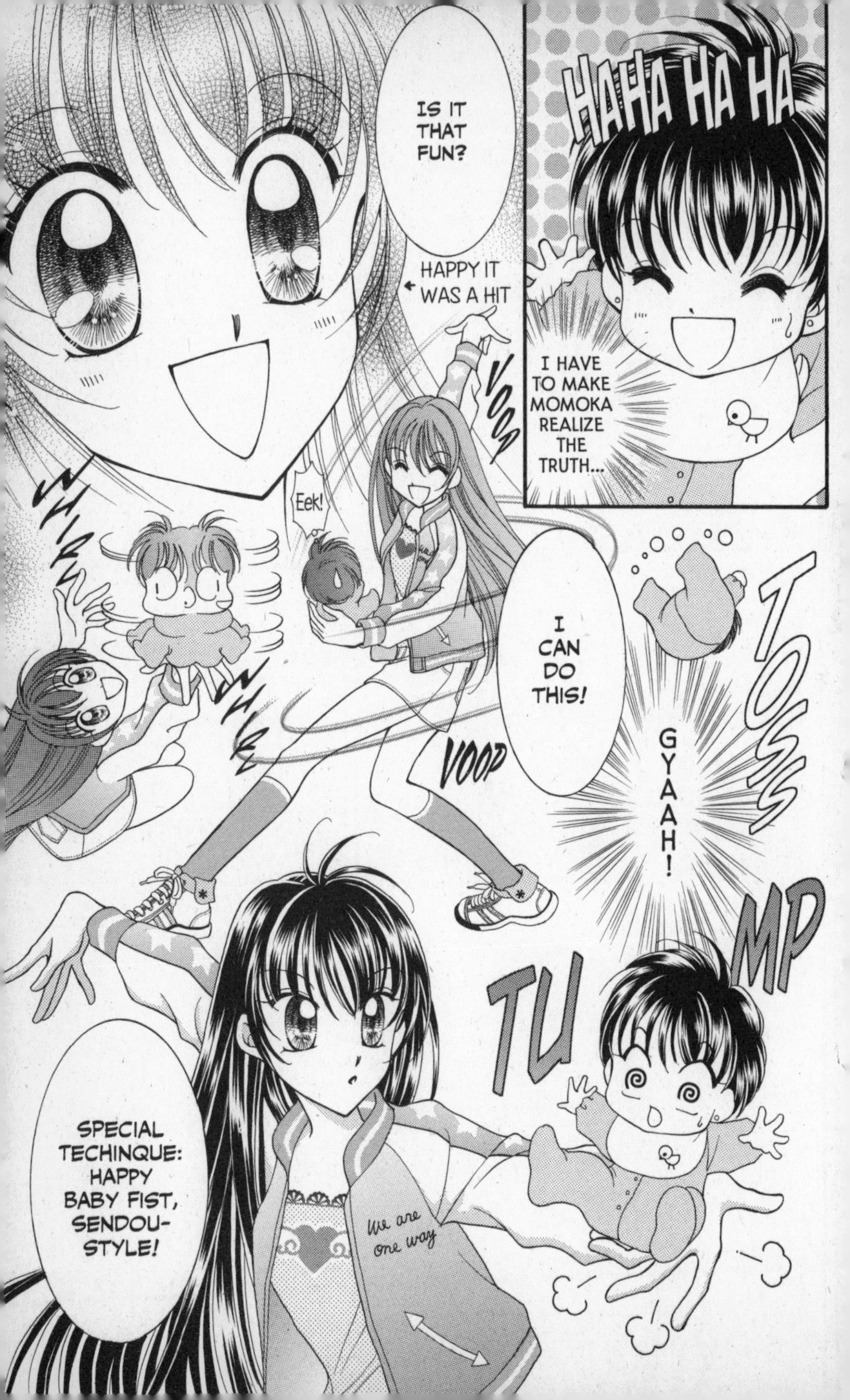
HAHA HA HA
I HAVE TO MAKE MOMOKA REALIZE THE TRUTH...
IS IT THAT FUN?
HAPPY IT WAS A HIT
VOOM
Eek!
TOSS
GYAAH!
I CAN DO THIS!
VOOP
TUMP
SPECIAL TECHINQUE: HAPPY BABY FIST, SENDOU-STYLE!
We are one way

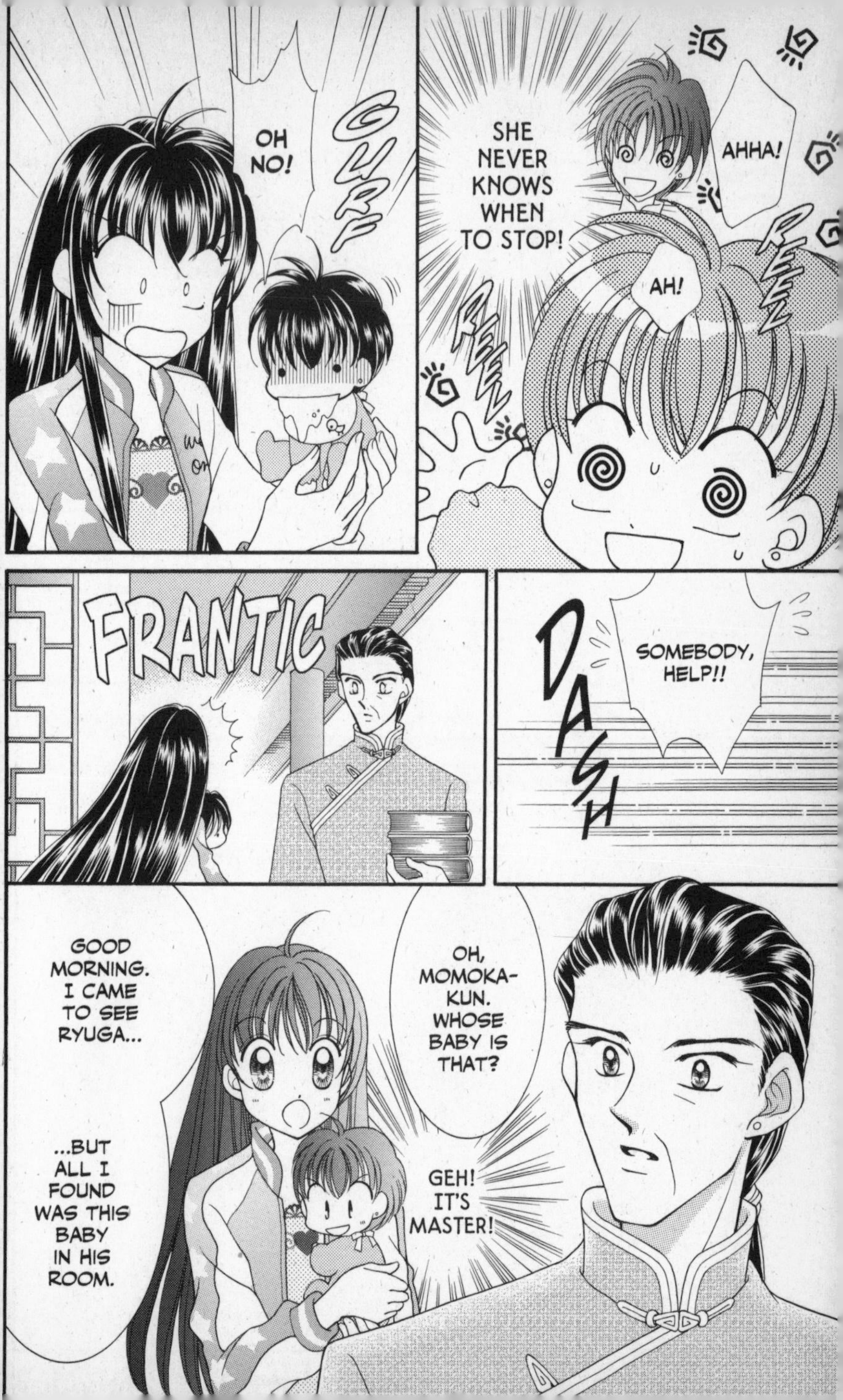
AHHA!
SHE NEVER KNOWS WHEN TO STOP!
AH!
OH NO!
DASH
SOMEBODY, HELP!!
FRANTIC
OH, MOMOKA-KUN. WHOSE BABY IS THAT?
GOOD MORNING. I CAME TO SEE RYUGA...
GEH! IT'S MASTER!
...BUT ALL I FOUND WAS THIS BABY IN HIS ROOM.

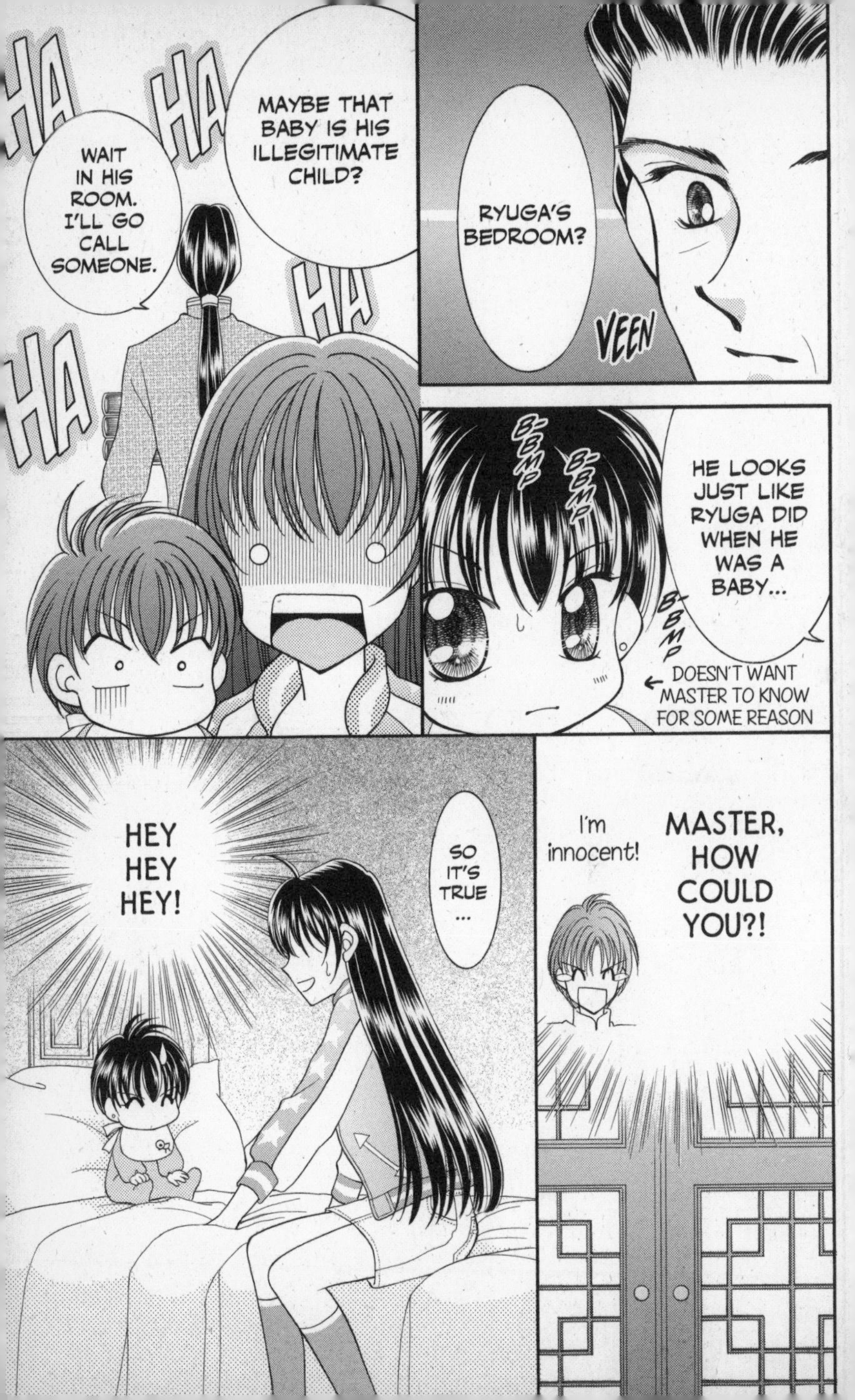
RYUGA'S BEDROOM?
VEEN
HE LOOKS JUST LIKE RYUGA DID WHEN HE WAS A BABY...
B-BMP B-BMP B-BMP
← DOESN'T WANT MASTER TO KNOW FOR SOME REASON
MAYBE THAT BABY IS HIS ILLEGITIMATE CHILD?
HA HA HA HA
WAIT IN HIS ROOM. I'LL GO CALL SOMEONE.
MASTER, HOW COULD YOU?!
I'm innocent!
SO IT'S TRUE ...
HEY HEY HEY!

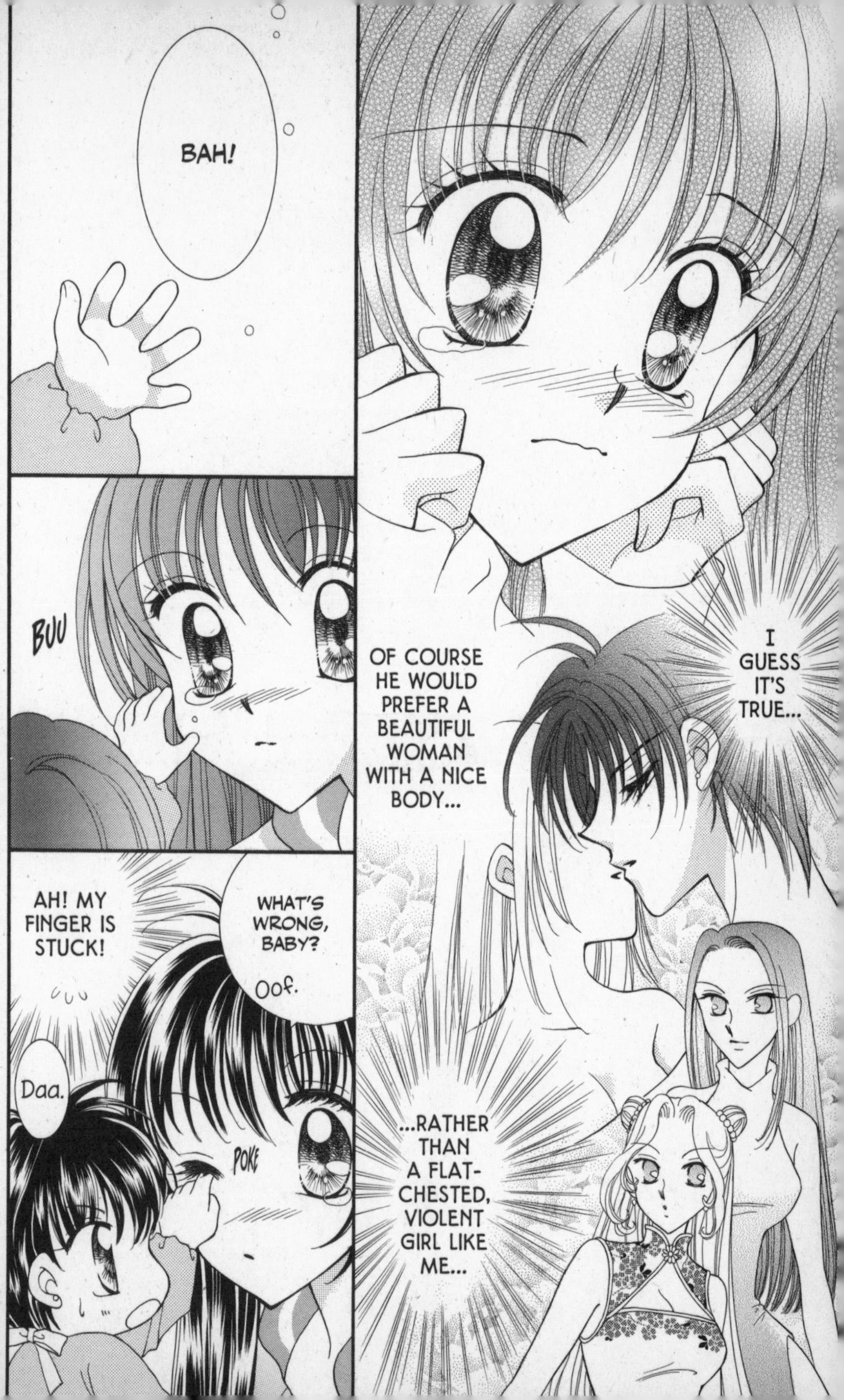
I GUESS IT'S TRUE...
OF COURSE HE WOULD PREFER A BEAUTIFUL WOMAN WITH A NICE BODY...
...RATHER THAN A FLAT-CHESTED, VIOLENT GIRL LIKE ME...
BAH!
BUU
WHAT'S WRONG, BABY?
Oof.
AH! MY FINGER IS STUCK!
Daa.
POKE

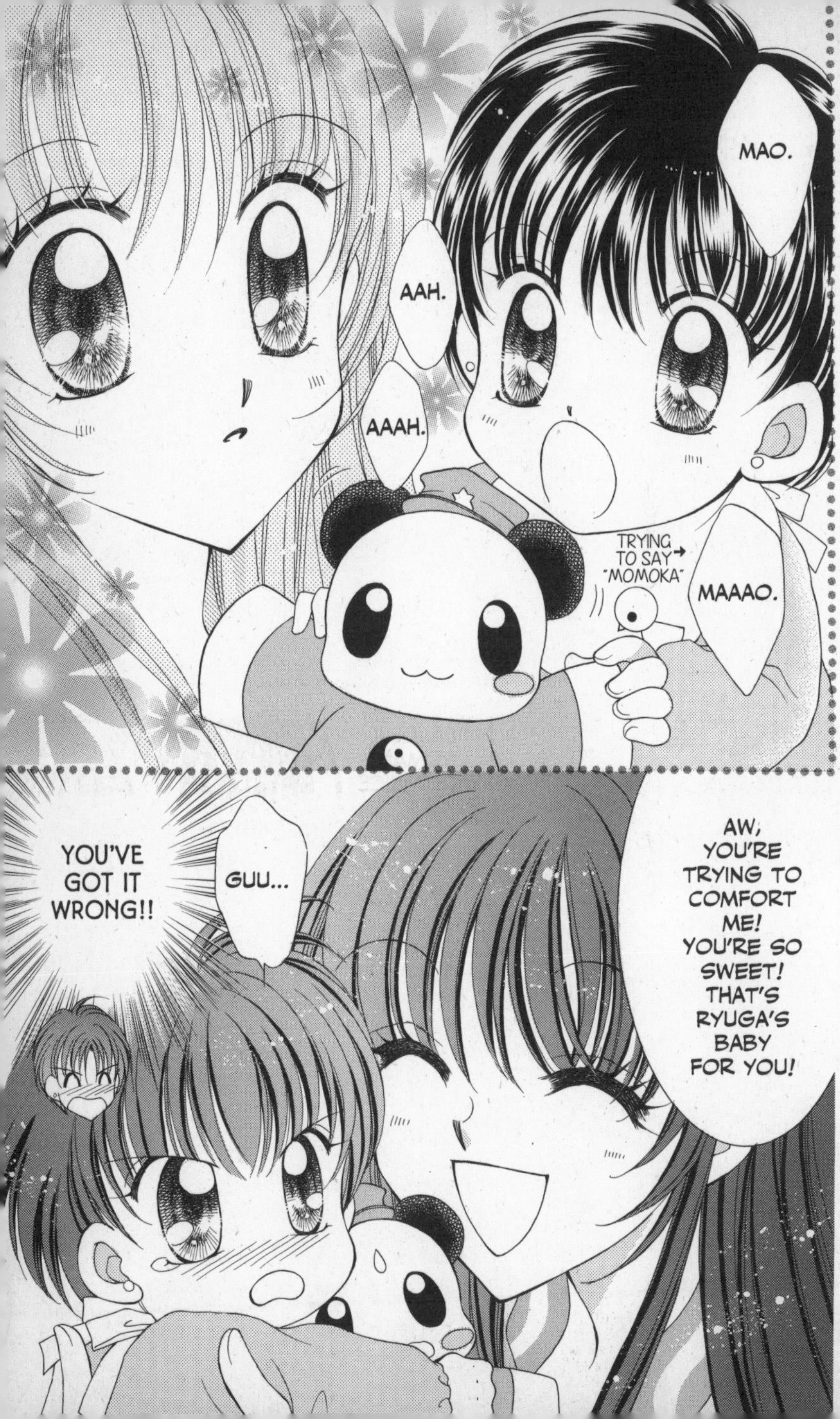
MAO.
AAH.
AAAH.
TRYING TO SAY "MOMOKA"
MAAAO.
AW, YOU'RE TRYING TO COMFORT ME! YOU'RE SO SWEET! THAT'S RYUGA'S BABY FOR YOU!
GUU...
YOU'VE GOT IT WRONG!!

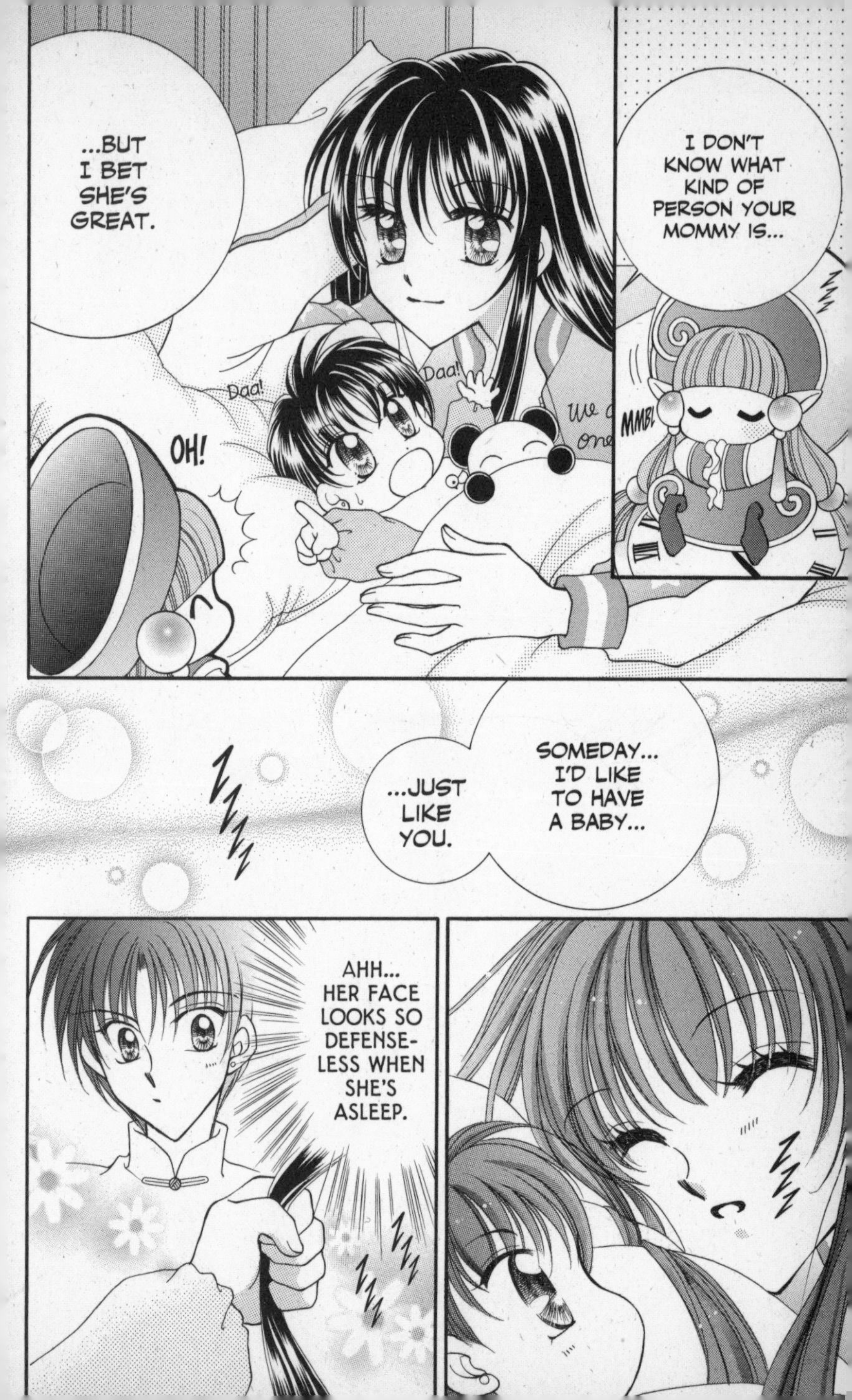
I DON'T KNOW WHAT KIND OF PERSON YOUR MOMMY IS...
MMBL
...BUT I BET SHE'S GREAT.
Daa!
Daa!
OH!
SOMEDAY... I'D LIKE TO HAVE A BABY...
...JUST LIKE YOU.
AHH... HER FACE LOOKS SO DEFENSE-LESS WHEN SHE'S ASLEEP.

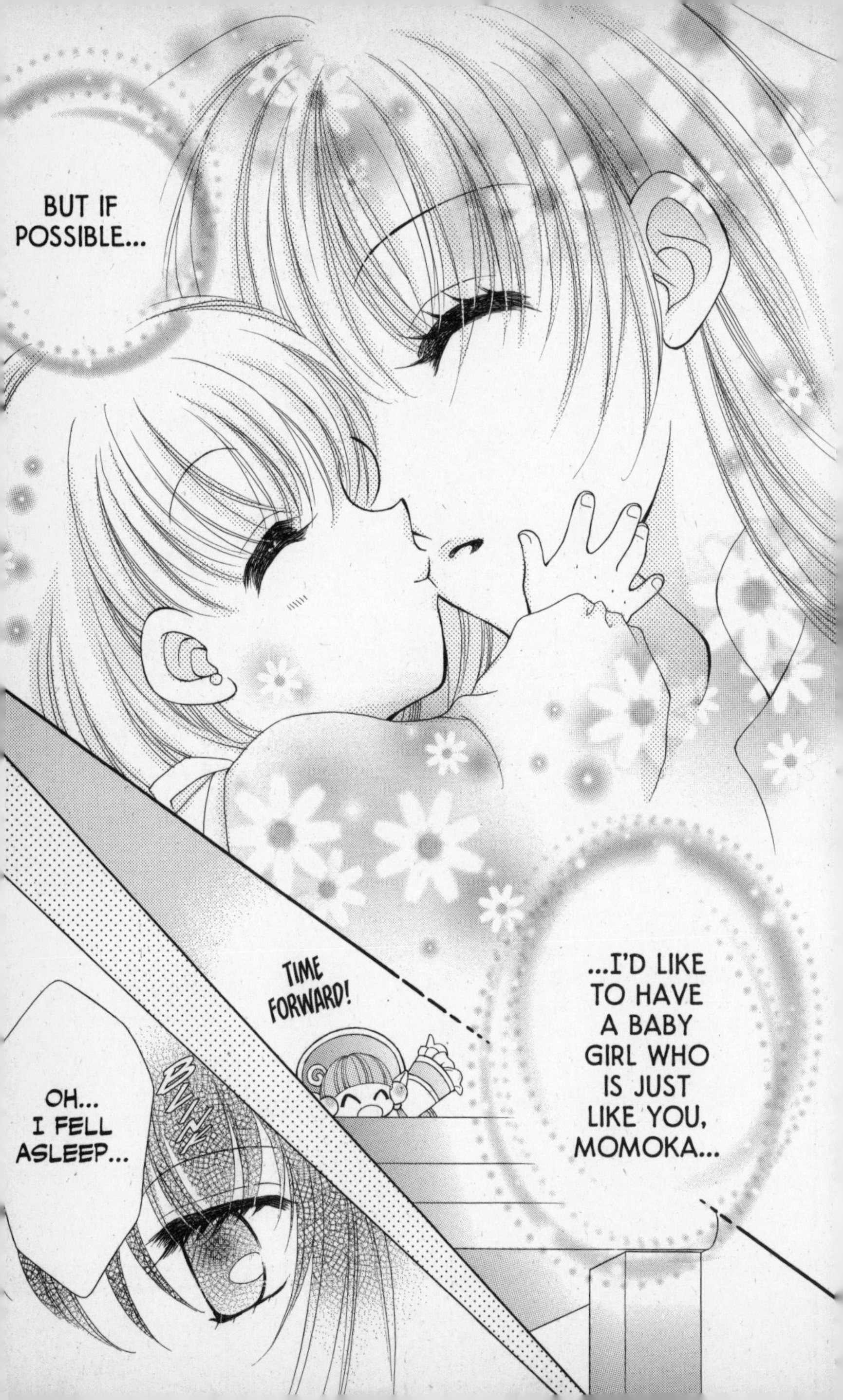
BUT IF POSSIBLE...
...I'D LIKE TO HAVE A BABY GIRL WHO IS JUST LIKE YOU, MOMOKA...
TIME FORWARD!
OH... I FELL ASLEEP...

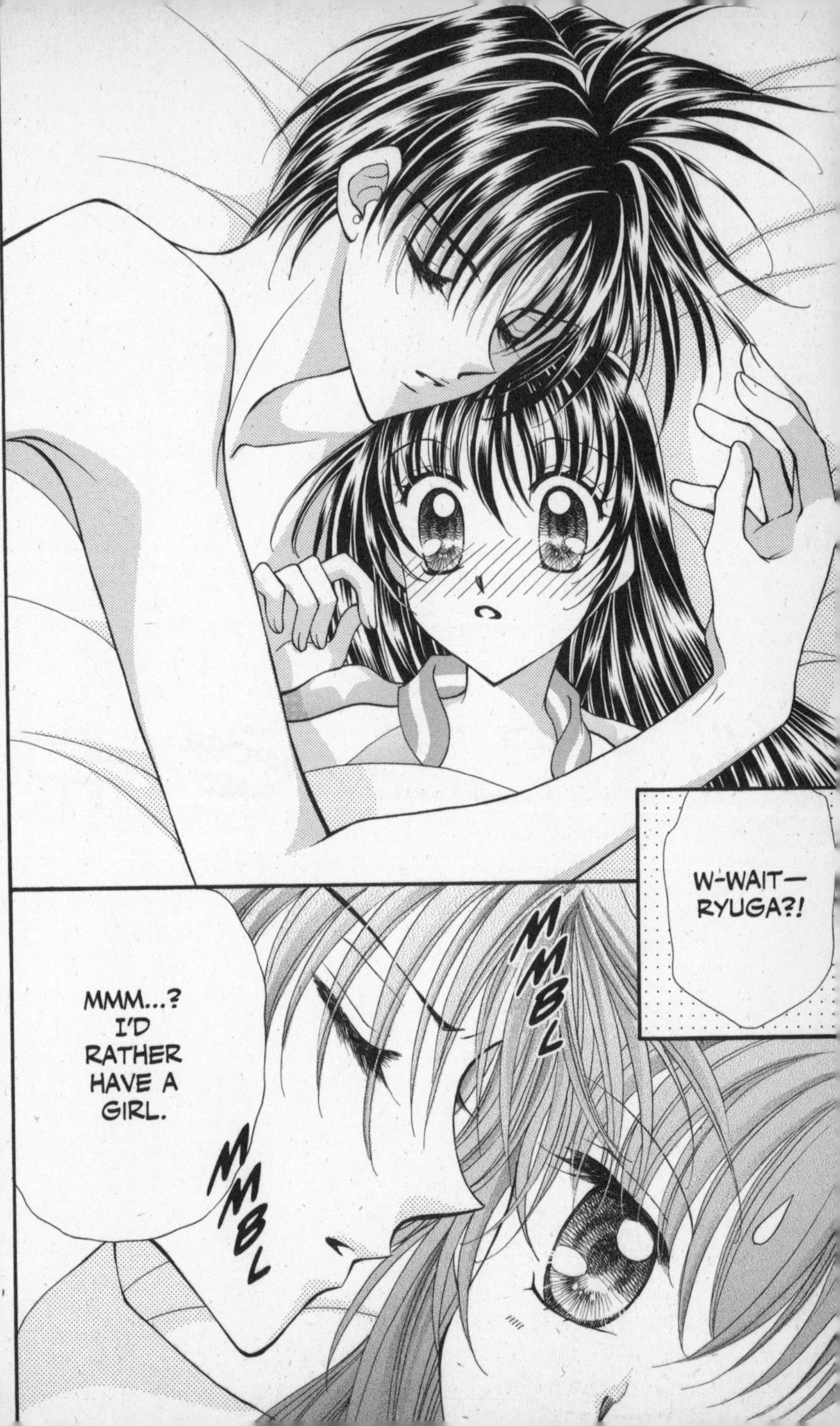
W-WAIT—
RYUGA?!
MMMBL
MMM...? I'D RATHER HAVE A GIRL.
MMMBL

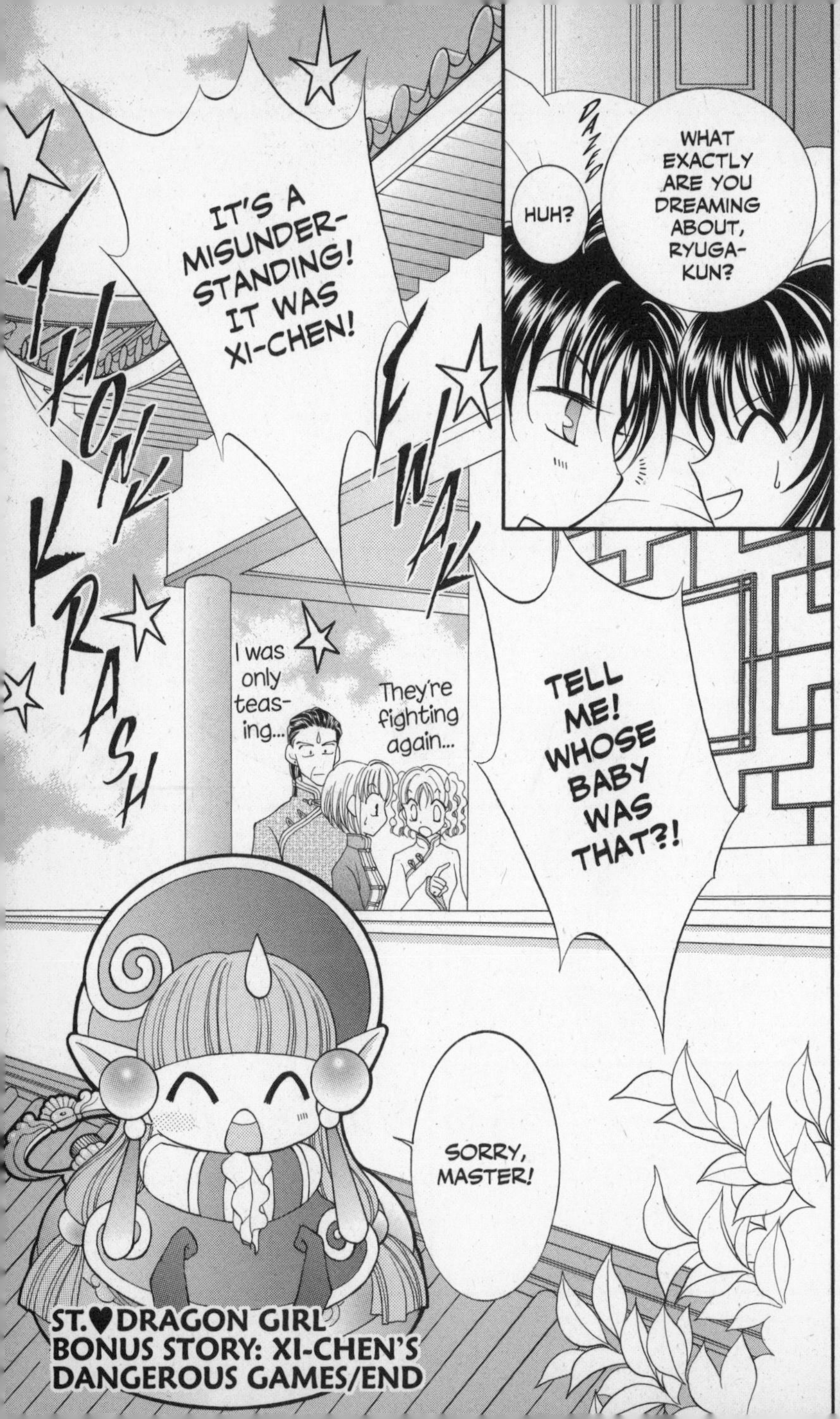

WHAT EXACTLY ARE YOU DREAMING ABOUT, RYUGA-KUN?
DAZED
HUH?
TELL ME! WHOSE BABY WAS THAT?!
FWAK
IT'S A MISUNDERSTANDING! IT WAS XI-CHEN!
THONK
KRASH
They're fighting again...
I was only teasing...
SORRY, MASTER!
ST.♥DRAGON GIRL BONUS STORY: XI-CHEN'S DANGEROUS GAMES/END

MOMOKA...

IDEA BY FUJI-SAMA (ALIAS)

Everyone always picks on Ryuga! I loved the last panel with him bawling. You guys are so great at these.

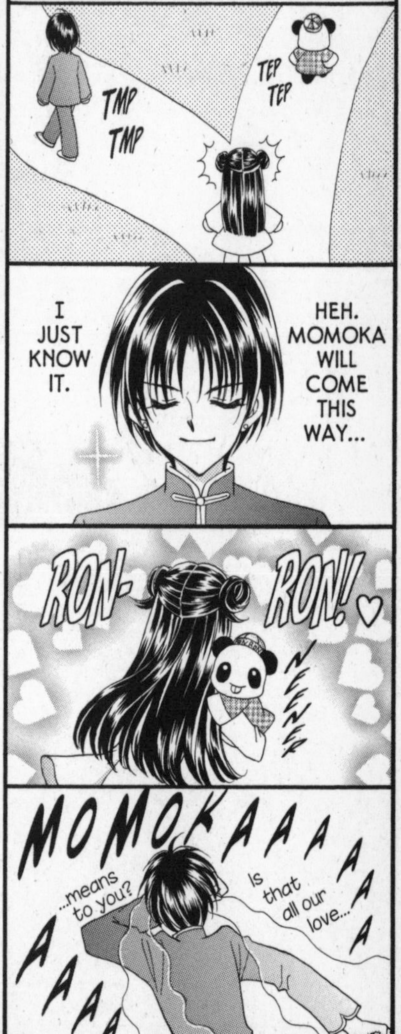
TEP TEP
TMP TMP
HEH. MOMOKA WILL COME THIS WAY...
I JUST KNOW IT.
RON-RON! ♥
NEENER
MOMOKAAAAAAAAAAAA
Is that all our love...
...means to you?

RON-RON'S FAILURE

IDEA BY TOMOKI KIYOMIZU

This strip has great pacing—I can tell Tomoki-chan is really talented. Her original art had a lot of style and was really cute. Thank you!

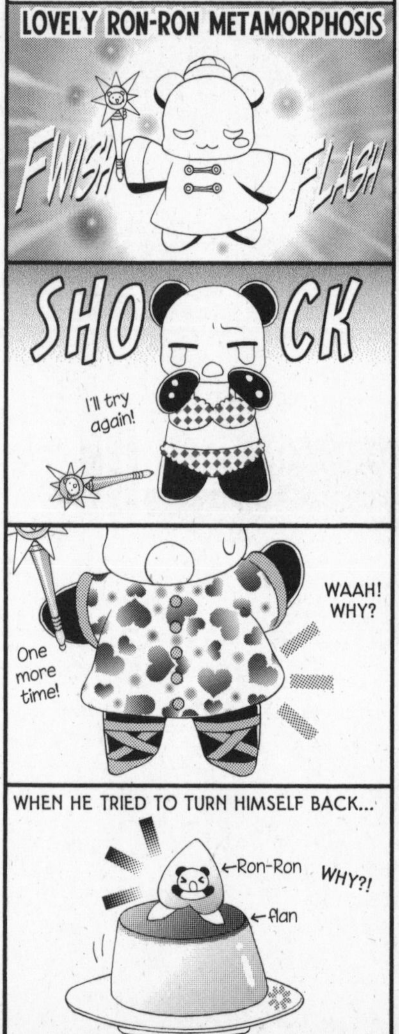
LOVELY RON-RON METAMORPHOSIS
FLASH
FWISH
SHOCK
I'll try again!
WAAH! WHY?
One more time!
WHEN HE TRIED TO TURN HIMSELF BACK...
WHY?!
←Ron-Ron
←flan

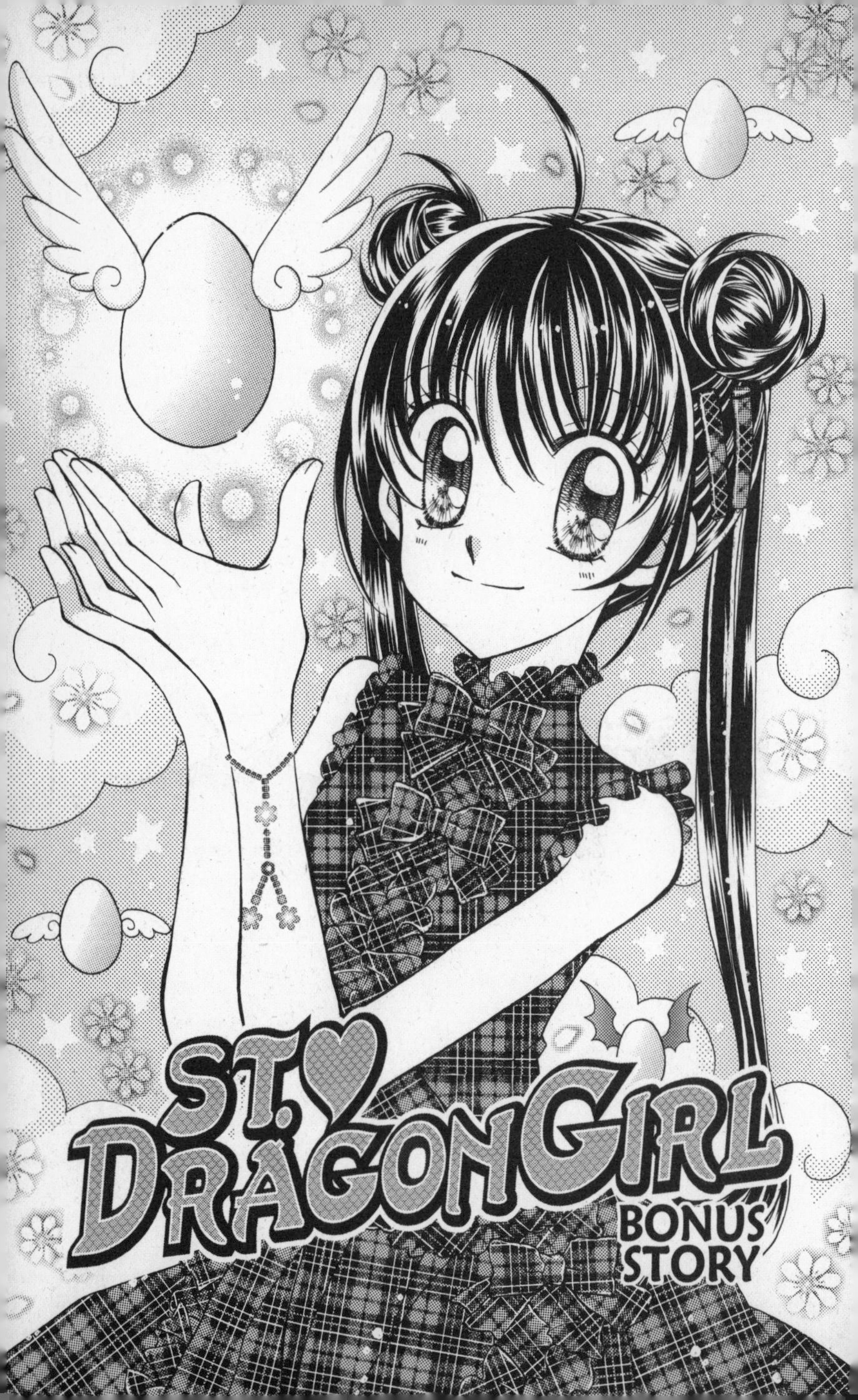
ST.♥DRAGON GIRL
BONUS STORY

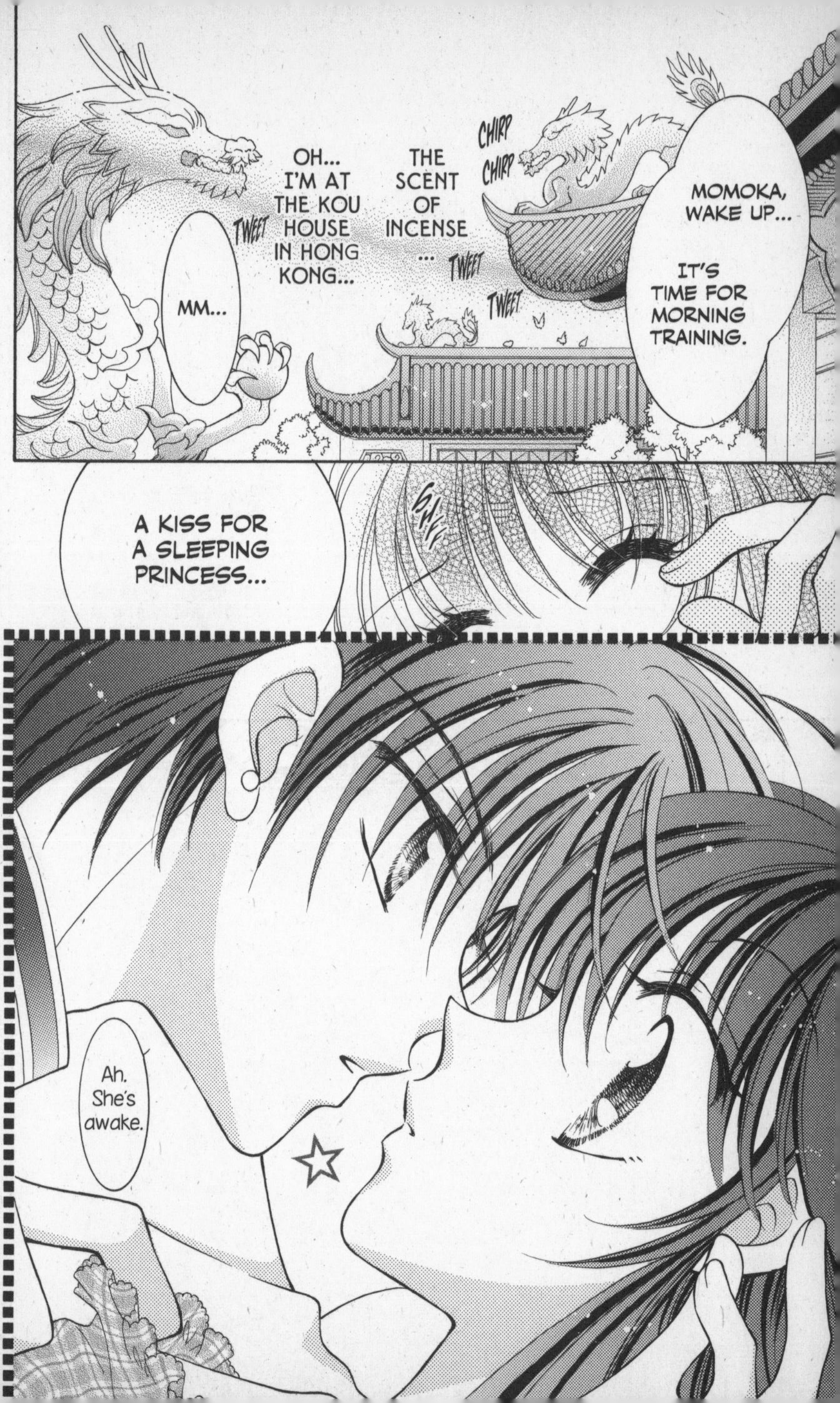
MOMOKA, WAKE UP...
IT'S TIME FOR MORNING TRAINING.
CHIRP
CHIRP
THE SCENT OF INCENSE ...
TWEET
TWEET
OH... I'M AT THE KOU HOUSE IN HONG KONG...
TWEET
MM...
A KISS FOR A SLEEPING PRINCESS...
Ah. She's awake.

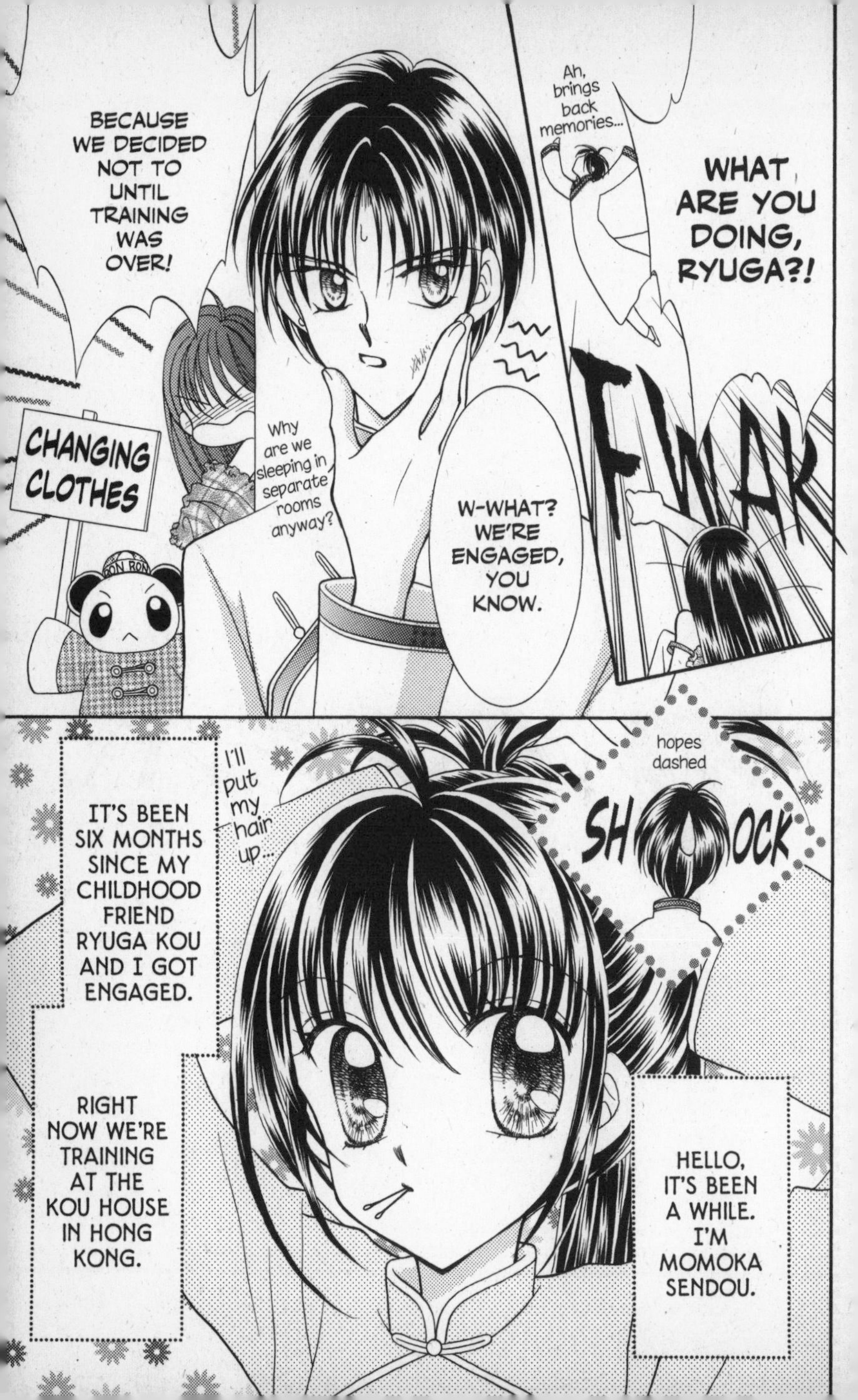
WHAT ARE YOU DOING, RYUGA?!
FWAR
Ah, brings back memories...
W-WHAT? WE'RE ENGAGED, YOU KNOW.
Why are we sleeping in separate rooms anyway?
BECAUSE WE DECIDED NOT TO UNTIL TRAINING WAS OVER!
CHANGING CLOTHES
RON RON
hopes dashed
SHOCK
I'll put my hair up...
HELLO, IT'S BEEN A WHILE. I'M MOMOKA SENDOU.
IT'S BEEN SIX MONTHS SINCE MY CHILDHOOD FRIEND RYUGA KOU AND I GOT ENGAGED.
RIGHT NOW WE'RE TRAINING AT THE KOU HOUSE IN HONG KONG.

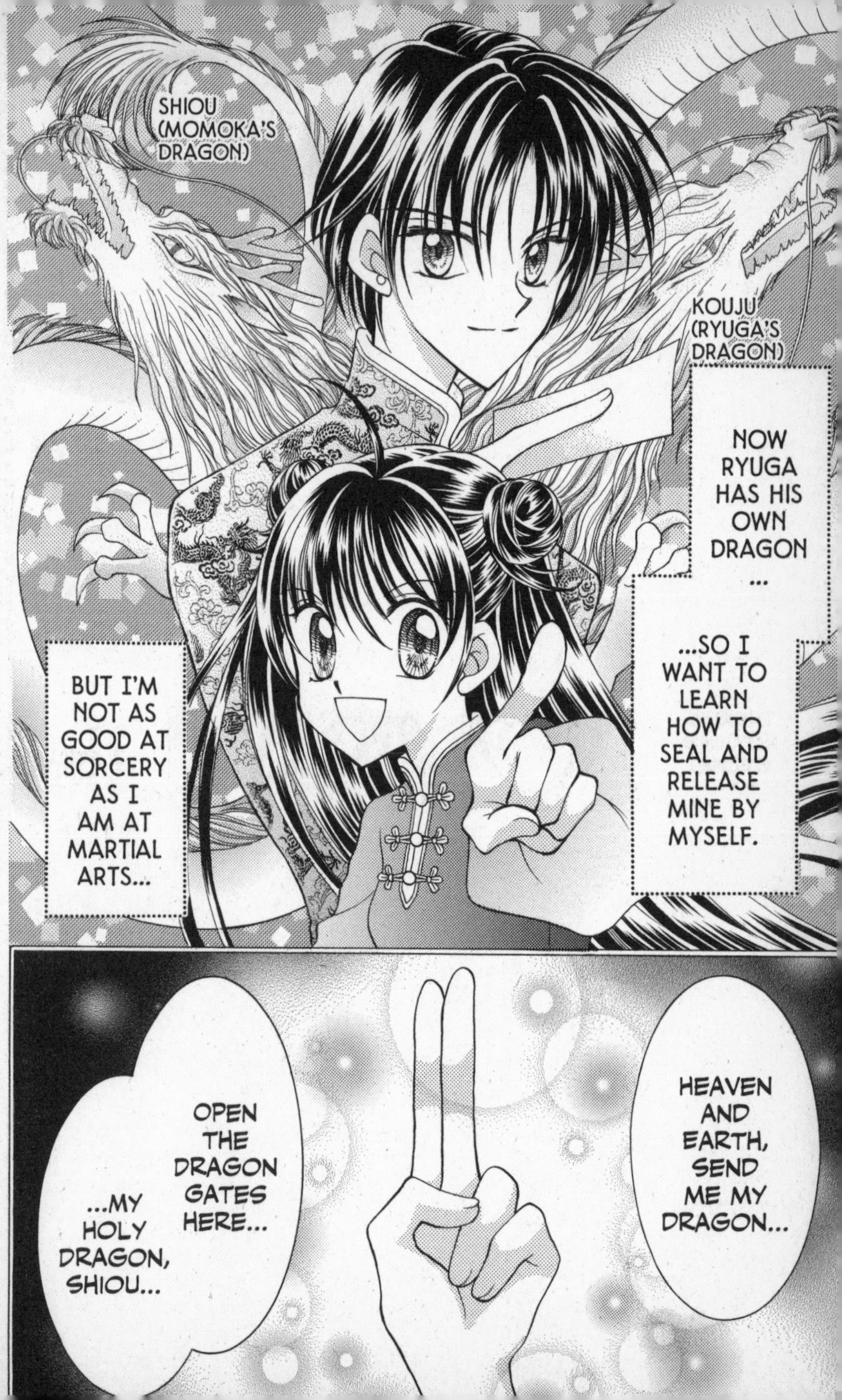
SHIOU (MOMOKA'S DRAGON)
KOUJU (RYUGA'S DRAGON)
NOW RYUGA HAS HIS OWN DRAGON ...
...SO I WANT TO LEARN HOW TO SEAL AND RELEASE MINE BY MYSELF.
BUT I'M NOT AS GOOD AT SORCERY AS I AM AT MARTIAL ARTS...
HEAVEN AND EARTH, SEND ME MY DRAGON...
OPEN THE DRAGON GATES HERE...
...MY HOLY DRAGON, SHIOU...

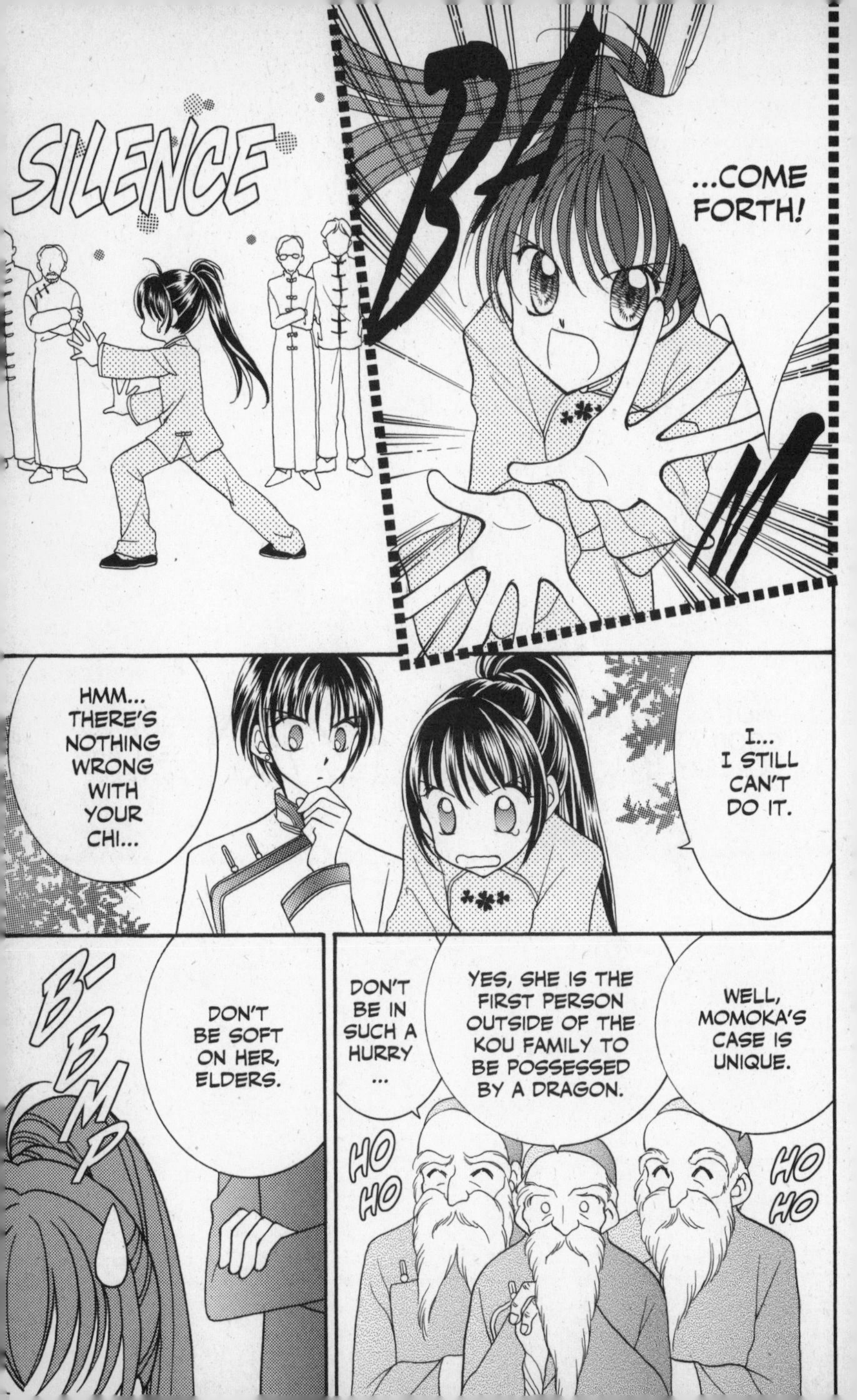
BAM
...COME FORTH!
SILENCE
I... I STILL CAN'T DO IT.
HMM... THERE'S NOTHING WRONG WITH YOUR CHI...
WELL, MOMOKA'S CASE IS UNIQUE.
YES, SHE IS THE FIRST PERSON OUTSIDE OF THE KOU FAMILY TO BE POSSESSED BY A DRAGON.
DON'T BE IN SUCH A HURRY ...
HO HO
HO HO
DON'T BE SOFT ON HER, ELDERS.
B-BMP

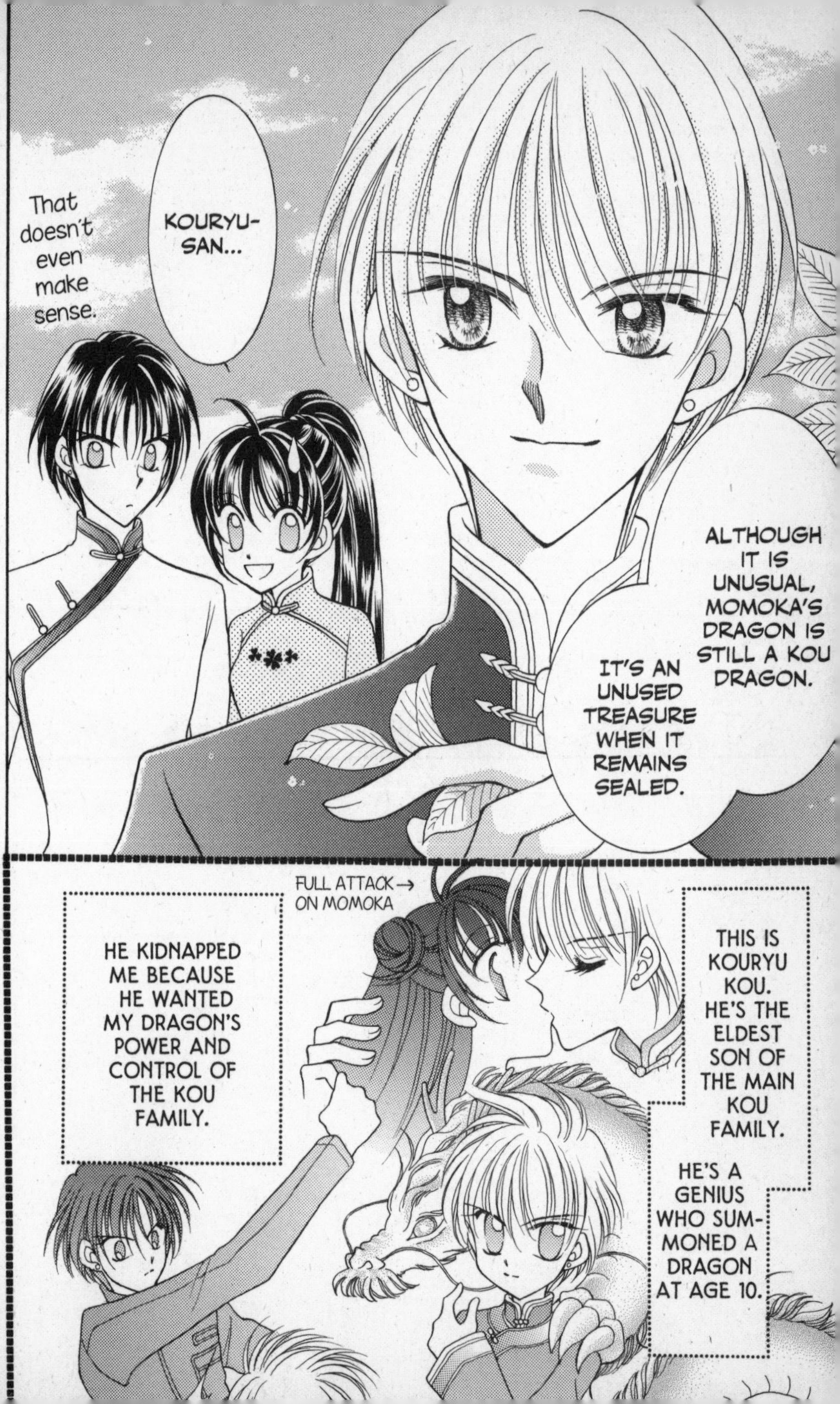
ALTHOUGH IT IS UNUSUAL, MOMOKA'S DRAGON IS STILL A KOU DRAGON.
IT'S AN UNUSED TREASURE WHEN IT REMAINS SEALED.
KOURYU-SAN...
That doesn't even make sense.
THIS IS KOURYU KOU. HE'S THE ELDEST SON OF THE MAIN KOU FAMILY.
FULL ATTACK → ON MOMOKA
HE KIDNAPPED ME BECAUSE HE WANTED MY DRAGON'S POWER AND CONTROL OF THE KOU FAMILY.
HE'S A GENIUS WHO SUMMONED A DRAGON AT AGE 10.

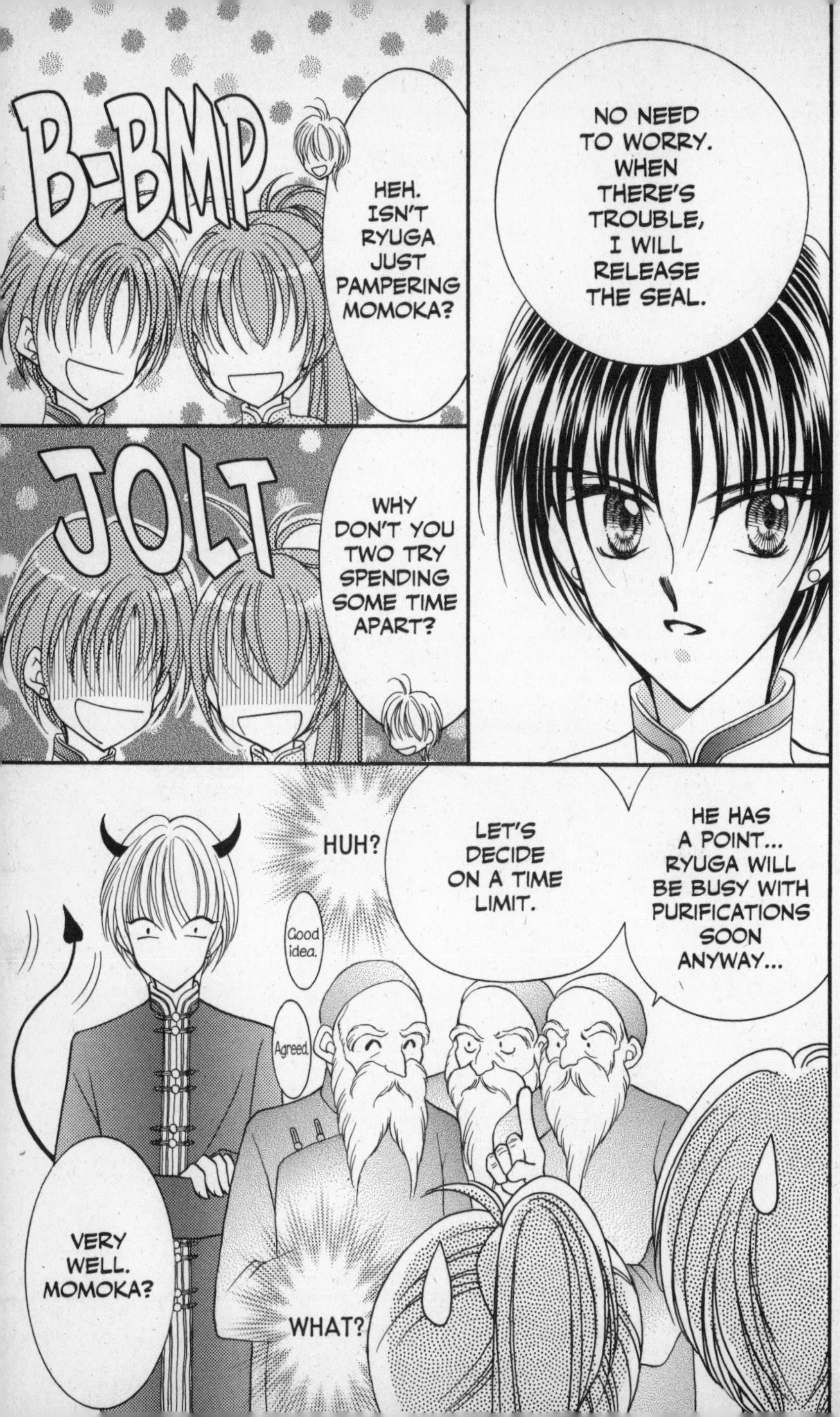
NO NEED TO WORRY. WHEN THERE'S TROUBLE, I WILL RELEASE THE SEAL.
B-BMP
HEH. ISN'T RYUGA JUST PAMPERING MOMOKA?
JOLT
WHY DON'T YOU TWO TRY SPENDING SOME TIME APART?
HE HAS A POINT... RYUGA WILL BE BUSY WITH PURIFICATIONS SOON ANYWAY...
LET'S DECIDE ON A TIME LIMIT.
HUH?
Good idea.
Agreed.
VERY WELL. MOMOKA?
WHAT?

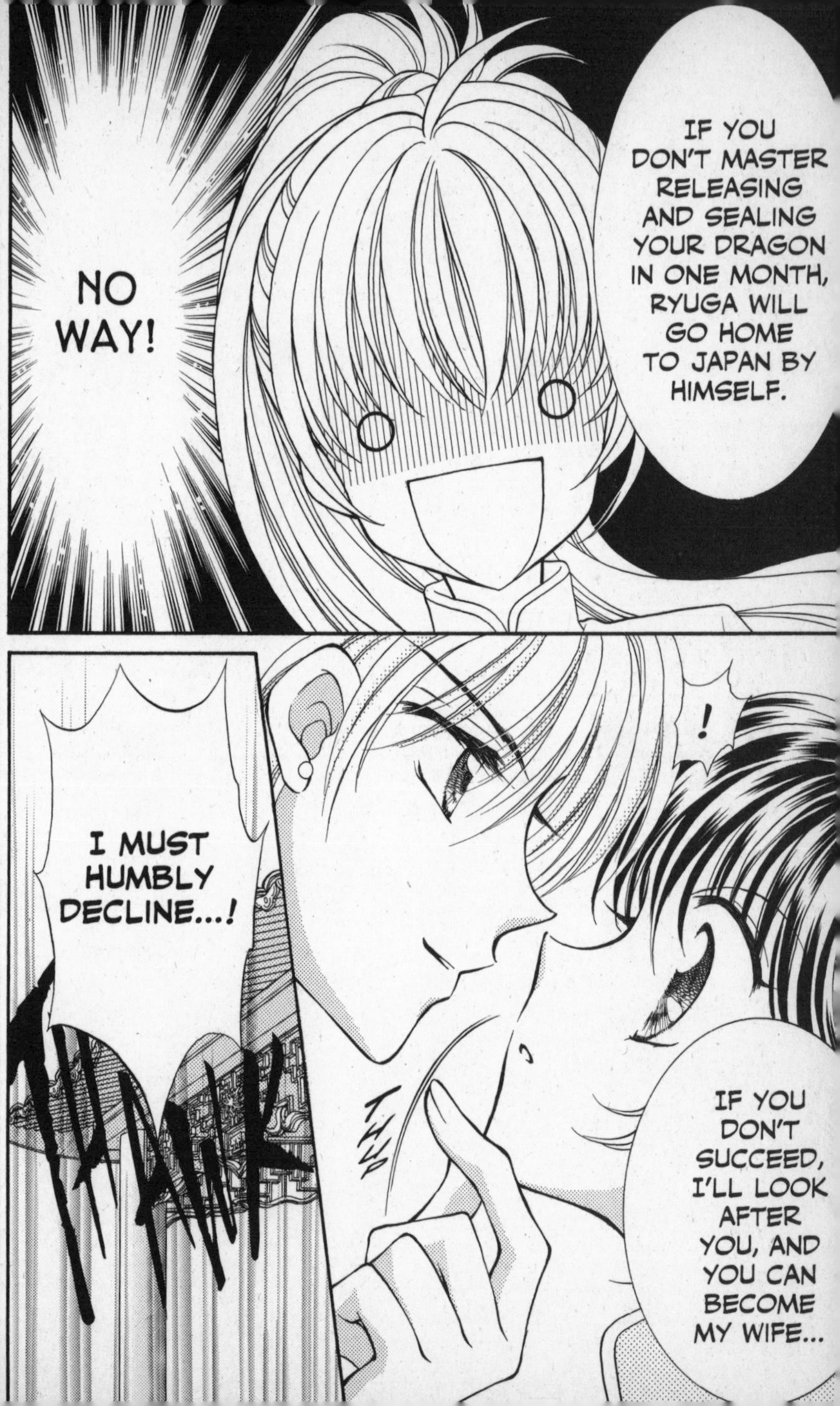
IF YOU DON'T MASTER RELEASING AND SEALING YOUR DRAGON IN ONE MONTH, RYUGA WILL GO HOME TO JAPAN BY HIMSELF.
NO WAY!
!
IF YOU DON'T SUCCEED, I'LL LOOK AFTER YOU, AND YOU CAN BECOME MY WIFE...
I MUST HUMBLY DECLINE...!

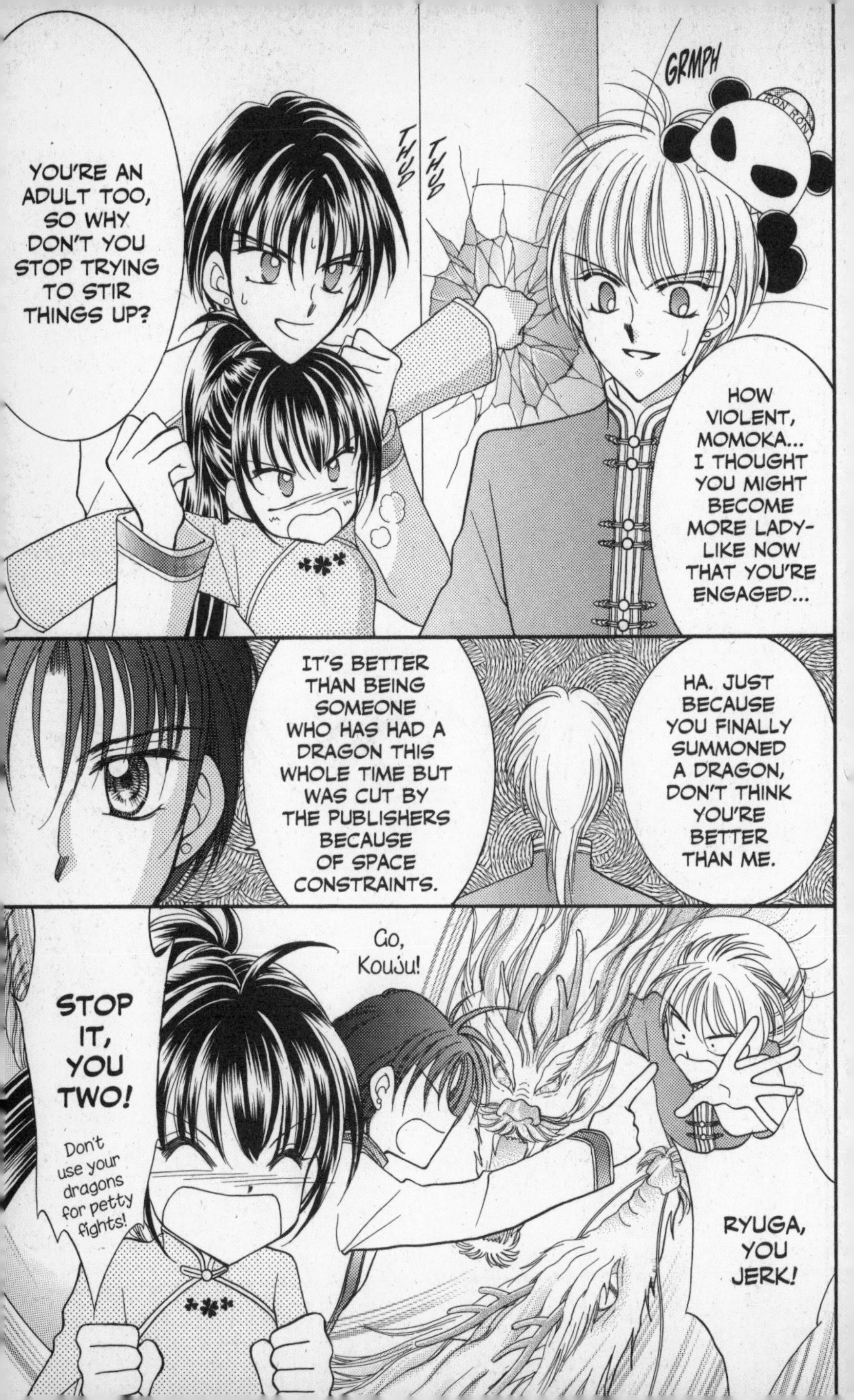
GRMPH
RON RON
HOW VIOLENT, MOMOKA... I THOUGHT YOU MIGHT BECOME MORE LADY-LIKE NOW THAT YOU'RE ENGAGED...
THUD THUD
YOU'RE AN ADULT TOO, SO WHY DON'T YOU STOP TRYING TO STIR THINGS UP?
HA. JUST BECAUSE YOU FINALLY SUMMONED A DRAGON, DON'T THINK YOU'RE BETTER THAN ME.
IT'S BETTER THAN BEING SOMEONE WHO HAS HAD A DRAGON THIS WHOLE TIME BUT WAS CUT BY THE PUBLISHERS BECAUSE OF SPACE CONSTRAINTS.
Go, Kouju!
RYUGA, YOU JERK!
STOP IT, YOU TWO!
Don't use your dragons for petty fights!

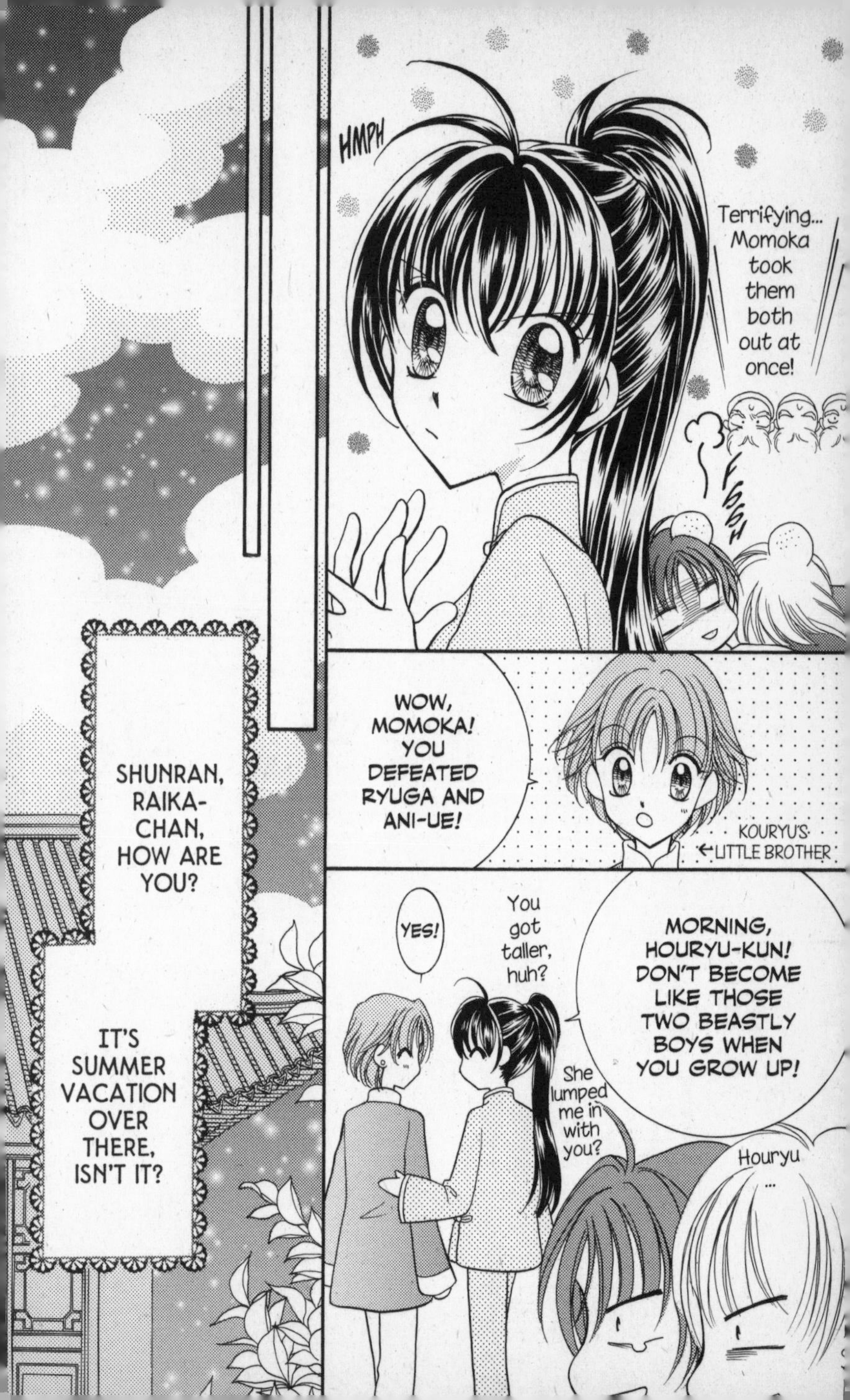

Terrifying... Momoka took them both out at once!
HMPH
WOW, MOMOKA! YOU DEFEATED RYUGA AND ANI-UE!
KOURYU'S LITTLE BROTHER
MORNING, HOURYU-KUN! DON'T BECOME LIKE THOSE TWO BEASTLY BOYS WHEN YOU GROW UP!
You got taller, huh?
YES!
She lumped me in with you?
Houryu ...
SHUNRAN, RAIKA-CHAN, HOW ARE YOU?
IT'S SUMMER VACATION OVER THERE, ISN'T IT?

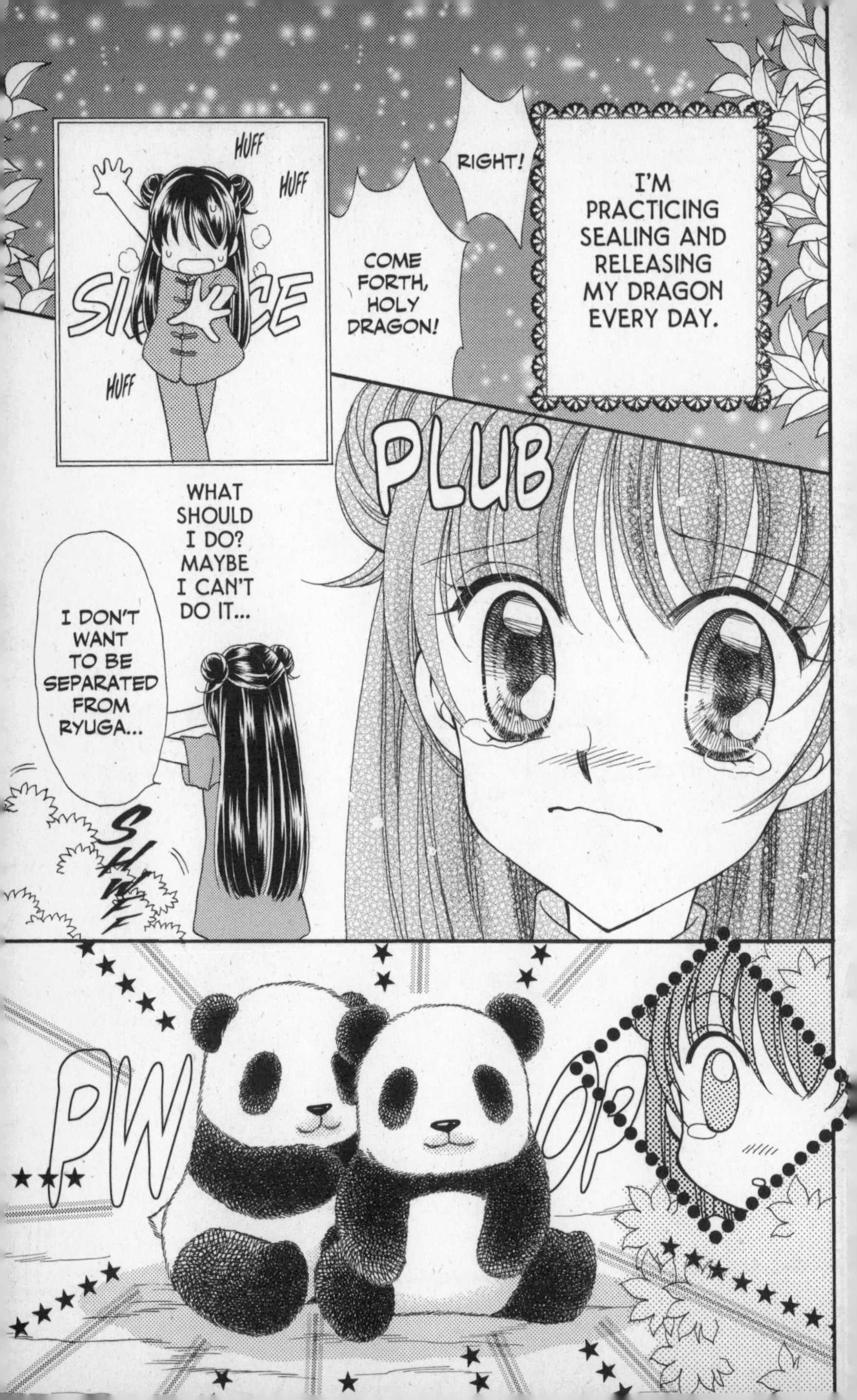
I'M PRACTICING SEALING AND RELEASING MY DRAGON EVERY DAY.
RIGHT!
COME FORTH, HOLY DRAGON!
HUFF
HUFF
HUFF
PLUB
WHAT SHOULD I DO? MAYBE I CAN'T DO IT...
I DON'T WANT TO BE SEPARATED FROM RYUGA...

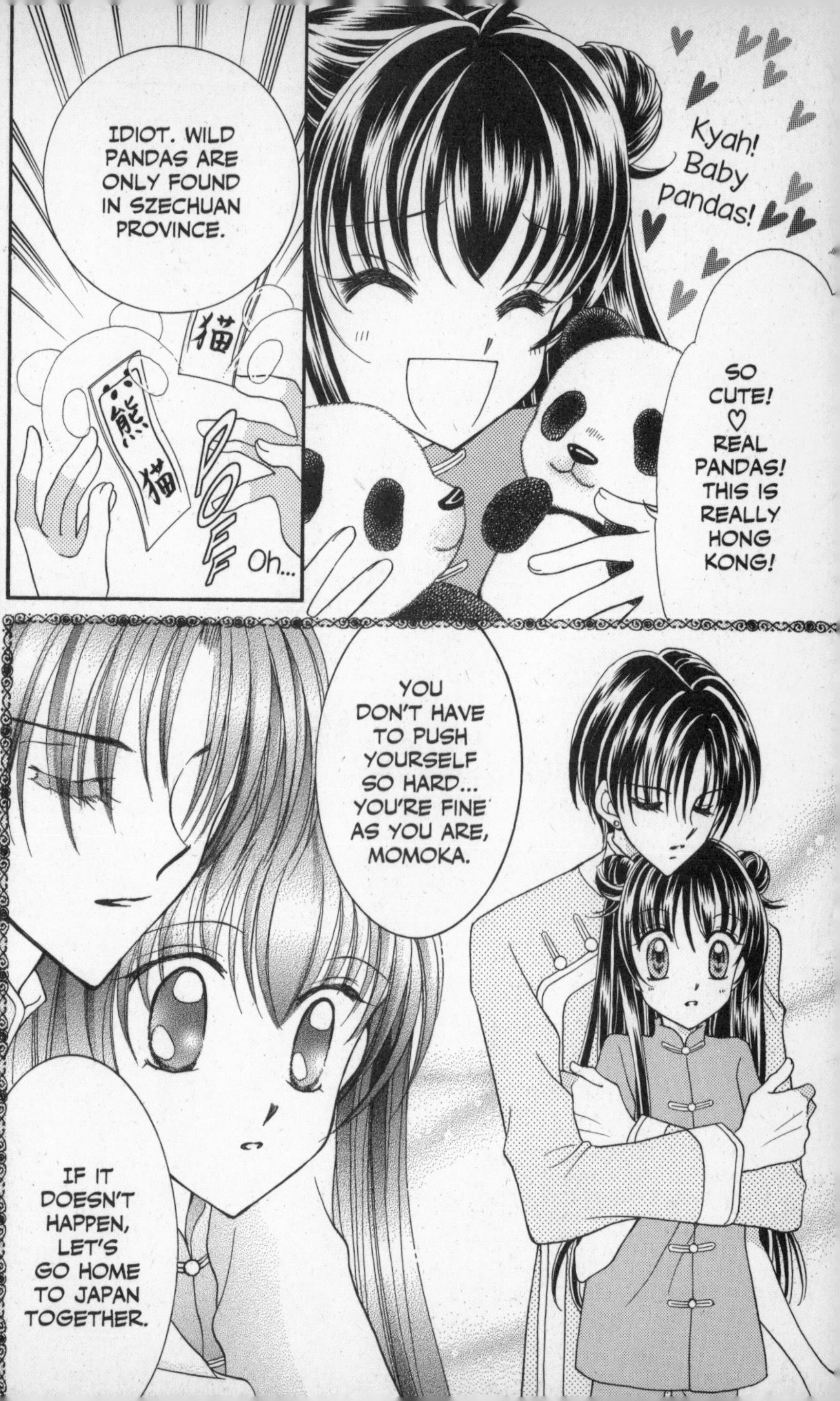
Kyah! Baby pandas!
SO CUTE! ♡ REAL PANDAS! THIS IS REALLY HONG KONG!
IDIOT. WILD PANDAS ARE ONLY FOUND IN SZECHUAN PROVINCE.
猫
熊猫
POFF
Oh...
YOU DON'T HAVE TO PUSH YOURSELF SO HARD... YOU'RE FINE AS YOU ARE, MOMOKA.
IF IT DOESN'T HAPPEN, LET'S GO HOME TO JAPAN TOGETHER.

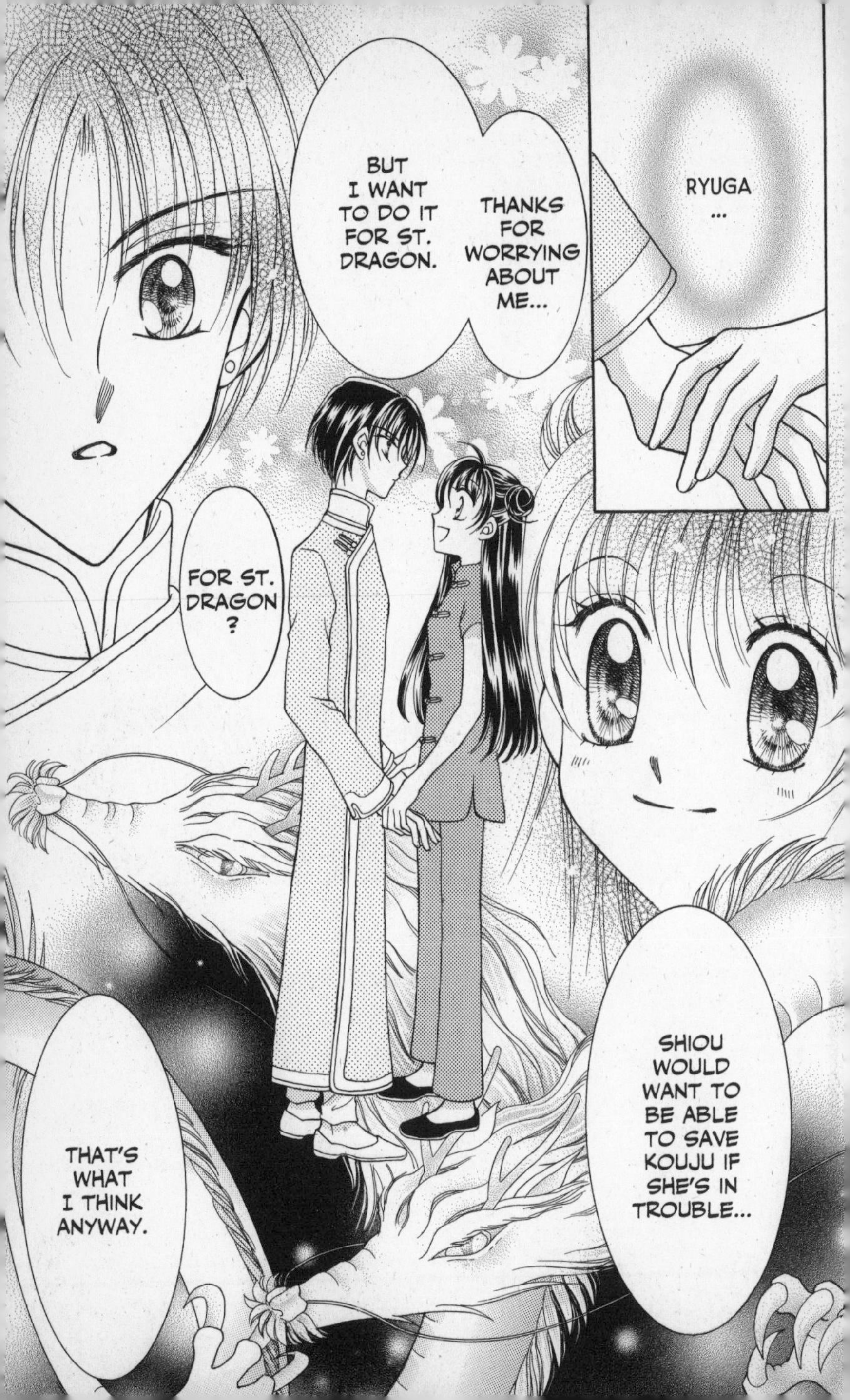
RYUGA ...
THANKS FOR WORRYING ABOUT ME...
BUT I WANT TO DO IT FOR ST. DRAGON.
FOR ST. DRAGON ?
SHIOU WOULD WANT TO BE ABLE TO SAVE KOUJU IF SHE'S IN TROUBLE...
THAT'S WHAT I THINK ANYWAY.

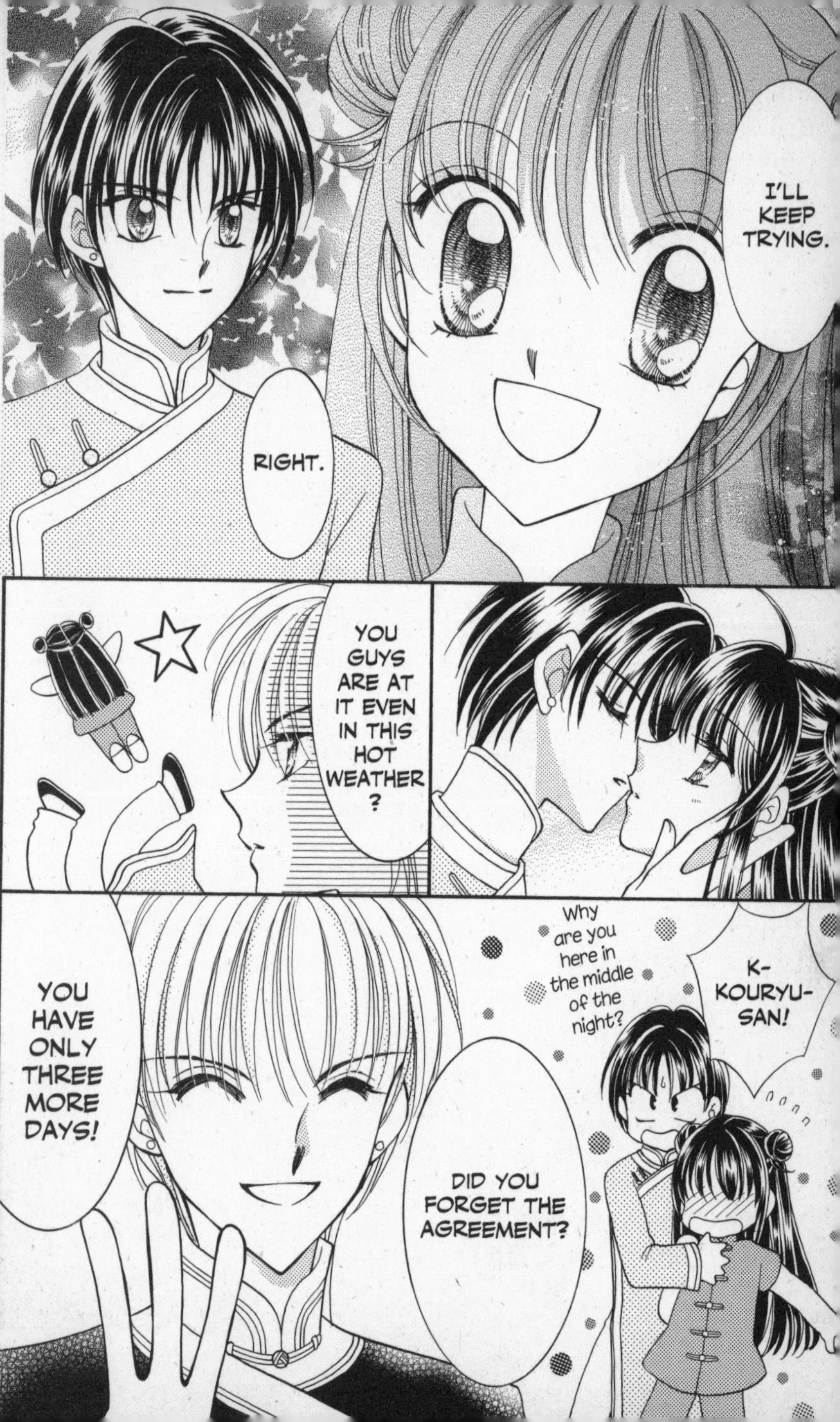
I'LL KEEP TRYING.
RIGHT.
YOU GUYS ARE AT IT EVEN IN THIS HOT WEATHER?
K-KOURYU-SAN!
Why are you here in the middle of the night?
DID YOU FORGET THE AGREEMENT?
YOU HAVE ONLY THREE MORE DAYS!

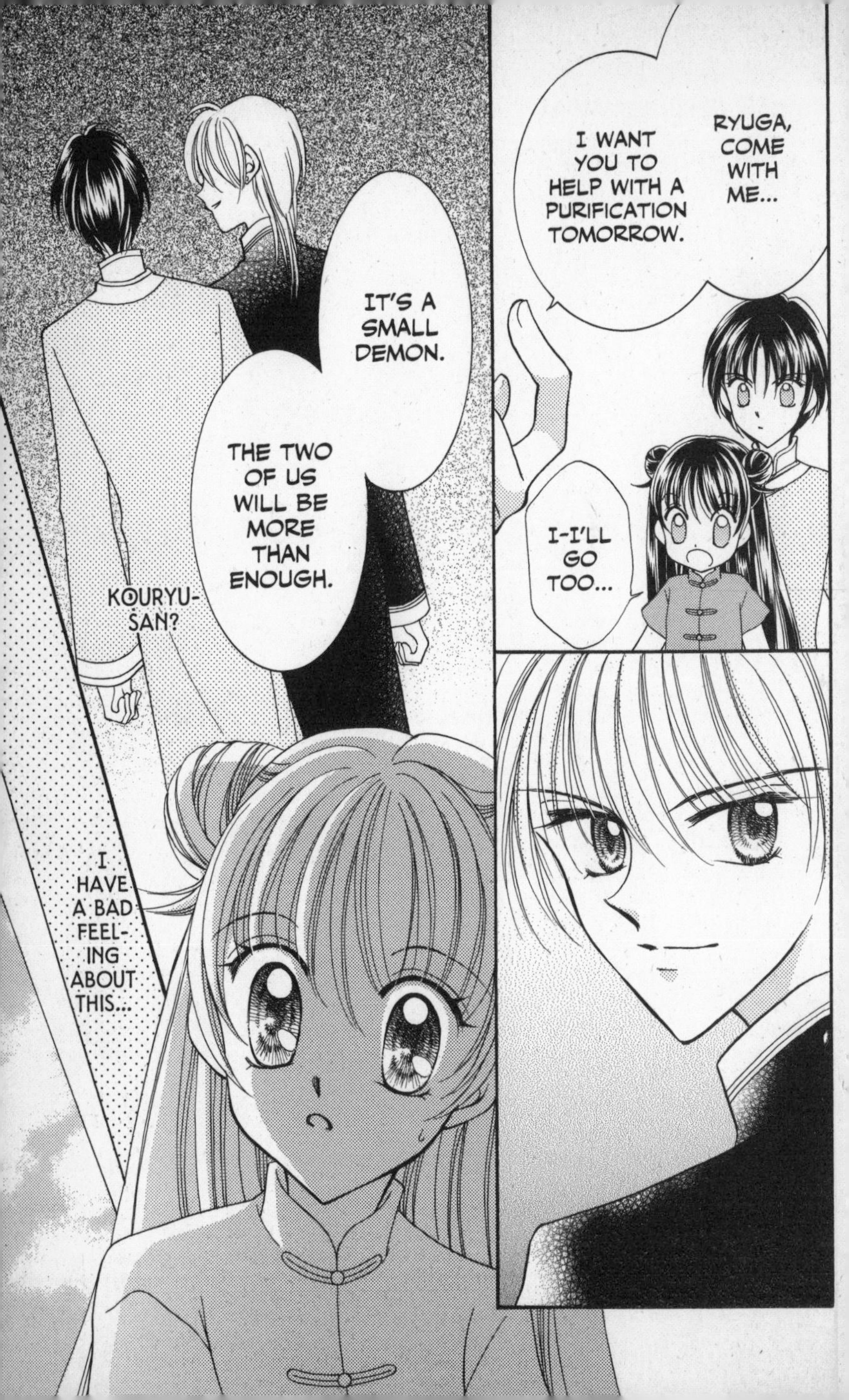
RYUGA, COME WITH ME...
I WANT YOU TO HELP WITH A PURIFICATION TOMORROW.
I-I'LL GO TOO...
IT'S A SMALL DEMON.
THE TWO OF US WILL BE MORE THAN ENOUGH.
KOURYU-SAN?
I HAVE A BAD FEEL-ING ABOUT THIS...

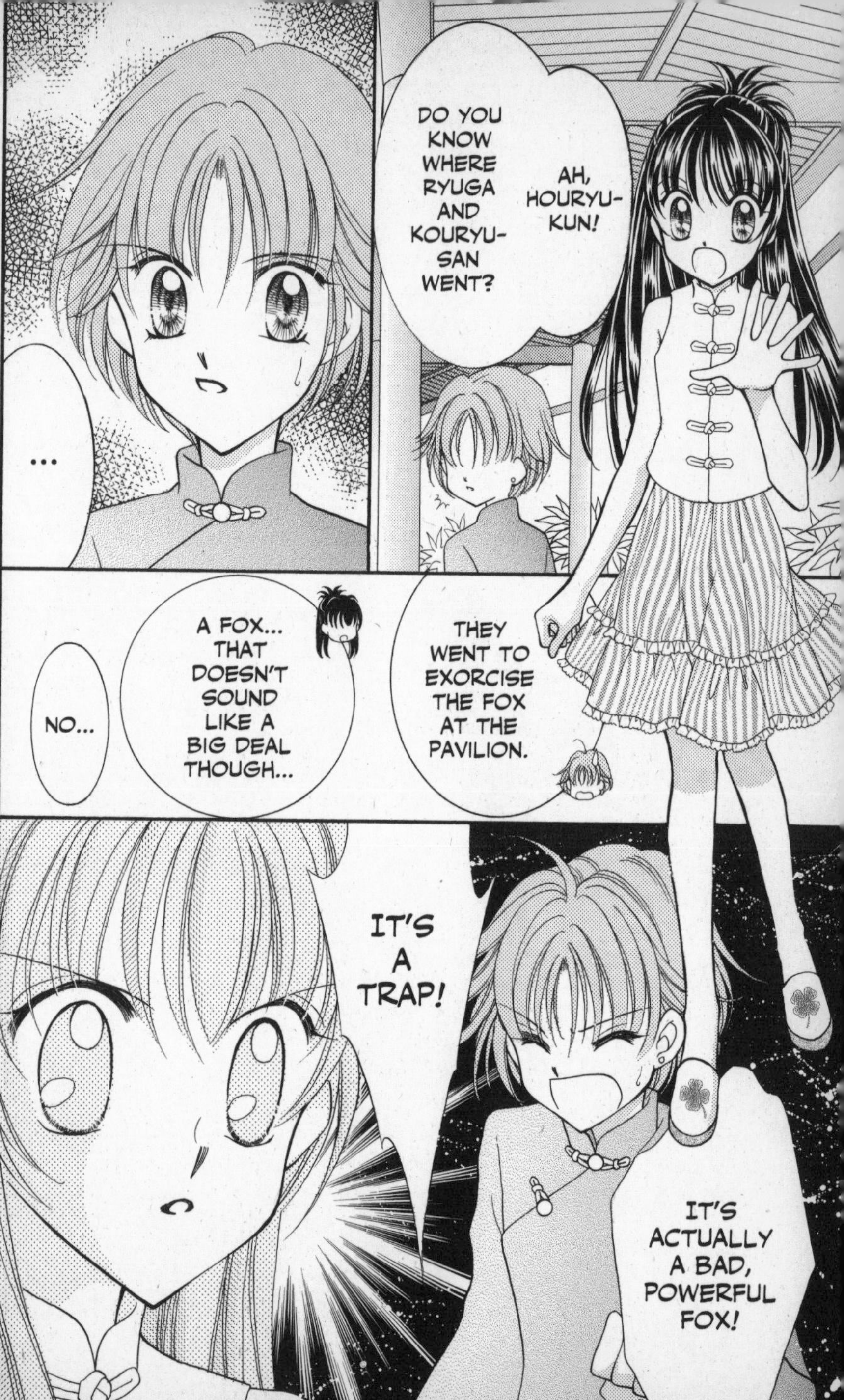
AH, HOURYU-KUN!
DO YOU KNOW WHERE RYUGA AND KOURYU-SAN WENT?
...
THEY WENT TO EXORCISE THE FOX AT THE PAVILION.
A FOX... THAT DOESN'T SOUND LIKE A BIG DEAL THOUGH...
NO...
IT'S ACTUALLY A BAD, POWERFUL FOX!
IT'S A TRAP!

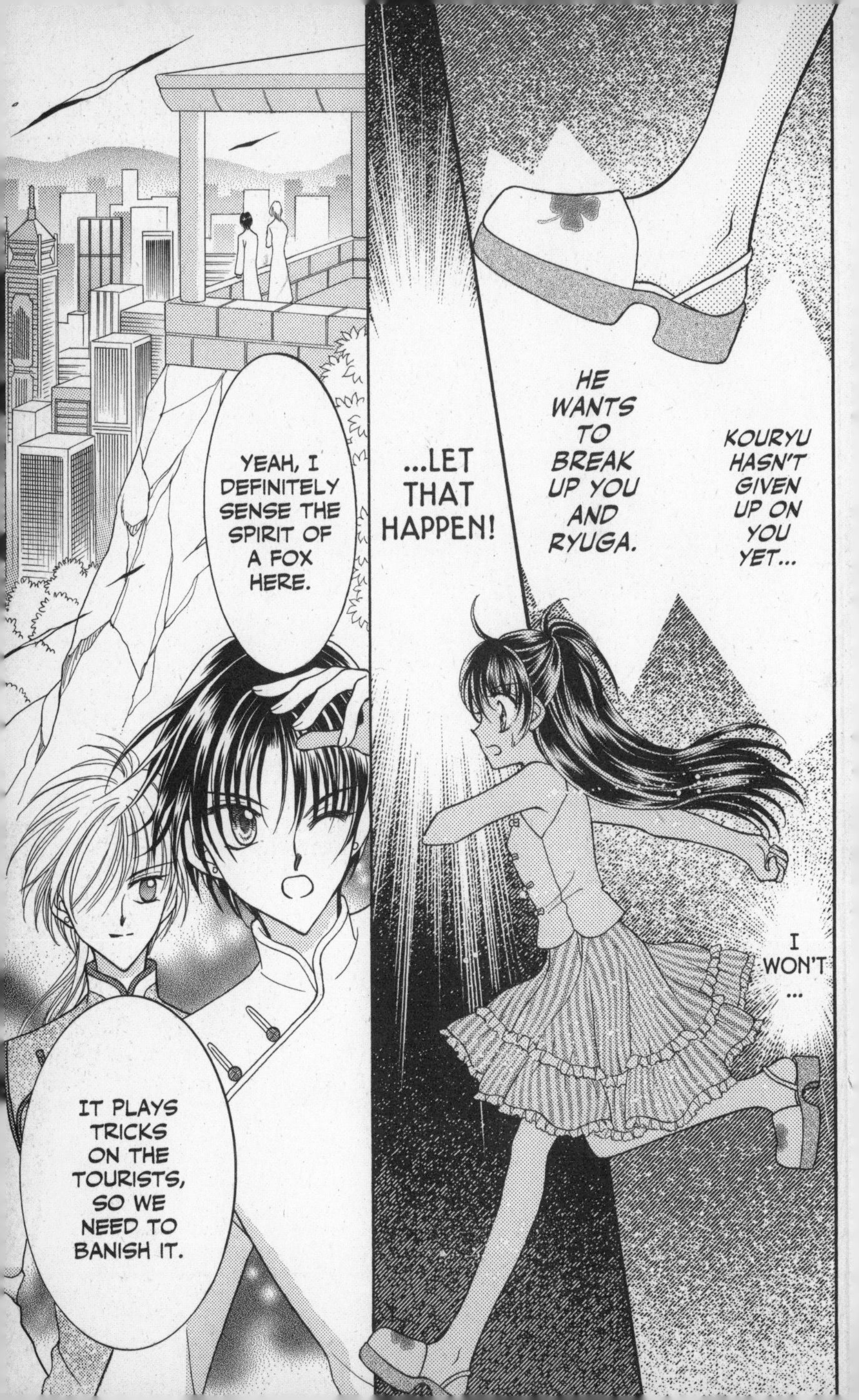
KOURYU HASN'T GIVEN UP ON YOU YET...
HE WANTS TO BREAK UP YOU AND RYUGA.
I WON'T ...
...LET THAT HAPPEN!
YEAH, I DEFINITELY SENSE THE SPIRIT OF A FOX HERE.
IT PLAYS TRICKS ON THE TOURISTS, SO WE NEED TO BANISH IT.

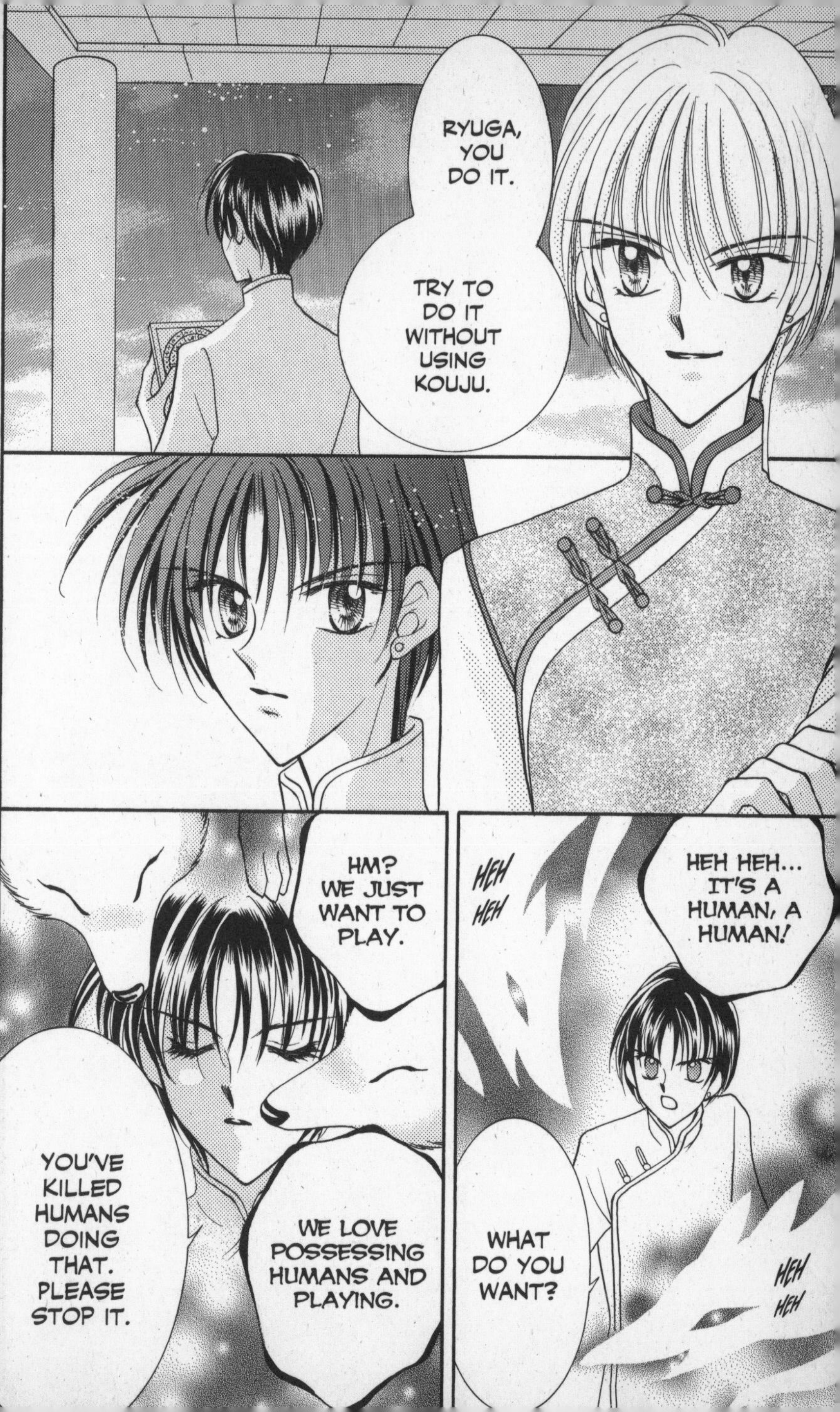
RYUGA, YOU DO IT.
TRY TO DO IT WITHOUT USING KOUJU.
HEH HEH... IT'S A HUMAN, A HUMAN!
HEH HEH
HEH HEH
WHAT DO YOU WANT?
HM? WE JUST WANT TO PLAY.
WE LOVE POSSESSING HUMANS AND PLAYING.
YOU'VE KILLED HUMANS DOING THAT. PLEASE STOP IT.

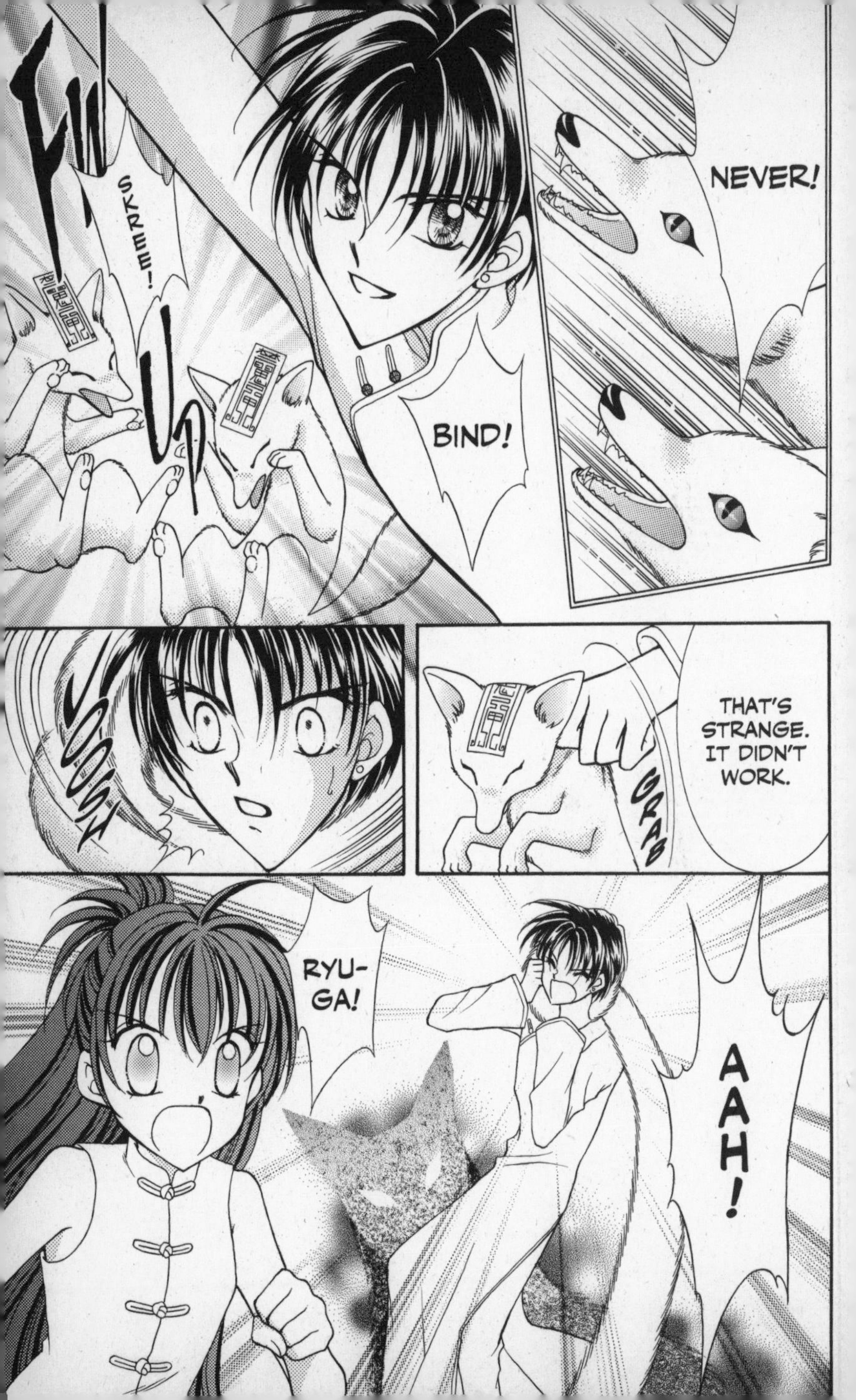
NEVER!
BIND!
SKREE!
THAT'S STRANGE. IT DIDN'T WORK.
GRAB
AAH!
RYU-GA!

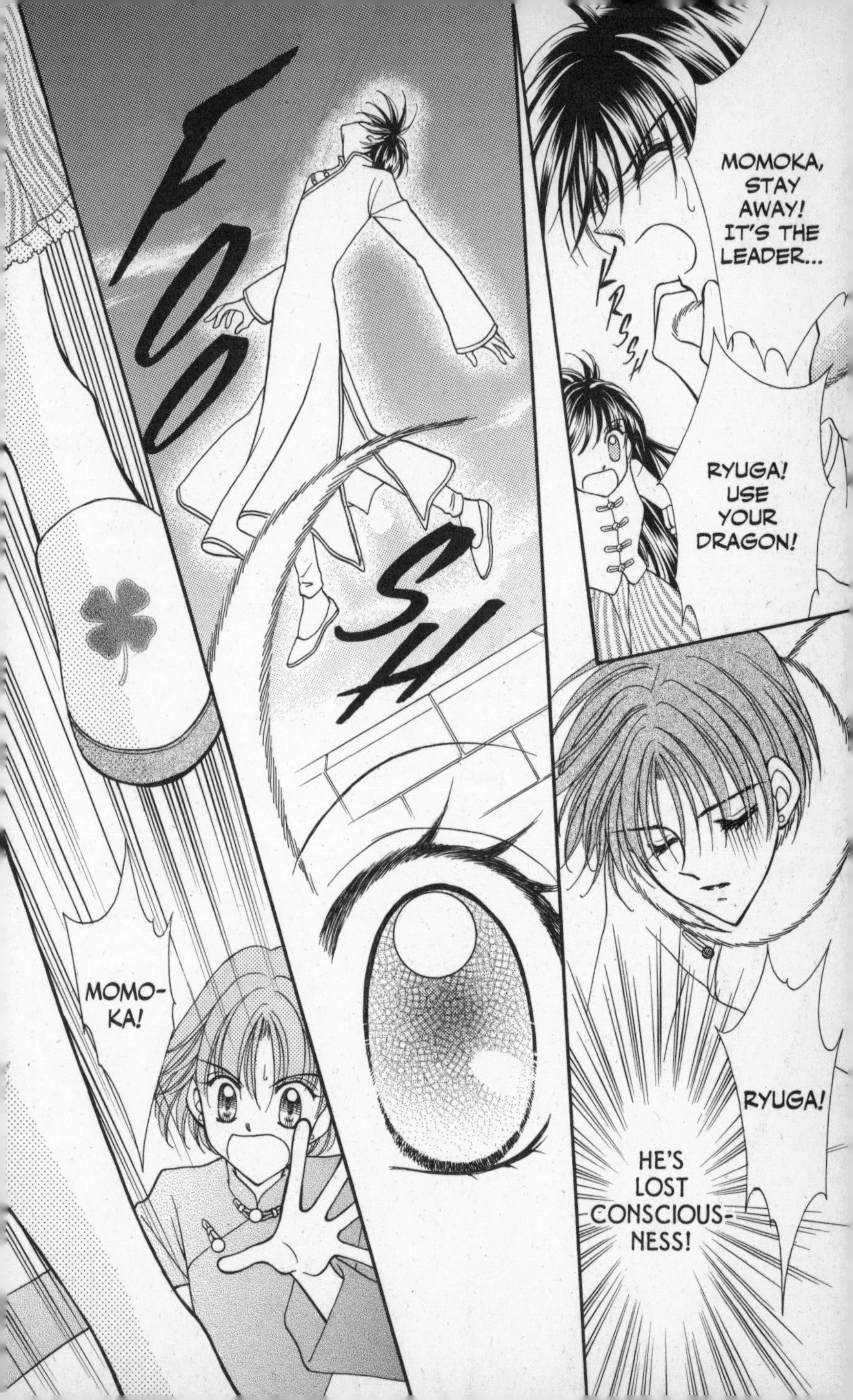
MOMOKA, STAY AWAY! IT'S THE LEADER...
KRSSH
RYUGA! USE YOUR DRAGON!
RYUGA!
HE'S LOST CONSCIOUS-NESS!
SH
MOMO-KA!

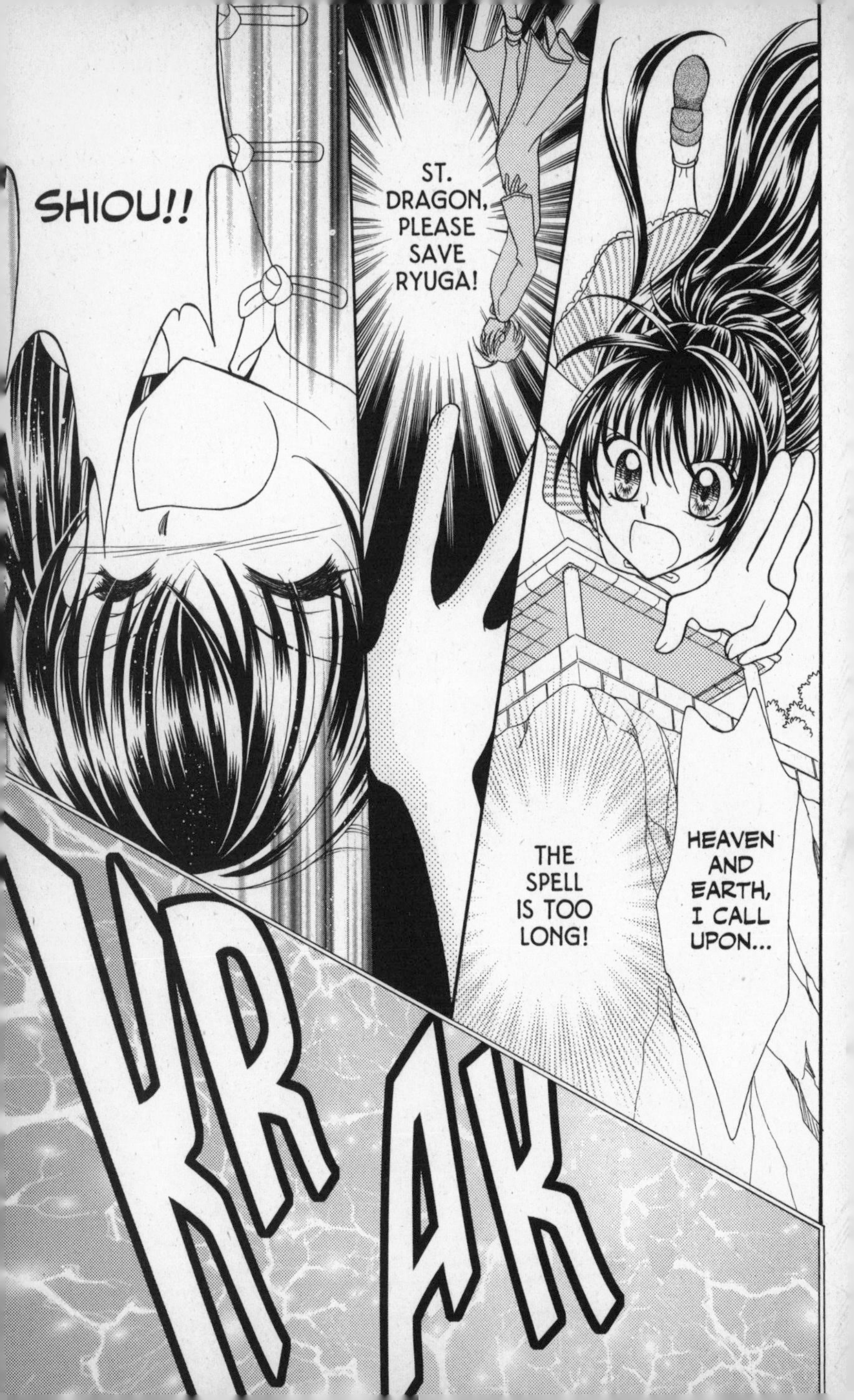
HEAVEN AND EARTH, I CALL UPON...
THE SPELL IS TOO LONG!
ST. DRAGON, PLEASE SAVE RYUGA!
SHIOU!!
KRAK

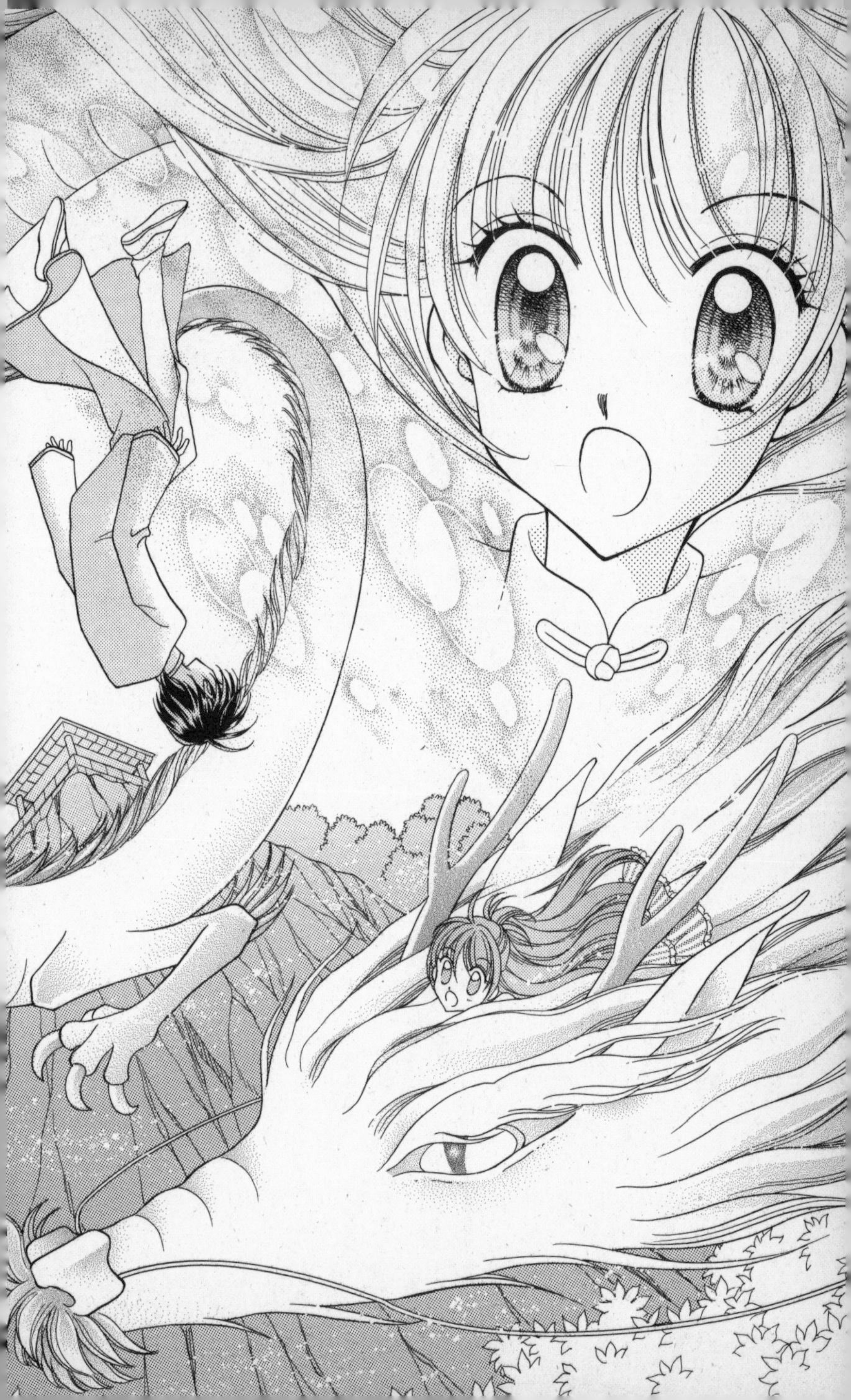

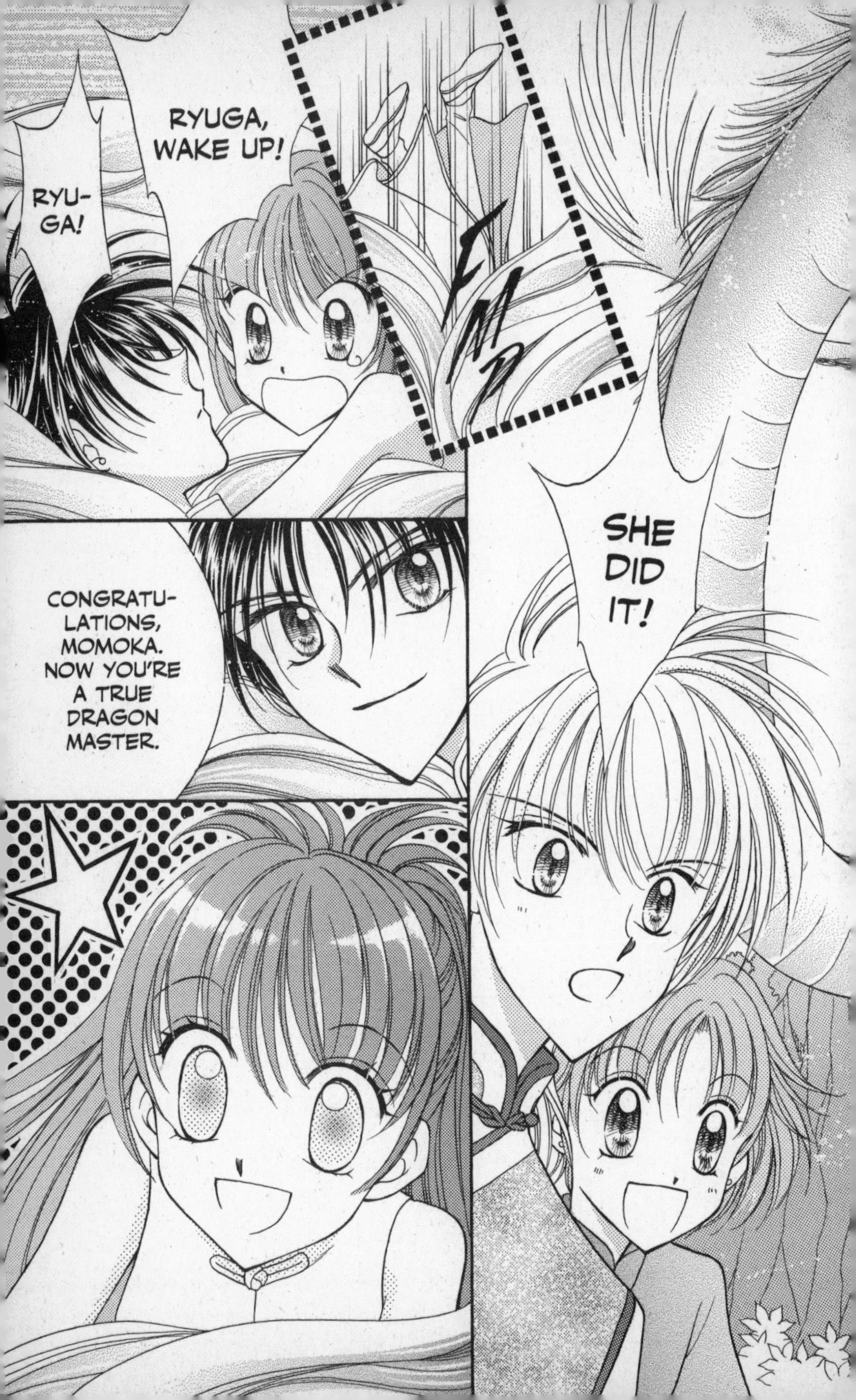

RYUGA, WAKE UP!
RYU-GA!
SHE DID IT!
CONGRATU-LATIONS, MOMOKA. NOW YOU'RE A TRUE DRAGON MASTER.

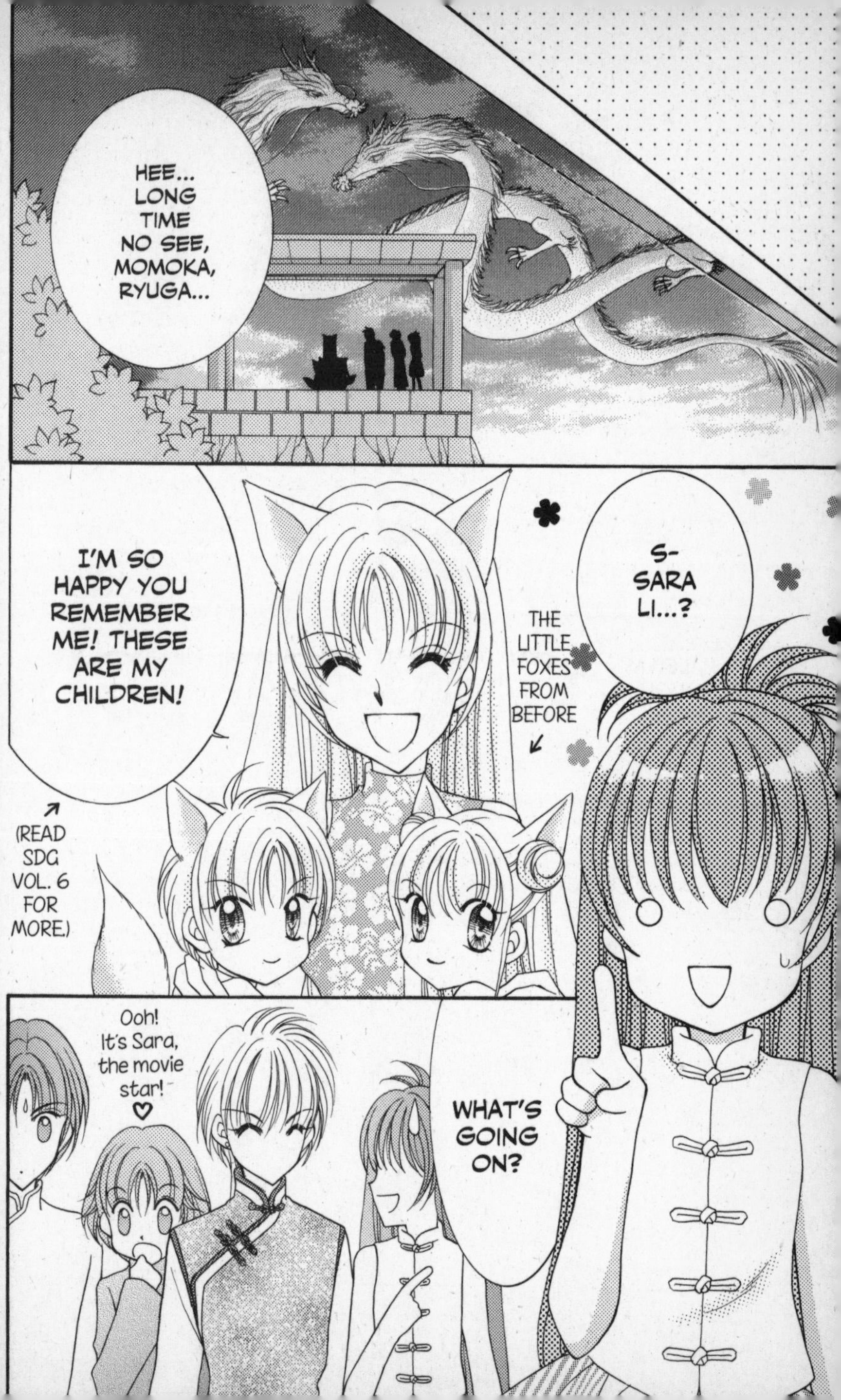
HEE... LONG TIME NO SEE, MOMOKA, RYUGA...
S-SARA LI...?
THE LITTLE FOXES FROM BEFORE
I'M SO HAPPY YOU REMEMBER ME! THESE ARE MY CHILDREN!
(READ SDG VOL. 6 FOR MORE.)
WHAT'S GOING ON?
Ooh! It's Sara, the movie star! ♡

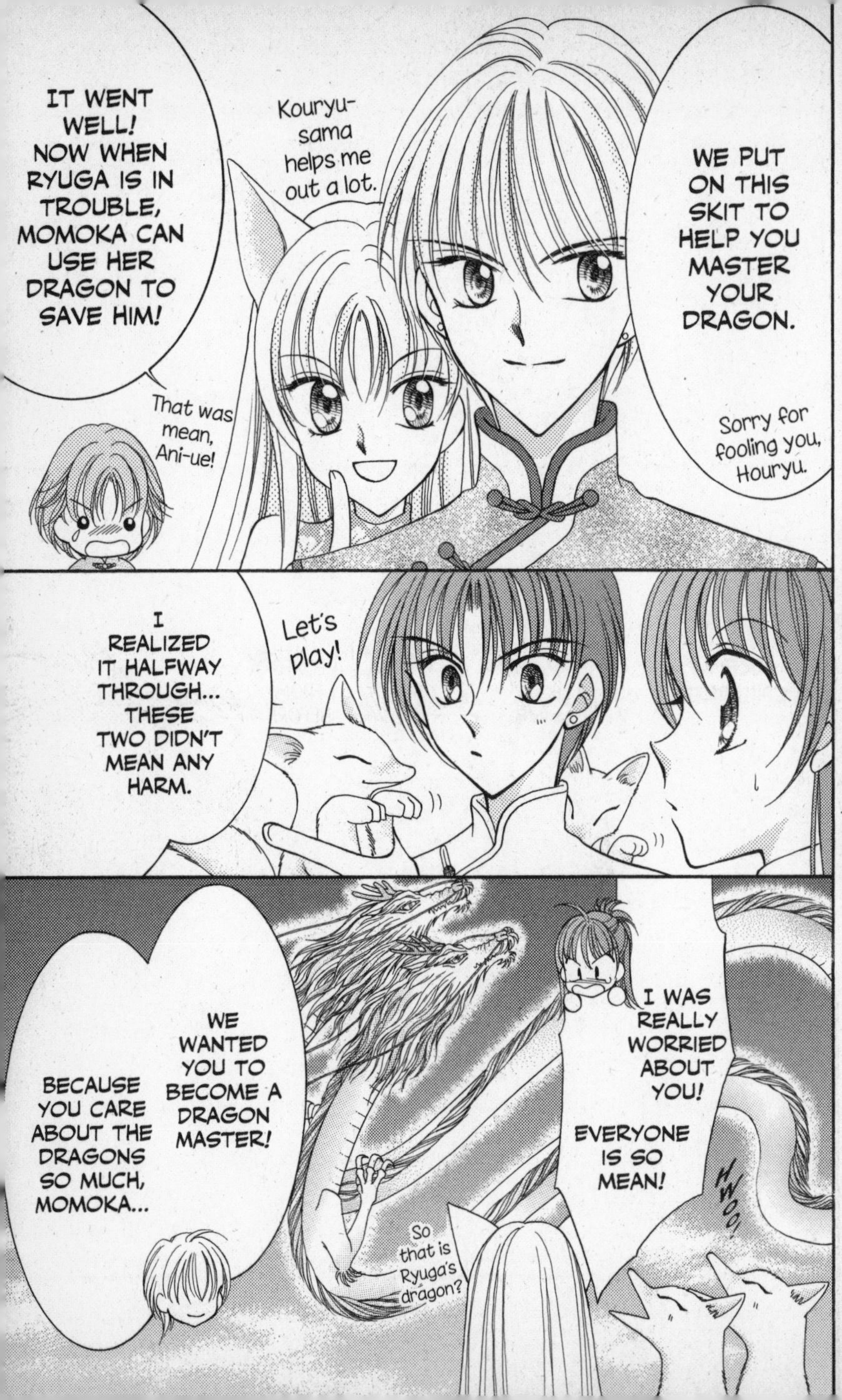
WE PUT ON THIS SKIT TO HELP YOU MASTER YOUR DRAGON.
Sorry for fooling you, Houryu.
Kouryu-sama helps me out a lot.
IT WENT WELL! NOW WHEN RYUGA IS IN TROUBLE, MOMOKA CAN USE HER DRAGON TO SAVE HIM!
That was mean, Ani-ue!
Let's play!
I REALIZED IT HALFWAY THROUGH... THESE TWO DIDN'T MEAN ANY HARM.
I WAS REALLY WORRIED ABOUT YOU!
EVERYONE IS SO MEAN!
HWOO!
So that is Ryuga's dragon?
WE WANTED YOU TO BECOME A DRAGON MASTER!
BECAUSE YOU CARE ABOUT THE DRAGONS SO MUCH, MOMOKA...

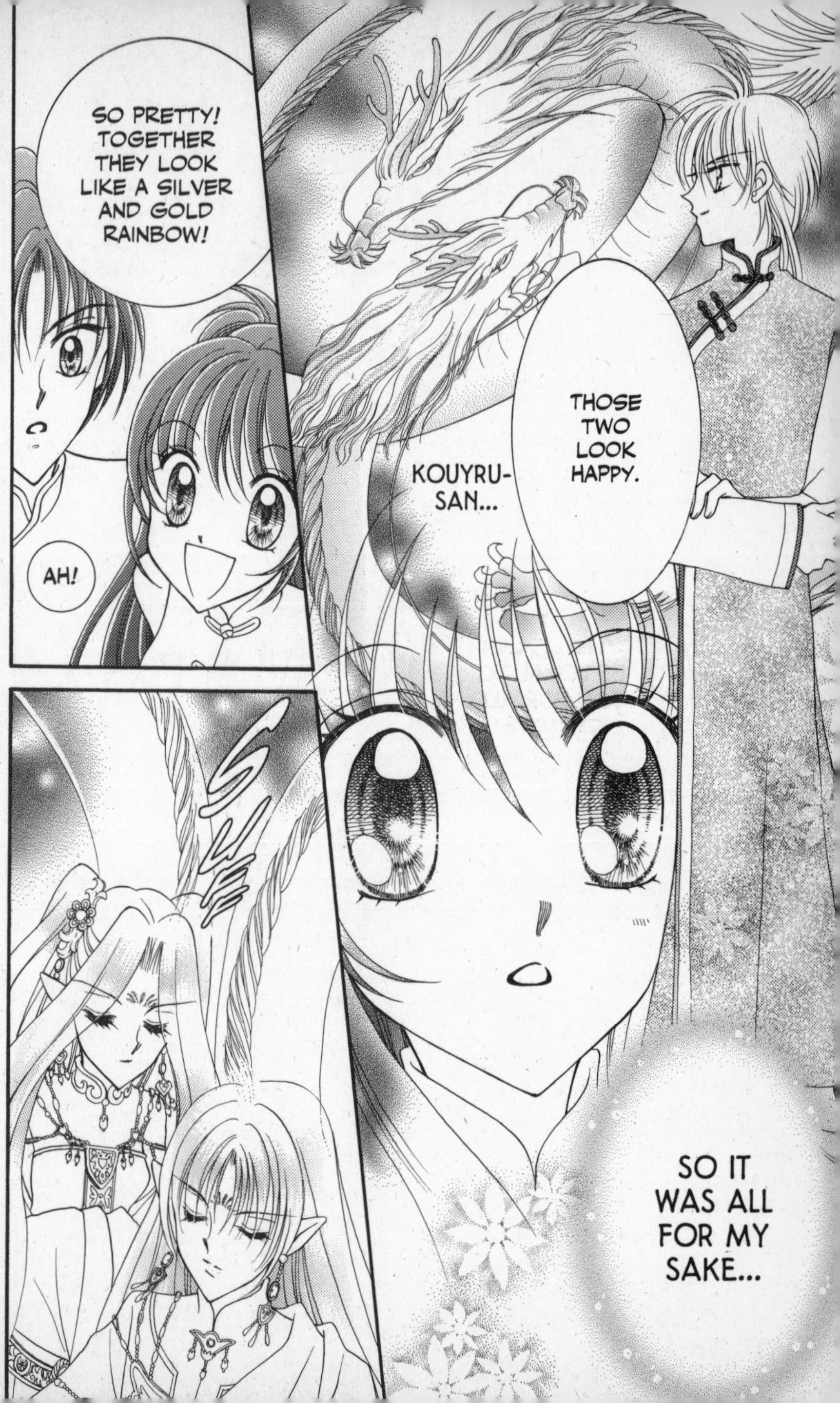
THOSE TWO LOOK HAPPY.
KOUYRU-SAN...
SO IT WAS ALL FOR MY SAKE...
SO PRETTY! TOGETHER THEY LOOK LIKE A SILVER AND GOLD RAINBOW!
AH!

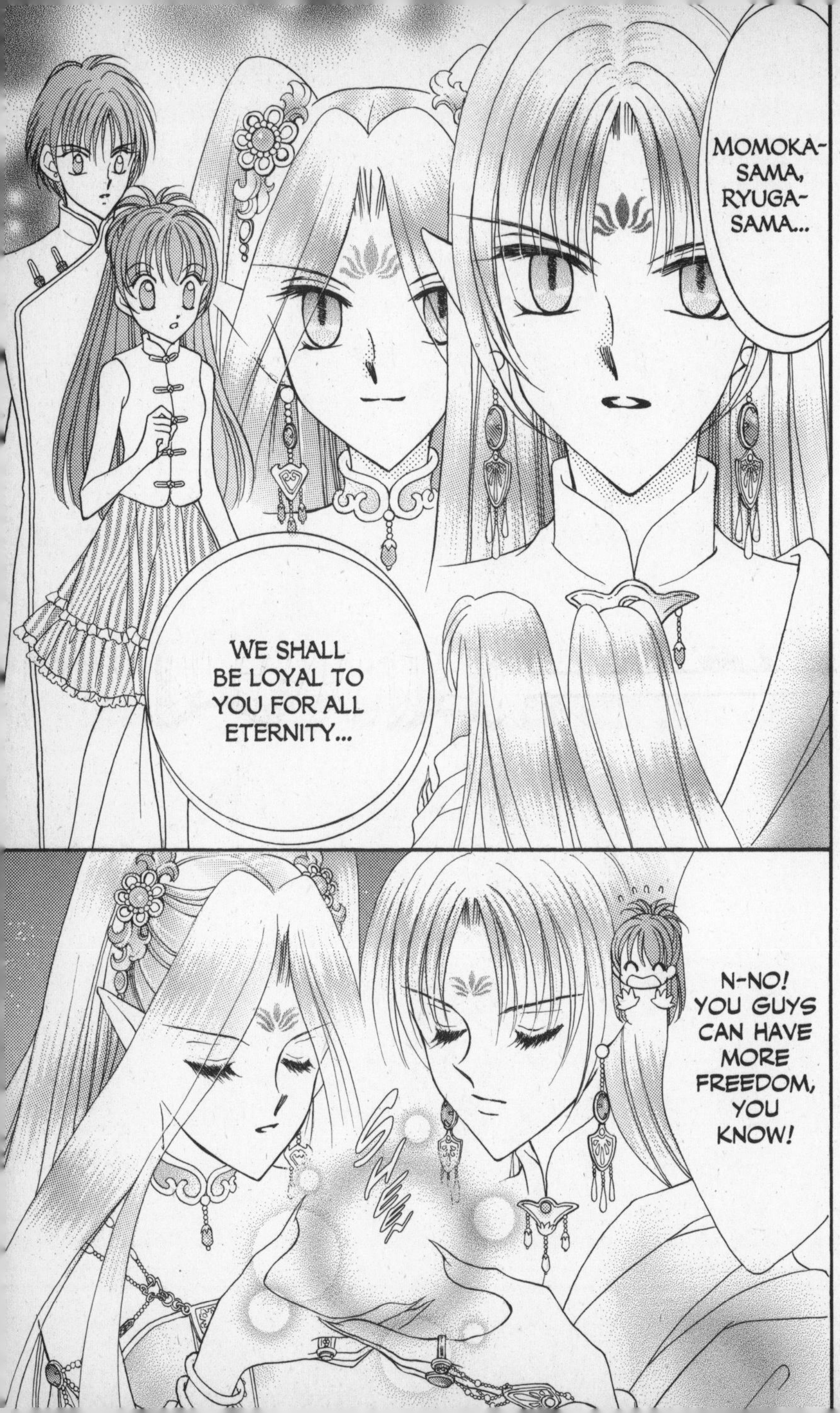
MOMOKA-SAMA, RYUGA-SAMA...
WE SHALL BE LOYAL TO YOU FOR ALL ETERNITY...
N-NO! YOU GUYS CAN HAVE MORE FREEDOM, YOU KNOW!
SHWAH

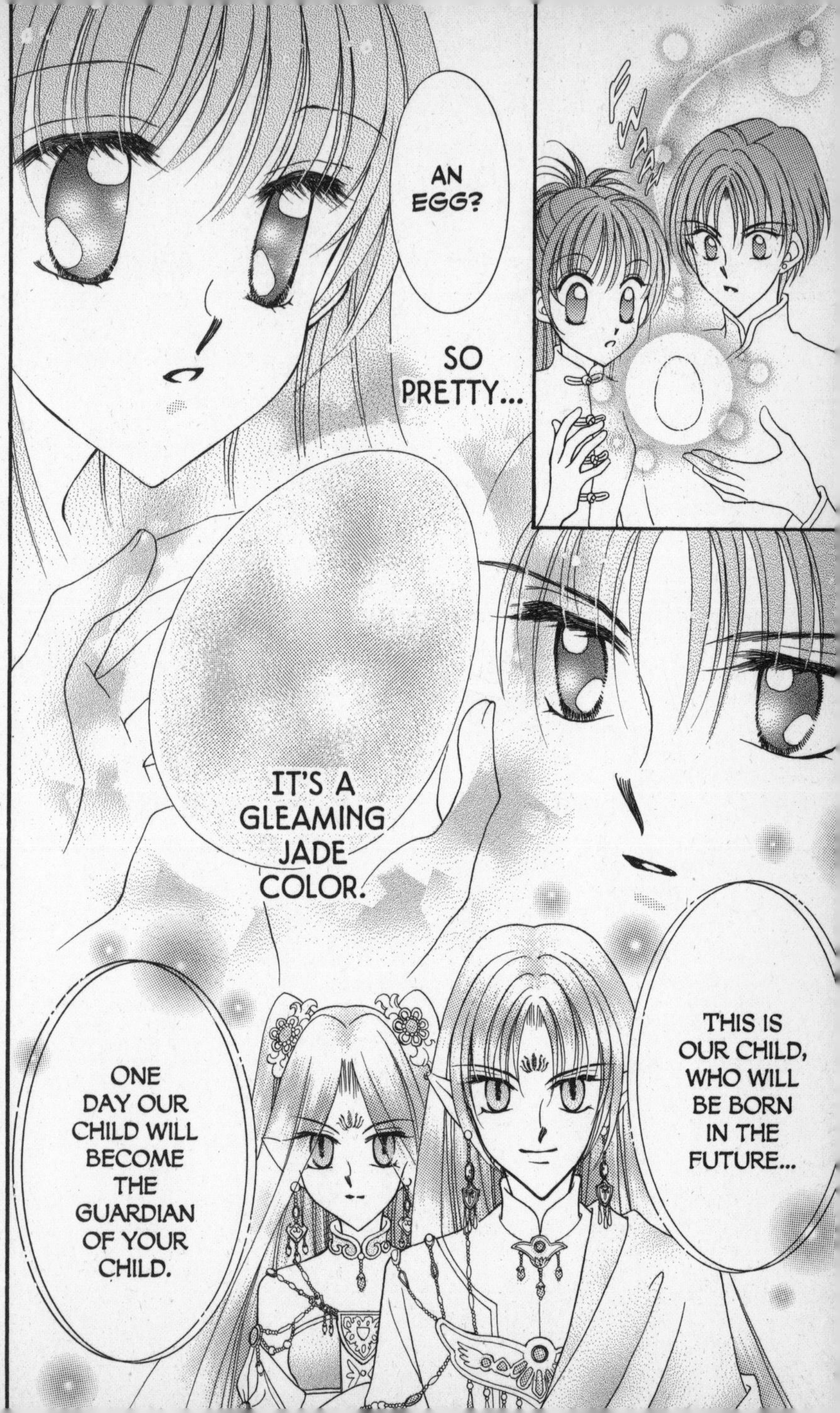
FWAAH
AN EGG?
SO PRETTY...
IT'S A GLEAMING JADE COLOR.
THIS IS OUR CHILD, WHO WILL BE BORN IN THE FUTURE...
ONE DAY OUR CHILD WILL BECOME THE GUARDIAN OF YOUR CHILD.

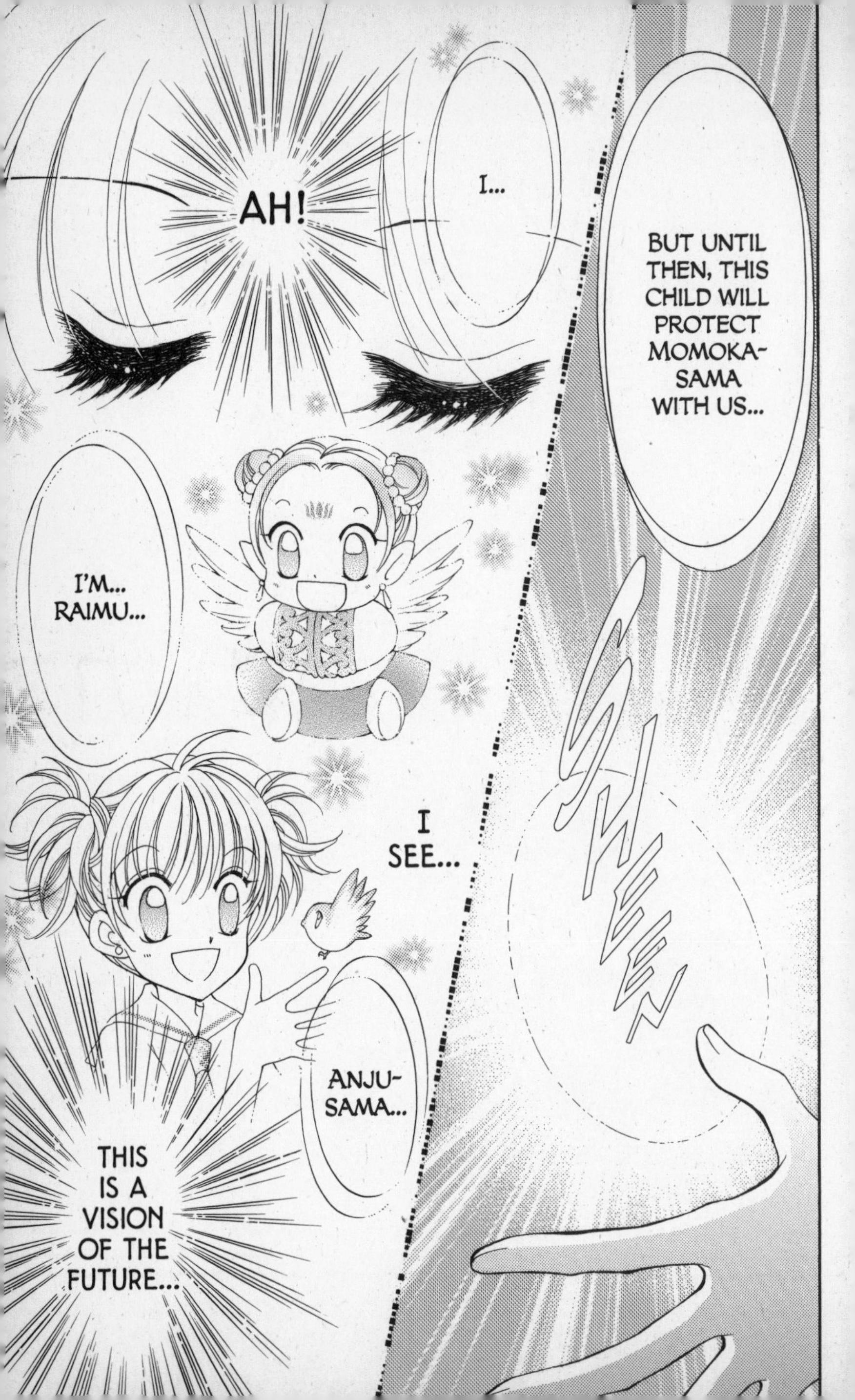
BUT UNTIL THEN, THIS CHILD WILL PROTECT MOMOKA-SAMA WITH US...
I...
AH!
I'M... RAIMU...
I SEE...
ANJU-SAMA...
THIS IS A VISION OF THE FUTURE...

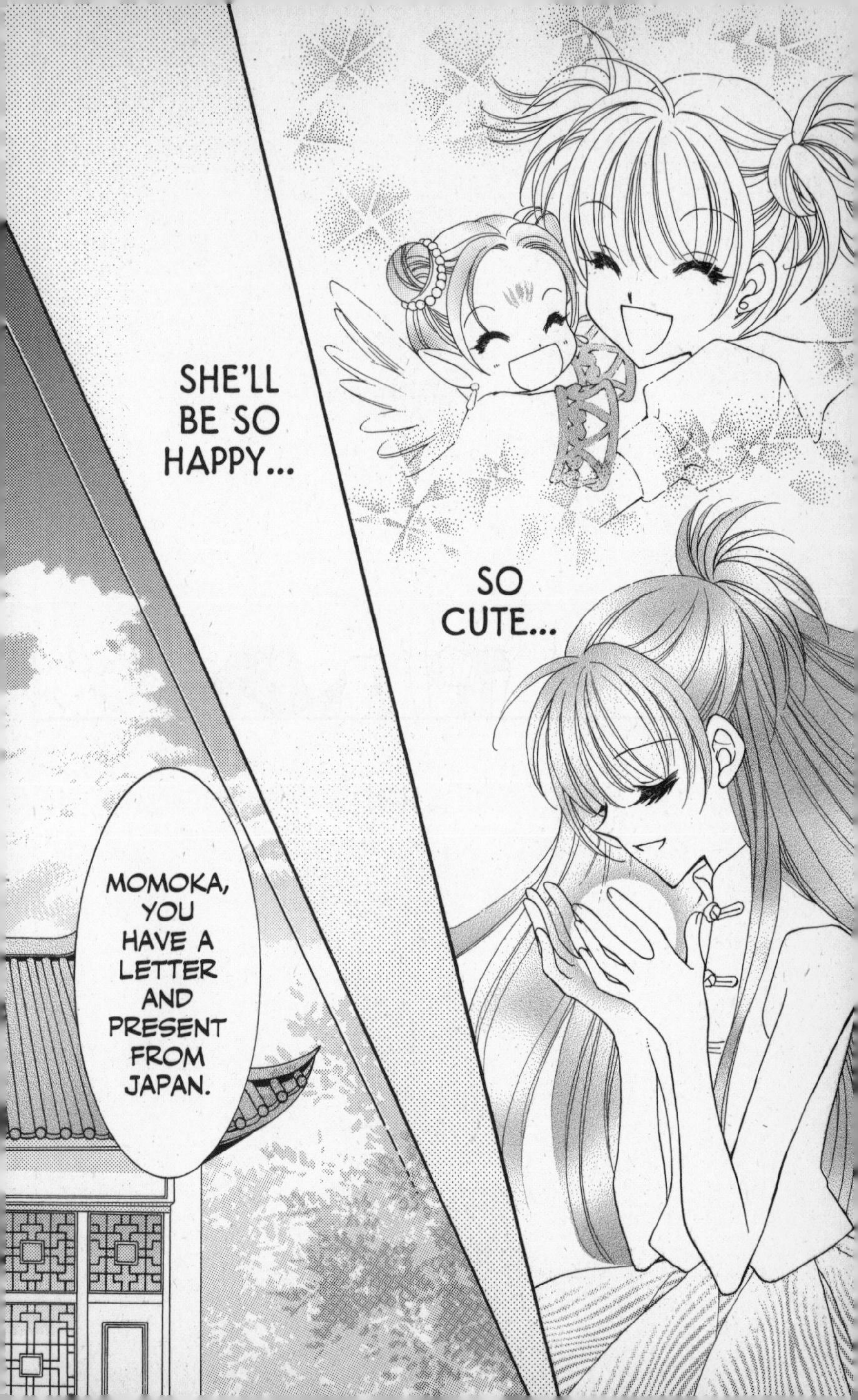
SO CUTE...
SHE'LL BE SO HAPPY...
MOMOKA, YOU HAVE A LETTER AND PRESENT FROM JAPAN.

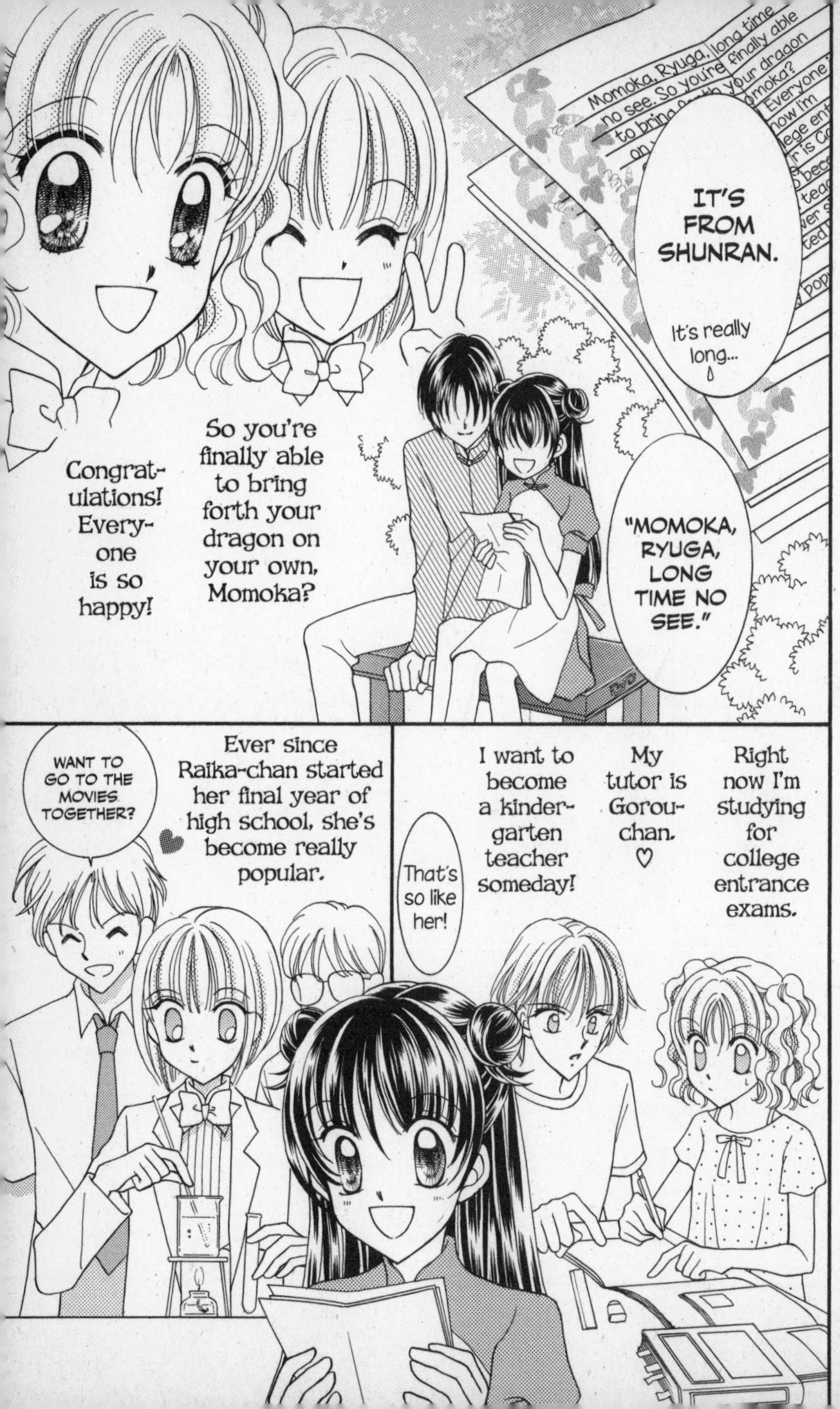
IT'S FROM SHUNRAN.
It's really long...
"MOMOKA, RYUGA, LONG TIME NO SEE."
So you're finally able to bring forth your dragon on your own, Momoka?
Congratulations! Everyone is so happy!
Right now I'm studying for college entrance exams.
My tutor is Gorou-chan. ♡
I want to become a kindergarten teacher someday!
That's so like her!
Ever since Raika-chan started her final year of high school, she's become really popular.
WANT TO GO TO THE MOVIES TOGETHER?

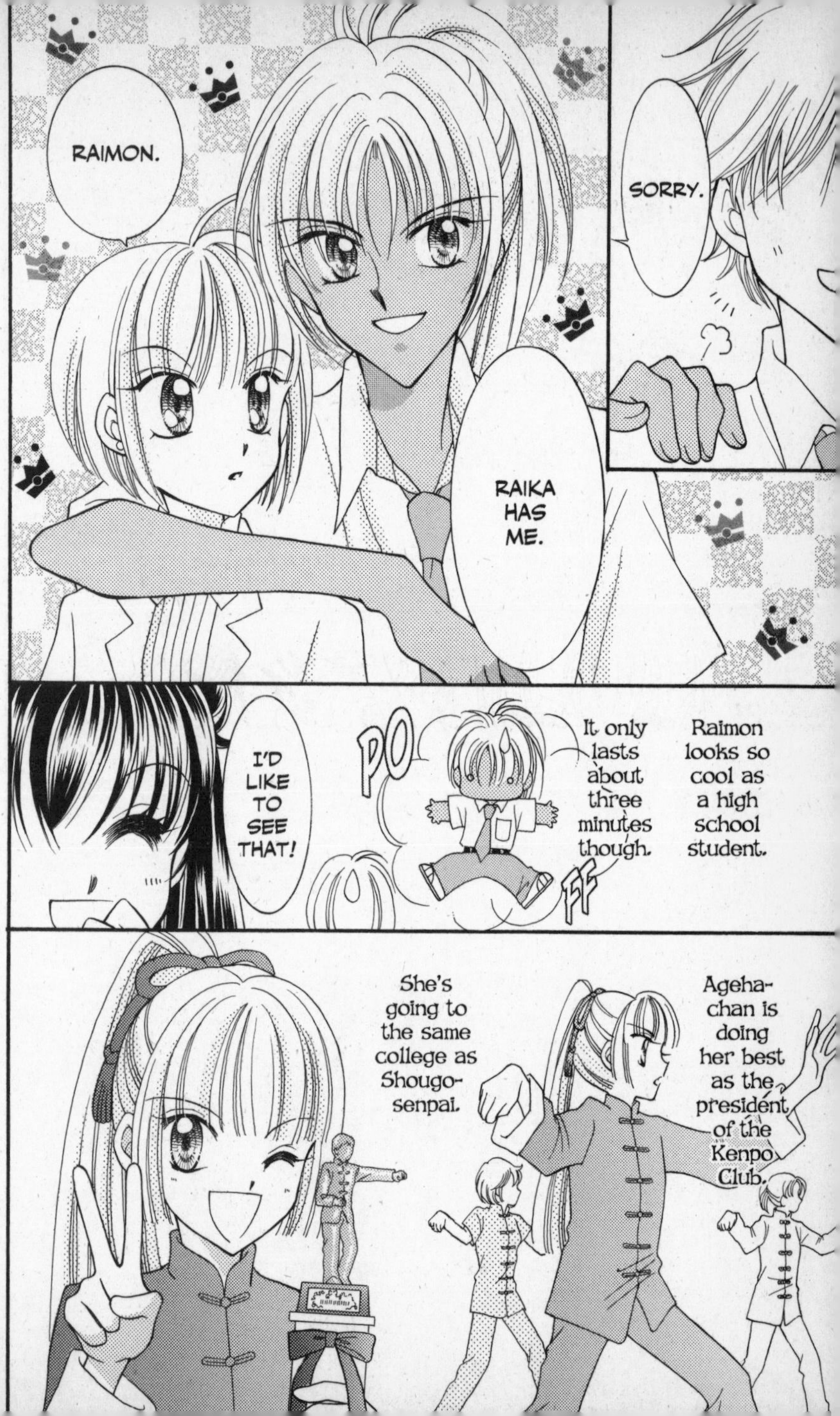
SORRY.
RAIMON.
RAIKA HAS ME.
Raimon looks so cool as a high school student.
It only lasts about three minutes though.
POFF
I'D LIKE TO SEE THAT!
Ageha-chan is doing her best as the president of the Kenpo Club.
She's going to the same college as Shougo-senpai.

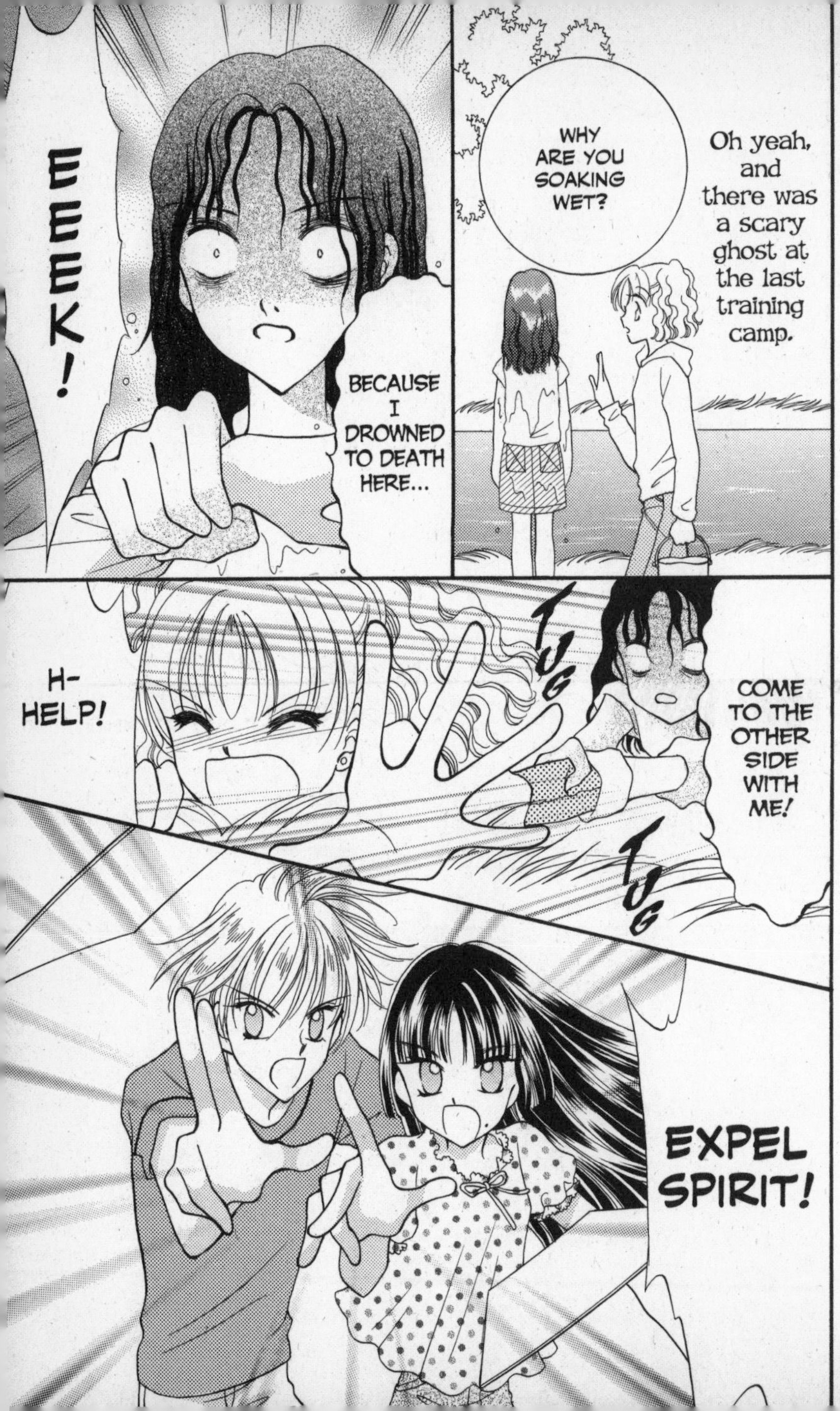
Oh yeah, and there was a scary ghost at the last training camp.
WHY ARE YOU SOAKING WET?
BECAUSE I DROWNED TO DEATH HERE...
EEEEK!
COME TO THE OTHER SIDE WITH ME!
TUG
TUG
H-HELP!
EXPEL SPIRIT!

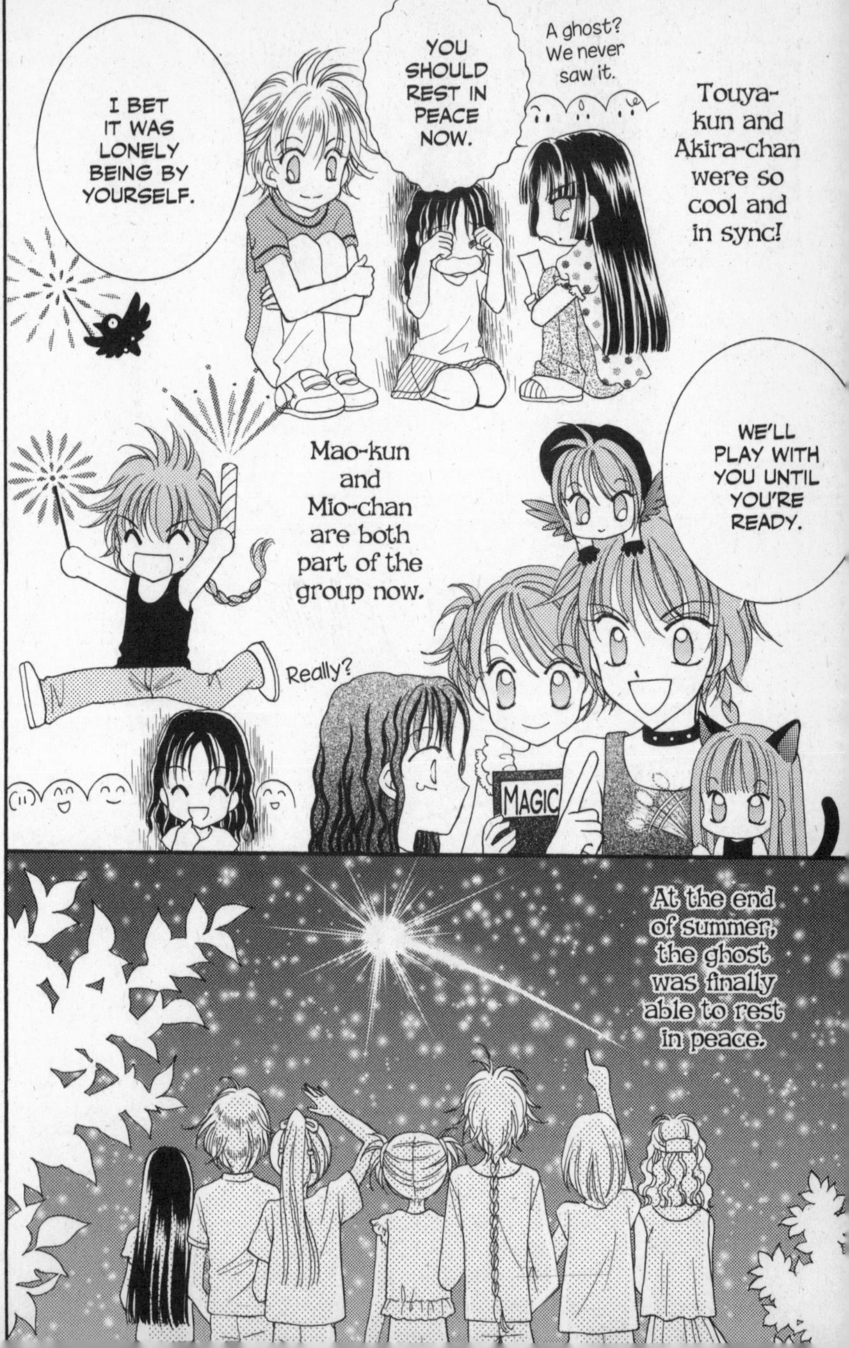
Touya-kun and Akira-chan were so cool and in sync!
A ghost? We never saw it.
YOU SHOULD REST IN PEACE NOW.
I BET IT WAS LONELY BEING BY YOURSELF.
WE'LL PLAY WITH YOU UNTIL YOU'RE READY.
Mao-kun and Mio-chan are both part of the group now.
MAGIC
Really?
At the end of summer, the ghost was finally able to rest in peace.

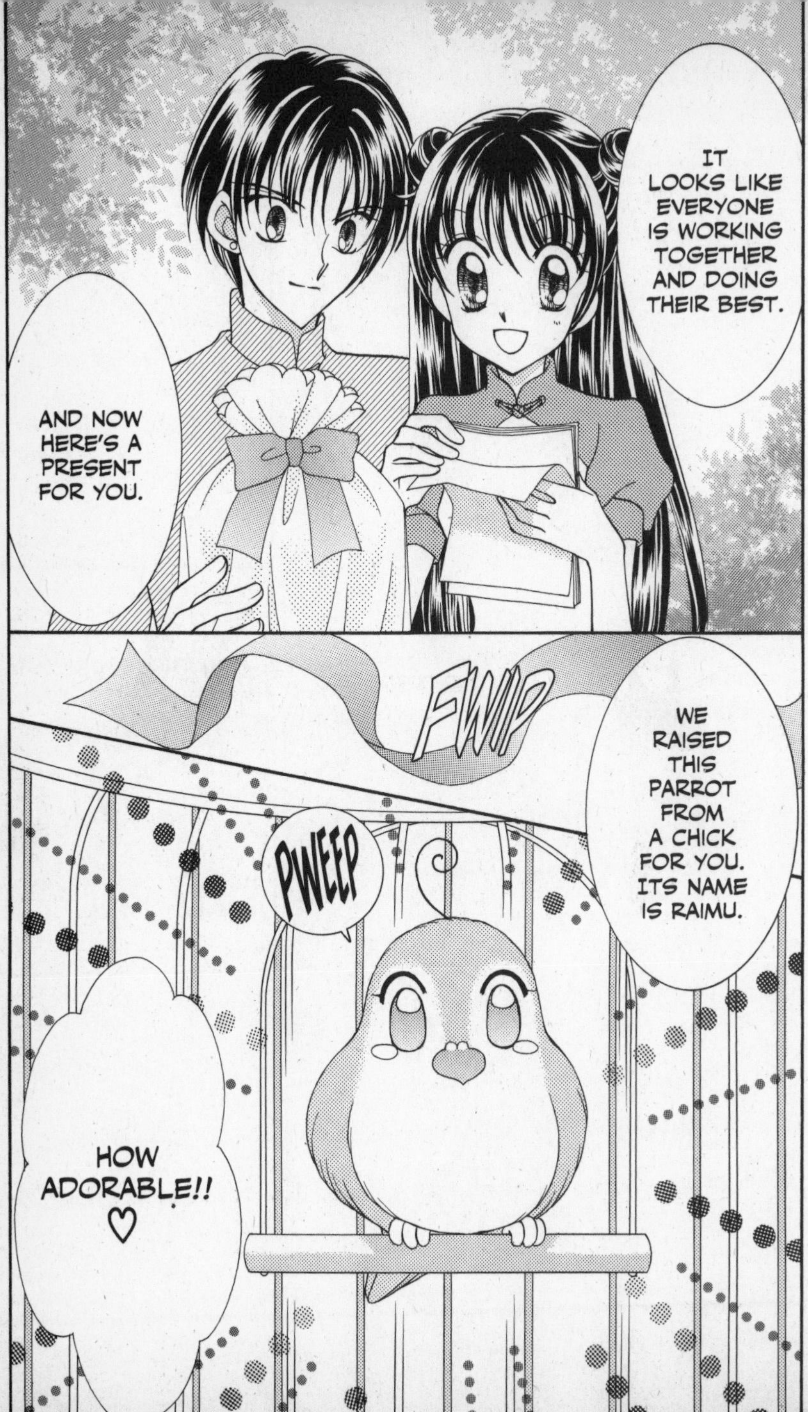
IT LOOKS LIKE EVERYONE IS WORKING TOGETHER AND DOING THEIR BEST.
AND NOW HERE'S A PRESENT FOR YOU.
FWIP
WE RAISED THIS PARROT FROM A CHICK FOR YOU. ITS NAME IS RAIMU.
PWEEP
HOW ADORABLE!! ♡

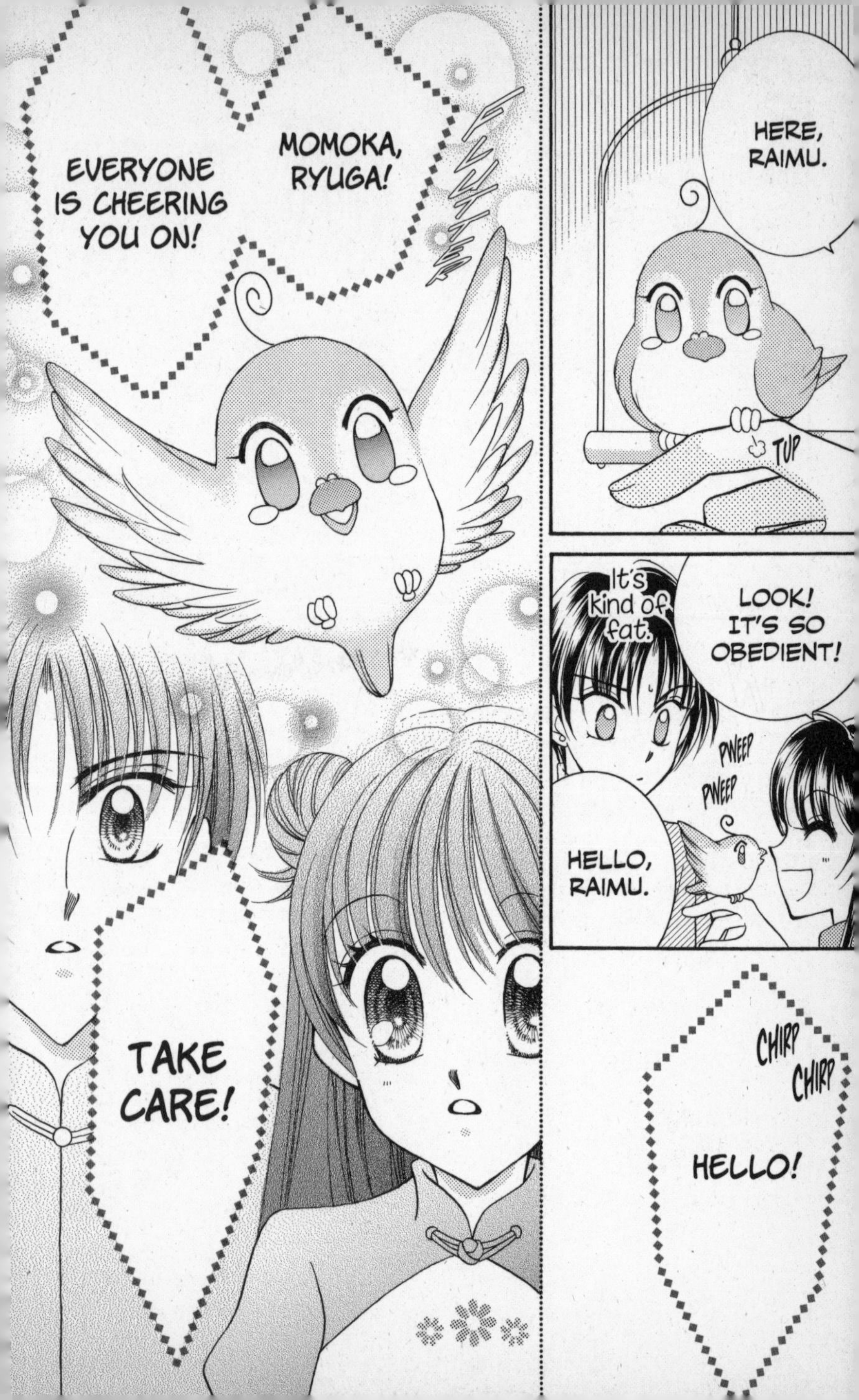
HERE, RAIMU.
TUP
LOOK! IT'S SO OBEDIENT!
It's kind of fat.
PWEEP PWEEP
HELLO, RAIMU.
CHIRP CHIRP
HELLO!
MOMOKA, RYUGA!
EVERYONE IS CHEERING YOU ON!
TAKE CARE!

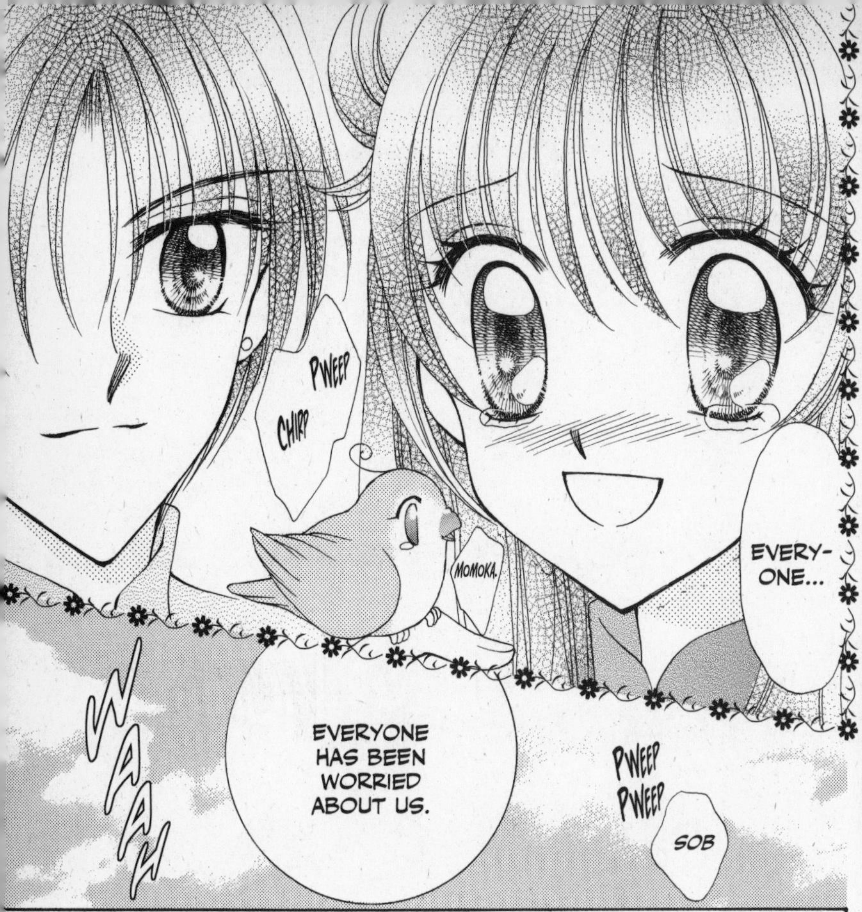
EVERY-ONE...
MOMOKA.
PWEEP
CHIRP
PWEEP PWEEP
SOB
EVERYONE HAS BEEN WORRIED ABOUT US.
WAAH
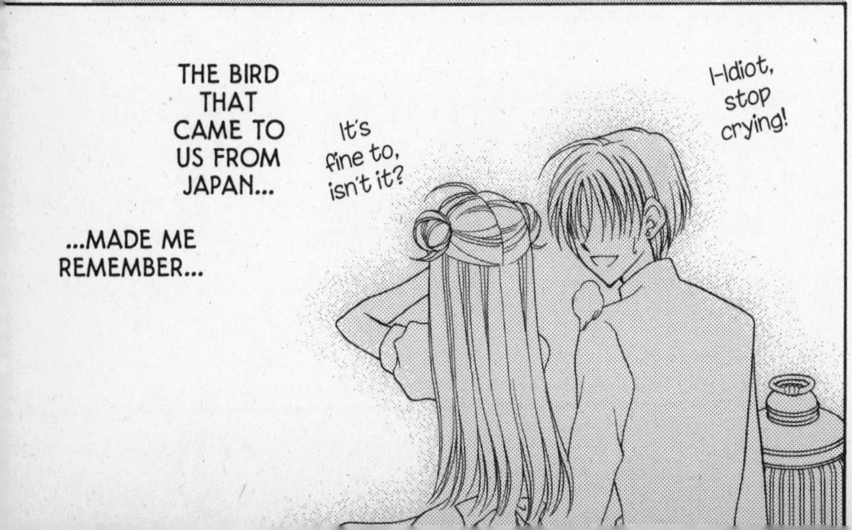
I-Idiot, stop crying!
It's fine to, isn't it?
THE BIRD THAT CAME TO US FROM JAPAN...
...MADE ME REMEMBER...

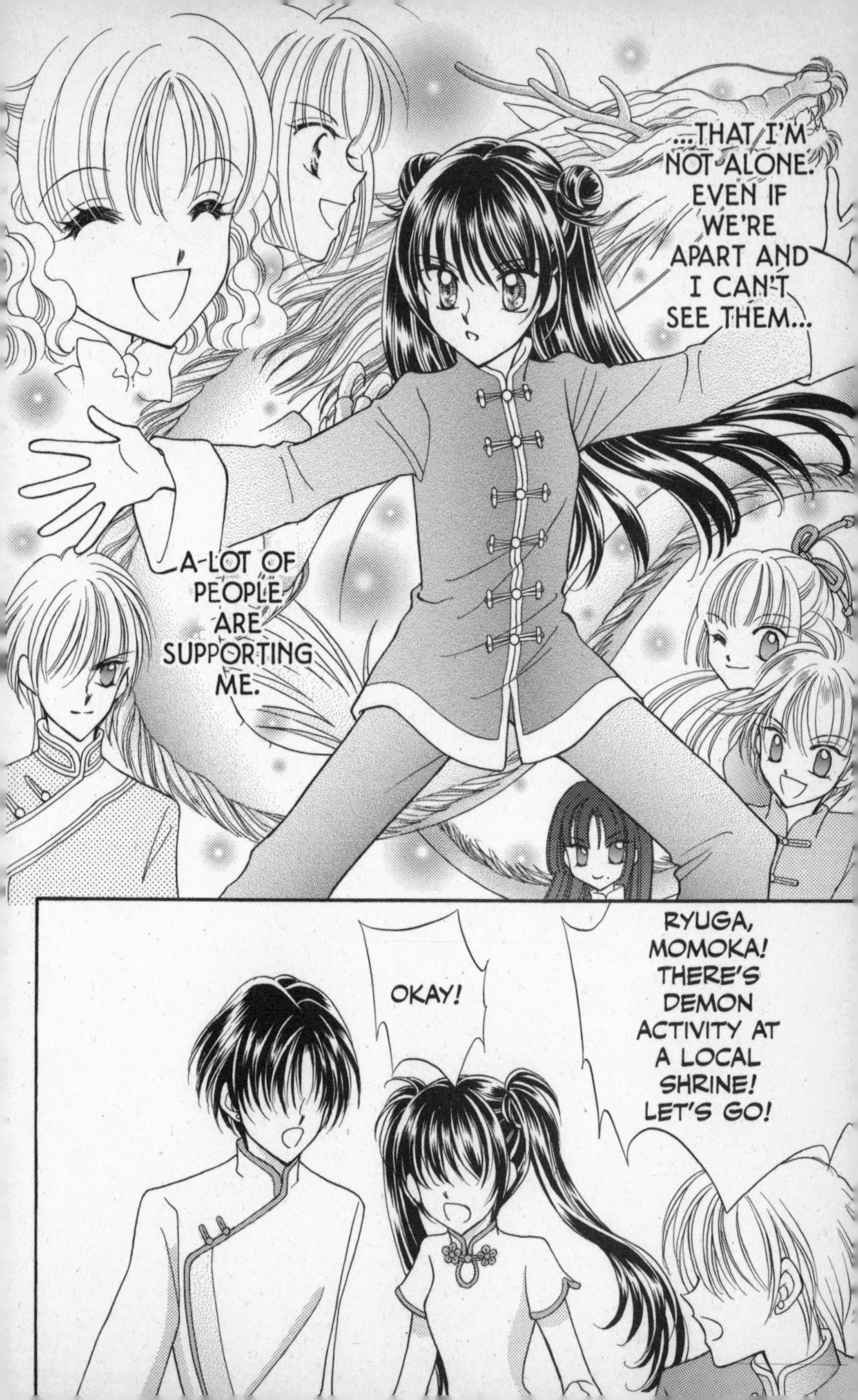
...THAT I'M NOT ALONE. EVEN IF WE'RE APART AND I CAN'T SEE THEM...
A LOT OF PEOPLE ARE SUPPORTING ME.
RYUGA, MOMOKA! THERE'S DEMON ACTIVITY AT A LOCAL SHRINE! LET'S GO!
OKAY!

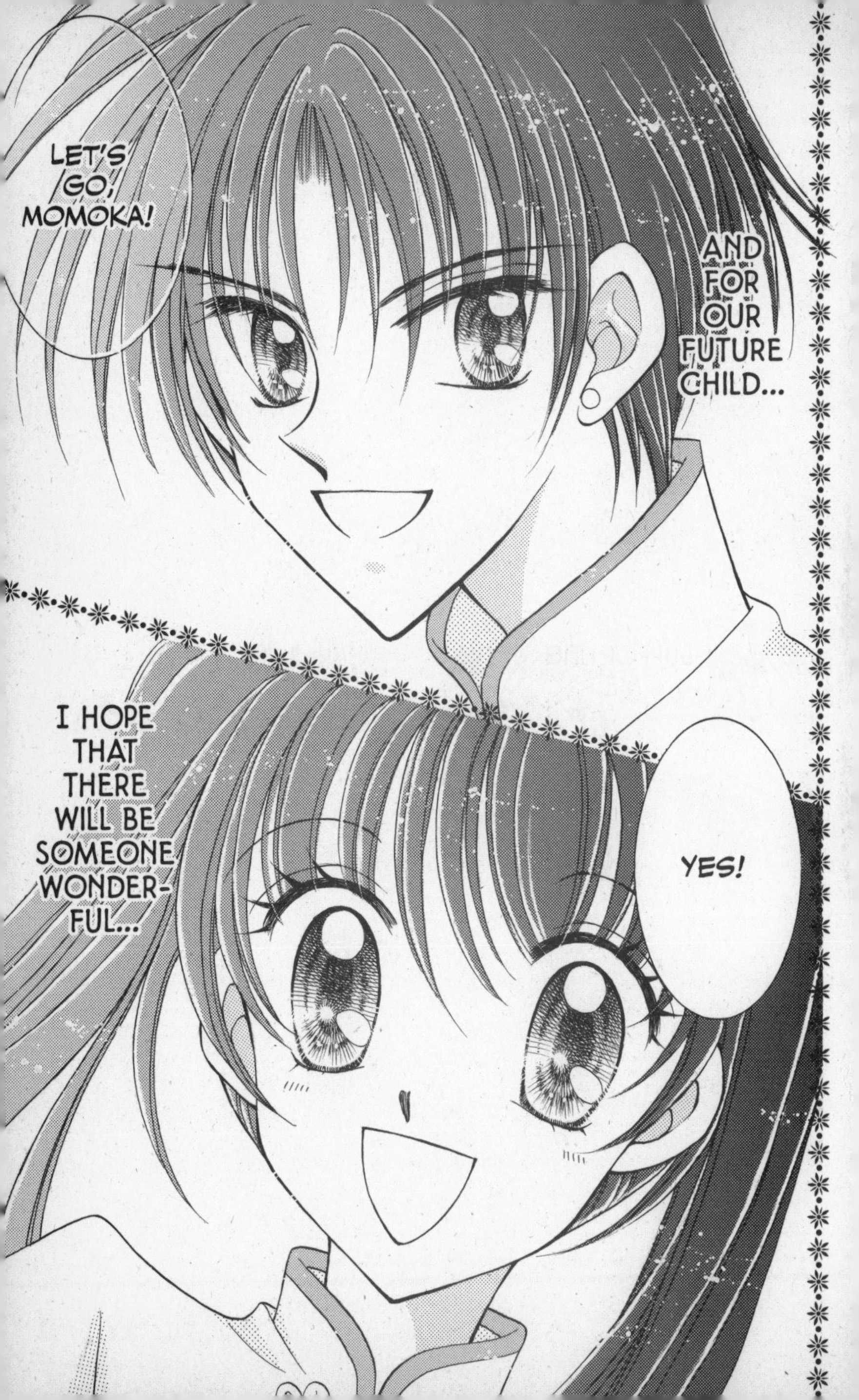
AND FOR OUR FUTURE CHILD...
LET'S GO, MOMOKA!
YES!
I HOPE THAT THERE WILL BE SOMEONE WONDER-FUL...

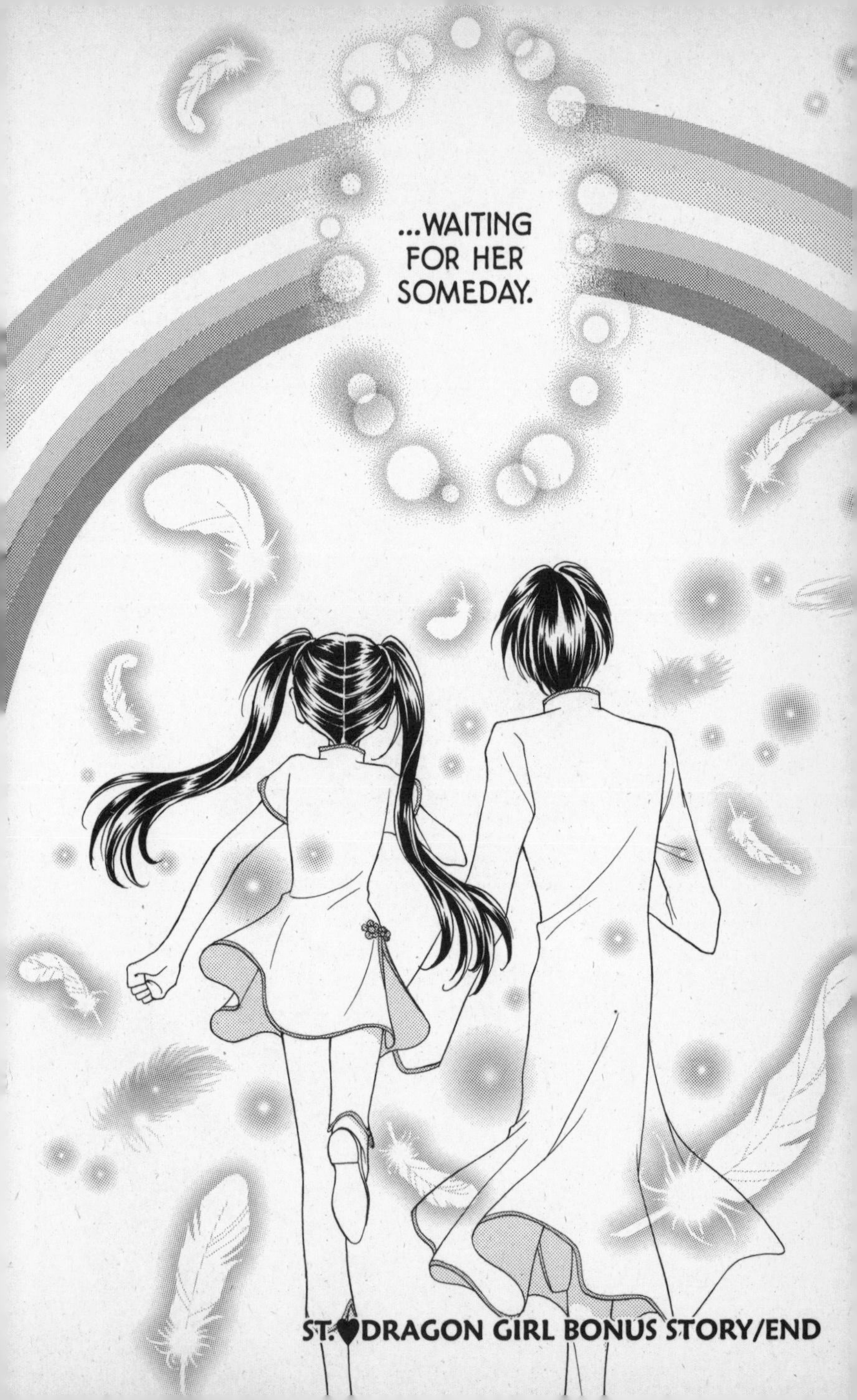
...WAITING FOR HER SOMEDAY.
ST.♥DRAGON GIRL BONUS STORY/END

As this is the last volume of SDG, I decided to let my assistants draw their favorite characters!!

This is Queen's drawing of Touya and Akira. I always wanted to draw an onmyouji like Akira. These two look like they could have their own manga together! Queen always draws such beautiful clothing. Thanks for all your help, and I look forward to working together in the future. Let's go to the movies again sometime! Ⓜ

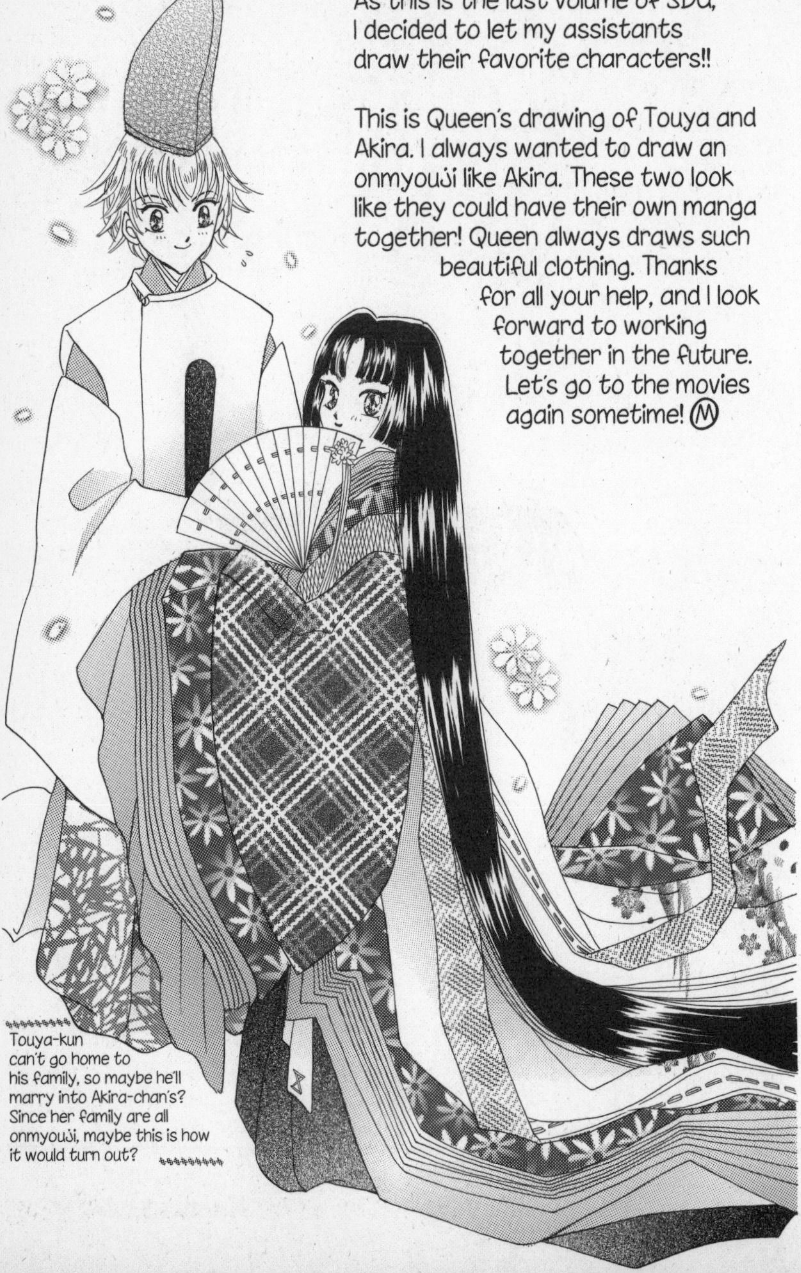

Touya-kun can't go home to his family, so maybe he'll marry into Akira-chan's? Since her family are all onmyouji, maybe this is how it would turn out?

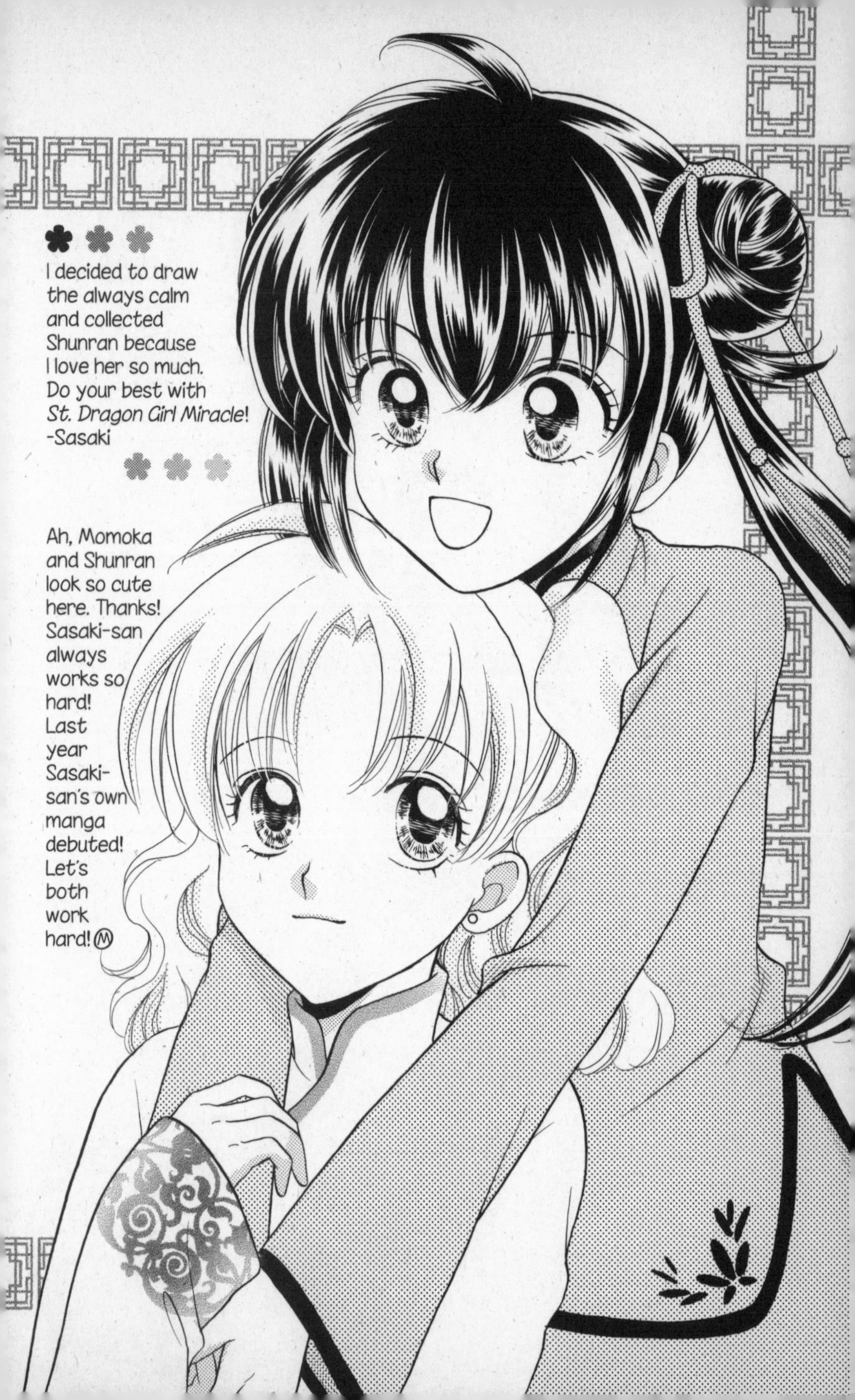
I decided to draw the always calm and collected Shunran because I love her so much. Do your best with *St. Dragon Girl Miracle*! -Sasaki
Ah, Momoka and Shunran look so cute here. Thanks! Sasaki-san always works so hard! Last year Sasaki-san's own manga debuted! Let's both work hard! Ⓜ

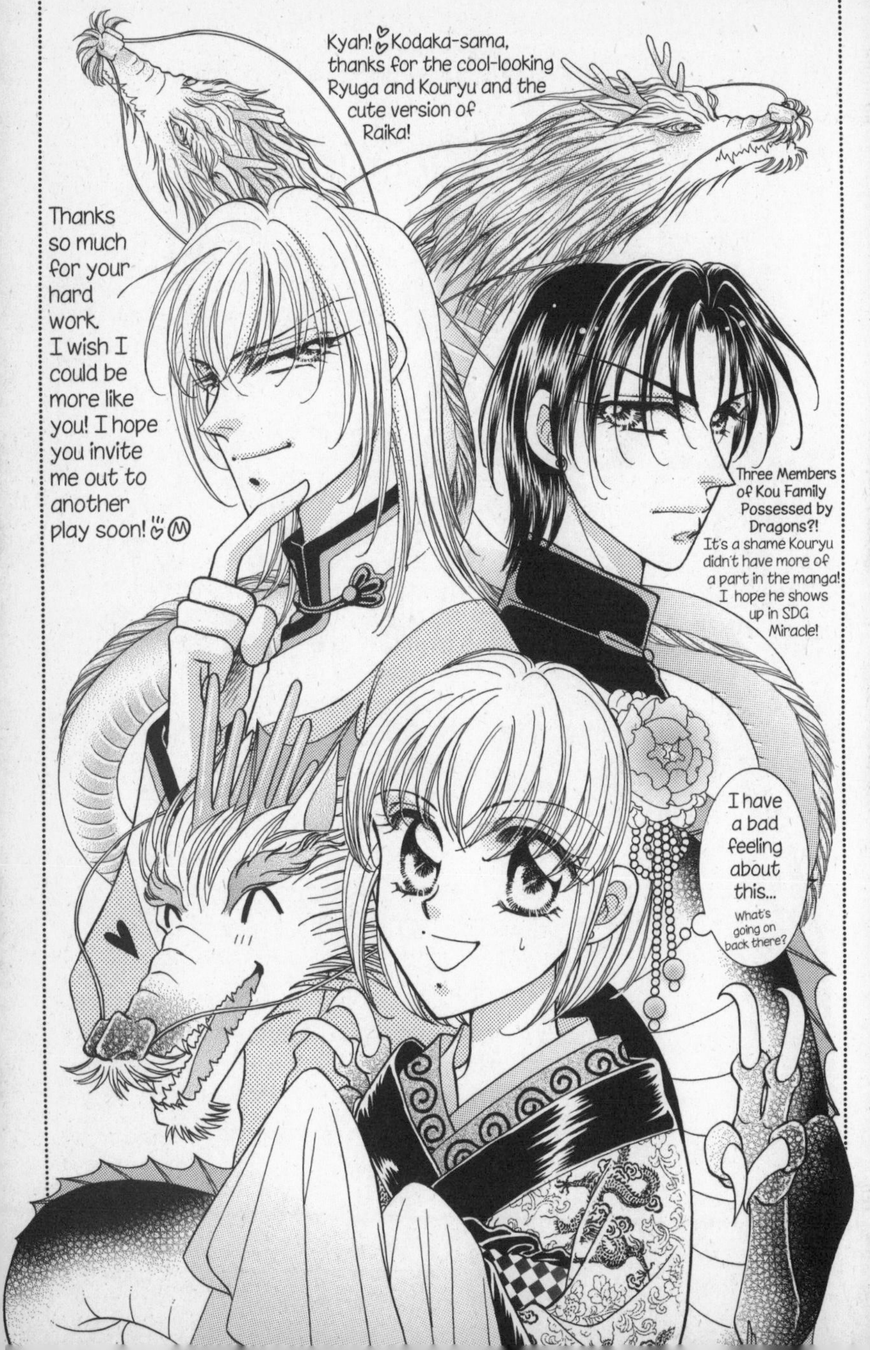
Kyah! Kodaka-sama, thanks for the cool-looking Ryuga and Kouryu and the cute version of Raika!
Thanks so much for your hard work. I wish I could be more like you! I hope you invite me out to another play soon!
Three Members of Kou Family Possessed by Dragons?! It's a shame Kouryu didn't have more of a part in the manga! I hope he shows up in SDG Miracle!
I have a bad feeling about this...
What's going on back there?

Lately Naruto Kakegawa from *Ribon* has been helping me. Thanks for the illustrations and the funny title!

SILLY ST.♡DRAGON GIRL

(Just a little fun!)

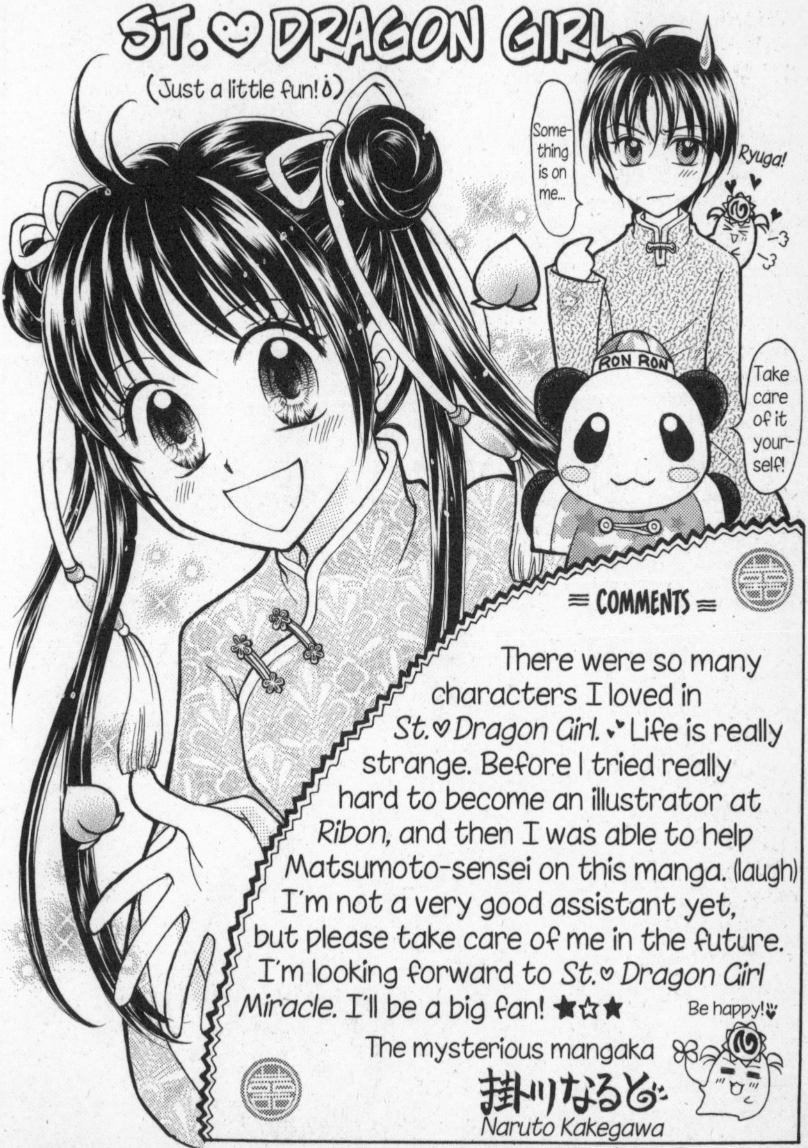
Something is on me...
Ryuga!
RON RON
Take care of it yourself!
Be happy!

≡ COMMENTS ≡

There were so many characters I loved in *St.♡Dragon Girl.* Life is really strange. Before I tried really hard to become an illustrator at *Ribon,* and then I was able to help Matsumoto-sensei on this manga. (laugh) I'm not a very good assistant yet, but please take care of me in the future. I'm looking forward to *St.♡Dragon Girl Miracle.* I'll be a big fan! ★☆★

The mysterious mangaka

掛川なると

Naruto Kakegawa

Let's go to a concert sometime together, Kakegawa! Ⓜ

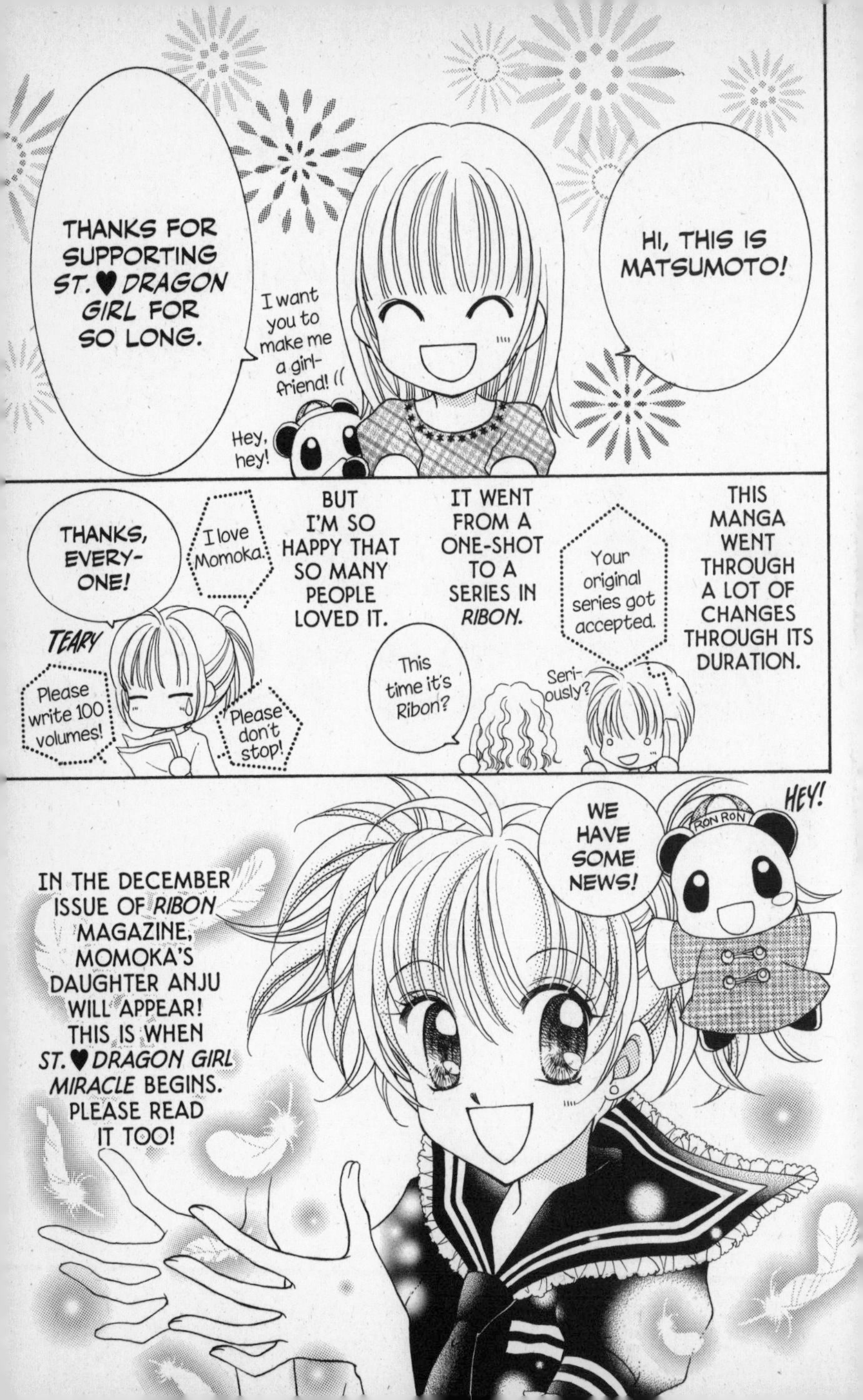
HI, THIS IS MATSUMOTO!
THANKS FOR SUPPORTING ST.♥DRAGON GIRL FOR SO LONG.
I want you to make me a girlfriend!
Hey, hey!
THIS MANGA WENT THROUGH A LOT OF CHANGES THROUGH ITS DURATION.
Your original series got accepted.
IT WENT FROM A ONE-SHOT TO A SERIES IN *RIBON*.
Seriously?
This time it's Ribon?
BUT I'M SO HAPPY THAT SO MANY PEOPLE LOVED IT.
I love Momoka.
THANKS, EVERYONE!
TEARY
Please don't stop!
Please write 100 volumes!
HEY!
WE HAVE SOME NEWS!
RON RON
IN THE DECEMBER ISSUE OF *RIBON* MAGAZINE, MOMOKA'S DAUGHTER ANJU WILL APPEAR! THIS IS WHEN *ST.♥DRAGON GIRL MIRACLE* BEGINS. PLEASE READ IT TOO!

HONORIFICS

In Japan, people are usually addressed by their name followed by a suffix. The suffix shows familiarity or respect, depending on the relationship.

Male (familiar): first or last name + kun
Female (familiar): first or last name + chan
Adult (polite): last name + san
Upperclassman (polite): last name + senpai
Teacher or professional: last name + sensei
Close friends or lovers: first name only, no suffix

TERMS

A *kotatsu* is a low, covered table with a heater underneath.

I'm thrilled when I read letters that say, "I received a lot of energy from Momoka and her friends." This is what I strive for in my manga. I also receive a lot of energy from my readers. Thank you so much for your support!!!

—Natsumi Matsumoto

Natsumi Matsumoto debuted with the manga *Guuzen Janai Yo!* (No Coincidence!) in *Ribon Original* magazine. *St. ♥ Dragon Girl* was such a hit that it spawned a sequel, *St. ♥ Dragon Girl Miracle*. Her other series from *Ribon* include *Alice kara Magic* and *Yumeiro Patisserie*. The popular *Yumeiro Patisserie* was made into an animated TV series in Japan. In her free time, Natsumi studies Chinese and practices tai chi. She also likes visiting aquariums and collecting the toy prizes that come with snack food in Japan.

St. ♥ Dragon Girl

Vol. 8
Shojo Beat Edition

STORY AND ART BY | **Natsumi Matsumoto**

Translation | **Andria Cheng**
Touch-up Art & Lettering | **Gia Cam Luc**
Design | **Fawn Lau**
Editor | **Nancy Thistlethwaite**

SAINT DRAGON GIRL © 1999 by Natsumi Matsumoto. All rights reserved. First published in Japan in 1999 by SHUEISHA Inc., Tokyo. English translation rights arranged by SHUEISHA Inc.

The stories, characters and incidents mentioned in this publication are entirely fictional.

Printed in Canada

Published by VIZ Media, LLC
P.O. Box 77010
San Francisco, CA 94107

10 9 8 7 6 5 4 3 2 1
First printing, September 2010

www.viz.com

www.shojobeat.com

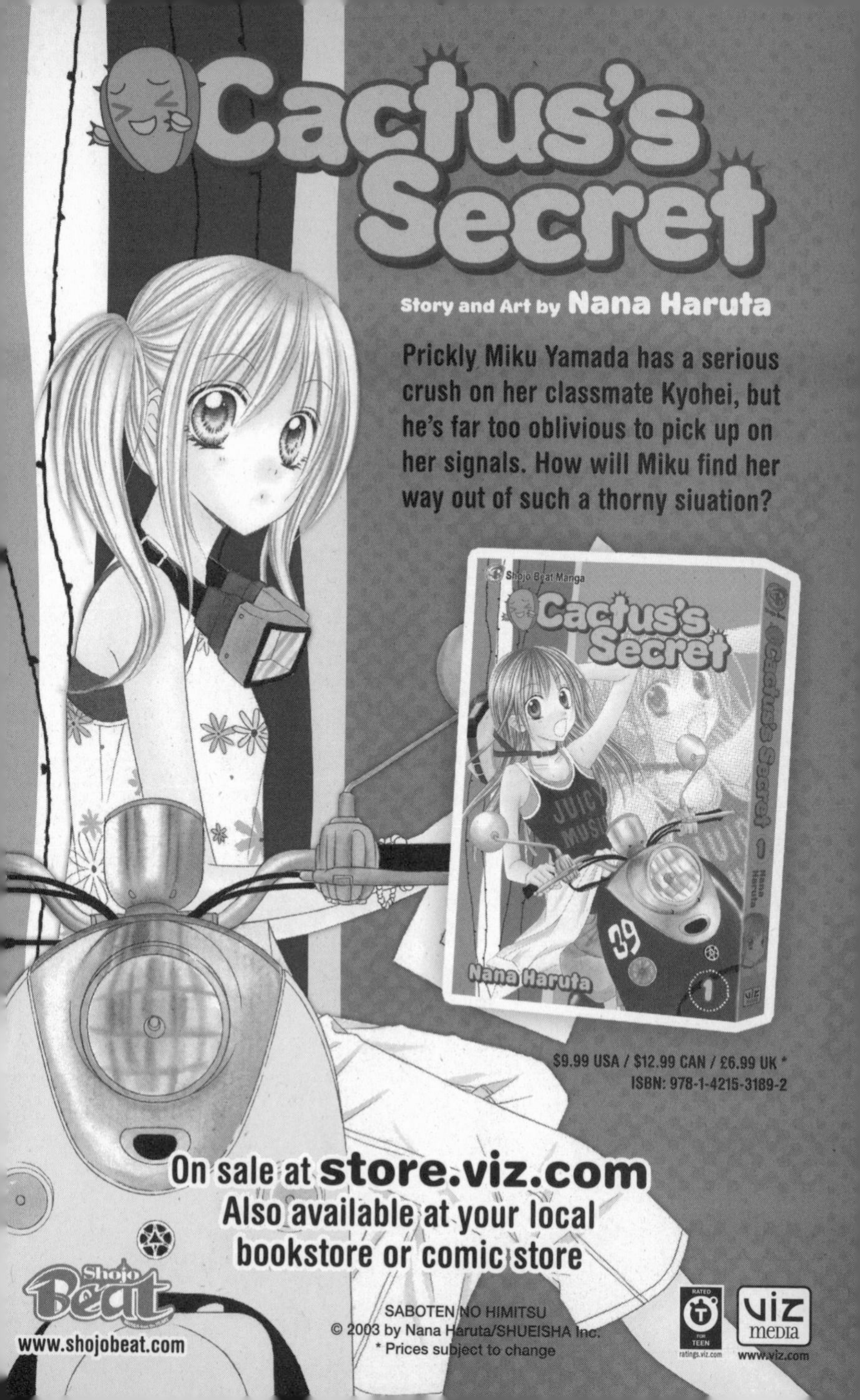
Cactus's Secret
Story and Art by Nana Haruta
Prickly Miku Yamada has a serious crush on her classmate Kyohei, but he's far too oblivious to pick up on her signals. How will Miku find her way out of such a thorny siuation?
Shojo Beat Manga
Cactus's Secret
Nana Haruta
1
$9.99 USA / $12.99 CAN / £6.99 UK *
ISBN: 978-1-4215-3189-2
On sale at store.viz.com
Also available at your local bookstore or comic store
Shojo Beat
www.shojobeat.com
SABOTEN NO HIMITSU
© 2003 by Nana Haruta/SHUEISHA Inc.
* Prices subject to change
RATED T FOR TEEN
ratings.viz.com
VIZ media
www.viz.com